THE SECRETS OF A KUTTITE

"CTESIPHON"
(THE FAMOUS ARCH WHERE THE WOUNDED WERE GATHERED AT THE HEIGHT
OF THE BATTLE)

THE SECRETS OF A KUTTITE AN AUTHENTIC STORY OF KUT, ADVENTURES IN CAPTIVITY AND STAMBOUL INTRIGUE BY CAPTAIN E. O. MOUSLEY, R.F.A.

The Naval & Military Press Ltd

published in association with

FIREPOWER
The Royal Artillery Museum
Woolwich

Published by
The Naval & Military Press Ltd
Unit 10 Ridgewood Industrial Park,
Uckfield, East Sussex,
TN22 5QE England
Tel: +44 (0) 1825 749494
Fax: +44 (0) 1825 765701
www.naval-military-press.com

in association with

FIREPOWER
The Royal Artillery Museum, Woolwich
www.firepower.org.uk

The Naval & Military
Press

MILITARY HISTORY AT YOUR
FINGERTIPS

... a unique and expanding series of reference works

Working in collaboration with the foremost
regiments and institutions, as well as acknowledged
experts in their field, N&MP have assembled a
formidable array of titles including technologically
advanced CD-ROMs and facsimile reprints of
impossible-to-find rarities.

SECOND EDITION

THE TREK

No pause, no rest ! Forward the column pushes
Across the stern and unproductive plain—
And Thirst, Satan's archfiend, darts at the brain
And the weight of the great heat their spirit crushes
To deeper silence and the tired feet bleed—
While the ruthless Turk with yells and sometimes blows
Urges them on beside his impatient steed
To a Future where and how no soldier knows
Beyond the dust-cloud on the horizon's rim,
Beyond the range of Hope—to memories grim.
But neither desert thirst nor fiercest sun
Nor dust-storms, nor the unknown miles ahead
Can touch their heart or clog its valves with dread—
These English lads that fought at Ctesiphon.

" SPARKLING MOSELLE."
From *Smoke*, the Kastamuni *Punch*.

TO

MY   MOTHER

PREFACE

THE following pages were actually written during the siege of Kut or during captivity. The original manuscript was concealed in Turkey and recovered months after the Armistice. I have been persuaded by my friends that to recast or add to the story would detract from whatever appeal it may have as a human document. As such, with all its limitations, it is offered to the public.

The exigencies of a captivity such as mine, even more than in the field, determine from moment to moment one's focus and perspective, and what to-day presents itself for record is to-morrow ignored or forgotten by concentration on the few things and the few moments that count. Added to this there is for the prisoner the pressure of existence when, so far from being allowed a pencil, he is considerably occupied with selling his last fork.

One moves on from minute to minute between walls that recede or converge, and one's experience, therefore, is a series of incidents often unfinished. A diary must reflect one's experience.

The secrets of every Kuttite would "make many books" as large as this. And from an experience more varied than fell to the lot of many prisoners the author hopes that the following extract, a simple story of incident, adventure and intrigue, may interest the British reader.

EDWARD O. MOUSLEY.

OXFORD AND CAMBRIDGE CLUB,
PALL MALL,
March, 1921.

ix

CONTENTS

PART II

THE TREK. KASTAMUNI

PART III

STAMBOUL AND BRUSA

CONTENTS

CHAPTER XV

CHAPTER XVI

CHAPTER XVII

LIST OF ILLUSTRATIONS AND MAPS

MAPS

PART I

TO THE FALL OF KUT, APRIL 29TH, 1916

THE SECRETS OF A KUTTITE

CHAPTER I

EN ROUTE FROM HYDERABAD TO MESOPOTAMIA—VOYAGE UP THE TIGRIS

KUT-EL-AMARA, December 22nd, 1915.—At the present moment I'm snugly settled inside my Burberry sleeping-bag. The tiny candle that burns gloomily from its niche in the earth wall of the dug-out leaves half the compartment in sharp shadow. But through the doorway it lights a picture eloquent of war. This picture, framed by the sand-bags of the doorway, includes a gun-limber, observation pole, rifles, a telescope, and a telephone, along a shell-pierced wall. Above winding mounds of black soil from entrenchments hang the feathery fronds of the eternal palm. Only some droop, for mostly they hang, bullet-clipped, like broken limbs. The night is still and cold, the stillness punctuated by the rackety music of machine-guns. As I write snipers' bullets crack loudly on the *mutti* wall behind my head. Another night attack is expected from the trenches in front of the 16th Brigade which we must support. When the battery is in action the most unloved entertainment that offers is the rifle fire that just skips the wall enclosing the date-palm grove in which we are hidden. Sometimes the sharp crackling sound of bullets hitting the trees increases as the flashes of our guns are seen by the enemy, and resembles in its intensity a forest on fire. One hears a sudden crack just ahead like the sharp snapping of a stick, and in the early days of one's initiation a duck is inevitable. I don't say one ducks, but one finds one has ducked. For a time every one ducks. It is no use telling people that if the bullet had been straight one would have been hit before hearing it strike the palm. Some people go on ducking for ages. Of course I'm talking of the open. In the trenches ducking is a fine art. The last time I ducked commendably, that I remember, was yesterday. I was observing from our front line trenches with plenty of head protection from the front, when a bullet came from an almost impossible direction. It flung a piece of hard earth sharply on my cheek, and I ducked. Afterwards I laughed and took more care.

By the way, as this is not a diary but an unpretentious record of things not forgotten, and intended on reference to dispel the illusion that all this is a dream, I may as well furnish an explanation of how I, Edward Mousley, a subaltern in the Royal Field Artillery, come to be in this dug-out here in Kut-el-Amara, along with the Sixth Division under General Townshend, that is to say, almost the whole original Force D, besieged by the whole Turkish army in Mesopotamia under Nureddin Pasha.

My brigade was at annual practice near Hyderabad Scind when a wire ordered another subaltern and me to proceed at once on service with Force D (in Mesopotamia) to replace casualties. Some very kind words and excellent advice from my Colonel and innumerable *chota* pegs from every one else and the next morning we left, the other subaltern and Don Juan and I, to exchange practice for reality. Don Juan is my faithful horse. At Karachi I found several gunners of my acquaintance who had come out from Home with me in the *Morea*, a few months before, including one Edmonds, who had tripped with me across India.

At Karachi I stored much useless kit, motor cycle, and spare saddlery, and notwithstanding a heavy bout of malaria just before, left for service fit and well equipped and with as excellent a horse as one could wish for. We sailed in the tiny mail boat *Dwarka* for Muscat, Bushire, Basra.

Muscat is a mere safety valve of Satan in his sparest wilderness, a lonely patch of white buildings completely shut in by awful mountains, rocks that in remote ages seem to have frowned themselves into the most fearful convulsions. And, even in November, hot !

After two days of scorching heat and tempestuous seas we arrived at Bushire, where a spit keeps shipping off.

Fifty Gurkhas, and a subaltern of whom I was to see something by and by, came aboard. Fine little fellows they are and very cheerful and contented even on the wretched deck of a tiny steamer loaded with fowls, food, a Persian donkey, vermin, and half-breeds.

Then, in a resplendent dawn, I saw the banks of the Shatt-el-Arab, verdant with the greenness of a new lawn, where millions of date palms clustered side by side on the flat, flood-washed shores. Here the river is half a mile wide. One may imagine its changed appearance when the great floods come, that are now three months off. Outside the entrance on the right bank, Fao, a tiny village and fort, marks the initial landing and conquest by Force D—General Delamain's brigade—in October, 1914.

Both banks of the river are thickly forested with date-palms right up to Basra, a crowded spot of a few hundred yards in frontage on both sides of a tiny creek Ashar, whence once Sinbad sailed. It was brimful of soldiers and Arabs, and quantities of stores and planks stood around half-erected buildings. It had the appearance of a very busy port, some dozen huge ocean-going vessels being anchored in the stream. There was no wharfing accommodation at all. One communicates with the shore by bellums. This is a flat-bottomed pointed boat and propelled by bamboo poles or paddled by sticks nailed on to a round blob of wood.

The shipping included H.M.S. *Espiegle*, the *Franz Ferdinand*, and the *Karadenis*, the two latter being large steamers captured by us and used as accommodation boats, each taking a thousand men if necessary. Pending the arrival of our upstream transport I was ordered with the other officers on to the *Karadenis* which lay in mid-stream. Some wretched-looking Turkish prisoners were aft.

We little knew it at the time, but our few days on this ship or mosquito-hive were destined to be our last in even moderate comfort. Henceforth we were to be playthings of the God of War.

There was a strange silence about news on this front. Some thought our army was near Azizie, over four hundred miles up river ; others that we were just outside Baghdad. We were chafing to get away to our units before we got malaria. A sudden chance with a detachment of the 14th Hussars was offered to a subaltern nick-named " Fruit-salt," because " 'e knows," and myself. We left on a paddle-boat called the *P*.5, a barge of horses, Don Juan among them, on either side.

To get on the *P*.5 again from the horse-barges we hop over to the paddle-box and clamber on deck. Our camp beds we stretched out forward, the men, arms, and maxims arranged aft. We had a comfortable mess table set so that we could see up-stream and also a good deal of the left bank. The officers of this troop of the 14th Hussars on board were all very young, very pleasant, and very keen. We sat and drank or smoked and talked, and war seemed then very far away. Or we watched a wandering tribe of Arabs trekking in the distance. The country was, of course, dead flat and except for a scrubby grass there was nothing to intercept one's eye reaching to the horizon. The river winds a lot and far away the *mahela* sails seemed to be making over land. One thought of the Norfolk Broads. Somewhere in the early morning we passed the confluence of the Euphrates and Tigris, and Ezra's tomb. (Maxim fire increasing : I must switch off here now.) *Later.*—No harm occurred except the heavy sniping has knocked out some poor horses and wounded a syce and spoiled some more palms. I continue.

There was also on board an excellent engineer, full of " sunny retrospect." He could talk or listen, which is like unto a horse that can gallop and walk. As he explained on inquiry, he had never married, nor had he ever avoided marriage. Altogether he was a delightful fellow for company.

We passed the marshes of Kurna of an earlier engagement in this campaign, where our army had dislodged the Turk with guns mounted on planks between bellums, and whole brigades punted and poled their way up. " Forward the light bellums ! " " Charge ! " were the orders the commanding officers yelled on that day. Britain was always irresistible on the water ! The whole affair is now called " Regatta week."

We also passed where the Garden of Eden was said to have been. As a matter of fact, the whole of this country, like the plains of India, is delta formation. The two rivers must have been higher up and consequently Eden also. The latter fact rather knocks out the little remaining romance about the place. Sir William Wilcocks puts the site at Hit, above Baghdad, and says that even going no further back than the tertiary epoch would place the delta there.

We reached Amara on the fourth day. It is a village of some considerable size pleasantly lining both banks of a beautiful straight reach in the Tigris. In the broad, clear water one sees reflected the languid droop of the eternal date palm, the great triangular sails of the *mahela*, the regular contour of the Bridge of Boats. It is not unpicturesque. Here, some months ago, a delightful *coup* was effected by the commander of H.M.S. *Shaitan* and about a dozen men. These were the first in the pursuit from Kurna, and the others not having arrived, determined on a bold policy, as at any moment the Arabs might have joined forces with the Turk and rendered the taking of Kurna quite difficult. These few men went ashore and, entering the barracks containing some several hundreds of men, demanded their surrender and the immediate handing over of the town. The prestige of the British Navy or the eloquent silence of the gunboat's guns did the rest. And so by this remarkable bluff Amara fell without bloodshed, and was held although reinforcements did not arrive until the next day.

Above Amara the country is still perfectly flat, but appears less marshy in winter than lower down. Here a thicker ground scrub teems with black partridge and quail, some of which we shot from the boat. A sub. in the Hussars, named Pope, brought off a wonderful revolver shot into a jackal's ribs from the boat : we practised revolver shooting hard.

Arabs clustered in tiny tribes every few miles along the river. The men, some of whom are quite naked, I thought remarkable for great size of limb and muscular development. They would sometimes accompany the boat for miles, doing their weird undulating dance, hopping round first on one foot and then on the other. They welcome us when we win and torture and loot our wounded when they get a chance. Here and there Jewish women and old men ladle water by a swinging scoop into a drain for their irrigation. The dress and general customs continually recall one's school days' pictures of Biblical times.

Two or three days later we got to Kut-el-Amara (pronounce Kut like foot), passing the battlefield of Essin *en route*. It was at Essin where Townshend, by leaving his tents on one bank of the river and crossing in the night, deceived the Turk into fancied security, and the next day flung him neck and crop out of a position of great strength.

Here the Hussars took my horse on by the desert and I left in the *Shirin* for Azizie. At Kut we had heard that Baghdad would fall that evening, and later that night reverse news that we had had very heavy casualties. The hospitals were removed from the barges, and reinforcements' kit of the West Kents and Hussars was left with us instead. "Fruit-salt" and I messed with the West Kents, awfully good fellows, one a youngster just from Clare College. The remaining West Kents marched, escorted by the 14th Hussars, and met us at some point on the river each day. One night we were stranded ashore and in awful rain. The *tatti* (rush) roof let most of the water through, and what it did not let through, collected in gutters that every now and then deluged over us. My sleeping bag became a tank. Suddenly came the dawn and we awoke to a steaming-hot sunny world.

A heavily-armed launch protected with *boosa* bales passed us. Their answer—"Headquarters"—was our first intimation of the seriousness of the position of our army. Two days after this, and about eight or nine since leaving Basra, we got to Azizie, a mere bend in the river with a few huts. There were many horses watering and several hundred Turkish prisoners on the bank. On every side we saw evidence of a hurried march. It was all hustle and haste. We went ashore, our last orders being to leave for Salaiman Pak, some thirty miles up river and fifteen from Baghdad. But once ashore, we saw from the ungroomed condition of the horses, the dust-covered harnesses and wagons, the exhausted men, many asleep in their roughly arranged lines, that our army after tremendous exertions had just arrived and halted. The C.R.A.'s flag hung over a mud hut. He explained that we had fought a big action at Ctesiphon where the Turks were heavily entrenched, that we had turned them out, and got into their second line when the enemy had retired to the Diala river, his third line. But the action, which was tactically a brilliant success, had cost us a third of our force. The word came that two Turkish divisions were reinforcing them, so we retired in the night. It seems that for a time both armies were in retreat, but the Turks, on hearing of our withdrawal, gave chase. They were, however, doubly respectful in having suffered casualties twice our own, and they held off some few miles from Azizie.

CHAPTER II

" FRUIT-SALT " and I joined our batteries, mine being the 76th R.F.A. All the force bore marks of a great struggle, great losses, keen hardship. The weary army was resting. That was well. Some kindly god that knew what still awaited them smiled on them, and they slept. Here at last, I thought, is the famous army of General Townshend, the fighting Sixth Division, that had overcome difficulties that few other armies had been called on to do, that had endured hardships of heat and thirst and pestilence in the cauldron of Asia, marched hundreds of miles with improvised transit, and moved from victory to victory until Ctesiphon. General Townshend's was the most loyal of armies in adversity. They knew that against his counsel he had been ordered to risk the action, where even if doubly victorious their tiny numbers would have been insufficient to hold Baghdad. There was also the haunting dream of that lonely river, our sole communication, winding through a hostile country five hundred miles to Basra. Reinforcements there were none at all in the country, which was a fortnight's distance from India and more from Egypt. Anyway, this was the army of which I, a subaltern in the 76th Battery, Royal Field Artillery, was now privileged to consider myself a member.

Rapid plans were in execution to strengthen Azizie, as the Turks might try a night attack. The troops had only arrived that morning, but by nightfall we had thrown up quite a bit of cover with gun pits and light breastwork for the infantry. Perfect order reigned over the customary military procedure. No Turks were in sight. Every man of the fatigued army worked as happens on manœuvres. It was only the battered condition of the gun carriages, the gaping wounds in the diminished teams of horses and that quiet "balanced up" look in the eyes of every Tommy that told of a reality more grim. On the flat mud desert, with no kind asset of nature to assist them, the nearest reinforcements hundreds of miles away, but with its own transport and some limited supplies, this lonely British army formed its semi-circle on the river. So it faced this unkind plain, its destiny in its hands.

An atrociously bad place to defend is Azizie, merely a meagre bend in the river, a floody or dusty desert with a few mud-walled buildings on the Tigris edge. Much of our baggage had to be left on a barge and the rest was taken from the Shirin into the R.A. shed. The first was ultimately sunk and the latter burned. None of it I have ever seen since—saddlery, coats, uniforms, camp equipment—all went.

All the officers of the 76th Battery had been wounded except one—Devereux, who had been with me at Hyderabad, and Captain Carlyle of the 63rd Battery was in command.

I slept by the gun pits. Beyond the line of infantry that separated us from the Turk, some jackals howled in ghoulish song. They had followed on the flank of our army and waited expectant, for they too had visited the field of Ctesiphon! Their devilish symphony grew fainter, and I slept. Now and then I was awakened by sniping.

The next day, November 29th, we got matters in order, rearranged teams and sections to replace casualties, and overhauled. We continued our vigilance. There was much to be done and, as might be expected after the recent ordeal, many were nerve-ragged and irritable, but all were light-hearted. We expected to move that evening, but did not. I slept on the perimeter by the guns again, and awoke to find my servant packing up. Orders to stand by to move in an hour set me going at once. After an early breakfast I had to go and relieve another artillery officer on the observation post, which was merely a few sandbags on the roof of a house, covered with rushes to keep off the sun. At 11 a.m. the greater part of the force had got on the road Southward ho! The Staff left about 11.30. General Smith, C.R.A., asked me my orders, which were to wait there until sent for, but which should have included "unless the Staff leaves first," as I was left without any guard and surrounded by hostile Arabs. I thought it better to wait a little and give a last attention to the column I had seen emerging from the northward clumps of trees where the enemy was waiting. I am glad I did so, for I was afforded the privilege of witnessing a spectacle at once unique and magnificent.

Below me the river lay blue in the morning sun between the black winding banks, and dark Arab forms dotted its shores. Somewhere ahead upstream was Baghdad. Distant horsemen scoured the plain. Some cavalry of ours lay hidden in an old smashed *serai* just north of the village. Moving south-eastward rose the dust of the main Turkish advance, mounting in clouds higher and higher. The quicker dust marked their cavalry, and here and there in dense column formation their wheeled traffic came on. To the southward in perfect order, and moving at an even pace, was our own army in retreat. The khaki column reached away to the horizon of dust, and the swarthy visages of our Indian troops doing rearguard in extended order, and the gleam from the accoutrements of the 14th Hussars were visible without field glasses. The village itself that was burning in a dozen places now broke into one great conflagration, and simultaneously some Arab bullets cut their way unmistakably near. I decided to rejoin my battery that was waiting half a mile off, as it was selected for rear guard. Fortunately, before climbing down the observation post I took the precaution to peer over the edge at the doorway. I saw about a dozen gigantic Arabs, one or two with knives, lounging round the exit, evidently counting on my uniform and equipment after they had despatched me. So I talked and answered for a minute, and shouted an order for them to think I was not alone. Then I ducked out the other side and jumped the back wall. I met my orderly coming with my horse. The Arabs around the doorway yelled in disappointment as we both galloped off. I brought the battery into action just south of the town, but we did not open fire. Then the C.O. signalled " Retire." It was " Rear limber up, walk march, trot, canter," then a mile farther on " Halt ! Action rear," and so on. A delightful battery, men and horses knew their job perfectly and foresaw the order every time.

We did about fifteen miles, and halted by the river side

at Um-al-Tabul, a mere locality without a building. I had scarcely seen that the horses were fixed up and fed, when an order came that General Smith, B.G.R.A., C.R.A., wanted me as orderly officer. I was to report immediately. An orderly officer, I was told at once, is responsible for the health and well being of his general, and has many details to attend to. In action there are countless orders to deliver and reports to make. The Brigade Major, mistaken for General Smith, had unfortunately been knifed by an Arab while asleep one night on a boat, so the Staff Captain and I were the only Staff. We shared a dug-out, or rather hole, eighteen inches deep and of course uncovered. Reinforced with some bread, meat, and whisky, I scooped a pillow place for the General's head, and in the darkness tried to collect some little of my kit, which, however, got lost in the subsequent events of the night. I completed arrangements for the morning and then slept.

General Townshend's *jugga* was next ours. We were on the river bank. Behind us lay H.M.S. *Firefly* and other boats and barges.

Presently from out of the darkness shells began to fall around us. We were right in the line of fire. It appeared that they were shelling the *Firefly*. One shell pitched just short of us and wounded the syces, another burst exactly over us, but too high for the spread to reach us. Then a brisk rifle fire commenced and here and there we heard a suppressed groan. These were my first real moments under fire. The darkness and scantiness of cover made it seem worse, but I was not half so frightened as I thought I should be, and after some minutes, when it was necessary for me to deliver some messages, I gave myself up to Fate with a light heart and blundered in the darkness on my several errands. That was infinitely better than lying pinched up in the inadequate hole watching the dried grass being cut by bullets a foot above one's head. It is a great thing to be occupied in times like this. In passing through my battery I heard that two drivers of my section had been killed. On returning to the dug-out I saw the Staff Captain ferociously digging with a mess-tin. I did the same for the General's side with his own shaving mug, —which I bent, to his disgust—and then got on to my own. About midnight the rifle fire thickened. Now of all entirely horrid things under these conditions you have first and foremost the bullet. It is a thing conceived by Satan for the dispatch of his outsiders and unbeloved. Invisible it comes from anywhere. You hear it and know you are safe. Or you feel it and know you're hit. Since then I have often been under rifle fire, but that night the devilry of the bullets was strange. At 3 a.m. General Townshend said he would attack in two columns unless the fire ceased. I delivered orders connected therewith, but the fire slackened. I slept, and awoke before the dawn, and bustled around after our headquarters' transport, as we expected an immediate move. I also got breakfast ready. This was December 1st.

At 8 a.m. the transport began to move. At 8.30 it had got fairly on its way. At nine I was standing by the Headquarters transport ready to move off, when the fog cleared as suddenly as the shadows lift when the moon comes from behind a cloud. Before us, some eighteen hundred to two thousand yards off, on the higher ground, we saw a host of tents. Even as we looked the guns of the Field Brigade on the outer perimeter were limbering up. But within two minutes they were down again in action, and the first shell sang out the delight of the gunner at the prospect of so gorgeous a target. For one minute it was splendid. The spirits of the incarnated field guns ripped their music across the morning sky and over the dewy earth in quick and lightning song. The next his shells came back. I relished much less the white puffs up in the air near us, each burst a better one. But almost immediately I found myself taking a professional interest in the faulty fuses of the Turk. Our own shells were cutting great gaps in the tents and in the columns of panic stricken fleeing Turks. I saw our bursts in excellent timing, quite low. But their fire also thickened, and converged on the mass of troops not yet under way, and also on our shipping, which was caught at a wholesale disadvantage. Still, a great mass of transport stuff and ammunition was on the move.

At last it was all off, and only the perimeter of our camp remained, the four field batteries and the single line of infantry close beyond them. Standing in the centre of the shell-strewn ground was General Townshend and his Staff. I stood for a while between him and General Smith, from time to time galloping to the several batteries with orders or inquiries about ammunition. Away to our right between the Turkish advance and our own, the 14th Hussars were very busy, now covering behind the knolls and now swooping upon the enemy, who, however, gave them no chance of getting in at close quarters. S Battery, R.H.A., which worked with them, was pouring shell after shell into the teeth of the Turkish force.

One could not but feel the keenest admiration for General Townshend, so steady, collected and determined in action, so kind, quick and confident. There, totally indifferent to the shell fire, he stood watching the issue, receiving reports from the various orderly officers and giving every attention to the progress of the transport. Some shells pitched just over us, one, not fifteen yards away, killing a horse and wounding some drivers. The restlessness of the horses, some stamping their feet, others tossing their heads, betokened their objection to standing still at such a time. It really is the most difficult thing to do. One's mind was left too free to prophesy where the next shell would fall. More than once I caught a humorous smile on the General's face as some shell just missed us.

Suddenly, to the southward, a thick dust wall appeared. The Turks had got round, and our transport, uncertain about advancing, was held up. For ten minutes it seemed that the issue might become general, but our gunners, and especially S Battery, kept up such a rate of fire that the Turks were paralysed. The officer commanding this battery, acting on local knowledge, remained in action after the order to retire had reached him, and by so doing contributed greatly to the success of the day.

About nine o'clock General Melliss' Brigade, which had preceded us from Azizie by several miles and which had been sent for during the night, arrived on the scene of action, appearing from the south-eastern quarter. That effectively threw back the Turkish attack.

Then, as we gradually gave way, the tide of action moved very slowly southwards. The General motioned us to take cover in a ditch. Our horses we had sent on. It was about this time that H.M.S. *Firefly* was hit in her boiler and captured by the Turks. Several barges filled with wounded and stores had to be abandoned.

First one battery limbered up and fell into action half a mile to the rear, then another, and so on. Several times I took orders over the intervening ground that was now being

plastered with shells bursting either too high or on graze.   Don
Juan behaved excellently.   He shied once violently when a
shell burst just behind us, and again as he took off to jump a
nullah at the bottom of which a medical officer, I knew, Major
Walker, was attending to a wounded man.   For the rest he
went in his best hunting style over ditches and holes and took
not the slightest notice of the noise or bursts.   I often give
him an extra handful of hay when I recall December 1st.

The transport was now some miles on its way and the mule-
drivers were doing their utmost.   Then the Staff mounted and
I was sent to see the whereabouts of the ammunition barge,
as the guns, especially S Battery, were running short.   Luckily,
I discovered where it had got stuck.   In feverish haste we
replenished the carts ourselves, General Smith, the Staff
Captain and I, our telephonists and horseholders, all loading
the first few carts at the run.   In less than five minutes the
cute little Jaipur ponies and mules had galloped to their guns.
The batteries remained in action as long as possible without
jeopardizing their safety, and each covered the retirement of
the other.   This went on for hours.   We, the Staff, walked
our horses half a mile, dismounted and waited.   Our pace was
the pace of the slowest fighting unit, *i.e.* a walk.   Gradually
we out-distanced the enemy, the Cavalry Brigade keeping him
back.   Once they caught us up and sent shells wildly over our
heads.   The Turks don't know enough of the science of
gunnery.   If their fuses had been more correct our casualties
could not have failed to be very heavy.   As it was they were
extraordinarily small considering the huge losses we inflicted
on them.

It was a most wonderful engagement, and General Townshend watched its every phase with great satisfaction.   An
exclamation of delight broke from him as he directed our
attention to a charge of the 14th Hussars.   Over the brown of
the desert a mass of glittering and swiftly-moving steel bore
down upon the line of Turks, which broke and bolted.   Then
the 14th came back.

My next job was to gather spare men and protect the
General's flank from Arab snipers.   Once or twice a bullet
hit the ground at my feet.   These Arabs use a tremendous
thing, almost as big as an elephant bullet.

At four o'clock I was ordered to ride ahead of the column

to find a watering place, which I did ; but the Turks still pressed in our rear, and we had to shove on without watering. I managed to water Don Juan, however, and gave him three of my six biscuits. The General had one and Garnett and I had half each. We pushed on, the horses showing signs of fatigue. At 6 p.m. it was dreadfully cold, and dark as Tophet. The order of the column had now been changed, the Field Artillery leading. The B.G.R.A. (General Smith), the Staff Captain, and I, rode at the head of the Division. The orders were seventy paces to the minute with compass directing. We took this in turns of half-hours. The strain was very severe. We had had no food except a sandwich for breakfast for twenty-four hours—violent exercise under exhausting conditions. The ten hours in the saddle had made me stiff, which was to be expected after the slack life of a month on board. We lost our way again and again as we got deeper into the dense black night. Road there was none, only a few hoof marks on the *maidan*. Tracks that went comfortably for a mile suddenly proved false, and then we had to hunt for the road. We all grew more irritable as we grew more tired, and I got an awful wigging about every two minutes. It's no joke leading an army on a pitch black night and endeavour- ing to keep to a road that doesn't exist, especially when thousands of Turks are in hot pursuit a mile or two behind the tail of the column.

" Is this the road ? " asks one.

" I don't believe it is."

" I think he's wrong. He's taking that fire for the star."

" He must be wrong. That fire has been directly ahead for hours and now it's to the left."

This was the eternal conversation behind as one tried to count the seventy and answer inquiries as to the magnetic bearing at the same time. With such preoccupations one could not very well suggest that the nearer one got to the fire, the more to a flank it must appear unless we were to walk on the top of it.

Then arguments would follow as to whether such a mark were really a hoof-mark or wheel track. The Staff Captain lost his way several times running, and I confess my heart rejoiced thereat. But we soon passed from levity that was born of nervous exhaustion, to silence, grim and impenetrable. I shall never forget that night. The want of sleep was maddening. Since then I have gone without sleep for days together, except for an hour or so once or twice. Then it came on one unprepared. We stumbled on. I thought of the army behind us, men as tired and hungry as I was, the army that had conquered Mesopotamia, all bravely staggering onwards in the darkness ; heroes of Ctesiphon, full of painful memories of lost pals somewhere behind, marching, marching, marching to the pace we set, and following the indication of my prismatic compass.

Some of the Staff suggested a halt. But our Napoleonic general drove us on. Again, as we learned subsequently, he saved us. That night the Turkish army, reinforced, was trying to outmarch us.

We pressed on and on. Don Juan followed with my orderly. It was awfully cold, but I preferred the cold to the weight of my coat. I slung it over Don Juan. The poor brute shivered from cold and hunger every halt. The march became a nightmare. With frequent drinks of water I managed to keep on. At eleven o'clock we were almost into the halting-place—Monkey Village by name—when the whole column, which was some five miles long, was compelled to halt owing to a block. The ground was very uneven and scored with nullahs, and had only the one narrow track leading to the village. Across this track the Cavalry Brigade, which had gone on ahead of us as advance guard, had bivouacked. The block took about an hour and a half to rectify.

At last we got to some open ground past the village. How cold it was ! We bivouacked on sandy soil. I scooped a dug-out for the General, got a few handfuls of hay for Don Juan, and a whisky and water for myself. General Smith got some sort of a meagre meal with me from a tin of jam, a little bully and a biscuit. We kept half for the morning. All our delightful *yak-dans* of stores, hams, fowls, biscuits, jam, tea and coffee were miles away with the transport, and I inquired a hundred times that night before turning in, without result. Those of our blankets which were not lost in the scurry of the morning fight, were there also with the transport. So in the bitter cold wind, feet numbed and teeth chattering, I scraped a hole for my arm and a sand pillow for my head, and shoving my topee over my ears to drown the nervy rip-rip of the Arab snipers, I slept. It was not for many minutes. The cold was too intense, without a coat. Then I had to ride to General Townshend for orders several times. Poor Don Juan was awfully done, but very game. There was a tiny stone bridge over a deep nullah near the village. Each time I was held up there. The scene was of the wildest confusion. Camels were being thrashed across, kicking mules hauled across, troops trying to cross at the same time. Several overturned vehicles complicated matters. The whole force had to go over that tiny bridge. After all had crossed the sappers blew it up.

I was quite an important person that night, what with orders and reports. The *Blosse Lynch*, with Major Henley aboard and also plenty of food, if I had known, was alongside. Captain Garnett was quite done up with continuous fatigue, although he had not ridden very much. We couldn't sleep for the cold, so we talked and hoped to get to Kut the next morning. That day, December 1st, he informed me, was his birthday. There could be many worse ways of passing one's birthday than in participating in the engagement we had fought that day. We felt a deep debt of gratitude due to our General for bringing us out of such a tight corner so brilliantly. At one moment the whole force was imperilled. The next our guns smashed lanes of casualties through the Turkish troops. I was assured by senior officers of much service that I had witnessed one of the most brilliant episodes possible in war, where perfect judgment and first-rate discipline alone enabled us to smash the sting of the pursuit and to continue a retreat exactly as it is done at manœuvres.

At 4 a.m. we were away again. We walked half a mile, then rested. After an hour or two of this the pace got slower and troops began to fall out and sit down. More than one dusky warrior unconsciously depicted the Dying Gladiator. We spoke kind words to them and where possible gave them a lift. Many mules were shot as their strength gave out. I ate my biscuit and gave Don a pocketful of hay I had kept for him. He rubbed his nose on my cheek and wished he were back in his excellent stable at Hyderabad.

Once this day my General's horse nearly unseated him as we crossed a nullah where a camel was lying stretched out.

"Come on," he shouted to me. "It's dead, and won't bite."

Don hates camels, and was rearing up in fine style. Therein he showed judgment more correct than did the General, for, in answer to my spur, he had no sooner drawn level with the beast than the "dead" camel swung its long snaky neck round upon us and opened eyes and mouth simultaneously. Don jumped the bank and the whole staff of telephonists and landed almost on top of General Smith, whose horse objected considerably. I laughed until the general restrained my humour.

The horses were awfully done, and in the batteries could just move the guns at the slowest walk. We did about a mile an hour. About 3 p.m. General Townshend shouted to General Smith that one of our batteries was shelling our own transport which appeared round the head of the river, miles ahead. My general apparently forgot me, and went off on his old charger. The transport could not have been saved by the time he got up to the guns. I put Don at a ditch and, racing up a knoll close by, blew on my long sounding whistle "cease fire," and held up my hand. The battery commander saw it, and when I galloped up I apologized for interrupting his shooting, and explained. They had bracketed the transport and a shot was in the breech of the gun, so my whistle had just got them in time. A splendid fellow is the commander of that battery, Major Broke-Smith, an excellent soldier and cheerful friend. Unperturbed, he said, "Well, if I'm to shell all Arab bodies, and the river will wind so——" And when I got back General Townshend thanked me, at which I was much elated.

In the afternoon we halted for two and a half hours to enable the straggling crowds to catch up. I rode miles trying to find our transport cart with the stores, but it had got somewhere in the front several miles off. Some one produced a cube of Oxo, and we had that divided and a whisky peg each. "G. B." slept, and I saw the horses watered and unsaddled. The general had some biscuits given him, and some signalling officer—whom the gods preserve !—gave me a sausage, which I ate before considering whether it would divide or not.

Then on again, on, on, for hours. Mules fell down and were helped up only to fall again a hundred yards further on.

Then word came by aeroplane that we might have to fight our way into Kut through an Arab and Turkish force. Later, to every one's dismay, we heard that we were not to reach Kut that night after all, but to bivouac five miles from it. In the last light of December 2nd, we saw the sun on the distant roofs of the village we had legged it so strenuously to reach. The brisk and prolonged marching of yesterday, and of last night, had reduced the present possible pace to a mile an hour.

We found a ruined *serai*, a four-walled enclosure of ground thirty yards square. Headquarters came here. A heap of dust and trampled chaff I selected as a sleeping place for the General, Captain Garnett, and me. It was colder than ever and a biting wind blew through our very souls. No one who has not sampled it for himself can credit the intense cold of such a Mesopotamian night. I have registered the cold of Oberhof, where twenty feet of snow and icicles forty feet high rendered every wood impassable. I have boated on the west coast of Scotland, where the wind from Satan's antipodes cuts through coat and flesh and bone. I have felt the cold from the glaciers of New Zealand. But I have never felt cold to equal that of December 2nd of the Retreat. Perhaps hunger and extreme exhaustion help the cold.

We lay close together for warmth. Late in the night some bread arrived from Kut. I had an awful passage of a mile, falling over ruts and into nullahs, and once very nearly into the river. We could not show lights as the opposite bank swarmed with Arabs. I walked with General Hamilton to the supply column. While we waited he told me of the battle of Ctesiphon. I got five stale loaves, two of which I gave Don Juan, who was shivering violently. Then I picketed the horses close together for warmth and we three ate our loaves. General Townshend occupied the far corner of the *serai*, and he spoke very cheerily to me for a minute or two. It was very extraordinary how well I had got to know some of the Staff during the last two days. Our acquaintanceship seemed of years. But then the retirement itself seemed that long.

CHAPTER III

W E left at 5 a.m. and trotted over the *maidan* to Kut.
The horses knew that there food and rest awaited
them. We got in at 7.30 a.m., but the column took
hours. I found Headquarters on the river front of the town
and our ill-omened transport already arrived there. I rode
on ahead to get things ready. First, I quieted my stomach
with some whisky and warm water, and then had a remarkable breakfast of bacon and eggs, cold ham, cold fowl, toast
and marmalade and coffee.

But there was no chance of rest yet awhile. A siege was
impending. No reinforcements were in the country and
Townshend's plan was to hold up the Turkish advance at Kut.
While we defended this strategical junction of the Tigris and
Shat-al-Hai, the enemy could neither get to Nasireyeh nor
down to Amarah. The river is the means of transport. And
so there was much to be done—wounded and ineffectives to
be moved downstream, trenches and gun-pits and redoubts
to be made, defences erected, and everywhere communication
trenches miles long to be dug and a thousand other things
arranged for. It was a race of parapet building against the
Turk. The army could not be spared much rest. I had to
collect the B.G.R.A.'s stores from *mahelas* and elsewhere, get
a secure place for ourselves and our horses, and buy stuff for
the possible siege, although it might be for only three weeks.

The river-front then became too hot for the Staff, so we
adjourned to dug-outs in the construction of which hangs a
story. In the meantime one learned that we had lost a barge
of wounded, several *mahelas* of supplies, supply barge,
H.M.S. *Firefly*, *Comet*, and *Shaitan* in the retirement. The

Firefly was an unfortunate affair, the shell striking her boiler. There might have been time to blow her up, but it appears that there was a wounded man down below. The breech-blocks of her guns were thrown overboard and the crew escaped. An excellent range-finder was captured on her. At the moment of writing she is pelting shells at us into Kut. We also heard that two cavalry officers who had ridden through the Arabs' lines to General Melliss' brigade with orders to join in the Um-ul-Tabul engagement on the night of December 1st, had been recommended for the V.C.

On December 4th, the day after we entered Kut, the last boat left for down the river. On the 5th the Cavalry Brigade and S Battery left Kut for down below, as they would not be of so much importance in a siege. Before they went Major Rennie-Taylor, commanding S Battery, had lunch with us. A day later the aeroplanes flew away. Then we were decidedly alone. Bullets fell from the north. Soon they came from every direction.

The dug-out for the B.G.R.A.'s Staff was to be made out on the *maidan* near the brick-kilns. The General added to the plans of the Pioneers for its construction, and so the thing was built like a long grave and the poles laid cross-wise. As a traveller of some experience myself I saw that trouble was obviously ahead. I hinted that as three poles were bearing on the centre one, that was insufficient to carry the total weight. My suggestion was dispersed by an eloquent explosion on the part of my General. So it was built ; and somewhere in high heaven a humorous Fate looked down and smiled. At midnight the roof that carried tons of bricks and soil collapsed without warning. It was the greatest luck we escaped without awful accident. I occupied the end farther from the entrance where General Smith slept, Garnett sleeping underneath beneath the ledge.

Luckily I was awake and, hearing the beam snap, I was out of my sleeping bag like a bullet, accidentally upsetting the General on top of Garnett. As I moved it fell in. I had taken the precaution to sleep with my head towards the entrance, else I had never escaped. For the rest of the night I shivered in the cold alongside the cook, without blankets, sleeping bag, or even jacket. All these were pinned down. In the morning when the working party came, we found that the central beam had broken and the two broken ends were forced a foot into the hard basement of my bed, just where my chest would have been. My General offered the remark : " An orderly officer is responsible for the health of his General." And remembering the mental curses I had manufactured at the time of the occurrence, and extracting further humour from having accidentally omitted to remove a stone from the part of the trench where the general had been compelled to lie, I proffered embrocation, and, being a dutiful subaltern, hid my smile. In the teeth of Turkish opposition the West Kents remade the dug-out that day. It has not collapsed yet.

To get from the dug-out to the town we had to cross a shell-swept zone. Every few yards was a splash of smoke and flame. That was, of course, at the beginning of the siege. Our dug-outs were near several brick-kilns, themselves sufficient target without our gun flashes. We had a battery of 18-pounders on one side, 5-inch on the other, and howitzers behind. So we came in for all the ranging. It was out of the question to leave any cooking utensils above ground, for they were certain to be perforated within a few moments.

A most wretched existence it was in that abominable little dug-out, but the balancing feature was our proximity to Colonel Courtenay of the 5-inch. A fountain of good-humour, ever flowing, an excellent story-teller, and a very human person. I delighted in his company. He was a very brave man, not of the defiant sort, but rather as one who has learned not to fear the inevitable. I saw him observing one day and a burst described a complete zone around him, but he went on stuffing tobacco into his pipe as if it was all November fireworks.

One evening I stood at the mouth of the dug-out giving orders. Some snipers from over the river must have seen me. A volley whistled past, one bullet cutting through the pocket of my tunic close to the hip. More extraordinary was the escape of the C.O. of the 63rd Battery, Major Broke-Smith. One morning he had a bullet through his topee and one through a pocket. In the afternoon another bullet got another pocket. Some one suggested his requiring a new outfit at an early date.

After the Cavalry Brigade had crossed our bridge of boats

THE BRICK-KILNS WELL REMEMBERED BY ALL KUTTITES. THE
GROUND HERE WAS HONEYCOMBED WITH DUG OUTS, GUN PITS
AND TRENCHES

below the town we found it necessary to destroy it, owing to a Turkish concentration upon that side. Its demolition was the occasion of considerable excitement. We lost an officer and men on the further bank. At the last moment it was found difficult to blow the bridge up. The heavy guns could not reach it, and I set off with orders for the howitzers to blow it up—an impossible target. The nearest shell was somewhere about 50 yards off. Then General Melliss rode up across the open to see what could be done, and interviewed my General. Finally, the bridge was destroyed by a very gallant subaltern assisted by another equally plucky in the following way.

At the further end of the bridge the Turks were in strong force. When night fell, and a dark night fortunately it was, a sapper subaltern started across the bridge with a charge, fuse lighted, strapped to his back. That was to ensure the explosion taking place even if he were hit. Strange to say, he got out, planted his charge, and got back without a shot being fired at him. The Turks must have been slacking. Then the other charge was laid. Both were quite successful and the bridge totally demolished. The officers have been recommended for the V.C.[1]

I was then quite busy for a few days with communications. We were very short of thick cable, and the thin stuff was being continually broken by fatigue parties. The General, as a rule, slept a little after tiffin, and at such times I would look up Colonel Courtenay.

" Hallo, Mousley ! How are you and the General ? Hope you are keeping him fit. Temperamentally of course, yes.

" Hello ? Oh, they're all right. Except lucky ones. Help yourself to that lot. But I've a cigar for you. Now let's talk about fishing."

Then there was Oxo (among the subalterns so named from resemblance to an advertisement)—a fiery ha ha, hum hum little colonel, as busy as a pea on a drum and exuberant as a thrush in June. He came to see us frequently.

On the 10th General Smith went sick. Captain Garnett followed suit. We left the dug-out for Headquarters, a

[1] Lieut. Matthews, R.E., and Lieut. Sweet, 2/7 Gurkhas.

building in the centre of the town with a courtyard. Like most others it was a two-story building with a promenade roof that was used for observation. Helio was used up there. Why, no one knows. Shells came on the building too, hundreds of them, and smashed the wall or thudded against it. The three legs of the helio disappearing over the balcony was the first sight I saw one early morning, and the signallers came down with white faces. The shell had smashed the helio without touching them. The Turks religiously refrained from hitting the mosque, but the hospital got it badly, and so did the horses which are stalled in the streets.

The enemy's lines have drawn much closer in some places, and are only sixty to two hundred yards off. The Turkish commander, Nureddin Pacha, sent word to Townshend that as our garrison was besieged by all the Turkish forces in Mesopotamia, he called on him to yield up his arms. General Townshend replied characteristically. Daily our General issued *communiqués* urging us to put up a good fight and to dig deep and quickly. Within a week we knew what that meant.

On the morrow I was brimful of influenza and chill contracted in the night the dug-out fell in, and was slacking on the bed when a report came from the 82nd Battery R.F.A. saying that a subaltern was wounded that morning and the captain was in hospital sick. The other subaltern, who had come from Hyderabad with me, had been slightly wounded days before. The message asked if the General could spare me. A very ardent soldier I was that morning. I jumped into my accoutrements feeling very weak from the influenza. However, I did not want to lose the opportunity, so with revolver, field glasses, and prismatic, I set off at once.

So delighted was I at the prospect of leaving the Staff for regimental duty that I had not noticed the artillery duel seemed to have developed into a general attack. No one seemed quite certain as to where the battery exactly was. It appeared to be somewhere in a palm wood some distance up the river. There were no communication trenches yet dug, so I went along the river-front which was shortest, and where I had heard there was also some rudimentary trench. It was a grave mistake, and I paid the penalty with as uncomfortable a half-hour as ever I had in my life. The *maidan* was deserted. Shells plunged into the first wood which I skirted. Rifle fire thickened and cracked fiercely in the trees. Snipers fired at me from over the river and I ran for it, stooping low, a hundred yards at a time. The Turkish gunners appeared to be sweeping all the woods. I got through to a little *maidan*, dead flat, not a blade of grass on it, and here was the hottest cross-fire I have yet seen. I crawled along back into the wood to get some way from the bank before going on. Then I raced for it and did about a fifth of the distance, bullets humming like bees in swarm. I took cover from the frontal fire, and then flank fire from over the river made it intolerable. About half way I saw a heap of rubbish and dirt about two feet high. I arrived breathless and fell flat. Shells came too, one burst on a building thirty yards nearer the river and the bullets splashed all round me. I had evidently been spotted over the river; bullets began to make a tracery around the rotten little heap. One dug itself in a few inches from my knee. The base of the mound stopped some, but when one bullet came clean through the middle, the dust being flung over my face and eyes, I got up and ran my best. This time I reached a nullah where a mule that had been hit was kicking to death invisible devils. From here I was fairly protected from flank fire so I bolted through the wood, and two hundred yards in I heard the battery in action. I shall never forget that horrible little affair behind the dust heap. I could see the Arabs' heads over the river as they shifted to take better aim, and the dust every yard or so that the bullets knocked up reminded one of Frying-Pan Flat in the volcanic region of New Zealand.

I sprinted over to the cover of a wall in the centre of the palm wood, and following it came across a gun-limber on end used sometimes as an observation post. It was protected by a few sandbags in front. I found the sergeant-major carrying on, the subaltern just hit being in a dug-out near by, where he was left until the " strafe " was over. The sergeant-major asked me to take better cover as several casualties had just occurred. I am now writing the first pages of this account from the identical dug-out near the limber. For hours I could not leave the post. The telephonist lay huddled underneath the wheels and orders coming by wire from the major I shouted on by megaphone to the battery, which was

dug in thirty yards in front.   Later on, reporting myself to
my C.O. and the colonel of the brigade, I was laughed at for
coming across the open, and they were astonished at my
arriving at all.

"It's a miracle you weren't knocked over," was the
colonel's comment.

The fire slackened and fell to mere sniping.   I looked
around.   The battery had excellent gun-pits, sandbagged in
front.   The dug-outs were very well built, the roofs being
supported by beams and trees.   Each detachment had its
own dug-out, and the men had furnished them snugly with
old horse-rugs and rush curtains and ammunition boxes
inlaid into the walls.   Our chief zone was directly up river.
My own dug-out was built up rather than dug out, being
constructed against a *mutti* wall which we believed was shell
proof until one day three shells plugged straight through near
by.   Then we dug down.   The mess was a very thick-walled
building and heavily sandbagged.   It also formed brigade
headquarters.   To get to the mess from the battery or from
one's dug-out, one had to run the gauntlet through the
incessant sharp music of rifle bullets cracking against trees or
branches.   As a rule, we one and all arrived in the mess
breathless from an ever-improving sprint.   This, of course,
and also the going from here to Kut, will be better when the
communication trenches have been dug.

On the same evening at dinner a native servant brought
in most startling news that a bullet had gone through the last
barrel of beer.   But jubilation succeeded dismay when we
found that a gunner, with the instinct of the British soldier for
preserving anything in the " victuals " line, had turned the
barrel over.   The bullet had entered near the ground, so
quite three-quarters was saved.   I hear on good authority
that the gunner will get the D.C.M.   We are almost out of
anything drinkable and the siege may go on several weeks.

At 9.30 p.m. I felt tired from the excitement of the day
and from the influenza, and turned in.   Ten minutes afterwards I was summoned on a night job.   Two guns of the
Volunteer Battery were in difficulties in an advanced position
near the river bank and just behind the first-line trenches.
They had been under heavy rifle and maxim fire at two
hundred yards range, and were enfiladed from over the river.

The guns were thus rendered unworkable. I was to take two gun teams and a G.S. wagon at midnight to retrieve them. This meant crossing the main *maidan* in the open without an inch of cover. It meant going almost under the rifles of the enemy scarcely two hundred yards off, and being visible in any sort of light to the enemy over the river. A guide was to await me at twelve midnight, near the battery.

I arranged for the teams and wagon to be there at 11.40 p.m., and for all links, swingle-tree hooks, drag-washers, and pole-bar to be bound up with rag so as to render them as noiseless as possible. The teams arrived punctually, their breath steaming up in the cold night air. The G.S. wagon had had a mishap over a rut just before pulling up, and the body was flung backward off the axle trees and jambed. We all tried our best to rectify it, but the jamb was so bad that it involved taking the thing to pieces. Here was first-rate luck already. The adjutant had spoken of the difficulties of the job, and strongly doubted the advisability of taking the wagon for the detachment's kit. A wagon is a rattling affair after any length of service. I utilized the accident as an excuse for waiting until the moon had gone down, which I thought advisable. I then awoke the battery sergeant-major and a detachment for a final attempt on the wagon. That was unsuccessful.

My drivers were all picked and excellent fellows. I mounted an old cavalry stager, and we set off about 1 a.m., when I met the guide, who, to my surprise, instead of being an officer or European N.C.O., was a half-caste, and as hopeless an idiot as ever got lost. His teeth were chattering with fright from the start. The *maidan* we had to cross was scored with trenches and barbed wire, and there was only one crossable place on each occasion that had been purposely made for us to cross. The guide could not even find the first flag. I threatened him with all sorts of disasters if he didn't find the place at once. We wandered about inside the *bund* of a communication trench for thirty minutes in awful darkness, that was at once our salvation and greatest difficulty. I rode along several trenches, and at last found the bridge the sappers had built for us. I believe they had measured the wheel-tracks of a gun-limber and deducted one-eighth of an inch from each side just to test the driving capacity of the field artillery.

We found a plank and shoved it down. It was quite dark, and any light was fatal. The drivers pointed out the difficulty. I told them to do their best. They deserved a medal, every man of them. The teams dressed exactly for the bridge, and then, when all was ready, moved forward and crossed safely. The noise brought rifle and machine-gun fire on us at once, but the bullets went high, a few hitting the ground with a sticky thud. I took the first team to a flank, and then we got the second over. The fire increased. I ordered the second gun team to keep one hundred yards behind the first in case of a volley. I didn't want to lose both. Again the guide was at fault, leading us bang upon our first-line trench some one hundred and fifty yards off the Turks. But the breeze came from the enemy to us, and, besides, the limbers moved almost noiselessly, so excellently taut did the drivers keep their traces. At last we found the small scrub and the guns. A subaltern rushed out and said we should be shot to the devil in two seconds if we came an inch further. Two days under continual rifle fire and no chance of doing anything had naturally not improved his nerves. I remember saying certain " things " about guides. I was much concerned with the state of his guns. They were in a banked hollow, close together in such a way as to render it impossible for the teams to hook in. Besides that, tins and rubbish were right across the track of any team attempting to approach the guns. As for the guns themselves, they bristled with the surplus baggage. All this meant noise, and my orders were for the greatest silence.

I ordered all baggage to be taken off the guns, and ammunition to replace it, as we had no wagon. We loaded all the ammunition, and after some trouble got the teams hooked in and away, following two feet of cover along the river edge. It was on the knees of the gods whether the enemy heard us. The fire had dwindled to sniping only, but we could see the lights of the Turks. A second guide now appeared. He was to conduct us to the new position for the Volunteer Battery guns in the middle of the *maidan*. To get there we had to cross three or four trenches and barbed-wire entanglements. The new guide, also a Eurasian gunner of the Volunteer Battery, was more confident than the other, but as utterly useless. He led us everywhere except in the right quarter.

Once he was certain he had found the crossing that had been shown to him that evening. On approaching it, however, I found it to be the flimsy roof of an officers' mess. In desperation I led the guns towards the original crossing, intending to reconnoitre for myself. The fire now increased, and a maxim opened. I believed we were discovered. But the bullets flew high. The Turks never dreamed that we could be so close.

At the bridge we made an awful row, the heavy guns straining and creaking abominably. It took some time to dress on to the narrow bridge. I wanted to get both guns over without delay, as I knew we should be spotted then. The first team refused to cross, but were persuaded to follow my horse, an old cavalry thing I had for the evening, that wanted to gallop on hearing the bullets. The drivers handled their teams magnificently. A few inches of error would have landed the guns in the deep trench—here quite ten feet wide on the top. The first gun got over, and something snapped in the bridge. I cautioned the drivers to have their whips ready. The second gun smashed the plank, and the bridge gave way. But the limber was over, and with whips and spurs the gun was bumped over also. We hurried to a flank, as several machine-guns opened on us. The fire was too high, and neither man nor horse was hit. One or two bullets cracked on a limber, and my old horse reared, breaking his girth, and the saddle and I found the ground together. I exchanged horses with a sergeant, and we went on. For the best part of an hour I rode alone up and down trenches, and at last found the crossings and the new gun emplacements. General Delamain, whose dug-out we missed by a few feet, asked if we had had casualties, and what had happened to our guide. We got back about 3.30 a.m. The sergeant-major had lain awake anxious. He is a father to the battery, and was delighted we had had no casualties. " Didn't expect to see you all back, sir."

My adjutant said he felt certain we were all done in when he heard the machine-guns open fire ; and Colonel Maule said : " Good show," and complimented me kindly on the affair. Looking backwards now, I am sure we could never have managed it with the G.S. wagon.

On the evening of the next day, December 12th, the Turks made an attack they had evidently been preparing some days.

It started so suddenly and decisively we felt no doubt as to the matter. The bullets came without warning, a veritable blizzard. I rushed out to the limber 'phone box, and we were soon at it hammer and tongs. The attack was on the fort, and a demonstration supported it from the trenches and scrub in the zone in front of our guns. We raked the trenches with shrapnel for hours. Subsequently the Arabs reported that while the Turks were concentrating in the scrub, our fire had killed a great many. We also fired some star shell, getting the burst well behind the enemy so as to show him up. Guns were booming all around, and the rifle fusillade on the walls and in the trees crackled like a forest on fire.

On December 13th I began duty as Forward Observing Officer for the field batteries. That meant that from our first-line trenches I was to range our guns into the enemy's trenches and saps. I was advised to dispense with helmet and wear a comforter as offering less target. I left with a signaller so as to reach the trenches at dawn, which was about 6.40 a.m. A surprise was in store for me. Instead of the roomy deep trenches with firing platforms, dug-outs, and so on, I found wretched little ditches, in many cases only three feet deep at the traverses. I did not know then, as I know now, the tremendous amount of work required in digging a good trench, and in Kut there were miles of them to be dug. The first few days I crawled miles on my knees. Every few yards some one had been sniped, so it came to crawling round the traverses. The trenches smelled horribly in the parts held by the native regiments. The dead were slung over the parapet, and sometimes not buried for days. The Gurkhas are truly gorgeous little men, patient, and very keen. They soon had their trenches wonderfully improved. The parapets varied most unreliably in thickness, and one had to keep one's head below the level, as bullets often came through. Turkish snipers were quite good. One day I saw a Punjabi carrying a pot of curry on his head and a bullet knocked it off. It spilled its hot contents over him and several others that blocked the road as they sat huddled up in the trench.

I ranged our fire on to the Turkish trenches that in places had got so close as fifty yards, and at one place where they were sapping, only thirty yards off. We were firing 18-pounders at very close range, the nearest being eight hundred

and fifty yards. It was great fun to correct back a few yards
and see the shell burst twenty yards in front of me, having
travelled about five feet above one's head. One such occasion
I was ordered to empty the trench for some yards in case of
accidents. It was as well we did so, for one or two prematures
burst behind us, and quite an appreciable amount of shrapnel
got in the trench. Several times after ranging I saw dead
and wounded among the digging parties of the enemy's trenches.

These trenches! They have their advantages, it is true,
for the Turks dare not shell them, and if you keep your head
down they are about the safest place in Kut ; but in the
course of their construction it was a case of a breaking back
from hours of stooping, or a bullet if one stretched. I've had
bullets knock dirt into my face, so that I thought that I was
hit, and had periscopes smashed to bits in my hand. Once a
bullet cut dead in the centre of the glass of the exposed end,
and pieces crashed all around my head, burying themselves in
the wall of the trench, and wounding a *naik* near by. The
Turks even came to know my yellow ranging flag, and cut the
bamboo rod time and again. They also had a nasty trick of
ricochetting bullets at us by firing them just ahead on the
ground. Not a few came into the trenches, especially before
they were very deep. Another factor that brought more fire
on us was the necessity of signalling from the trenches to the
battery by flag, and also having a danger flag. The reason
for this was the shortage of wire. The Turks always opened a
hot fire in the vicinity of the flags, and observation was very
difficult, except by periscope, as the loopholes were most
unsafe.

One afternoon I had been trying to discover a hostile
maxim that was playing havoc in our main communication
trench. A native reported that he had located it, and while
looking through a tiny loophole in plate iron he was shot
through the forehead, the bullet making a ghastly mess of
his head. Such a quick, silent death makes one careful. By
and by more periscopes were made by the sappers, and there
were fewer casualties. One mistake is enough, unless one is
very lucky. Turkish snipers lay with their rifles ready on a
part of our trench that was insufficiently deep. The first
sign of a movement there was the signal for a volley. After
a time we got accustomed to the dead things in the trenches,

D

and ate by them and slept by them.   After all, they are only earth full of memories as is an old coat.

Direct hits were very rare, but on one occasion I had the satisfaction of seeing a machine-gun hurled over the Turkish parados.   The 82nd was an excellent battery, and shot well. It was great fun ranging on the new trenches that had begun to appear since the night.   We blew one whole trench completely out of shape and there was a stampede of Turkish heads.

Great luck decreed that two shells, on different days, both premature, should scatter shrapnel in our trenches, while emptied for safety.   On one occasion Major Nelson, of the West Kents, I, and my signaller were there standing at the end of a traverse.   A kerosene tin and some utensils were scuppered between us, and dozens of our shrapnel bullets buried themselves in the wall of the trench.   But incidents of this nature grew too numerous for mention, and happened to many.   Another round from a cold gun landed into the cookhouse of the 76th Punjabis.   No one was there, but the cookhouse was not improved.   Another tragic premature killed a private of the Hants and badly wounded a second. Some of the shrapnel of this burst reached to where I was in in the trenches nine hundred yards away.

We were in daily dread of another attack, and at night all our guns were placed on their night-lines, each to its zone, just over our trenches.   On the first indication of a general attack we thus made a curtain of fire that the Turks funked breaking through.   Two or three times a night we would sometimes have to go into action for this purpose.

The West Kents improved their trenches splendidly, and made them quite comfortable.   A very nice regiment they were, and on many occasions I have been grateful for their hospitality at a breakfast.

They had a wee wooden home-made trench-mortar that we christened " Grasshopper," as every time he was fired he jumped, sometimes several feet back over the parados, out of the trench, and had to be recovered with lassos.   Once he tried to range to some trenches farther away, and blew himself to small bits.   The casualties during these first weeks were very heavy.   Our line was short, scarcely more than a mile and a half, and the enemy swept this with fair regularity.   The fatigue parties often had to risk going over the top in the night, and there was almost always a casualty.   I often think of my great luck on that night when I went for the guns.

Nor shall I easily forget the first time I was in a trench when an attack began.   This trench was about eighty yards from ours, and the rate of fire was terrific, but not so fast as ours.   The Turks well knew that although only eighty yards had to be crossed nothing human could arrive.

My trench incidents would fill a volume, which I have no time to write, and even with time it would be difficult to isolate individual instances of extraordinary routine.

What a kaleidoscopic mixture this diary is, to be sure.   I confess that on reading a passage here and there it seems merely an autobiographical sequence, and egoistical into the bargain. But the truth is, that personal experience in this thing called war is at best an awakening of memory from a dream of seas and foggy islands bewildering and confusing.   A few personal incidents loom a little clearer, deriving what clarity they have from the warmth of personal contact.   Then incidents fraught even with the greatest danger become commonplace, until the days seem to move on without other interest than the everlasting proximity of death.   Even that idea, prominent enough at first, gets allocated to the back of one's mind as a permanent and therefore negligible quantity.   I firmly believe that one gets tired of an emotion.   A man can't go on dreading death or extracting terrific interest from the vicinity of death for over long.   The mind palls before it, and it gets shoved aside.   I have seen a man shot beside me, and gone on with my sentence of orders without a break.   Am I callous ?   No, only less astonished.   Death has lost its novelty.   I am tempted to diverge into a speculation as to the necessary permanency of Heaven's novelty, a novelty of which one can never tire.   Alas, I am not now up in the cloistral peacefulness of Cambridge, so I can't follow up that speculation. Life never seemed so wonderful a thing as it does now.   I am extracting more fun and fact to the square inch here than I ever did before.   Now we know death as a tangible and nonabstract affair.   Let me not be accused of irreverence if I say we walk in his shadow and lunch with him.

Every evening I return to the battery and enjoy a meal in mess or relieve my major at his post.   Then follows a look around my section and inspection of the night-lines, and then bed in my dug-out among the date palms. Our sergeant-major is the best I've seen yet. The other day, just as he put down his megaphone in the speaking hole, a bullet plugged clean through it into the opposite wall, a vicious twang. He laughed quietly. " I believe it was alive," he said.

The Turks have moved their big guns closer, and their shells crash straight at this wall, which before was perfectly safe. On the 20th, two days ago, a shell smashed into our ammunition boxes after coming through the wall, a few yards from my dug-out, which I have been deepening this afternoon. It is a quiet day, and I left the firing-line early. The enemy can't locate our guns, as there is a wall some eighty yards ahead of the battery, so his gunners range just over the wall and search. Several shells have been through the gun emplacements, and some trenches have been smashed. Now and then a palm tree goes down with a crash. I've often awakened in the night thinking the whole place on fire. Sometimes, again, I awake to the sound of soft ceaseless swishing, that full and incessant sound of early morning in England, dear England, when the gentle rain washes open the eyelids of the waking world and green trees murmur, and birds begin to sing—but I look outside my dug-out and see only a mass of black crows flying over a palm-dotted wilderness to their Tigris haunts.

This morning the Gurkha regiment relieved in the first line. I am quite keen about them, a manly, silent, respectful set of men ; but children, too, mere children, for all that they are tigers in a scrap. Their genial colonel and I had a pleasant conversation after my morning ranging was done. We discussed the war and the Mesopotamian campaign and the eternal question of relief. He is a most active C.O. of a sprightly regiment. It yet remains a wonder to me how these full-sized colonels can possibly get along the half-completed trenches, which the first fortnight were only some 3 ft. 6 ins. deep, and often barely 2 ft. wide, and partly filled with ammunition boxes, stores, men's kit, and sundry cooking pots.

Among the gunner subs. is one known as R. A., which some say means Royal Artillery, and others the Ricochetting American. He has just returned from ranging, with the announcement that he knocked out half a dozen maxims with his 18-pounders. We have been ragging him by suggesting his field-glasses must be faulty, and asking to see them.

At a conversation in Kut to-day one heard many conclusions about America, who is not yet in the war. "It is a terrible New World," as Dooley said of the war ; "but it is better than no world at all." Not the least of our blessings is the gift of Time. Time it is that invites us to sit tight and say nothing while bounders and cleverly veneered barbarians romp rapturously through an applauding world. We have found them out. In time others will find them out. In the meantime we wait patiently. And patience is life. This has no connection with America, except that the Americans, with all their virtues, and they have many, have adopted impatience as their national characteristic. And Impatience is the off-spring of Ambition, and Ambition is forgetful of many things.

"Hitch your wagon to a star," suggests Emerson to his countrymen. "I guess I'll do better," says the American citizen, "I'll hitch it to a comet." At what time the shade of Don Quixote, that excellent gentleman, smiles quietly as he recalls having once hitched his charger to a windmill !

Later. Quos Di Amant.—I hear that poor Courtenay and Garnett are dead. Some days have elapsed since writing the last lines owing to a severe engagement we fought on the 24th and 25th. I will revert to that in a moment, but just now, as I sit here writing in the Fort, my narrative seems incapable of any reference quite fitting for that excellent soldier Colonel Courtenay. My General was ill when I left Headquarters to replace a casualty in the 82nd Battery that day under heavy fire.

Colonel Grier became C.R.A., and got hit in the head with the splinter of a shell. Then Colonel Courtenay became C.R.A., and Captain Garnett, Staff Captain of retirement memories, removed with the office of the B.G.R.A. on top of the building where the helio men had been. It was quite a good place, but conspicuous and dangerous, and shells struck incessantly on the wall behind. It was also in line for Headquarters, which the Turks had located. Not long after my leaving the building a disastrous shell killed Captain Begg instantly, an awfully nice fellow, with whom I had often had a joke, wounded and burned Captain Garnett severely in the leg, and hit Colonel Courtenay badly in the lower leg, smashing it. I tried hard to get along to see them, but urgent duties prevented. Garnett's case was complicated with jaundice. He died suddenly, to our great surprise and grief. I thank goodness I am not married just now. The General, he, and I, were together in that awful retirement, and during that time we exchanged many confidences, and he had censured me for taking risks. Now he is fallen already. Colonel Courtenay died heroically two days after the amputation. He was known throughout India as " Mike." After the operation we were discussing how fine it would be for him to be able to ride still. They had amputated his leg some few inches below the knee, leaving plenty for a grip. I suppose the shock took him away, that and the inadequacy of medical conditions. He was a robust soldier, and every one says the Service has lost a great sahib and an excellent officer.

Several other amputated cases have died with equal suddenness. It seems that they are mostly run down with the effects of this dug-out, exerciseless life. And the strain is constant. No part of Kut escapes the shell and rifle fire. The hospital has several casualties daily.

We have been on half rations in some things, and others have ceased altogether. Tinned milk and fresh have both stopped. There were a few goats, which have gone under from shell fire. Drinks have become a memory, except for the lucky ones who had huge mess stores awaiting them in Kut. The bread ration is one half, bacon twice weekly, (a tiny portion), no potatoes, and some cheese. Bully and bullocks will last for some little time longer. The trouble is that very many have dysentery, or colitis, or acute diarrhœa, and cannot take much except milk and eggs. These are almost unobtainable. What little there is, goes to the hospital.

The weather is bright and sunny, quite warm at midday and freezing at night. The extremes serve to emphasize the cold, and I find I require more blankets than ever I did even in the coldest weather at Shoebury. I have contrived to be comfortable by the help of my Burberry sleeping-bag and riding coat, combined with a travelling rug that is warm with distant and pleasant memories.

During the week preceding Christmas the assiduous Turk completed alternative positions for most of his guns, and it became necessary for us to do the same, so that at emergency we could shoot over the river also. For this a place was selected on the *maidan*, as we call the bare flat plain. We began with the pits by night fatigues, under fire the whole time. The high parapet of a communication trench probably saved a lot of us from getting hit. In two nights we equipped my section, which was on the right, with a communication trench, and I then fixed up an excellent little observation post by a wall for myself. Long ramps were made for the guns, so that we could get them into and away from the pits without difficulty. It was to be my show, and I was very keen on it. Then I chose a dark night and took my section down on the edge of the *maidan* near the river to demolish a *mutti* building that came in the way of our fire zone. Very heavy fire, but fortunately much too high, broke out from over the river. One man had a shovel hit, and another bullet struck a huge lump of *mutti* two men were carrying in my direction. Then we built a wall with the *débris* to screen us from machine-gun fire immediately over the river. Altogether we made a good job of it.

The horses are having many casualties daily. Already we have lost a fourth of their number.

The relieving force is rumoured to be expected about January 3rd. It cannot be a very large force, although on the date of Ctesiphon large reinforcements were wired for immediately. At first we were told that our concentration was taking place near Shaik Saad, some thirty miles below, on December 15th, but the rumours and counter-rumours cast considerable doubt on the whole thing.

On December 24th the enemy tried to storm Kut with a surprise attack by way of the Fort. It was a cold but eventful Christmas Eve. About 12.30 midday a hot rifle fire broke out over our trenches, and within a few seconds the symphony of bullets crackling in the palm trees swelled to a roar like the falling of fast and dense hail.

We went into a fast rate of fire at once with the battery on our prepared zones, and immediately put up a heavy barrage of shrapnel just in front of our first line. At first the densest fire seemed to come from in front of the 16th Brigade, but soon it extended right round our perimeter.

Woolpress appeared to be busy in action also, and then

our guns were hotly engaged by enemy guns of varying calibre, but chiefly 16-pounders, shrapnel, and high explosive. From our concealed position in an old orchard surrounded by a high thick wall we were not definitely located, and the Turkish gunners, often after having got our exact range, went on sweeping and searching, hoping to get us. More than one dug-out and gun-pit was entered by a shell, and one particularly narrow shave was when a 16-pounder crashed through the revetment of sandbags, smashed the shield of the gun, and buried itself in the earth behind without exploding. The rifle fire was so thick that our telephone wire in the trees was cut through the first two minutes. Major Harvey, our adjutant, had selected this position for the guns. The dug-outs of the gun detachments and the communication trenches were by this time well and deep down.

The fire became general all round Kut. High above the roar of rifle fire and scream of shell rose the sharp high note of the Turkish mitrailleuses. Suddenly most of his guns concentrated on the Fort, a salient by the river, none too strongly held. The Turk was evidently merely demonstrating on our sector, and intended to attack through the Fort. All our available guns in turn were switched on to their Fort lines, *i.e.* for a barrage, already prepared, just over the walls of the Fort. We increased our range and searched, getting in among the Turkish reserves all piled up and awaiting ready to support. A red glow hung over the low mud walls, and reports said that the Turks with great gallantry and determination had rushed up to the outer ramparts with grenades and charges of dynamite. By this time their guns had made a breach or two in the eastern sector known as Seymour bastion, and heavy hand-to-hand fighting ensued. Grenades and the bayonet were chiefly in operation. At one time some hundreds of Turks had entered the ramparts, and it was touch and go. The Oxfords and Norfolks were hurried up to stiffen the Indian regiments, and every available man, sappers or pioneers included, was given a weapon and pushed into the fray. The Volunteer Battery did extremely well with rifle and grenade. Instances of pluck and daring were many. Handfuls of men from the British regiments in little knots formed the backbone of the struggle, and, nipping around behind the attackers, dispatched them to a man. Finally, thanks largely to the terrible casualties our guns had inflicted on the enemy supports, the pressure slackened, and the last Turks were bombed out of the bastion. It was a great resistance, and successful chiefly owing to the outstanding merit and fighting quality of the British regular infantry.

Firing continued intermittently all day, and while on duty at the guns pending any renewal of the attack, I inspected the Christmas decorations of the men's dug-outs.

Above ground we saw merely the several sandbagged emplacements of the guns among the long grass and fruit trees, with six ominous muzzles peering through the revetments, and ammunition awaiting ready near the pits, the limbers drawn up snugly in rear for protection. Below, the communication trench ran into and through the dug-out of each gun detachment. The men had made those comfortable by letting into the wall ammunition boxes as receptacles for their smokes and spare kit. Rush curtains hung over the entrance, and matting purchased from the bazaar was on the ground. To-night decorations of palm-leaves were spread out gaily on all sides, and the artistic talent of the various subsections had competed in producing coloured texts: "God bless our Mud Home," " Merry Xmas and plenty of Turks," "Excursions to Kut on Boxing Day." One humorist had hung up a sock without a foot, and suspended a large bucket underneath to catch his gifts.

Our mess secretary, Captain Baylay, an officer of much resourcefulness in cooking and making shift, arranged an excellent plum-and-date duff for the men.

Several alarms were given through the night, and we stood by our guns hour after hour. However, nothing much happened, as the Turks had evidently had enough. Orders came for me to proceed to the serai, River-Front Artillery observation post, and to be ready to open fire, if necessary, at daybreak, and to have my telephone wire already laid. This entailed getting up early, so after an hour's rest without sleeping, I set off with my telephonist. We laid the wire accordingly, direct on to our own brigade headquarters, through the palm grove to the serai. Dawn found me among the sandbags and *débris* of the dismantled heavy gunners' observation post, looking around on the vast plain, seemingly quiet and deserted and divided by the great broad sheets of the Tigris. Gradually the darkness rolled away. The soft glow of approaching day climbed up in the eastern sky. Ray after ray stole across the water-dotted plain and revealed to me the coloured minaret of Kut silvered in the dawn, emerging from the night. The outlines of Kut followed, our defences, river craft, the palm groves, a few Arab goats grazing out on the Babylonian plain. Less than fifty miles from the scene of my Christmas morning once arose the Babylon of the Ancient world, and her chariots coursed all around this vicinity. Babylon has gone. For thousands of years her memory has slept wrapt in the silence of oblivion except for the passing of Arab or Turkish heel. Perhaps the war is to see this ancient land once again awakened by England to life and a new destiny.

Wild geese and duck were the first to stir. Buffalo far down stream followed. Then small dots began to move along the black lines. They were the heads of Turkish soldiery moving along their trenches.

Suddenly a rifle fusillade broke out, and bullets ripped into my sandbags, and some flew just over. I moved my telescope, for the light of the sun was on it. At the same time one, two, three, four small white fleecy puffs appeared away to the north-west. Immediately after one heard the report. Before the shells had reached us my message was through to the brigade. " Target ' S ' opened fire. Bearing so-and-so, new position." Our guns engaged them. Other targets opened, and the morning entertainment began. I was joined by the garrison gunners, Lieutenants Lowndes and Johnston, who took me down later to a wonderfully good breakfast.

I was relieved at lunch, and finding my way back to the battery slept a little before having to stand by for action again. In the evening I had permission to go into Kut to attend a Christmas dinner at the Sixth Divisional Ammunition Column given by " Cockie " R.F.A. It was dark when I left the battery, and rifle fire became lively. The communication trench, however, had progressed considerably, and one went most of the way under cover. I overtook some stretcher parties bearing wounded men from the first line. Arrived at the D.A.C. I found a most cheerful entertainment in progress. A long decorated table seating a dozen guests was full of good things. We commenced with a gin concoction

MAP of KUT.
Scale 2" = 1 mile.

Turkish First Line

4.12 cm Krupps
B target

L 9 pr. Mtn Howr.
Y Target.

FLOODED

Positions

Turkish Forward

FLOODS

FORT

Bridge 6.12.15"

Sandbanks

A

B
Gurkha
LINE

C FIRST
OUR

Q Target

Site of Reduced Gun
Vol. Bty.

MIDDLE LINE

82 Bty.

Anti Aircraft Gun

SECOND LINE

76 Bty.

63 Bty.

K
Captured British 18 pr.

Site of
Demol.
Bn. 8.12

Mortar.

Turkish Trenches

Wool press.

Snipers Nest.

SHATT-AL-HAI

Names

Brick Kilns
Hows.

Palms

Mosque

O.P.

6 D.A.C. Mess
Cemetery
Gen. Townshend's
House

KUT

Vol r. Bty.

Palms

H.M.S. Sumana

Maidan

N

RIVER TIGRIS

MAP OF KUT DURING SIEGE

of considerable potentialities. There was Tigre Crème, Turques Diablées, Nour Eddin Entrée, Donkey à la lamb, Alphonse pouding. I sat between Cockie and Major Henley of Dwarka memory. The Navy, Indian Cavalry, Flying Corps, and the Oxford Regiment and West Kents were also represented. A limited supply of whisky was available, and with such a good fellowship we abandoned ourselves to a joyful evening. Anyone hearing our shouts of laughter would not have imagined we were in a siege.

From the pudding I drew a lucky coin, a brand new half rupee, which I am keeping as a mascot. A sweepstake on the date of relief was opened, Lowfield January 1st, Highfield (which I drew) the 31st. So optimistic were we on immediate relief that I was offered for it only four annas. We had a miniature game of football in the tiny quadrangle to terminate proceedings, and at ten o'clock, in joyful frame of mind, I struck out in the pitch-dark night for the palm grove. I missed my way again and again before getting the trench, and finally found the many turnings so bewildering without a light that I got up on top and followed the river-front once more as I had on joining the battery. A faint moon emerged, and the Turkish snipers followed me along. Several shots striking the wall alongside me I went inside it at the first breach and came across a dismantled tent behind which dark forms moved stealthily. On looking to see what it was, I found several jackals and pie-dogs mangling a horse that had strayed and been sniped. They sprang out with most dreadful yells. This commotion was heard across the river, and the Turks turned a machine-gun on. I lay quiet in the wood for some time listening to the rain and the bullets in the palms. It was a most ghostly spot—what with dead horses and mules, dismantled tents, graves, cast clothing, and shell-stricken trees. At this minute I became aware that I was not alone, a feeling one can very well have on such occasions. And I watched a certain shadow move by inches along the ground. It had been hiding behind a tree, and I imagine had been following me some little distance. There were from time to time rumours that the Turks sent Arab spies into Kut to pick off stray people in the hope of getting any plans. With my cocked Webley in my hand I called out. It proved to be an Arab who took to his heels and vanished like a wraith. He

had probably been salvaging. I reached my dug-out very
tired an hour later and found all the battery asleep. An order
required me to stand by from four to six, so I slept with my
boots on. At four I went around the battery and had the
men standing to, which means awake and dressed ready for
action but resting. Nothing happened. At dawn I was told
to get my kit and report for duty at the Fort as Observation
Officer to the Tenth Field Artillery Brigade, the other officer
having been wounded the preceding day. Slinging a few
things together to be brought along by my servant, I walked
the two miles of trenches to the Fort, which I entered for the
first time.

It proved to be a mud-walled enclosure of about seven
acres with a few bastions extending beyond. The garrison
of the Fort were all underground and dug in. In fact, the
place was a network of communication trenches, dug-outs, or
store-pits. It was an easy target for the Turkish artillery,
and shells of all sizes kept leisurely arriving from all sides, and
at this close range we hadn't any warning report of the Turks'
guns, besides which, grenades and bombs were slung or fired
over the wall indiscriminately into any part of the Fort. In
the centre an observation mound of bags of *atta* (flour), some
fifteen feet high, commanded quite an extensive view over
the walls on to the plain beyond. One could see three-fourths
of the horizon and a very good view of Turkish activities upstream. This observation post was frequently a mark for
the Turkish machine-guns, and one had to run the gauntlet
in getting up to it by making a sudden bolt, and frequently
a r-r-r-rip of bullets into the flour-bags followed. Sometimes, generally during the firing of a series, the Turk ranged
several machine-guns and small pounders on to the post.

Besides myself there was an observer for the heavy guns.
When registering we seized the most favourable hour of the
day for the minimum of mirage, usually just after sunrise or
before sunset. As the artillery duel became general, one had
to range on several targets in succession and sometimes two
simultaneously. When one was too preoccupied the services
of the machine-gun officer were utilized. Although not trained
for artillery observation, and talking of " degrees over " or
" short," which frequently puzzled the gunners, he nevertheless
had a good eye for a bursting shell. He was a big-game shot

endowed with a large imagination and a bad memory, as he constantly varied the same story, but what one lost in veracity one derived in entertainment. I liked especially to get into the " stack," as we called it, at dawn, and watch the shadows lifting over the plain and the wild duck and fowl flying away to their feeding-grounds.

On one such early occasion, after a heavy " strafe " the night before, I had no sooner entered the " stack " than two or three of the several bullets hitting the bags came through and struck the inside wall. We placed another bag or two on the spot, and then in the afternoon a bullet came through between another officer and me. We could not understand why this had happened, as the "stack" had frequently been subjected to the heaviest Maxim fire, and if there had been any flaw we must have been riddled several times. Late at night, before the moon was up, I climbed on to the bags from the outside and found that the machine-gun fire had cut grooves into two sacks and the flour had run out on to the ground, making an excellent mark, and what was worse, the outside bags were three parts empty, allowing the bullets to come through the second.

The long tedious hours of the day were diverted by the Volunteer Battery Section firing at any target that offered. Other things failing, a basket ferry at near range was engaged, and excellent sport it made, the Arabs or Turks ducking out of it into the river. A small mountain gun called Funny Teddy was ubiquitous, appearing on all sides. He was extremely annoying to us, and once several guns were turned on to him. He was fairly well protected, but one round turned him completely over. Great joy reigned over the Fort, and word was sent into Kut. But the last message had scarcely been dispatched when he appeared behind a tent and spat out several rounds almost into the " stack " just to show his spite.

Early one morning, a few days after I had reached the Fort, I observed that the *Firefly*, formerly H.M.S., now S.A.I., was not in her accustomed spot. We usually located the ships of the Turks and reported any activity to G.H.Q. Suddenly there caught my eye something like a perpendicular stick moving at a rapid rate downstream towards Kut. Her funnel appeared immediately after. We informed Kut and a fire was opened on her from our five-inch and four-inch River

Front Guns. This stopped her, but not before she had got some of her 4·7's into Kut. This gun, with some small supply of ammunition, was captured on the *Firefly* and was the hardest hitting gun the Turks had.

January 1st.—I was up a half-hour before the dawn on first spell of duty, Captain Freeland taking the second hour. We usually took breakfast in turn. Food at the Fort I find much worse than in Kut, the distance out being accountable for that, and the special chances of getting horse-liver or kidneys, a great delicacy, quite a remote one. We live in a tremendously large dug-out, some sixteen feet by ten, the roof being spanned by great beams of wood, eight by six inches, but much too low to allow one to stand upright. The beam is already bent considerably with the great weight of some feet of soil on top, and one lies smoking on one's back staring at this beam and applying the Aristotelian axiom that just as " some planks are stronger than others, so all will break if sufficient weight be applied," and hoping a 60-pounder won't just add the difference.

I am writing alone in the observation post. The New Year has just been heralded in with a wonderful dawn. Shades of mauves and heliotrope and violet are diffused over the most extraordinary geography of floating cloud islets, continents, and seas, sailing and sailing up and away. From a belt of electric blue fringing the southern horizon down to Essinn past the Tomb, and over the Eastern desert, cloud island after island has broken from its aerial moorings speeding like sailing ships across the ocean sky up past Shamrun Camp of the enemy towards Baghdad. The first streak of dawn beheld this phenomenon of smartly moving Change. How much more prophetic this than the stillness of a static dawn. As Horace says, one sees not into the future, but such a moving dawn may well be taken as an augury of big happenings in the year just born and, ultimately, let us hope, of a convergence of British destinies moving onward like these cloudlands to Baghdad. But I for one as a traveller do not believe we have yet nearly appreciated the tremendous vitality and potentiality of Germany or fully realized the great strength and solidarity she draws from her geographical centrality.

In the meantime, here am I in a siege, believing in a certain relief within a few days or two weeks if British luck holds, sitting in an observation post of many tons of *atta* (flour) which seems to have been used for defences on all sides and no tally kept of it at all. Sitting on an *atta* stack talking of dawns ! !

Evening.—Quite a few shells fell about our dug-out, and machine-guns were turned on the stack while I was ranging on to a party of Turks working on two distant gun-emplacements. The Turks seem to know most of the ranging is done from the Fort, and when our guns in Kut open fire the northern sector invariably strafes our observation stack. The working party we can observe quite well taking cover when the shell is heard coming, and immediately after the burst away go their shovels and picks again. We fired sectional salvos, and I believe did good execution, as we observed carts coming out from their hospital and some stretcher parties. The work evidently proceeded nevertheless, and this afternoon two guns in the new position opened fire on Kut. Our heavy guns, however, soon silenced them.

This afternoon I visited the battered sections of the Fort known as Seymour Bastion, still in a most dilapidated and shattered condition from the heavy assault of the 24th, and only roughly reinforced as yet with corrugated sheet iron, barbed wire, and trestles. The bombs and shells have made great breaches in the wall. We went along in the dusk to the listening post and along the bastion, a corridor running out past main wall towards the Turks, and enabling the defending party to enfilade an assaulting party on the outer wall. However, on the 24th, the bastion itself became the scene of a hand-to-hand struggle and it got choked with dead. It is a pity we haven't Lewis guns as they have in France, which are much lighter and more portable in case of an assault. But when our machine-guns were out of action, bombs and bayonets and rifles held him off. The bastion, I was informed by a man of the Oxfords, was a most unhealthy spot. It proved so. As we passed a loophole, bullets entered that one and the one ahead. The Turk here is ever alert, and he has a big tally to account for. One passes a loophole (they are quite low and unavoidable in walking), and then waits for the rifle fire before rapidly crossing another. In one place bullets simply pour through a cavity or chink in the mud wall. This is to be built up to-night. The Oxfords and Norfolks are very proud of the part they took in the fight and showed me scores of dead Turks scattered all around. There were hundreds, only many have been removed by the enemy during the truce. In this heat of the day, the odour that comes to the stack from the " unburied " is at times almost overpowering. More than one Turkish " trophy," rifle, belt, or helmet has been boldly retrieved by our men, and one sepoy has recovered no fewer than three helmets and an officer's sword.

Our frugal breakfast is rice and bully and tea. We have no butter nor sugar. For dinner we are to have a small ration of potatoes, fillet of horse, date and *atta* roll, and to divide two bottles of beer the Mess has providentially saved—a very good New Year's Day meal considering one is not a Scotsman.

Later, 7 p.m.—Dinner over. I feel in conscience bound to say it was excellent and almost half enough. I have a Burma cheroot from a very precious supply of a kind-hearted subaltern here from Burma.

January 2nd.—The event of to-day was the arrival of an enemy aeroplane flying quite fast. It came from the Shamrun Camp and flew over taking observations, followed by a fusillade from every available rifle and machine-gun.

Later in the day another aeroplane flew over us likewise from the north. Our big-game friend insisted that it was a Turk. One could not see the colour, but I saw what looked like rings. General Hoghton, who came into the stack, agreed with me about it, and on its return so it proved to be. A Turkish plane has a crescent on its wings or generally the German cross. This brigadier is a most intrepid and fearless man, and is to be found everywhere at the loopholes, digging-parties, and observation posts. The Fort is merely part of his command (the 17th Brigade), but one sees much more of him than the C.O. Fort. He is a most genial and kind general and very cheerful about everything. To-day I met Colonel Lethbridge, now commanding the Oxford Regiment, and one of the few officers of that regiment to survive Ctesiphon. We had a most interesting and diverting talk on European politics in general. He is an extraordinarily well-read man and over everything he says plays the quiet light of a well-focussed intellect. We talked of Germany, where I had spent a considerable time before the war, and he asked me many questions of the French front. I hear I am the only one of the garrison who was in France in August, 1914, and only two other officers have been there at all. In fact, one notices that this Division, having come direct from India early in the war, has, for the most part, no idea of the significance of the war and of the new armies. Neither has it, or could it be expected to have, any sort of perspective of the many fronts of the war. They allow either too much or too little. They are focussed sharply on to Mesopotamia and the Sixth Division, and the perspective of the World War suffers. Moreover this front is not contiguous to any other front. But this Colonel of reserved utterance in his grave way dismissed many of the current rumours of Kut as being out of proportion, and made one feel at least how very vast and far were the ultimate issues of the war. And for listening respectfully I had a most entertaining hour and two large whiskies and water. On my way back I saw the work of the Sirmoor Sappers, a most keen and enthusiastic body of men who are never idle.

January 16th.—I am writing in an excavation of four mud walls and beneath a tiny roof of corrugated iron topped by some feet of earth. Two tiny camp chairs, a wooden table with legs driven into the earth, and two niched candles form the furniture. It is the mess of my battery, 76th R.F.A., whither I have been ordered some days since from the Fort to replace Lieut. Edmonds who was wounded while mending a telephone wire. The man accompanying him was killed outright, and Edmonds had a narrow shave, the bullet cutting a deep groove across his neck and just missing the spinal column.

Captain Baylay of the 82nd Battery relieved me at the Fort. He has about eighteen years' service and is by general admission a very good gunner, quick, resourceful, and of instant decision. Apart from the fact that I am getting back to my own battery I feel he will be more able than I am to deal with the ever-increasing responsibilities of observation officer out there, which goes pretty close to having two or three targets almost simultaneously. It will also enable the machine-gun detachment commander to devote his attention to his own particular job and incidentally to become conversant with the theory and terminology of field-gun ranging.

My battery is just behind the middle line out on a solitary

E

position on the *maidan*. Unlike any other field battery we have no cover whatsoever except that of the earth. Every time a gun fires the flash is visible to every Turkish gun on the north or eastern sector. We are swept by rifle fire all around, the nearest some few hundred yards over the river, and we get all the " shorts " intended for the heavy guns at the brick kiln, five hundred yards behind us. Our Major (Lloyd) is away at the Brick Kilns from where he can observe much better than in the battery, and he messes more comfortably with C.Os. of other batteries there. The only other officer in the battery is Lieut. Devereux, my junior of a few months, who had been sent from Hyderabad before me. He has a keen sense of devotion to duty and is most conversant with every detail of horse management, harness, and guns, but less quick at figures and in making up his mind. I leave much to him, as for some months he had been a sergeant-major of M battery before coming to Hyderabad, and we owe more than one good meal to his knowledge of the Q.-M. department in Kut, and " Coffee-shop " official ropes. We live and sleep in the mess with our boots on, as we frequently go into action during the night.

The new dug-out for myself, just behind my section of guns, is almost complete. It is large and deep, and although in danger of floods, I am content. Some trestle beams from a dismantled dug-out I am using for the roof. The difficulty is to find wood of sufficient strength to support the weight of earth necessary to keep off rifle fire.

The 40-pounders we cannot compete against. For a radius of one hundred yards the battery is thick with holes which in one place have joined up and made a pond where I have counted over sixty unexploded shells. Before I came one of these arrived in the mess, having entered through feet of soil and beam and iron. The thrilled occupants had reason to be thankful that it did not explode. It has been inserted in the hole, which it fits exactly, just above the doorway, its nose pointing at the table, a standing reminder of the thinness of line described by the Circle of Destiny.

We are awfully short of firewood, only enough being available to cook one meal a day for the men, and provide hot water besides for breakfasts. Sometimes there is not even that. Theft of wood is punishable with death. The G.O.C.

is loth to destroy the town. We shall, however, have to do that very soon.

News there is none, except that on January 12th General Younghusband smashed into heavy Turkish forces at Wadi, a stream coming down from the Pusht-i-Kuh mountains, and got through with the tremendous losses of four thousand. The liner *Persia* has been sunk by a submarine.

The patience of the garrison is beyond all praise. I can honestly say I have learned to love the character of the British soldier who has acquired the habit of doing cheerfully what he does not want to do, at the moment when he just does not want to do it. In other words, bigger than himself is the momentum of years, discipline become a habit. There are rumours that the Relieving Force has retired. The fighting, we hear, is in deep mud and must indeed be terrible.

CHAPTER IV

JANUARY 21*st.*—A black-letter day for Kut in general and myself in particular. About 6 a.m. in the pitch-dark, the water burst into our front line by Redoubt D and flooded the trenches up to one's neck. All the careful and dogged efforts of our sappers could not stop it. Lately the weather has been what an undergraduate would call the last edge. On the 17th it poured. In fact the heavens opened and lakes of water tumbled down. It has kept this up on and off ever since. To-day we have had to abandon our first line from Redoubt B to the river on the north-west sector, and the line now falls back at a tangent. The salient at the Fort has been kept with the greatest difficulty; but the enemy on the flooded sector has had to go back likewise. It was a queer sight to see them all running over the top where we had previously seen only their pickaxes and caps. Our casualties from rifle fire during this movement were not so many as his. We shelled his ragged masses with great glee. A mile or more of silver water now surrounds this part of the line. As to food, we have eaten up some very tough bullocks, and I much prefer donkey to mule. We are down to horse in a day or so. The floods have put our meagre fires out, and for dinner we had half-raw donkey, red gravy, and half-cooked rice with some date stuff that made me feel like an alarm clock just set off.

January 26*th.*—The weather gets worse. I am in my new dug-out, cold and shivery. In fact my lower half is almost without feeling. The water percolates from the four sides and from the roofs in several streams. This I have diverted into buckets and ammunition boxes by means of pipes and waterproofs strung up with any available tackle. The various sounds of water falling into its several receptacles remind one of fishing in the rain by a cliff-side.

Our trenches are half full of water, and as we have no change of dry kit we run the gauntlet along the battery to the mess. It is difficult in the dark to get along, and of course no light is permitted, as every day some one pays the penalty of chancing it. One runs low and slides along the mud. In the day a heavy fire is invariably opened. But one just gets through in time. I can tell where I am by the sound of my boots in the water. Once I slipped down with my megaphone, and when I found it a second later it was pinked with two holes from a bullet.

To-day General Townshend has issued a lengthy communiqué dealing with the failure of General Aylmer to get through, and predicting relief by the middle of February, but noting our last day of resistance under reduced rations as reaching to about April 15th excluding horse rations. We are, however, beginning to see how vital a part the floods play in every movement of troops. Here in this dug-out, streaming with tiny rivulets and squelchy underfoot, one feels rather than sees the plainness of the issue between the Turks and us—our advance of four miles with four thousand casualties, a rumour of repulse with as many more, a sequence of Turkish trenches similar, floods rising, etc., etc.

Kut-el-Amara,
January 26th, 1916.

The relieving force under General Aylmer has been unsuccessful in its efforts to dislodge the Turks entrenched on the right bank of the river some fourteen miles from the position of Es-Sin, where we defeated them in September last when the Turkish strength was greater than it is now.

Our relieving force suffered severe loss, and had very bad weather to contend against. More reinforcements are on the way up river, and I confidently expect to be relieved some day during the first half of the month of February.

I desire all ranks to know why I decided to make a stand at Kut during the retirement from Ctesiphon. It was because, as long as we hold Kut, the Turks cannot get their ships, barges, stores, and munitions past this, and so cannot move down to attack Amarah, and thus we are holding up the whole of the Turkish advance.

It also gives time for our reinforcements to come up from Basrah, and so restore success to our arms. It gives time to our allies the Russians, who are now overrunning Persia, to move towards Baghdad, which a large force is now doing.

I had a personal message from General Baratoff in command of the Russian Expeditionary Force in Persia the other day, telling me of his admiration of what you men of the Sixth Division, and troops attached, have done in the past two months, and telling me of his own progress on the road from Kermanshah towards Baghdad.

By standing at Kut I maintain the territory we have won in the past year at the expense of much blood, beginning with your glorious victory at Shaiba ; and thus we maintain the campaign as a glorious one instead of letting disaster pursue its course to Amarah, and perhaps beyond. I have ample food for eighty-four days, and that is not counting the 3,000 animals which can be eaten. When I defended Chitral, some twenty years ago, we lived well on atta and horseflesh, . . . but, as I repeat above, I expect confidently to be relieved in the first half of the month of February. Our duty stands out plain and simple. It is our duty to our Empire, to our beloved King and Country, to stand here and hold up the Turkish advance as we are doing now ; and with the help of all, heart and soul with me, together we will make this defence to be remembered in history as a glorious one. All in England and in India are watching us now, and are proud of the splendid courage and devotion you have shown ; and I tell you, let all remember the glorious defence of Plevna, for that is in my mind. I am absolutely calm and confident as to the result. The Turk, though very good behind a trench, is of little value in the attack ; they have tried it once, and their losses in one night, in their attempt on the fort, were 2,000 alone ; they have already had very heavy losses from General Aylmer's musketry and guns, and I have no doubt they have had enough.

I want to tell you all now that when I was ordered to advance on Ctesiphon I officially demanded an Army Corps, or at least two Divisions, to do the task successfully, having pointed out the grave danger of attempting to do this with one Division only. I had done my duty: you know the result, and, whether I was right or not, your names will go down to history as the heroes of Ctesiphon, for heroes you proved yourselves to be in that battle. I, perhaps, by right should not have told you of the above, but I feel I owe it to all of you to speak straight and openly and take you into my confidence, for God knows I felt our heavy losses and the sufferings of my poor wounded and shall remember it as long as I live. No general I know of has been more loyally obeyed and served than I have been in command of the Sixth Division.

These words are long, I am afraid, but I speak straight from the heart, and you will see that I have thrown officialdom overboard. We will succeed, mark my words, but save your ammunition as if it were gold.

(Sd.) CHARLES TOWNSHEND,
Major-General,
Commanding Sixth Division.

I grow sleepy. Two nights ago we had a disaster I have not recorded. The flood burst a *bund* adjacent to us, and surplus flood water travelling fast swept across the battery carrying along with it the revetments and emplacements. The soft side of the trenches collapsed with a sickening thud, and in places filled right in. I was awakened by the sound of trickling water pouring down the earthen steps of my dug-out. It overflooded the *bund* which I had taken the precaution to build between the battery trench and my cavern. On climbing out I saw that the whole plain was a reach of water. I shouted to my orderly. We seized spades and shovels and filled in. This kept out further water which was still rising. The men were similarly engaged. One dug-out was close to the main trench and only supported by a tiny wall of earth which collapsed when wet. Trench and dug-out then ceased to exist. It was a pathetic sight to see the men, eight to a detachment, diving in five feet of mud and water for their belongings, some of their friends holding up the roof of their dug-out with poles. No bunnies flooded out ever felt more " out " of it than the men of my section. I had all their clothes dried as best as our scanty firewood could do it, some hot tea made for them, and their spare kit put into my dug-out. All night long the fight continued. My floor was two feet under water. In the gun-pits it came up to the breech-blocks of the guns, some of which had collapsed through their planks which had sunk into the mud. This I had foreseen weeks before. In fact, I had drawn up a simple scheme for putting in each gun-pit a foundation of filled ammunition zinc linings, then the planks, and on top the bricks from the brick kilns close by. There were a great quantity of these. My Major, however, possibly for some good reasons of his own, thought this unnecessary, and I was not permitted to go on with it. To-night, as I lay in my dug-out after hours of useless battling with the floods and in endeavouring to get the guns into action, I felt glad that my scheme had proved well-justified, for the ammunition pit which I had made as an experiment was the only dry part of the battery. We had the greatest difficulty in endeavouring to traverse the guns. After getting the wheels level we found every movement of the trail brought it off the scanty planking, and our many targets required considerable traversing. We reinforced the telephone compartment but the mess was feet deep in water. About two dug-outs remained more or less habitable, and in these the men crept while a few still went on trying to retrieve lost kit.

"'Ere, Bill, 'old me 'and, while I reach for this boot." The next moment oaths followed as the unfortunate pair fell in owing to the bank collapsing. Gaspings in the dark indicated where the unfortunates were. "'Ere I tell yer! Take me 'and! That ain't me blanky 'and. That's me blanky foot."

In the morning a most deplorable sight met our eyes. The trenches were unrecognizable, and from six feet had become in places only two feet deep. We had to go into action with the guns in this state and had to depress the gun to get the shell home into the breech without wetting it. Then we elevated the gun. After hours of bailing and bunding we reduced the water in the gun-pits to about eighteen inches, but two guns were still out of action. We now put all hands on making a bunded wall right around the battery, and on this we worked for two days and nights. On this second night I went to Kut and had dinner with " Cockie." We dined on horse and dahl peas quite satisfiedly. My way home was in the

REMAINS OF MY (76 R.F.A.) BATTERY-POSITION ON THE MAIDAN.
THE GUN EMPLACEMENTS AND DUG-OUTS ARE STILL DISCERNIBLE

pitch dark. Myriads of starlings were screaming and wheeling
in the sky. On the plain the high yelping chorus of jackals
arose over the steady crack, crack of the enemy's snipers.
Beneath all as an accompaniment was the rippling music of
the running floods.

From a reminiscent I got into a prophetic mood, and then
I suddenly found myself tumbled headlong over some obstacle
on the *maidan*. The trenches were for the most part eighteen
inches deep in mud and water, and apart from the discomfort
took hours to negotiate, and I had leave only until 10 p.m.
from the battery. One therefore walked on top. I found I
had stumbled over a horse that had no doubt strayed and
been sniped. His four feet turned skywards. As I got
up, the moon appeared and played full on his ghastly
head with bared gums and teeth. Assuring myself, from an
inspection of his hoofs that he wasn't of my battery, I moved
along and got into quite an amount of rifle fire. I ran and ran
until I almost fell again over Number 2 gun emplacement.
Two large saddles, a limber pole, and packal very much
known to me, located my tiny boarded bed staked into the
wet earth.

Everything is wet. I must stop smoking this drenched
Arab cigarette. These are like small spills filled with bad
tobacco dust and invariably burn one's clothes. Last
night again the rain came! The tackle did not work.
Streams poured on to my head and chest. I lit the tiny rope
that floats in my dubbin tin. I lit my pipe that had belonged
to Colonel Courtenay, my good friend, now resting among the
date palms. This tobacco burns well. I listened to the roar
of the four sectors of heaven all raining. Heaven, earth, and
the waters under the earth, all rained. A raining world, in
the centre my dug-out, a beleaguered town, a Turkish rampart.
Outside the desert, and somewhere across it home, home,
home! One searched oneself to see if one could do ought
else, but ever returned to the sound of the rain. . . . It was
at this moment that I bethought me of Timon. . . .

Now Timon was a wee green frog that came to me some
days ago from out the deluge. I fed him on many things, and
he couldn't escape over the line of my dug-out. Him I
watched and addressed on more than one occasion, and our
talk found common history. [My notes here are broken, but

I find them continued with an address to Timon before going to bed, written probably an hour before the procession of mule carts wound their way out to the Fort with rations, as I frequently smoked in the rain near my doorway until they passed, somewhere about 9.30 p.m. They were my signal for sleep———]

"And so, Timon, thou tiny frog, now shalt thou hear more of thy long history. Before Daly's Theatre or America was, before 'dry land was or ever the sea,' before there even roamed a Brighton bather along the shore, nay even before the forests themselves had appeared, thou wert. That, wee frog, was long, long ago to us men. It was in the twilight days when this round earth beneath our feet had just rolled out of primeval Night, and upon her still hung the shadows of Tehom which is Chaos. Then all was still, there were no forests, and no birds sang. In that deeper silence was only the whispering of racing stars and the humming of the spheres. A great symphony was that, the lullaby of the earth's infancy. After a long time and many changes, came the marsh reeds and the squashy moss plants that did for vegetation. It was all bog, wee frog—all. No wonder thy eyes grow big with wonder. And somewhere in that great marsh that covered the world was thy first great ancestor born. God knows what freakish fancy of a frolicsome couple in that distant Walpurgis night brought *him* forth. He was a salamander and he had the world to splash and croak in. Thou hast a question? Ah! Yes to be sure there were many insects and pulpy sedge for thy meat and vegetable. Wouldst have been there, my Timon? Well! and then alongside the salamanders came toads, and these multiplied and filled the world with noise. Such was the first chorus that arose from the dank, dark reeds—ten billion million jumping, diving, frolicsome little fellows, all lifting their voices in one tremendous croak—croak—croak—croak in perpetual chorus. Then was thy ancestor, the salamander, the largest animal or moving thing. But in time the water receded and shrubs grew, then themselves fell and sank deep down to form the coal beds of other ages. That was the coal plant. And then small trees appeared, later forests, and great beasts hung therefrom or walked beneath. But thy line remains distinct. Ages flew by and then I found thee, Timon, in my trench.

" Thou listenest intently as if thou rememberest it all. Canst hear the voice of thine ancient father still echoing adown Time's corridors ? 'Tis a great thought, is it not, my Timon, that the earth, being a female, possessed herself of many-coloured draperies and the moving fancies of ten thousand hues, and man, that extraordinary biped, then appeared, and invented locomotives and whistles and violins and guns. Truly we are large frogs equipped with ancient instincts. Imagine thine ancient ancestors in the primeval swamp ahorseback on tiny horses, or standing boldly up to their guns from which they shot fire at other obstinate frogs. It's a lovely idea is it not ? Of course at the first shot there had doubtless been a tremendous plop and a universal view of disappearing hind feet, but they would have got accustomed to it as have we. Thou hast forgotten. Man never knew. But the earth hath a memory long and sad, and it is said that she longs for the ancient stillness and turns yearly more cold. And one day when the sun no longer warmeth her glaciers and frozen seas she will return to that cold contemplation of the eternal problem from which she was diverted to watch the careering antics of man. A mere wraith of memory will she retain of tiny bleached bones gripped once again in the eternal snows—the last relics of that small and daring race of unaccountable beings. And then the wraith will be closed over by the mists, and Night shall descend once more. Thou, Timon, and I, will be what Thomas Atkins calls ' done in.' Hast still a smile ? 'Tis well ! 'Tis very well. Thou art a game little devil, and altogether the queerest little cus I've ever come across. So ! Thou wishest a stroll after our long talk. Bravo, thy profile is absolutely wreathed in smiles. That was a right merry little hop. I wish dearly that I could teach thee to dance. Thou would'st make Gaby blush, and she is no small fish at the game. Now what in the name of the Seven Gods art thou at, poking thy head in that fashion ? Thou shalt to supper and bed. Here are three flies and a squashed worm. Fill thy small green belly and sleep. *Pax*, I say, *vobiscum*. For thou also wert made by God."

February 13th.—I have had a half cup of milk. This morning I awoke feeling abominably seedy with sharp pains across the small of my back, awful head and wretchedly feverish. Devereux and I are suffering from dysentery, as,

in one form or another, are many others. This complaint in
its mildest form is diarrhœa which becomes colitis, which
becomes dysentery, which turns sometimes to cholera. The
doctors shake their heads and say : " Diet." They might as
well recommend a sea trip. But of course they are right.
Some fellows in their unwillingness to enter hospital stuff
down dozens of leaden opium pills, various powders, much
castor oil with chlorodyne and camphoradyne in between.
The last is an excellent drug. It's all a matter of constitution,
but sooner or later it's a case of hospital and injection of
emmatine. A hostile aeroplane flew over to-day and dropped
bombs on the town and brick kilns, evidently potting at the
5-inch guns there. A brisk rifle fire from our trenches
followed it. Accounts suggest the unpopularity of this
demon bird with its unhappy trick of laying, in mid-air, eggs
that explode on reaching the earth. Another danger is from
falling bullets fired at the place. The circuit is now complete.
We are shot at all round and from on top.

General Aylmer's forces concentrated on the 6th for a
new effort in a new position. It wants two days only in which
to disprove General Townshend's prophecy about the date of
relief. We hear that a Division has left Egypt for here.
Every one is asking why it didn't leave months ago. Impatient
questions are quite in vogue, but then we are many of us
seedy and " siegy " and " dug-outish," and the end does not
seem in sight. The latest news is that at Home no one knows
a word of it all. We are merely "hibernating in Kut." Well,
if it isn't known now it will be one day, that the siege of Kut
is probably the most important and vigorous siege in modern
military history.

I finished a novel to-day. It has at least made me long
for England again. We are all full of longings ; and the
chief blessing of civilization is that it supplies the wherewithal
to quieten them. Lord ! for a glass of fresh milk and a jelly.
Temperature 103° and shivering. I am going to have an
attempt at sleeping. Everything is very quiet. The sentry's
steps beside my roof make the earth shake.

It is the seventieth day of the siege.

February 14th.—Well, here am I again in my sleeping-bag
at six minutes past eight p.m. Everything is dead quiet.
Stillness itself is throbbing with the pulsation of a very real

thing. Two sections are away digging at the alternative position by the kilns which faces both ways. There is a great deal of work required to complete such emplacements for a whole battery. Besides the gun-pits and parapets and communication trenches, there are ammunition dug-outs, a telephone and battery dug-out where the battery headquarters are, officers' mess, officers' dug-outs, men's dug-outs, cook-houses, and water dug-outs, and latrines. Then a trench and *bund* must be made around the position to keep out rain floods.

Dorking came to see me this morning for a time. The fever has decreased but my boasted fitness seems to have deserted me for good. I believe those wretched floods did the damage. Sleeping more or less under water tells on one in weakened condition.   I have no cold though, luckily. Number 3 gun's detachment has appalling coughs, and every dug-out is the same. They have two blankets, but when the dug-out gets wet they have nothing even wherewith to dry themselves.

Cockie, who rather prides himself on some rudimentary knowledge of Egyptology, sent me a perfectly undecipherable note in hieroglyphics to come and dine. At least I guessed this out. What other interest could men have in common so much at such a time ? I sent a figurative reply with a linear representation of myself 'in bed, a procession of ancient Thebans filing out of the dug-out with fowls, snipe on toast, puddings and fruits—all untouched. I hope to be able to toddle out for a walk to-morrow.

We have laid in a stock of Arab tobacco—half branches and twigs, and make our own cigarettes. Our reserve bottle of whisky to be drunk the night of relief we have divided, as firstly the relief may never come, and secondly we may be bowled over beforehand, in which case the one concerned would lose his share. Finally, I suggested that when the relief does come we shall be sufficiently intoxicated with joy, even supposing no refreshment is with the relieving force on that fortunate day.

The Turkish aeroplane bombed us again to-day. Yesterday thirty-five people including Arabs were wounded.

The sniper fellow over the river hit a gunner in the back yesterday at the next gun. The poor fellow is mortally wounded I hear. I was at my own gun at the time and heard him sing out. He didn't fall but walked about a little, " just," he said, " not to let the swine know he had been lucky." We sent him to hospital and will visit him to-morrow.

How very horrible to be quite poor ! Here am I longing for hot milk and buttered toast, and instead I have a coarse slice of black *boosa* bread with the chaff sticking out of it— and a tiny portion of tinned cheese ! But I will forget these abominations of the flesh and hope my twenty-one aches and pains won't pursue me into dreamland.

Venus, in her whitest robes, is shining resplendent over the Eastern horizon above my mud staircase.

February 15*th.*—I am feeling somewhat better, thank goodness. I hear that Pars Nip, the garrison gunner sub that came out from India with us, is in hospital with dysentery.

There is quite a deal of sniping. A bullet whinged off a limber a few minutes ago. My candles are finished and I don't like sitting alone in a dug-out on a foggy evening without any sort of light. It suggests being buried alive.

A shocking report is to hand concerning Don Juan. During the last two days he has taken advantage of the cold weather to eat three successive blankets, four jhuals, and his companion's head-collar. I suggest turning him loose in the dismantled hospital camp on the *maidan,* now a wilderness dotted with rotten tents. Some horses have commenced to eat their tails and are not above snapping at their mates' tails if they get a chance. It's great fun watching them all on the qui vive sparring for an opening to attack one another's tail, or cover, or head collar. Don has even gnawed his wooden peg to chips and swallowed most of them.

February 16*th.*—This morning we had a heavy artillery duel. Fritz, the Turkish planist, flew over several times but did not bomb. He is evidently observing. His plane proved to be an old pattern Morane and is certainly very fast.

I have been for a little walk in the trenches. I felt awfully groggy and returned to R. L. Stevenson's " Silverado Squatters," which rings so very true even in a Mesopotamian dug-out. In this volume Robert Louis, without the addition of the terrible occurrences so dear to the sensational writer, and so rare to the lives of most of us, has left the beauty of simplicity unadorned.

February 17*th.*—Fritz flew back this afternoon and dropped bombs on the town. The one nearest to us was 300 yards towards the 4-inch guns. One bomb fell in our horse lines in Kut, just missing several drivers in a harness room, and taking the adjoining room completely. Everything therein was wrecked, but the effect of a bomb is very local. They are as yet only 30-pounders, all of which along with some larger ones, 100-pounders, were captured from us on a barge in Ascot week. Ascot week represents the temporal series from Ctesiphon to Kut. The passing overhead of Fritz's Morane we view with feelings compatible with our universal conception of him as the Destroying Angel. All deeply detest his tricks and damn him most devoutly, and I have heard many say that to be bombed by an aeroplane is the worst experience in the field. Not in the trenches, for there one is comparatively safe unless it pitches to a yard. Who doesn't take many more risks motoring? But when one's duty requires one to move about a battery in action, the fire of which is a perfect target to the plane hovering overhead, or to move about Kut or the horse lines, it is a considerably smaller joke. For the most part the dug-outs are entirely unproof against bombs, or, of course, a direct hit by a shell. The town quarters of the regiment on relief from the trenches are dug-outs covered with canvas or straw *tatti*-work and three or four inches of soil. The only safe place is in these Arab houses of two floors. The roof explodes the bomb which wrecks the upper room and possibly the first floor if not very substantial. Now an S & T walla sprinting for cover is considered, not being a combatant, quite in order, but an infantry officer not so. As for an artillery officer, he is supposed to be so used to high explosives that if the table and everything thereon blows up while he is drinking his cup of coffee, he must nevertheless not take the cup from his lips until he has drained it dry.

The first indication of his visit comes from the alarm gong which hangs near the river front observation post. All eyes strain skyward and a little black speck scarce distinguishable from a bird dots the blue sky. It approaches, and our improvised air-gun, a 13-pounder worked on a circular traverse at a high angle, has a pot at it. This gun was set up by Major Harvey, R.F.A., our adjutant, a most efficient gunnery expert from Shoeburyness. He worked out the mathematics, too, with schemes of ranging in the two planes, perpendicular and horizontal. A little white puff of cloud appears near the plane and one hears the report. Then another shot is fired and the plane mounts or swerves and still comes on. His propellers and engine are heard quite distinctly as he gets within range. A fierce burst of rifle fire and the still sharper maxim gun's staccato music is the signal for all to take cover. One sees him now directly over the Gurkha regiment's bivouacs, and hears a faint hissing noise as of rapidly spinning propellers. The hissing increases for several seconds until it becomes quite loud and terminates with a crashing explosion. One bomb has dropped. The air is full of other hissing things in various stages of their careers. A creepy feeling suggests that the bomb with its tiny propellers rapidly spinning, is going to pitch on the top of one's head and blot one out of existence, like stamping out an ant. It strikes a building a hundred yards off and the resounding smash of falling timber is caught up by another smash which has struck earth, a third that has landed in the hospital, scattering death all around, a fourth that has splashed small pieces of horseflesh and hair on the surrounding walls and trees.

All these are our captured bombs. A Tommy to-day observed that the Turk was flinging our bombs about as if they belonged to him. Another wag suggested Fritz was merely returning them.

February 18*th*.—This afternoon we had to shoot at a gun target that was pestering the Fort, and as a consequence drew thick shell fire on ourselves. Shells fell all around every gun. We went to the fastest rate of fire, gun-fire, the first heavy firing for over a month. Last evening the 82nd Battery, R.F.A., had its turn when, although concealed in the palmgrove, it was bombed by the plane and shot over by three or four targets.

There were several wounded and two killed. The guns on the water front are very active. The greater attention which the Turks have paid us during the last few days suggests that something startling is doing.

4 *p.m.*—I have just received orders attaching me temporarily to the ammunition column, which is practically without any officer as Cockie has several guns on the river front, and is continually up in the observation post there. I am to take

charge of the column and incidentally relieve him at observation. It is thought that the enemy may try to rush boats down the river. They could never get past our four-point-sevens in horse barges moored on the river, or the 5-inch or the 18-pounders or the 12-pounders from the Sumana. But great vigilance is necessary. The river is at least 400 yards wide.

It is quite good business getting attached to the column. I shall be practically C.O. with all the horses and wagons and ammunition, and two guns to keep my eye on, and observing between whiles. It will mean living in a house, for which I am very thankful. Anyway, I have been moved about owing to casualties certainly as much as any other subaltern, and up till now I have been fairly fit all along. Those early days in the brick kilns, then in the shallow trenches, then in the Fort, and especially during the floods in this battery, absorbed my fitness, and I am now a bag of pains and have lost ten pounds in weight.

I have had tea, and am already packed up. Farewell my dug-out, in which I have spent many wonderful hours and thought many strange thoughts. I am wiser at leaving than on entering thee. Timon, also my friend, thou hast earned thy freedom. Thy supper eaten, I shall put thee near the pond behind the old communication trench near the palm woods. I have no time to write an elegy upon thee. Thou camest sharply into my life and leavest it as suddenly. It is the way of the army and of life. Thou hast been a soldier's companion. Many, many are the fantasies we have indulged in, have we not ? Many thoughts exchanged that could never be set on paper, oh dear, no. What better confidant than a wee green frog ! Mind not thy unceremonious dismissal. My advice is to smile. When thou seest thy fly, go for him between wind and water, and smile even if thou art unsuccessful. Joyful days and full rations I wish thee. Never think ! Farewell !

February 19th.—Graoul removed my kit to the building in the town occupied by the 6th D.A.C. near the Minaret, where I had enjoyed my Christmas dinner. It is close to the mosque, and two minutes from the guns on the river front. There is the usual tiny concrete square with rooms all around it, mostly occupied by the servants, and one large room with wooden shutters which was the mess. Cockie sleeps in a basement room as being presumably safer and wishes me to share with him. But he is such an extremely exuberant and nervy companion, I have taken a small room on the first floor which has a thick wall on the side from which the shells come. Of course the doorway is also there, directly in line of the usual fire direction, and many bullets have at one time or other entered there and gone through the front wall which is quarter inch wood only. However, I have enough room for my bed, and must learn to lie close. Outside my room is a tiny promenade space of the flat roof and the basement rooms, and bounded by a low wall which stops a lot of bullets. I have often sat up there close to the wall and read while bullets cracked into the other side of it or flew overhead. Looking over this wall, one may see the deserted shell-ploughed ground between the battery and the palm trees that fringe the river, the river itself and the Turkish trenches beyond.

I dined with Cockie and Edmonds, who is convalescing, and enjoyed an excellent cup of coffee with tinned milk.

I commenced duty this morning by inspecting the horse lines. Cockie has not been near the lines for months, and the general condition of things is highly creditable to the N.C.Os. who have carried on. The horses, I find, are easily the best conditioned in Kut, but that is because they are by far the youngest, and also have not had the work of the battery horses. The wagons and harness require attention, and I have ordered inspection of each in sections. We are almost out of dubbin, which is in great demand for light. A twisted piece of rope, or wick, if possible, gives a mild, dull light.

Graoul I had to send back to the battery, which is too short-handed to spare men. My new servant is a Punjabi Mohammedan from the lines, by name Amir Bux. He is a good, silent lad, and very attentive. This morning the aeroplane got up and then went down so we have been spared one entertainment at least.

This afternoon I spent some hours in Cockie's observation post, river front, which is a tiny sandbag affair arranged around an opening in the roof to which a ladder leads from the first floor of the heavily bricked and sandbagged building on the river bank, and some forty yards from the water. This tiny strip of land, once the wharfage, is now grass green. To cross it is certain death. The observation post is certainly the most exposed in Kut, being nearer the river front than the Heavies', and getting all the 5-inch over and shorts. The Turks are thickly entrenched on the other side of the river, and have a bee line on every brick on the water front. The two-horse artillery guns and the 18-pounders are behind emplacements just below, and are within megaphone distance from the observation post. Our telephonists are at the foot of the ladder on the first floor. The post commands a view of three quarters of the horizon, the whole of the right bank, and has artistic advantages all its own. The solitary waters of the sunlit Tigris and the misty distances between and beyond the palm trees invite one to pleasant dreams after the strenuous times of trench days, and fort days, and perpetual dug-out days.

Edmonds returned to the battery and my dug-out. He has had a delightful period of convalescence here on the balcony, and seems much more fit.

This afternoon there was quite a strafe. The Turkish snipers' nest near the mouth of the Shat-el-hai, opposite our observation station, became troublesome, and we popped a few into them from the 13-pounders. That shut them up. Then Fanny, the huge Turkish trench mortar near the Woolpress post we hold on the other bank, popped her bomb of 150 pounds weight towards us. The bomb comes slowly at about the pace of a falling football, and of course is quite visible. It burst about a half-minute after reaching this bank, but did no damage. Then Fritz flew over and dropped three crashing bombs on the town, and returning to the Turkish lines for more ammunition, dropped four bombs near the 104th heavy battery. We gave him a hot rifle fusillade, and our improvised anti-aircraft gun did quite well. One burst was just below and two just in front. Fritz mounted very hurriedly.

As I write, guns are rumbling downstream in a most pessimistic way. Reuter reports this campaign has been taken over by the British War Office. The reinforcing division is said to have embarked at Port Said on the 10th. That would remove the date of relief at least to the end of March. Food may be made to stretch, but the casualty list of sick will be very high.   Even now some castes will not eat horseflesh, and the Mohammedans have refused to touch it.

To-night for the first time in three months I am sleeping in pyjamas, as my only duty with the guns is to relieve Cockie.

February 20th.—I have to-day continued inspection and altered the horse-lines in case of a flood.   I also went to the first-line trenches for a walk, the second line that was, for the floods compelled us to abandon the original line.   I scarcely knew the place.   The trench was a fine broad pathway ten feet deep with firing platforms several feet wide where the men bivouacked and the officers had tiny mess tents.   A wall or *bund* loopholed at the top, some five or six feet high, sloped towards the Turkish position for fifteen feet.   Beyond it, in patches, are the waters of the last flood.   The loopholes lend this firing-line an appearance of mediæval embattlements. My old acquaintance, Dinwiddy, in the West Kents I found doing awfully well under awnings, but looking very thin. This flood scheme is one of the most praiseworthy incidents in the siege of Kut.   Every day the flood waters of the approaching annual floods are creeping across our front.   We believe the *bund* will save us.

It was a beautiful day, and I enjoyed my walk immensely. At midday the sun is unpleasantly warm, and the nights are quite cold.   We have all gone back to helmets, and perspired freely in the day.   We hear the *avant-courrière* of the summer.

Last night Wells of the Flying Corps came into the mess, and " re-flew over Ctesiphon."   I should like to fly.   He has had the bad luck to lose all the fingers of one hand while engaged manufacturing hand grenades for the trenches.   The old Flying Corps has been of great assistance to us in Kut. Another Flying Corps officer, Captain Winfield Smith, rigged up old engines and made our corn grinders and mills practically out of scrap-iron.

Cockie wants me to promise to go Egyptologizing with him after the war!   Fancy a mummy awakening from a silence of three to five thousand years to hear a voice like Cockie's !

Frolicsome Flossy, that very aggressive female, made four overtures to the gunners on the 4·7 barges.   Needless to say her warm attentions met with the cold reception they merited.

I also visited the hospital to look up some sick friends. One who was in with jaundice had a complexion like grass-green oil flung into a bowl of rich Jersey cream. The sight made one bilious. I'm not so seedy as I was, but the universal complaint still pursues me.

Don Juan is in his new lines with a native syce. He has already eaten both tails off his new companions, one of which is Cockie's charger. Cockie is furious, but seeing that Don has eaten his own tail also I don't see much for Cockie to grumble at.

Erzeroum has fallen. That may relieve the pressure here.

I have just come across Longfellow's "Daybreak," an old favourite of mine that I once heard that excellent song writer Mallison and his wife render in a most delightful manner. One misses any music except this endless fire symphony!

February 21st.—The eightieth day of siege. We fired at Snipers' Nest across the river, otherwise the day was very quiet except for the visit of Fritz who had evidently had sufficient taste of our anti-aircraft gun, and he flew diagonally across the town and right around to avoid it.

Upon the tiny observation station, which is scarcely large enough for two to sit down in, Cockie entertained me with antiquities. He likes to talk of empires and dynasties falling, and thousands of years gone by, and Good-God-look-at-it-all-now sort of thing. To which I always lend a careful ear, and if he ever asks me a question to see if I am attending, I say, " Good heavens! How extraordinary! Don't spoil it by inter-rogations. Go on!" Not that I'm not interested in such things, far from it, but Cockie gets impatient with his in-adequacy of description.

Sealed orders arrived at 10 p.m. to be opened at 4 a.m. Something is agog! I must sleep again in breeches and field boots.

February 22nd.—At 4 a.m. by the dusky dubbin's misty light, Cockie opened the secret orders with an air of mystery becoming an Egyptologist having the secrets of forgotten worlds beneath his thumb.

The General Staff has been hatching a scheme for some time past, and this is why I was wanted in the column so urgently. Cockie is to remain C.R.A. of the river-front artillery. I'm in command of the ammunition column. General Townshend, our G.O.C., intends to attack in two columns, Column A comprising General Melliss's 30th Brigade and one battery R.F.A. to debouch through Redoubt A, Column B with the 17th Brigade and two batteries R.F.A. to debouch through by the Fort. The show is conditioned to take place if the Turkish forces retreat past Kut to their main camp on this bank—or if any reinforcements proceed on their way to the Turkish Essin forces downstream. The latter condition makes it appear that something should happen soon.

Some say it is a risky thing for us to move outside our position, but somehow one has every confidence in such an old campaigner as the Sixth Division. The intention is for the 16th Brigade in front of the 82nd Battalion position, to demonstrate, holding the Turks there and thus enabling Column A to move on. One section per battery (R.F.A.) will remain to cover the advance. The advance of either column must necessarily be subjected to a lively enfilade fire from across the river and by the transverse trenches rounding the Fort. Enfilade from our left, *i.e.* the right bank of the river, must be kept down by the river-front artillery. The sappers will go ahead to spring the many-rumoured mines of which I doubt the existence, as the Turks are not very up to date this way.

I have everything ready, wagons loosened up, shovels and picks on, ammunition filled, double feed in horse bags, men's rations ready for one day. The ammunition column does not move off until the last guns of the 63rd have moved clear. So we are not harnessed up, as there will be more than doubly sufficient time when the batteries get the order to go—and it will save the horses a lot, as it may be a long waiting affair. Our job will be to keep in touch with both columns and have a first position outside Kut only if either column advances into the open. The trip will have to be done again and again, so we shall not escape without casualties.

It is on the knees of the gods, and I for one hope it comes off. In fact we all do. An impression has stolen upon us that if we don't help ourselves we shall stay here altogether.

2 p.m.—There is heavy firing downstream. Fritz has just flown by to see what's doing. The G.O.C.'s intention, according to rumour, is to consign matters to final issue, and to force a great battle, provided the show downstream goes decently well.

I am glad the horses have not been in their harness all day. Four teams have had to be lent to the batteries as theirs have been eaten more largely than ours.

Now I'm off to have another look round my show and then on to the observation post.

6 *p.m.*—There has been nothing to report except a decided Turkish movement downstream from the right bank. It has been a beautiful day with plenty of cloud.

Downstream the firing, which had lulled this afternoon, is increasing. I have been on the *maidan* near the pine woods watching distant bursts.

February 22nd.—There has been another hitch downstream. The Turkish position blocking the relief advance is evidently much stronger than was anticipated. This we hear in the form of a rumour that there was insufficient artillery preparation of the position before the infantry got in. Also a lot of difficulty and uncertainty has arisen over some of the native troops. Two or three times to-day the heavy bombardment downstream has suddenly ceased, a phenomenon pregnant with meaning in war, for it means that the infantry has advanced to the last stage and awaits the cessation of gun-fire to spring up and rush the position. But as often as it ceased, it recommenced an hour later and continued until the next break.

As yesterday, we are all ready and awaiting the order for immediate debouch. I am " booted and spurred " and feeling very important. The Turks are reinforcing heavily on the other bank, the sly dogs, as appears from the movement in their trenches. Our little affair is supposed to be awfully secret, but there is no doubt that Arabs scuttle away across the river or swim it and keep their religious pals in the know.

February 23rd.—Last night at 11.30 p.m., as a counter demonstration, there was a night attack on Woolpress Post, our village over the river. This induced an attack from the enemy facing our 16th Brigade. The town was alive with bullets that cracked incessantly on the *mutti* walls of the town. Through the deserted streets I ran to the observation station, river front, in case the field-guns were required to go into action. For forty yards I had to run the gauntlet from the street end to the door. There was not an inch of cover and the bullets were splashing on the road and into the buildings on my left. The fire was swishing as thick as water from a powerful fire hose. Goodness knows how I got through. I passed several poor wretches on stretchers and ran up the ladder.

On the first floor bullets were viciously cutting through the *tatti* and interstices, and some plopped into sandbags, and the air seemed full of that tiny buzzing music as from some lightning-winged bee.

When I returned I found that some men and several horses had been hit, and in my room one bullet had ricochetted across the bed and three others had entered by the doorway and gone out by the window. Anyway it is more pleasant up here, and the bed zone is safe enough, so I'm going to risk it. And I must dress on the far side of the room. I am sure, after the awful air in that wretched dug-out, with swamp water oozing through it, that most people would risk something for this comparatively delightful air.

February 24th.—We are to remain in a state of diminishing expectancy and increasing disappointment. We acknowledge the colossal difficulties that beset our friends downstream, nor do we forget one division there has been previously decimated in France, and has many recruits. The fighting is against the pick of Turkish troops entrenched behind seas of mud.

The Mussulman soldiers here will not eat horseflesh. Among their excuses is one that the signature from India of their High Priest's permission to eat it is not authentic. It came by wireless !

Generally speaking, the native soldier for first-rate work in the field is only third class if he has no *khana* (food).

February 25th.—The show downstream has been postponed. More reinforcements are necessary. History repeats itself, and we are down to three slices of bread a day. It is a lovely morning. Some gunners and Fritz, R.A.M.C., were around to dinner last night bringing their own bread, as is the correct order of things in Kut. We had an excellent roast of horse. For sweets we had rice and date juice, and instead of savoury, " post mortems " on Ctesiphon.

Our friend, Tudway, R.N., has been awarded the Military Cross for Essin services. This we celebrated.

February 26th.—Much firing downstream. Last night I dreamed that Alphonse (Townshend) was communicating with Aylmer by megaphone, all Kut excepting I being asleep. And this is what happened—

" There, Aylmer ? "

" Of course."

" Why didn't you attack on the 22nd ? What happened ? "

" Sweet damn all. Didn't even get a look in ! "

" Then why on earth didn't you ? You've had your reinforcements and sufficient time."

" 'Tis not in the nature of mortals to command success. We've done better, Townshend—we've deserved it ! "

" Rot ! There's a screw loose somewhere. At Essin I turned him out of a much stronger position than he's got now, and with one-fourth of your force. Do you suppose we like being here or can hold out indefinitely ? "

" Don't gibe ! Do you know you're certain for a peerage —Townshend of Ctesiphon, I hear—nice alliteration too."

" No, really ? Well, old chap, get through when you can. Some old time ! We're eating door-mats and dubbin [Liar] ! My pigeon though."

" Oh, I say ! Last night I thought of suggesting we risked a plane landing in Kut for you and bringing you away so that you could have had the honour of relieving Kut."

" Then why didn't you ? "

" Well, I thought what a godless ass you would look if you didn't succeed. Nothing seems certain except these floods ! "

" Do you really think there is any chance of your getting through ? "

" Not in the least ! Even Lloyds wouldn't look at it. But the Bishop of London says you are making a glorious page in British history ! "

" Page, sir, be damned ! We've finished two volumes long ago. Is there anything else ? "

" Yes ! The people in all the churches at home are praying for you."

Loud laughter sounded through both megaphones, and I bethought me of the queer temperament of our race—and awoke.

10 *p.m.*—Cockie has retired to bed. I am alone with the

" dim glim." The Turkish aeroplane has left us unmolested to-day, and for a change one of our own machines from below flew past us and bombed the Turkish main camp. It also dropped some money for the troops and letters for the General, as it has several times previously. There has been a considerable increase in the scurvy cases lately among the native troops. Of course all the drivers in the ammunition column are native troops. I had a scurvy inspection to-day, and the regimental surgeon picked out the grubby ones. It is due to total lack of vegetables. This is what we must chiefly guard against—disease.

Anthrax also has broken out in a few isolated cases and the orders are for livers of all animals to be buried.

I am much more comfortable here, as we have a long table and chairs and two or three stock books, " Monte Cristo " and Longfellow. That simple poet's lines in " Sand of the Desert in an Hour Glass " seem to have added to themselves additional appeal since the siege.

> "Or caravans that from Bassorah's gate
> With Westward steps depart;
> Or Mecca's pilgrims confident of Fate,
> And resolute in heart ! "

That is the old Basra downstream : I must, if possible, visit the ruins of Babylon some sixty odd miles from here and forty directly west of Azizie. Also I would like to see Istamboul as they call it : and if Aylmer doesn't hurry up I possibly shall.

February 28th.—Alarming reports are to hand that the river is rising. It is already three feet higher than it was two days ago. The Shat-el-hai now has changed from a watercourse to a broad deep river that *mahelas* can navigate quite easily. It is worthy of mention how very close the *mahela* resembles one's nursery pictures of the Ark and possibly most correctly so, for with its great beams and high bow and stern it has remained unchanged for thousands of years. This land, we are told, is God-forsaken. Animals there are none, beside the goat, sheep, camels, donkeys, jackals, and river buffaloes. A few herds of the latter used to bask downstream near Kut. Now they too have deserted us.

It is reported that the Russian General Baratoff has taken

Kermanshah on the road to Baghdad. We are all anxiously hoping he may get through.

A large sweepstake on the date of the relief has been started for all European troops. Relief is defined as the time when our first boat passes the Fort. The contingency of our having ultimately to surrender is not included. For who could entertain that possibility except in the extremest banter ?

A Reuter tells us of a big German shove at Verdun. What an awful slaughter yard that will be ! The news has become most unsatisfactorily fragmentary. We hear that something or other is about to take place ; then subsequently the wireless is blocked and we never know whether it happened or not.

There is much anxiety in the town about the floods that must soon come, and the river's level is the all-absorbing topic.

The fine spell of weather seems about to break.

February 29th.—It is raining in a most shocking fashion. Lord ! How it does rain here—when it wants to ! The sun goes, the sky shuts its eyes and rains with all its might, so that it is difficult to believe there ever was a time when it did not rain.

Cockie is sick. I took his duty on the river-front observation post and watched for hours the deluge of water falling down and flowing past in a yellow turgid current. The reports are that it is hourly rising. Every endeavour is being made to strengthen the *bunds* and build others. The main *bund* across our front still holds and the other side of it is already a great lake where our former position was. The Turks have had to leave this part of their line and go back a few hundred yards to the sand-hills. Through my telescope I can see tiny waves dashing up against the *bund* like a drifting sea against a breakwater. I met Captain Stace, R.E., to whom I lent a clinometer while he worked at this invaluable construction. He is most reassuring in his quiet optimistic way.

The next most important event of to-day is that Dorking was persuaded to exchange seven cigars for my ten cigarettes. I came by them yesterday in a special issue " found " by the Supply and Transport people. By the way, there are more things in the Supply and Transport philosophy than heaven and earth ever dreamed of.

It is the gala-day of Leap Year, but I have no extra proposals to record—not even from Sarah Isquashabuk, the Arabian lady with bread-plate feet and small gate-post legs and a card-table back on which she carries small trees and walls of houses. She is a hard worker and always cheerful, but with a most murderous-looking eye, and I confess that one doesn't always see daylight through all her actions. This morning I saw her dragging a stalwart Arab along by the unshaven hair with much laughter—possibly her truant Adonis.

The Arab population have done themselves fairly well until recently, for they had hidden much foodstuff and stolen considerable supplies since. But the last few weeks they have been begging, and the children search corners and rubbish heaps.

If the siege goes to extremities it will be ten thousand pities that the Arab population was not removed out at the outset. For the laws of humanity would restrain our pushing them out now—the Turks or surrounding hostile Arabs would murder the lot. But we should have had the food they are getting now for rations, and that might have saved the lives of thousands of British downstream. All we did was to invite them to stay at their peril. They accepted.

March 1st.—A most eventful day. Cockie is still down with dysentery, and I have relieved him all day at the observation post. Everything was very quiet on my way to tea. I walked through the palm grove intending to examine the mountings of the anti-air gun when I heard the muffled boom of guns to the north. Then others sounded—that ruffling sound of a blanket being shaken. I hastened back to the observation post, shells falling in the trees and alongside the trench. I got on top and ran until I got back. The fire increased into the biggest artillery bombardment the enemy has yet made, lasting for two and a half hours. About ten batteries opened out on us, searching the palm grove for our 4-inch, and then four batteries concentrated on the 4·7 guns in the horse boats and barges moored in the river 150 yards from them, and also on the 5-inch heavies immediately below them but thirty yards to a flank. Thankful I was indeed for that thirty yards respite. At least fifty shells pitched at exact range for my few sandbags that any direct hit would knock flying—exact range but always within those thirty yards to a flank, and of course on the other side into the river dozens of them. But not all, for sometimes they " swept "

and the heavy Windy Lizzies tore up the green ground all
around, and the building, on the roof of which were my bags,
shook so much that the bags moved. Then one lucky shell
struck the *mahela* near by, another got the building I was on,
smashing down the end room, and yet another pierced the
side partition ten yards off, and for a few seconds I didn't
know whether I had been blown into the river or not, for the
shock was severe and all was yellow darkness. Large pieces
of wood and *mutti* were hurled all around my sand-bags, one
piece fetching me a clout on the helmet and denting in my
megaphone. I remember a faint cheer from the Supply and
Transport shelters when the smoke cleared away and the
observation post was seen still to exist. All this time I had
been engaging one target with our 18-pounders, and keeping
the rifle fire of Snipers' Nest down with another.

It all seemed to come about so very quickly. One moment
I was walking out of the trench in the date grove threading
my way over the slippery ground when the first three muffled
booms told me B target had opened fire. The next, without
wondering what the grimy Turkish gunners at B were shooting
at, or what the result of the shells still in the air would be, I
was tearing back to the river front. One counted the usual
twelve seconds from the distant boom of these targets and then
heard the invisible singers in the mid-air, and then krump-kr-
rump-sh-sh-sh-sh as the shells struck with a deep bass explosion
followed by the swishing sound of falling earth that had been
hurled up aloft. I recollect now seeing a mule bolt as it heard
the increasing hits, and although I felt quite as uncomfortable
as the mule I was tickled with the notion of a mule developing
the fire instinct, for it bolted intelligently to a flank. That
mule deserves to live.

From the observation post there was no need of a telescope
to tell me that B was in action. The three puffs stood out
very clearly and three more to the right. I reported a new
target, gave the bearing, and watched our 5-inch and 4·7's
reply. This brought A and B targets to engage our 4·7 and
5-inch below me. The 40-pounders tore up the water, going
very close to but always missing the barges, and the shock
from a Windy Lizzie hitting the water was always much greater
to my sandbags on the roof, than when hitting the earth
beneath us. In the former case my six-foot stack vibrated

several inches. I saw one shell actually enter the 5-inch emplacement. It exploded on touching the other side, missing a gun-layer by inches. The shock knocked him down—that was all. Ten minutes later another shell got there again, within two feet of the former one. This time the men were taking cover. It was now that the battery opened on the town with 16-pounders, and on my engaging them the Turkish heavies lengthened and shelled my observation station, also the other observation station for our heavies 100 yards away. As I have noted, they got me in a beautiful 100-yards bracket, the one crashing into the poor devils in the hospital amid awful yells, and the two nearest getting the end of this building and smothering me with débris. Some pitched into the hospital forty yards away, their trajectory just above us. It is extraordinary the tricks one gets up to on occasions. The sergeant-major, an excellent soldier and very cool fellow, stuck his hands on his head more than once, and I found myself leaning hard up against the sandbags the hissing Lizzies were directly making for, just as if my doing so would help the bags to stick there. They came with a slow hiss that finished in a vicious whip past for the last bit. The sandbags stopped scores of bullets this afternoon, and that is all they are meant to do. I had very good luck with the target we had previously registered on. It is a target of three guns over the Shat-el-hai. I shut them up with half a dozen rounds, and then took on another new target that opened further south. Then still another target on the Woolpress sector shelled Kut and the 82nd engaged them. We had barely shut up this target M, and also S, when several other Turkish batteries that had been silent for months opened up on the town. This proved too much for the youthful spirit of Funny Teddy, that ardent and sprightly young mountain gun, which just as a puppy watching a fight between his seniors tries to have a look in too and barks and bucks about in the most promising style, opened up on H.M.S. *Sumana*. From my observation post I could see targets all round the compass being engaged by our guns. The Turk was out-gunned and out-shot absolutely, but his target was Kut and ours merely his guns.

A hot rifle fire sprang up from the Snipers' Nest, Shat-el-hai, and from across the river by the tomb. This we kept down in a fashion in our sector, and the 12-pounders of the *Sumana* also gave them hot music, as the men call it.

The town then came in for it badly, the hospital especially catching it. We may thank heaven the Turks haven't anything much in the way of high-explosive shell. They use old stuff, common and segment, and the thick crust of baked mud wall is usually sufficient percussion to bring about the burst. The danger then is from the fragments. The building usually escapes. I have seen segments of a Windy Lizzie as big as a half loaf embedded in a wall opposite to the aperture it made on entering. High-explosive shell would demolish the building altogether.

At the height of the show the sharp notes of the alarm gong rang over Kut, and Fritz, with a second machine accompanying his Morane, was seen approaching rapidly from the north. Our machine-guns opened on them and also a brisk fusillade from the trenches as they came over. They bombed Kut and then returned to their camp for more bombs. This was repeated again and again, making a dozen trips in all. Every one took cover in basements. Scarcely a soul was to be seen. We had to stick where we were, as our guns were still in action, but one had plenty of time to look skyward and see the death-bird there, as I did three or four times this afternoon, directly in a plumb-line over our heads, and to hear the whirring propeller of the bomb increasing in loudness and pace as it fell. One trusted in Providence or luck. He got the bank of the river and the hospital several times, but his nearest to us was at least forty yards off. The bombs cannot be placed with great accuracy, so they drop three or four close together to make a zone. Some of the bombs were 100-pounders, which would blot a fellow out as effectually as an hydraulic stamp.

Funniest of all, the heavy mortar, Frolicsome Fanny, tiring of acting wallflower on the other bank, chucked her big bombs at us. But she is a left-handed and cross-eyed filly, and the gods have set a limit to her range for evil. Some went in the river near the horse boats. These were received calmly by the Tigris. Another got into the sand-heap near our butchery and fell into it without exploding. Some scientifically minded Arabs charged up to secure it and were within thirty yards when the thing went off to their huge astonishment.

We had a good laugh at the way they sprinted back jabbering with rage and fear. The mules have got to know her, and, keeping one eye on the bomb as it comes over the river, continue grazing until it is nearly across and then bolt the opposite way.

One of Fritz's bombs, a 100-pounder, we saw toppling over and over in the air quite plainly. It didn't go off. But another such sent a table at least two hundred feet into the air. This is true. I won't spoil it by saying that the cloth was laid and set. It was merely a table and its four legs stuck up towards the evening moon.

The bombing raid continued until it was too dark for Fritz to see. Then I went home, and on my way saw interested little crowds that had emerged to examine various shell-holes. Arabs ran up and down the streets howling for their dead. Over a thousand shells have been flung into the town and there were a good few hit among the hospital patients, and the Arabs lost many. About a score only were killed, but many more were injured. Considering the intensity of the bombardment this is an excellent tribute to the shelters of Kut.

10 *p.m.*—Every one is extra vigilant to-night although we think it hardly likely the Turks will try to storm us. That they cannot easily do now, and the floods increase their difficulty daily.

March 2nd.—The whole night long wild howlings and dismal wailing of the Arabs for their dead and wounded continued and kept me awake. Now and then some other Arab extra full of despair would let out a yell like a steam-whistle that rose high above the universal hubbub. The Jews here cry in a different key altogether, a wobbly vibrato long sustained, much less sweet but not wholly unlike the *tangi* of the Maoris in New Zealand. A Jewish funeral is a sad little affair. Dressed in long black robes and carrying lights in little tins they escort the dead to a grave way out on the *maidan*. They walk with bowed heads in twos, a tiny column and a sort of acolyte person following the body. They perform their ceremonies by night so as to avoid drawing fire upon themselves.

It is a peaceful day, the peace that follows a violent storm. Rumour has it that various Turkish guns which had been withdrawn for service downstream have been brought back here, and the bombardment was intended to acquaint us with the fact. Or else they are thinking of sending the guns down and wanted to disillusion us on the point. This is most likely. It certainly hasn't done much harm, and surely Khalil Pacha does not suppose he can give us " nerves " by this sort of thing.

A beautiful aeroplane of ours flew over, her wings resplendent with the morning sun.

It has been very cold and windy all day, but so very peaceful—not the peacefulness of calm but of a windy, lonely day.

During the show yesterday I was practically doing C.R.A. River-front, a high-sounding title especially pleasing to Cockie, but as a matter of fact it is merely an observation job, as all he does is to command his own three guns. He is still seedy and inconsolable at his inaction.

March 2nd.—An uneventful day. We fired a few sniping rounds. I hear the 76th Battery got its share of shelling the other day, and a bombardier was killed.

I persuaded Cockie to talk about ancient Egyptian kings. He annotates himself in a most delightful way in talking history, and has an extraordinary imagination for detail. This imagination it must be admitted does not get much of a chance in Egypt, which has been fairly well explored. I would suggest turning him loose among visions of the lost Atlantis. I believe he would even produce the history of the other Adam's first love affair in that continent. Some such sentence as this—" Yes ! In that extraordinary land which history has almost forgotten and which geology never knew, Phargon the bog-king, the præcursor of Romeo, proceeded to divest himself of shoes and jacket, and taking in another hole of his belt, plunged, according to Whinny, feet foremost after Phargette."

March 3rd.—The cold wind, or the wet, or something, has made my back so rheumaticky that I can hardly turn round or get down to tie my bootlaces. I am very lucky to have kept as fit as I have. Dozens of men from the trenches are in hospital with muscular rheumatism from the floods—the source of many evils.

I have finished " Monte Cristo." What an artist he was ! And I have started " David Copperfield " again.

I omitted to record that a shell tore down the house at

G

the front of this, and one wrecked the base of the column office.   Several horses were wounded during the bombardment.

We had a parade of Mussulman drivers, and I read a communiqué asking them to eat horseflesh, as their Mullah in India requested, this being required by the exigencies of the service.   Not they !   I believe, nevertheless, there is only one thing rooted deeper than a man's religion, and that is his appetite.   This proves it, for hunger is driving them to eat it. What an awful joke on the part of Charon if, when these fellows reach the banks of the river Styx, he informs them the only available ferry is astride of swine.

We have finished the inspections.   The horse rations have fallen away to very little.   We give them pieces of palm tree to gnaw at.

March 4th.—The rheumatism is much worse.   It is bleak and cold in the observation post.   On such an occasion the vigil is a wretchedly dull one.   I'm too cold to dream.   One can only psychologize viciously on the difference in point of view between a full man and an empty one.   Eating maketh a satisfied man, drinking a merry man, smoking a contented man.   But eating, drinking, and smoking maketh a happy man—that is, the heart of him glad.

It is not far from the truth to say I have to-day done none of these.   For by *eating* one cannot mean half a slice of chaff bread, nor by *drinking* a water-coloured liquid like our siege tea, nor yet by *smoking* a collection of strange dried twigs and dust.   Man, it has been excellently observed, cannot live by bread alone.   How much less, then, can he live upon half chaff and half flour ?

Far away on the edge of the western horizon I watched for hours, through my telescope, a convoy of camels, each with a tiny white dot of humanity aboard, striding away with delightful patience to the Turkish camp downstream.   They were conveying stores from Shamrun, the enemy depot on the river above us.

General Smith, of former mention in these notes, has been dangerously ill in hospital, but the crisis has been passed.   He contracted pneumonia on the retirement.   I have been to see him.   He is very full of pluck, and gave me a *Times*.

Tudway, R.N., dropped in for a pipe.   We talked of the sea, and he spoke of the soft life on the Chinese station.

The adjutant of the Dorsets was killed while strolling in a communication trench yesterday—a chance bullet getting his heart. The D.A.A.G. is being operated on to-day with an abscess in the thigh. The facilities for operating on such cases are very modest. But nothing less than raising the siege could alleviate these matters. And in this little maelstrom of destiny here at Kut, we and our weaknesses are whirled around together. Some of us disappear in the vortex, and others continue circling around the swift walls, and may or may not be fortunate enough to so continue. But from this seething cauldron none can escape by his own effort, for we are all up against a thing greater than ourselves.

March 5th, 6th.—Shortly after daybreak, as usual, I got up, feeling awfully full of aches and unsteady. Cockie, however, being still seedy, it was necessary for me to be on duty on the observation post, so I flannelled myself up and went. I stuck it until 9 a.m., when I returned for breakfast. Our Parsee regimental doctor, from whom I required a dose of rheumatism physic, sent for a major of the Fourth Field Ambulance, who pronounced me bad enough with muscular rheumatism to have to go into hospital. I was awfully disgusted at this after holding out so long, and begged to be allowed to stay in my billet. But it was of no use. He said strict orders made it imperative, also that in hospital eggs were forthcoming. Four native bearers and a stretcher turned up shortly afterwards, much to my disgust. Anyway I walked, after fixing up for the sergeant-major to carry on.

I entered a ward too terrible for words, next bed to a most sad and awful apparition of a poor fellow who had been very ill. It was a long skin-covered skeleton with skinless ears, eyes protruding so far that one wondered how they stuck up at all, teeth on edge, legs thinner than a pick handle, and two arms like gloved broom-sticks catching frantically at various parts of his apparel where creatures of the amœbic world fled before those awful eyes. Add to this a half-insane chattering, punctuated with a periodical sharp crack as louse after louse was exploded between the creature's two thumbs, and you have the picture entitled, " A Hospital Shikar." Altogether it was a sight utterly terrible.

I thought of flight, and other things, but the hospital was small, and there was no other available room. So I wished them all good morning, and sat on the side of my bed farthest away, and having undressed got into bed as the assistant-surgeon, otherwise apothecary, directed.   I had not been there for more than three minutes when the Enigma's Hindoo bearer entered.   He became quickly engaged with his master in strenuous argument relating to curry, what time the Enigma ricochetted on and off the bed, and his mouth became the exhaust valve for his pent-up opinions of the world in general and his bearer in particular.   I discovered later that malaria and dysentery had between them rendered him temporarily insane. He had been in the hospital for the whole of the siege, but was now slowly recovering.   While he was *in extremis*, however, I should say from all accounts that he must have been by far the most interesting person in Kut.   For many days it seems his main hobby was in trying to make his bearer precede him through a door which did not exist at the foot of his bed. Another diversion was in seating himself on the window-sill stark naked about 1 a.m. in the night and mimicking, often with ghastly relish, the sounds and noises of various members of the Turkish artillery from Windy Lizzie to Naughty Nellie, the buzzing howitzer.   I believe he was quite good at the bullets, and very promising on Frolicsome Fanny, which was easy, and only required an awful noise without warning—for as I have noted Fanny's jokes sometimes held fire for minutes. But in reproducing vocally the aeroplane's 100-pound bombs he is reported as having outdone even the bomb itself.   In fact his own nerves could not stand this performance, and he generally wound up the item by taking cover under his bed.

Other nights he has been known to get behind his over-turned bed and preach in a most entertaining way.   Why he took to preaching was, he explained, due to the fact that he had been to church only once in his life, and that was his wedding-day.   His sermons may be described as unorthodox, and varied from blatant sarcasm in such texts as, " When ye hear of war and rumours of wars be ye *not* troubled " ("Not" being considerably emphasized) to sheer optimism, one being, " Eat, sleep, and be merry, for to-morrow ye starve."   But he did not always stick to his text, and in the last-mentioned sermon made a humorous digression on Kut, the way in and the way out, this being, as he informed his midnight audience, the prelude to a book he had recently written called " The Last of the Sixth Division," by a Field Officer. One day he insisted on believing he was on board a P. boat going downstream in charge of Turkish officers, and having attempted unsuccessfully to rejoin his boat in scanty apparel, finally consoled himself with fishing out of the window. However, he is now supposed to be more or less permanently located in the sane region, but this from the other would seem to be separated by a mere dividing line, and he occasionally strays back.

But these interesting events are past, and the poor fellow is a dull subaltern once more. Other occupants of the ward were the Welsh Bulbul and an awfully decent subaltern in the Territorial Battery named Tozer, whom they called the Eye-Opener, because he never slept.

An awful place is this hospital. Our ward is on the first floor on one side of the yard, and the barred windows are sandbagged up part of the way.

I read and slept, and then stole downstairs to interview " G. B.," who was in a most kind and amiable mood.

The only advantage to be derived from being in hospital here is that one has facilities for dying under medical supervision. Not that the authorities don't do all they can, for the officer commanding the officers' hospital is as kind and thoughtful as he is able, and altogether the best of good fellows. But his difficulties are enormous. There is the scantiest of sick diet left, medicines are more or less exhausted, only the simplest drugs remaining. Besides, the pressure of work on all the medical people here necessitates the use of untrained orderlies. One of these, a podgy and giggling recruit, enters twice daily with a handful of pills in his fist, and distributes them as per order, but it is well to know one's ailment and the remedy, for sometimes the ardent youth is forgetful. The C.O. comes round once a day, which is the event of the twenty-four hours. He is all patience, encouragement, and industry. The orderly rubs the backs of the rheumatic patients, and this is a delightful relief.

As for food it matters not. Dysentery and rheumatic cases can be safely starved, I believe, and if this is the chief way of getting well there is every facility here for rapid recovery. Two small portions of Mellin's food and one egg with a small piece of white bread are the daily ration. A few extra things came for me, but I could not eat them.

From 6 to 8 p.m., as we have no candles we have a spelling game, each one in turn adding a letter that continues to spell a word. The object is to avoid saying the last letter of the word, and consequently the words changed or lengthened in an extraordinary fashion. One-syllable words were barred, and we had challenging for bluffs. Each fall meant a life, and three lives was the total. Thus o-s-t-r-a-c-i-z-i-n-g. The defeat was staved off " ostrich " and " ostracize " on to some one else. It proved highly entertaining, and abuse flowed freely, especially as the abuser was more than once let down deliberately by all hands. Doubtful words we voted on. I got into trouble with " phrenolophaster," which we carried by three to two, I pointing out other words, poetaster, philosophaster, etc. One wouldn't dare to tell Dr. Johnson so, but it " did."

There joined us in these evening orgies a subaltern of the Oxfords named Mellor, otherwise Square-Peg, who was convalescent from a bomb wound in the arm. On the morrow I got out of bed and walked with him to the vegetable gardens, which were planted at the beginning of the siege, like they were in Troy. I hate bed when I'm not fit, and the walk was refreshing. I am trying to get permission to go back to my billet and do duty on diet.

6 *p.m.*—There is an order for the Arabs to remain confined to their houses as another sortie is imminent.

I have just been talking to Woods, a cheery fellow who got the Military Cross for saving men from a dug-out at the Fort during the heavy bombing of December 24th. He is gleefully nursing the stump of an arm, and tells me how he proposes to still enjoy himself in life with the other. " The Enigma " has just begun another *shikar*, the severalth this day.

March 7th.—Late last night there was talk of a brigade going over the river to stop the enemy's forces attempting to retreat that way. We had no bridge, but Major Sandes had prepared a trestled bridge for the Shat-el-hai, and if wanted the brigade was to be ferried over in *mahelas*. We were all wound up and restless in hospital, and did not wish to miss a show. All night long there was the clang and clump, clump, of marshalled forces, and the champing of bits and the tramp of men under full arms. A few rounds were fired during the night, and at the dawn a signal awakened us, but nothing else happened. Anyway orders for the debouch were about to be issued the second time, and with this as an excuse I persuaded the C.O. to let me out to resume duty, and I was to remain on diet issued from the hospital. I left the Enigma my midday's rations. It was a relief to escape from the dreadful ward. This I did at 11 a.m.

But before I left I visited General Smith's room on the other floor. From him I learned that Verdun is raging with unabated fury, and Epinal and Belfort still hold out. The Russian General Baratoff is almost on to Khanakin through the mountains. If this were only true the Turks hereabout would have to retire on Baghdad.

The general was what girls call " very nice " this morning. He reads three books at once, so that when he is tired of one he changes to the other. We talked more fishing, and what we would do when we returned to India. This I find the most interesting topic for invalids.

9 *p.m.*—It is rumoured from headquarters that an attempt is being made by General Aylmer to get through to-day or to-morrow with a dawn attack. The weather is favourable to a long march. We are all ready with our *mahelas* and launch and *Sumana* to convey a brigade across, if necessary to cut the Turkish retreat or assist General Aylmer. It is, however, a serious impediment that we have none of the bridging trains which were so famous in the history of the Sixth Division and so efficiently handled by Major Sandes. The last was blown up on December 5th.

Later.—We partly expect some orders this evening. I find I am almost too stiff with this rheumatism to mount my horse. I have been practising on the table, but once in the saddle I shall be perfectly right.

I am overjoyed to have got back to my billet from that hospital ordeal. Have played chess with Mellor.

There is sound of distant firing—a dull smothered roar of an engagement down at el Hannah.

Everybody is talking about Baratoff, and hence this verse:

> "The mountains looked on Baratoff
> And Baratoff looked on me;
> And in my evening dream I dreamed
> That Kut might still be free."

CHAPTER V

*M*ARCH *8th*.—In the night a terrific explosion from
the direction of the Shatt awoke Kut. Someone
says it was caused by a floating mine going aground.
It had been intended for the bridge some distance up the
Shat-el-hai. Not long after dawn we awoke to the sound
of intense gun-fire so close to us, that for a time it seemed
like our own guns in Kut. At first we surmised this to be
Turkish artillery turned on positions won by the Relief
Column, but, on climbing on to the roof, we saw the flashes
came from what the experts knew as Dujaila Redoubt.
Our own guns were preparing on the Turkish position!
This in itself seemed difficult to believe, although, no doubt,
some good reason existed for it. As the light got better,
before eight o'clock, we saw quite clearly hordes of Turks
rushing up towards the Shat-el-hai support trenches, and
some troops were being ferried over near Megasis from the
other bank. General Aylmer's night march had evidently
been a complete success, and the Turks were taken by surprise.
Why, then, were we waiting to prepare ? The fire grew heavier,
the bursts thicker, and all the while the Turks were rushing up
troops. Then the fire ceased. We held our breath and waited
for news, knowing that the bayonet was busy, and the men at
handgrips. No news has come. We have waited hour by hour.

Is anything amiss ? Why haven't they got through ?
Was our artillery preparation intended to be so deadly as to
pulverize the Turks' whole series of trenches ? Could so
many heavy guns be got up ? If not, why did we wait ?
We only know that up to 9 a.m. the Turks' trenches were
rows of moving heads, and many went over the open. The

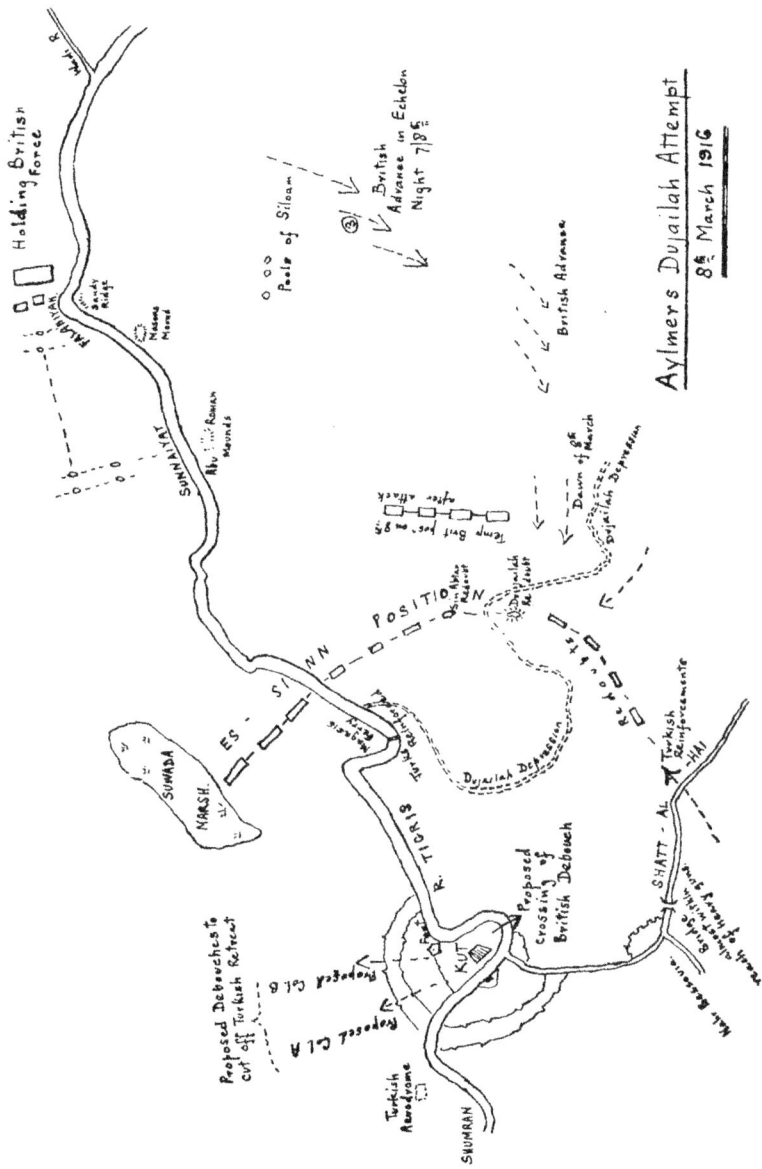

Aylmer's Dujailah Attempt
8th March 1916

Holding British Force

Pool of Siloam

British Advance in Echelon
Night 7/8th

British Advance

Sandy Ridge

Nasooa Mound

FALAHIYAH

SUNNAIYAT

Abu Rinan Mounds

Dawn of 8th March

Dujailah Depression

Temp Brit pos. on 8th after attack

POSITION

ES - SINN

MARSH.

SUWADA

Dujailah Redoubt

Sanaiyat Nacut

R. TIGRIS

Turkish Entrenchment

Turkish Lines

Dujailah Depression

Turkish Reinforcements

SHATT - AL - HAI

Proposed Debouches to cut off Turkish Retreat

Proposed Col.A

FORT

KUT

Proposed Col.B

Proposed Crossing of British Debouch

Turkish Aerodrome

SHUMRAN

Main Road to Baghdad

fact seems to be that our arrival at the redoubt was absolutely a surprise, and yet, through not pushing on, the benefit of surprise has been lost.

March 9th, 3 p.m.—The relieving force did not get through. We have heard this unofficially. We all have the feeling it is " the big effort," and not a side show. We are disappointed, but having had little else than disappointments we are accustomed to them.

March 10th.—There is another famous *communiqué* from General Townshend, our G.O.C. It is interesting to see how " Alphonse " improves every occasion. Here it is :

Communiqué to troops.

" As on a former occasion I take the troops of all ranks into my confidence again, and repeat the two following telegrams from General Aylmer from which they will see that the relieving force has again failed to relieve us.

" *First telegram : March 8th.*—' To-day's operations terminated in a gallant but unsuccessful attempt to storm Dujaila Redoubt. Our troops pushed home the attack and carried out the operations with great gallantry, but the enemy was able to mass great reinforcements which arrived from the left bank at Megasis and Shamran, and we were unable to break through. Unless the enemy retires from his present position on the right bank, which does not seem probable, we shall be unable to maintain ourselves in the present position owing to lack of water, and unless the enemy evacuates the Essin position to-night, we shall be obliged to withdraw to our previous position at Wadi.'

" *Second telegram : March 8th.*—' We have been unable to break through to relieve you to-day and may have to withdraw to Wadi to-morrow, but hope to make another attack before long and relieve you at an early date. Please wire movements of enemy, who in any case suffered most severely, as their repeated counter-attacks have been repulsed with heavy loss.'

(End of Telegrams.)

" I know you will all be deeply disappointed to hear this news. We have now stood a three months' siege in a manner which has called upon you the praise of our beloved King and our fellow countrymen in England, Scotland, Ireland, and India, and all this after your brilliant battles of Kut-el-Amara and Ctesiphon and your retirement to Kut, all of which feats of arms are now famous. Since December 5th you have spent three months of cruel uncertainty, and to all men and all people uncertainty is intolerable ; as I say, on the top of it all this comes—the second failure to relieve us. And I ask you also to give a little sympathy to me who have commanded you in these battles referred to and who, having come to you a stranger now love my command with a depth of feeling I have never known in my life before. When I mention myself I would couple the names of the generals under me whose names are distinguished in the army as leaders of men.

" I am speaking to you as I did before, straight from the heart, and as I may ask your sympathy for my feelings having promised you relief on certain dates on the promise of those ordered to relieve us. Not their fault, no doubt—do not think I blame them ; they are giving their lives freely and deserve our gratitude and admiration. But I want you to help me again as before. I have asked General Aylmer to bring such numbers as will break down all resistance and leave no doubt of the issue. Large reinforcements are reaching him, including an English division of 17,000 men, the leading brigade of which must have reached Wadi by now—that is to say, General Aylmer's headquarters. In order, then, to hold out, I am killing a large number of horses so as to reduce the quantities of grain eaten every day, and I have had to further reduce your ration. It is necessary to do this in order to keep our flag flying. I am determined to hold out, and I know you are with me in this heart and soul.

> " (Signed) CHARLES TOWNSHEND,
> " Major-General,
> " Commanding the Garrison in Kut.

" Kut-el-Amara,
" 10th March, 1916."

The rank and file of the garrison, from what one over-hears, are all for sympathy with their G.O.C. They are quite sure that " Alphonse would have got through " and have altered the name of the relieving general to Faylmer. Why wasn't the action delayed until the new division could have taken part ? As a matter of fact, one should suspend judgment until all the facts are in, and in the last analysis the blame must rest on Governments rather than on generals. When first besieged we expected to be relieved within a month, and so far as the Government knew we could hold out for about two months. Fortunately we secured various supplies of corn from Woolpress, and from dismantled engines we erected milling facilities which enabled us to turn corn and barley into bread.

But reinforcements have been sent into the country at a slow trickle and the enemy has found no difficulty at all in out-reinforcing us. When one considers the state of Turkey this is most incredible. One would think that the lesson of Ctesiphon was sufficient to chasten the authorities out of the belief that the Mesopotamian campaign could be dallied with. By sheer brilliancy of arms a whole country had been conquered by a single unsupported division. This achievement was not enough, however, and the cheap methods in vogue further required this one division to risk the whole fruits of a campaign in a single doubtful throw, and this against the advice of its generals. Through the same cheap methods of having insufficient forces to follow up a brilliant victory, our army was badly let down and several thousand lives flung away. Then only the same brilliant generalship of General Townshend disengaged the division from a force several times its size, and completed a masterly retirement for ninety miles, with the whole Turkish forces on top of it. Extraordinary success of the rearguard action at Um-al-Tabul enabled the division to reach Kut, where it is intended to hold up the Turkish advance and keep back the enemy tide from reswamping Mesopotamia. The post was surrounded and bombarded at once, but the public evidently does not know this owing to very necessary censorship. The garrison, then, can hold out for a certain time. It can forestall disaster for that time only.

One might imagine that the Indian Government would by this have become awake to this aspect of the crisis, have taken prompt action and sent out three or four divisions at once. Even admitting the difficulties of river transport, six weeks from the date of Ctesiphon, *i.e.* January 9th, would have allowed ample time for arrival at Basra. But the first reinforcements did not arrive in the country until considerably later, and then only depleted divisions. British divisions, which are really required, were only sent for recently and have hardly started. And now difficulties of transport will delay their transit up river. One cannot help recording these facts in black and white. Every day lost now is piling up tremendous difficulty for the future and swelling the list of lives downstream that, please God, will one day retrieve a disaster that might easily have been avoided. The world knows nothing of the siege of Kut, and the authorities are not being goaded by public opinion. In other words, the Indian Government has played with a serious situation. The price will be disaster. I am not setting this down as my own opinion merely. It is the point of view of every one in Kut. As a soldier one must refuse to believe that the position has been mishandled or that Kut will fall. But if I were a politician, which I am not, then would I add a lot of things here which I will not.

As I write it rains, and with every drop of rain the time within which the garrison, and, more important still, the strategic position at Kut, can be relieved, shortens. Soon come the annual floods, and when the whole country is under water reinforcements will be of no avail. And the time is short. It is the eleventh hour, and unless considerable forces are already on the way it is even now too late. But that is an affair between the authorities and the floods. Our problem is one of food.

The position here is much as it was in the Dardanelles. Excepting for floods and natural conditions we can outgun and outfight the Turk every time here. Moreover, we are tremendously relieving Aylmer of pressure, as the Turkish river communications must stop at Shamrun above us, and then his transport has to go overland. This is the marvellous thing about our enemy. He is daily carrying on a colossal bandobast of transport away from the water.

5 *p.m.*—Reuter reports the Verdun battle is going satisfactorily. One imagines that the German Kultur Geist must be bilious by this time, according to the numbers they are offering at his shrine. I am wondering how Nietzsche's Zarathusa would speak now if he saw the Verdun shambles. And what his blonde-haired, pink-limbed Über Mensch would

say about it too. Somehow I can see old Rudolf Eucken at Jena with outspread hands invoking " Schicksal " (destiny) as once he used to " Die Unendigkeit, Die Ewigkeit." Deep down in the German nature is a connative impulse towards the dramatic, and this is fed by a presentiment coloured with all the hues of harmony sweetest to them. It is not unknown for students at Jena and Heidelberg to extract such exquisite juice out of the word " Unendigkeit " (Immortality) or " Ewigkeit " (Eternity) as to become intoxicated therewith and commit suicide shortly after in the pine forest, or near a ruined " Schloss " (castle) what time the sun sets.

He loves the experience of the actor, likes to feel his gamut of emotions considerably twanged. This dramatic tendency showed itself on the occasion of that delicious utterance of the Kaiser on the eve of the Great War : " Now let my ministers put their hands through mine in token of fidelity, and let the nation follow me through Need and Death." Now, the Roman did this sort of thing rather well, but the German makes an ass of himself. One feels the Kaiser said it to see how it felt to say it.

The Germans tell us they are doing well, but I believe there is a sight becoming more familiar to their eyes, a phenomenon it is their daily delight and wish to behold, and that is the altar of this " Schicksal "—Fate. The Germans think in battalions. They have yet once again to go mad as a nation, as they did on the outbreak of war—absolutely " verrückt,"—and to bolt with competitive haste towards the national funeral pyre. They are not fanatics. They are temperamentalists—and from the spleen of a German musician it is said that in successful operation you can cut a piece of temperament nine inches long and twenty-five ounces in weight. Apropos of this general digression one may consider their " New Year's Picture " of " Tod " (Death), of which a copy reached us in the autumn of 1914 in France, and cheered us up considerably. " Tod " (please pronounce " toad "), an awfully unpleasant looking " Death," a snobbish skeleton with a bad seat, rode a heavy horse through a smitten land, a tremendous scythe over his shoulder and his metacarpal bones holding his reins incorrectly. The scythe flung a gigantic shadow, and as for Tod, his shadow reached almost to the horizon over black, burned villages, sacked cities, and many corpses. The horse had reached a double signpost which showed the way to St. Petersburg and the way to Paris. But, more interesting still, the skeleton had the lantern jaws of a Prussian. Fancy turning such a fellow loose! Truly the " God of Want and Rapine and Death ! " and a most excellent subject for the Germans' accepted New Year's Picture.

I remember my limber gunners having the same picture, months afterwards, at Aldershot. And Chopin composing the " Marche Funèbre " with a skeleton between his legs while he played wasn't in it with them. They had stuck the picture on the muzzle of the gun while they cleaned it. I hope every one of them goes untouched through the whole war.

Poor Germany ! I have had some happy days there, but when I compare the Kaiser's words to his nation on the eve of war with those of our own dear King, how I thank God I am an Englishman. And who would not mind being a Pharisee at the price of being an Englishman ? I ask you.

It may be suggested that when Germany falls, the same cement that holds that extraordinary nation together will assist it in falling together. In the meantime it will be an interesting spectacle for history to observe—the German nation sprinting on hot foot towards the registered funeral pyre, with all the dramatics of the bolting horse that gathers speed and insanity from its own flight.

Talking of horses, I hear that to-day is the slaughtering day for numbers of them. This is good-bye to any possibility of debouch, for there will be insufficient horses to move the guns. It will eke out our corn and barley that can be made into bread ; but what is wanted is sugar or jam for the body, and tea for the spirit.

" You are," says Townshend, " making a page of history."

" I would rather," thinks Tommy, " make some stew."

March 11*th*.—We have all been made acquainted with Sir Percy Lake's condolences on our misfortune, but also promising us relief ; but the floods are gradually increasing, and we fear it will be a case of Lake *v.* Lake, and there will be no appeal.

Sir Percy Lake is the Army Commander in place of Sir John Nixon, and General Aylmer is Army Corps Commander. Before going to bed last night we told fortunes by cards. The results in short were these : Firstly, a climax is to be reached shortly. (I quite agree.) Secondly, March 27th, my birthday, will seal my matrimonial affairs, the marriage to take place before the following March 27th. (Doubtful, unless I marry an Arab or Turk, or get freed for the event.) Thirdly, the star of the Fortune-God is in the ascendant, and his horoscope is wreathed with smiles. Which we two subalterns, and Cockie (a junior married captain), devoutly pray may come true.

Personally, I hold with that excellent fellow Horace that "the gods only laugh if they behold mortals showing an unseemly interest in their destiny." It is essentially a plebeian instinct, a relic from barbaric days when the world was brimful of curiosities for the twilight intelligence of recently-born man. But many decades taught him that unbridled curiosity ended in burnt fingers. Then he avoided with a fearful dread all that he did not know, and not the least of his tortures was occasioned by the Inexplicable straying upon him across the border from the Great Unknown. Later on he gets more nerve and he pioneers—still later he becomes scientific and investigates. And when the facts are more or less all in, his curiosity instead of his investigativity once again gets the better of him, and he fortune-tells and goes table-rapping, and tries to lassoo his astral body and to open up direct communication with those "not lost but gone before." It is, one might say with some truth, a mark of spiritual breeding to know how to acquiesce. Somehow one cannot picture the greatest of the gods tremendously excited. Equanimity is at least more dignified and always useful.

Nor should prophecy be confused with fortune-telling, for it is to the latter what investigation is to inquisitiveness. And inquisitiveness was always bad form. The personal factor looms too large.

Ah! how infinitely colossal and strangely beautiful is that great thing the Future, that ever bears down upon us from across the seas of Time. That dark tidal wave bearing great histories in its bosom and pregnant with joys and sorrows for us all. The gymnastics of living philosophers teach us that Time does not exist—but to me here in Kut it is almost the only real thing. O Futura Divina Ignota! thou mighty engulfing wave advancing from horizon to horizon upon us, with Change and Hope lightly treading thy combing crest—how pricelessly excellent a thing art thou, and what could we do without thee ? Whence art thou ? From what distant regions of Eternity art thou sped, on what strange shores do thy billows break ! We know not. It is beautiful not to know. And thus is Faith born. Thou art a beautiful stranger. We dread thee not. We trust thee—for thou art God.

Truly it is a great and wonderful world, and considerably reflected upon before patented. Some day a great man will write a book on " Some Attitudes to the Future "—wherefrom it will be gathered that the happiest is he who trusts but does not seek to know. " If," writes the prospective Plato, " it were permitted me of God to be the only mortal in the history of the human race to discover the lever that raises the curtain between us and the next world, and even if by so doing we might at once behold the flight of angels, the life of the spirit world, the procedure of heaven, yet would I certainly refuse to reveal the secret or to use it. Because to behold that Ultramontane would be to remove from life the two essential factors of discipline and hope. Moreover, if likewise I only were accorded the power of turning the searchlight on that land of mists we know as the Future so that all might see what is ahead of each, yet again would I not do so." And on second thoughts, who would ? It would indeed be a dreadful ordeal to have to live. And if you don't believe this, then go and ask a certain gunner subaltern in Kut.

9 *p.m.*—My hospital acquaintance, Square-Peg of the Oxfords, came along this afternoon for a game of chess, and asked if he might join our mess, as he is convalescent. Square-Peg and we talked 'Varsity gossip by the pipe-dozen. He is at present doing light duty on patrol of the gardens, technically known as " C.O. Cabbages."

I managed to best Edmonds later. He conceded me a knight, but then he is a very good player.

I made another acquaintance at the hospital, one Father Tim, the Catholic padre, who called to see me to-day.

A few rounds fell into the town. We did not reply.

We are informed that the English division of which we have heard so much is coming up-river now.

Rations have been still further cut down. We get bread and meat, nothing else, and of the former merely four ounces per diem. The garrison is in a bad way. Men go staggering about, resting every now and then up against a wall. I hear that the number succumbing in the trenches is daily increasing. As for the native hospital, the sight is too appalling for words. Skin-covered skeletons crawl about or turn over to receive their scanty nourishment, but nothing else, not even shell fire, engages their attention. One sees a coma stealing over them, a coma not less relentless than the Arctic Sleep of Death in the snow. The poor devils cover up their faces with blankets or tattered turbans, and dream of Home. One told me the other day that he heard the steps of Kismet.

It is roughly estimated that this further reduction of rations will give us two to three weeks—not more.

There is every confidence in our army below. One thing, however, we dread : that is the floods, which may or may not leave sufficient time.

March 12th.—Rain fell last night and again early this morning. Then we heard the sound of distant artillery, which increased to the subdued throb of gun-fire far away. But this was drowned in the grander music of a thunderstorm. How splendid is the artillery of the gods ! How majestic their salvos billowing across the heavens !

Last night we felt what we believed to be an earthquake, but which proved to be the sappers trying to dynamite fish in the river, which experiment was completely unproductive.

5 *p.m.*—It is still raining, which is bad for the river. I did my rounds and straightened up pay books, etc., in the office, and then played chess. I am a little better, and Amir Bux is an excellent masseur, a distinct improvement on Graoul, who used to treat my shoulders like a punch ball.

The soldiers have renamed this place Scuttle-Amara !

March 13th.—More rain has fallen ! The Tigris is almost bank high, and still rising.

I have been around the horses. Every tail is bare, and the *jhuls* and head ropes disappear as fast as they are put on. They all remain perpetually on the *qui vive* to prevent their stall-mates from biting them. Some are scarcely horses, but rather half-inflated horse skins.

Father Tim, the worthy Irish padre, who divides his attention between wistful ultramontane meditations and an excellent appetite, played chess with me to-day. He rooked me beautifully once.

H

March 14th.—Heavy gun-fire has been heard downstream. The irrepressible humours of Tommy inform us that it is our own guns covering Aylmer's retirement to Basra.

5 *p.m.*—The rain has stopped. I have been writing to King's College, Auckland, of many memories, and also to my acquaintance, "the delicious Conservative," at Corpus—Cambridge.

I find in the latter's epistle this sentence : "To-night I shall think of you in that delightful room with chairs so easy and cheroots so persuasive, soliloquizing on the eternal destiny of the American Conservative candidate."

He does not regard all Americans favourably, and I remember well how once when a Southern son of that enterprising nation averred that in the Northern States there were no aristocrats or conservatives, still the South was full of both, that he replied he had always understood it to be merely this way, that the Northern States had neither, and the Southern believed they had both. Which was very severe. But then he had a delightful, disarming smile. Oh, for a disarming smile ! ! !

March 15th.—The Ides of March ! Moreover they are come and gone, for I am making this entry, I find, on the 16th. The river rose eighteen inches, and for some hours lapped over the banks. Then it subsided a little. I had a walk through the palm grove and back via the Gurkha communication trench.

March 16th.—It is a beautiful day, warm and sunny, and the only blurr on the silvery brightness is the muddied Tigris winding like a yellow ribbon over this flat desert land. I felt so weak during my walk yesterday that to-day I merely strolled about the " gardens."

It was a fine sunset. Away over the muddy plain the Western skies were dragon-red, and clouds stirred by the evening breeze sailed in and out of the luminous belt which reflected a soft pink on the face of the rising moon climbing over the Eastern horizon.

I stale-mated a game of chess. Also received a gift of three brace of starlings that are the veriest God-send for the seedy.

March 17th.—We had an extraordinary breakfast of kedjereed tinned salmon Square-Peg brought with him.

Cockie's temperature is increasing and ought to be diminished.

I played patience a little, which I can't stick for long. There are not many books circulating.

March 18th.—Another beautiful day ! I stale-mated a game of chess with Square-Peg, and then had a walk round the trenches almost up to the Fort. There is an old disused trench skirting the river on the eastern side, where we sat in a hidden nook and let the cool breeze from the river play on our feverish dank foreheads.

Grass is beginning to grow in patches here and there on the *maidan ;* and here and there a truant mule did himself well behind the *bund.* Presently the Turks or Arabs spotted us, and we reluctantly had to leave the blissful spot.

Rumour says that the Turks have some new 7·5-inch guns coming. If so, the damage done will be ten times what it has been. And if they only had high-explosive shell the smashing up of the fort wall and the town would be a very short affair.

A bombardier of the 76th Battery, an excellent lad, has just died of wounds from the aeroplane's bomb. I remember upholding him in a matter of duty once.

Every day some one goes, either from wounds or sickness. And so far as we know the end is not yet.

March 19th.—Rheumatics bad again. They remind me I lived in feet of water in my earthy dug-out during the floods, even my bed sopping wet. However, in the heat of the day the aching is less intense. More serious are the increasing cases of entritis everywhere in Kut. I believe this is essentially a siege malady. The symptoms are violent pains in the intestines and a wish to vomit. It is, I hear, due to bad and insufficient nourishment. I know many who have already succumbed, but so far in my case these pains have been rather stomach than abdominal.

A bombardment started while I was in the gardens, and I hastened back to Cockie's observation post. It lasted the best part of an hour.

The floods have necessitated removing the 5-inch guns on the river-front, which are now in a dead line for our observation post, so any accurate one will be not far away. Anyway they can scarcely be closer than they have been. One shell

we felt certain was making dead for us, but it went by with a
fearful swish and burst ten yards off, killing one man and
wounding another after penetrating two feet of brick wall.
The fumes and filthy gases well-nigh choke one.

Another shell got the *Sumana* through the funnel and
bridge, killing one of her crew. Tudway's cabin was completely wrecked. Tudway is a deserving, hard-working
subaltern, the only R.N. representative in Kut. He always
takes it as a personal insult if his gunboat is hit. She is the
apple of his eye. H.M.S. *Sumana*, an improvised gunboat, is
of the greatest importance, as she keeps us in touch with
Woolpress, our tiny stronghold on the other bank, which
prevents the Turks from coming right down to the river-bank
and thus rendering our water-front totally unendurable. She
takes across a barge with provisions and reliefs, and makes
three or four trips a week. This the Turks know full well, and
do their best to send her under during the day. However,
she is fairly well protected with *mahelas* and rafts, though by
no means completely. It is a difficult problem to know how
to protect her, and engages all Tudway's thoughts. In fact,
how she remains afloat at all is a puzzle to every one.

The last trip of the Morane plane was sufficiently disastrous, one bomb dropping into the hospital ward, killing a
dozen men and wounding many others. These large bombs
are dreadful things, the splinters of the outer case being very
thin and sharp as razors. Square-Peg's servant was among
those hit. In the 1907 Convention at the Hague we tried to
get all the Powers to agree to refrain from this abominable
trick, but it was not to be. Anyway war is now full of
abominable tricks.

March 20th.—Cold and windy, an ideal day for a leather
chair with book-rest in one's study before an open fire, or for
Grieg's music, for there is a whip and a whistle in the wind,
and Peer Gynt is passing over us.

Another small strafe started, and H.M.S. *Sumana* stopped
quite a few. She received five direct hits from 9-pounders,
and one from the 18-pounder field-gun the enemy captured
from us at Ahwaz.

To be shelled by one's own gun and ammunition adds
humour to injury. And we have learned to respect the fearful
rip of this weapon. She hits ten times harder than any other

gun they have got of the same size.   But as Cockie says, " If British workmanship will be so thorough—— "

The Morane flew over us last night in the moonlight and dropped several bombs, one of which cut through an ammunition wagon, setting off several shells.   We give every credit to this intrepid flyer.   He came quite close.

For dinner we had a very excellent roast joint of horse and some rice.   I find that first-class horse is better than second-class mule, and only second to second-rate young donkey.   It beats camel and eclipses buffalo altogether.   The horses decrease most sadly.   Poor Don Juan!   No insurance company on earth would look at him.

We smoked lime-leaves and talked rose-leaves, which means Omar Khayyam and Hafiz.   But it lacked much—for we had no drinks more Khayyamnian than water.

March 21st.—To-day it is a world of brightness.   One has in one's self a feeling of joy and rejuvenescence, and outside there are the strong lines of a matter-of-fact morning, bright with the spangled beauties of ten thousand sheets of sunlight. They are the banners of approaching summer, and beneath the palm trees one hears the sweet voice of that ardent goddess and the elfish cadence of her myrmidons.

Gorringe, promoted to lieut.-general, has succeeded General Aylmer in the command of the relieving force, and has wired that he is making his final plans.

The river has fallen three feet, and so to-day the whole garrison is keen with expectancy and buoyant with hope.

A few details are to hand with regard to the recent unsuccessful dash by General Aylmer up the right bank.   From all accounts it was an excellent scheme, and came very near being a brilliant success.   The Turks were completely hoodwinked, expecting the attack on the left bank, but Aylmer's flying column, by a commendable night march, got up to the main line of the enemy, and struck Dujaila Redoubt.   The British troops got into this, but the story goes that General Aylmer then chose to wait for his guns and prepared before pushing through.   This took two or three hours, and the Turks, who had scanty troops on that side, immediately rushed over every available man from the other bank, and Aylmer, in attacking again, found the position too strong, and had to

cut his way back. If he had shoved on at dawn he must
have carried it easily.

Another version is that he had to go back for water, which
is almost incredible, the show not having miscarried at all in
length of time, and the river lay before him. One thing is
certain : if he had got through, the Essin position would have
had to be abandoned by the Turks, and, incidentally to the
relief of Kut, our debouch would have brought about a
heavy capture of the enemy. The difficulty now is that the
floods are daily rendering more and more of this table country
impassable. The soil is such that a shower of rain makes it
a quagmire, and stagnant water turns it into the stickiest
paste. Guns cannot be moved a yard, and it is almost equally
impossible for man or horse to move. This means that the
enemy's line downstream is shortened considerably, as they
have to depend mainly on the dry land for transport.

To-day there is artillery fire below. Our guns exchanged
a few rounds with his, and then Square-Peg and I strolled to
the middle line and managed to procure some saccharine.
We are spending every available sovereign to buy anything that can be got to see us over the last days of the
siege.

It is needless to remark that the only foodstuffs now for
secret sale are those that have been stolen or illicitly concealed.
But even these have long since been purchased, and it is only
by secret-service methods that an Arab is fossicked out who
will sell a tin of milk for fifteen rupees, a pound of rice for
five rupees, or atta for ten rupees. Officers and men, we are
all on the same footing, and the extra that one can buy is,
after all, such a very small supplement. There are many
besides myself who have to starve completely if eggs or milk
are not obtainable. Of the latter I have had one on issue
per day when they are available. This just keeps one going,
and after a few days of it one can manage with potato meal
and a small portion of horse.

Tudway has joined our mess altogether on account of the
Sumana being untenable. One shell has completely smashed
his cabin, luckily during his absence. Her 12-pounders are
ashore and he has a little nook which enables him to see a fair
zone on the right bank which he periodically shoots over like
a luxurious lord his pheasant coverts.

March 22nd.—During the night the enemy's plane visited us and the sharp staccato notes of our anti-air maxims rapped out a brisk warning to the sleeping garrison. The others took shelter downstairs, but my bed was so very comfortable that I waited for the music of the first bomb before jumping out. It didn't come. At 5.30 a.m. we were awakened by a sudden and intense bombardment. This building is not far from the mosque and quite close to the anti-air maxims, so-called because they never hit anything but air.

The bombardment seemed concentrated a good deal on this part of the town. Cockie went to observe. Then the plane came back and bombed us, circling across the town, after which the bombardment again opened. Square-Peg developed a spasmodic sprint of extraordinary alacrity every time anything happened or the plane gong rang out, and dressed downstairs. This proved such a nerve-racking ordeal that I proposed to have my tea in my room and then go below. The shells were thumping on the houses just behind us, and I took the precaution to shift over the thick wall side of the room which left just space enough for my servant Amir Bux to miss the doorway. Shell after shell struck the adjoining buildings, shaking our house considerably. Then suddenly there was an awful roar and splitting crash. The room was filled with smoke and dust and plaster, and a terrific thud shook the wall just behind my head. Two segments of shell had flown through the doorway and embedded themselves in the opposite wall. That excellent fellow Amir Bux suddenly asked, " Master thik hai ? " And on my assuring him I was all right he pointed to the embedded segment and smiled, muttering " Kismet ! " On inspection I found that a Windy Lizzie had crashed through the slender wall of the upper enclosure around the roof on which my room opened (there was no door), and about half the fore-end of the shell had struck the thick wall of my room a few inches behind my head and had gone halfway through the plaster. Another foot and it would have got my scalp precisely.

The show kept on intermittently until 8.30 a.m. The horse lines and hospital have again caught it rather badly. One shell passed under a patient's bed in the General Hospital and exploded on the far wall without hurting anybody. There is not any backward zone worth mentioning in some of these shells. High explosive would have been a different story.

9 *p.m.*—A few more shells fell this evening. We hear that after all the plane did bomb last night and altogether made a most daring raid. We must give Fritz full marks for excellent bombing. He attended chiefly to Woolpress village over the river. More serious was the damage done by the same plane to the 4·7-inch guns in the horse boats—a very small target. One barge was almost sunk, being suspended by her cables only, and the other gun was jerked out of its socket by the force of the explosion. It appears the bomb touched the edge of the horse boat and fell into the river, exploding under the water. The result was a deluge that heaved the gun out of its pedestal. Reports from Woolpress say he flew within thirty yards of the barges, which for a night performance was highly commendable. Fritz is a German. He had hard luck in not getting one gun at least. We contemplate painting in large letters on the roof of the Serai, our condolences over his bad luck. Tudway is busy towing the barge to the *Sumana* shelter where it is to be repaired.

Cockie is a first-rate chess player, at least so he has repeatedly informed us. He knows the whole history of Ruy Lopez even to his private affairs, and can at any stage of any game tell you the exact measurement of the sphere for evil of any piece on the board. He does not finger his piece and wave it in mid-air before moving as do smaller fry at the game. Neither does he hesitate for four minutes ever. Attacks, counter-attacks, demonstrations, feints, holding and flanking —he is an artist at them all. At every exchange he gets an advantage in pieces—*or position.* " Position," he assures us, " is the all in all." He can even nominate the moves without looking at the board. In short, if he did not invariably get beaten, he would be a perfect player, and even Lasker would have to look out. Square-Peg once brilliantly remarked that this tendency to get beaten was the tragedy of it all, but with infinitely more tact, at least to my mind, I added that Cockie was merely a great player and not infallible ; in other words, that there were limitations in us all. This Cockie said he denied. And I agreed.

That may seem illogical. But it was necessary. If to beat Cockie is a misdemeanour, then to allude to the fact is certainly a crime—in his eyes. Besides, he isn't invariably beaten, as I have said. That was a mis-statement. For when he has made a bad slip or, let us say, paid too big a price for " position," such as losing his queen for a bishop or maybe a pawn, he frequently goes very red in the face and knocks all the pieces from the board on to the floor, which shows he has the foreseeing eye, a faculty absolutely necessary to a first-rate chess player. Maeterlinck, we are told, has the seeing eye. How much greater, then, is Cockie, who has the foreseeing eye ? If, thinks Cockie, it is not always the province of man to anticipate disaster, he can at least forestall it.

" I had the game on my head," Cockie usually bursts out as he sweeps the board. "And it wasn't lost either, don't forget—but the interest in it had all gone."

He did the same the first time he played me when he showed me a new opening—about three moves. He got a piece or two ahead, when after an hour or so I evened things up. Then he made his invariable slip, and before one could strike a match Cockie had the board clean as a skating rink, remarking hotly, "When I play against myself I'm always beaten."

" Thank your God, Cockie," I retorted, " then you admit some one can beat you." Which remark somehow or other he didn't appreciate.

However, since then I'm more awake, and when, which is not often, I bag his queen, or when, which is very often, he makes a slip, my arms are around the board before you could smile. It's the only way to keep the men on. If we were in America I should practise " getting the drop on him with a Colt's revolver " at each crisis.

Poor Square-Peg came to me in trouble on this point the other day.

" We have to be thankful, S.-P.," said I, " that Cockie has not yet commented on our morality."

" But it's coming. He's saving it up. I'm sure of it. Why, this morning I had a certain mate in two moves, but my dread of what he would say in another explosion was such that I thought it necessary to extend the check to six times before finally checkmating him. It was a hard job and might have cost me the game. But then, since that last show, my nerves are none too good."

"Well, you got off lightly! I heard him merely knock his chair over and say that your playing was only better than mine. Did he not?"

"Yes! he's a blank, ten to one."

Whereat we both laughed as only subalterns can. At this point Cockie, who wanted my field-glasses, looked in at the mess. Now, if one thing annoys him more than another it is to see two people laughing and not to be in the joke. He always presumes he is in it. This time he was correct. Turning to me venomously Cockie said, " I suppose you'd like a game?"

"Rather not, thanks awfully, I might get beaten."

Cockie snorted in disgust, and I had to give him a last cigarette I had just made for myself.

"The truth is, Cockie, that Square-Peg and I are hopelessly deficient in this chess business, and we have to fluke to win as they say in ' pills.' That churns you up and you can't see the pieces, and consequently move the wrong one. Don't swear. I've a proposition. ' Nellie ' is coming to lunch and will give you a game. He's very hot stuff."

So it was settled. Square-Peg and I made our plans and fixed it all right with Nellie, who tries to be a very dignified and silent person of the cutting variety, and dislikes Cockie.

After our lunch of stewed horse and horse-beans and rice the game began. After a few moves Cockie had a slight advantage, and I took this opportunity to whisper to him that Nellie had a weak heart and it was dangerous to shout at him. Cockie nodded approvingly and the game went on. Half an hour later Cockie lost a bishop which he could only retrieve by uncovering check.

His face went red and he took a breath. " Don't forget," I sang out, and I and S.-P. each seized a glass of water and an almost empty rum bottle for any emergency.

Cockie glared at me in a cannibalistic fashion, and eyeing Nellie carefully the while, addressed some superlatives to us, saying that the interruption had spoilt his move. Nellie sat with steady countenance while I replied that the interruption came after the move. But Cockie played brilliantly and recovered a piece, whereupon he got quite genial and addressed conciliatory remarks to me.

Twice Cockie forced exchanges, and as in both instances

he got " position," which means that he was a pawn to the bad each time, we quietly stood up with the water in a first-aid attitude. But Cockie was playing as he never played before, and was nodding his head in a queer way. I thought he was so blind with annoyance that he was counting the pieces, but Square-Peg assured me that his engine had got hot and was running free. Cockie went on serenely for about another half-hour when, after a pause of several minutes, he suddenly discovered himself to be mated, for Nellie had said only the word " check " and now added " mate " in the most matter-of-fact voice.

" Damned fluke," screamed Cockie, forgetting himself, and springing up he banged the chessboard down fiercely on the table with an awful smash.

Poor Nellie gasped and said " Oh-o-o-o," and apparently stopped breathing and reeled in his chair. Not having brandy we gave him the last of Cockie's rum, which he managed to negotiate, and then, as usually happens, felt better. We three preserved a frigid silence towards Cockie, who said he was damned if he knew what was the use of people on service with weak hearts, and then strode off, Nellie in the meantime pulling hard at the bottle for an extra drip or so. How we laughed. For Cockie was really scared. It's not the sort of story to make you popular if it gets about—wilfully startling a fellow to death with a weak heart merely for beating you in a game of chess.

Later on Square-Peg and I joined Cockie on the observation post and a battle royal ensued.

" I tell you," said Cockie to me, " it's fearfully difficult to give the whole of one's attention to the game when one is playing an absolute novice. So things are missed. But if you will back me for five rupees against Square-Peg to win ten games out of ten I'll do it, you see. That will supply the interest."

I complied at once, offering one game in, which he proudly refused. With a vicious jab to Cockie to please remember it was " my money and not his " that was concerned, and to have no nonsense, he grew demonstrative, and I fled to pay a visit to Tudway on the *Sumana*.

" I tell you I can't lose," he had said. When I returned to the mess, there I found Square-Peg, who announced that he had left Cockie in a fury, he having lost the first three games. I insisted on Square-Peg's taking the five dibs. It appears that during the first game Fritz passed him and said " Good afternoon," to which interruption Cockie stormily attributed his subsequent beating. . . .

Later.—This very morning the other half of the shell that crashed outside my doorway (there isn't a door) went through the roof of Cockie's bedroom and simply smashed most things in it. A foot of *débris* from the roof lay on the floor. It was lucky for Cockie that he was on duty. And luckier for me that I did not accept Cockie's many invitations to share his room. Only yesterday he asked me again to do so. But Cockie generally has two or more rounds with Curra Mirali and pursues him round the yard, leaving the door open—every morning about 6 a.m. when I am doing my best to have one other dream.

To-night after dinner Fritz, Cockie, Square-Peg, and I discussed the proposition that the hole a shell makes is the safest place, as no two shells ever fall in exactly the same spot. One recalled that very good Tommy story from France when, on being asked why he hadn't taken cover in a Jack Johnson crater as he had been ordered, replied, " Unsafe, sir. I'd rather try another spot and chance it."

" But you know that the same gun never shoots into exactly the same spot twice ? "

" Yes, sir. But another gun might."

Fritz and I upheld the theory of probabilities as being against a second shell getting into Cockie's room. For that meant a very precise elevation just clearing the back houses and wall, and meant also the range to a foot or it would get the yard.

Cockie and Square-Peg, on the contrary, held that because one shell has got there and so proved that a shell *can* get there, another might get there also. I remember painfully suggesting that Cockie ought not to sleep in the room if he thought that another shell might come in, especially as he had no doubt offended the gods over the Nellie incident. This is altogether an extraordinary affair and I am recording it in detail. Well, Cockie went to bed, taking the precaution from my incident of the morning to sleep with his head to the door instead of his feet. We were half undressed when the bombardment reopened. It became so hot that we all took shelter in the mess, the safest place. Indeed the back wall was stopping dozens of them. Later it slackened and we went to bed, whereon it gradually increased. After I had tossed restlessly for half an hour it exceeded the limit, and the plaster and dust were being flung through the doorway of my bedroom. On my way down I inspected the whole of the wall and found the roof all around pulverized. Five minutes later Square-Peg and I were smoking half undressed in the mess when the stunning noise of a splitting crash seemed to burst the world in halves. *Débris* came into the mess. We thought the shell had entered the tiny yard, but Cockie's voice in unearthly yells quickly disillusioned us.

I shot into the room, which was stifling with fumes and dense yellow gas and smoke. The lamp went out. I told Square-Peg to fetch a doctor and tried to strike a light, but nothing would burn in the thick fumes. I felt for the ruined bed and managed to get him out of the room into the mess. There was a nasty deep gash over the tendon of Achilles, but no bones were broken, although the ligaments were gone and it was bleeding freely, so I applied a first field dressing, as I had so often done in France, and assured him it was not at all serious and that now he was sure to get downstream. Nevertheless poor Cockie's many nerves had been badly shaken. Fritz came and said :

" Let me see. That's good—no bones. Bleeding stopped. Move your foot. Nothing much really. Where else ? "

After a fresh spasm Cockie complained that his back seemed cut in two, and this proved a nasty bruise, although the skin wasn't gone. It was a black bruise, and he must have got a pretty hefty knock from a piece of the bed. How he escaped goodness knows. The room was two feet deep in rubbish—topees, uniforms, cameras, bed, everything was wrecked.

We got him to the hospital, and on the way he invented extraordinary futures for each of the stretcher bearers.

Arrived at the hospital I am afraid the whole place was awakened, and some poor fellows whose dying was only a matter of hours or days turned from their fitful sleep on the ground floor to ask who was hit.

He wanted me to sit up with him, but General Smith

insisted that I went back to bed, assuring me I was far too ill, and he kindly gave me an excellent cigarette.

Cockie is intrepid under fire even to the point of recklessness, but is also of the kind that feels pain tremendously. It is, I suppose, a matter of temperament and nerves.

This has released me from the river-front and I succeed to the command of the ammunition column, and am now running our mess.

Tudway, Square-Peg, and I are now alone here. We have a little potato meal and rice, and I have procured a tin of jam. I could not have two more generous companions with whom to share our last food.

March 23rd.—The servants won't sleep in that part of the building where the shells came, so we have vacated a room for them, and Square-Peg and I have moved below into the basement.

I saw Cockie this morning and heard him from afar.

Near him is an officer lying very still and white and quiet with his whole leg shattered, silent with the paralysis of extreme pain.

I assisted Cockie with letters and other things, and got away as quickly as I could, as I felt this other sufferer wanted silence.

March 24th.—Some shells fell in the town during the night, and once again the horses got it badly.

The 4'7-inch gun which was bombed by the plane is now under-water, as the river has risen five feet, the highest level during the siege.

It is a clear, beautiful day and appreciably warmer. Already the flies are dreadful and swarm everywhere in billions. The Kut fly is a pronounced cannibal.

I walked through the palm woods to the 4-inch guns, where I found Parsnip alone in his glory. There he has been the whole siege with a very comfortable tent under the trees, and his only job is to repeat orders from the telephone to his two antediluvian guns. As a field gunner I am not enamoured of his monotonous and stationary job. Parsnip is a subaltern also and has two characteristics. In playing chess he seizes the pieces by the head, and after describing an artistic parabola, sets them down. He is a Radical, as you would expect of any fellow so handling a pawn, let alone a queen. His second claim to notoriety is said to be as author of a future publication entitled, " Important People I intend to meet." As a hobby he kills mosquitos with a horse flick.

For over an hour beneath those biblical palms Parsnip, or Pas Nip, and I stood by his guns and smoked and looked out over the darkening plain where shadow chased shadow under the capricious moon, and where, like will o' the wisps of an extravagant dream, tiny flashes tempted us still to hope on. For what ? Well, there were the flashes. They were the flashes of our guns. And I longed for tobacco and wine. Parsnip, on the contrary, was a married man !

March 25th.—This morning I had a thorough inspection of the horse and wagon lines and inspected shelters previous to my visit to headquarters to report on ammunition. Orders are out for all ranks to prepare to receive heavy bombardment. I am having the ammunition shelter even further reinforced against shell or bomb. The present scheme is to have two thick roofs each topped by kerosene tins packed close and filled with soil. One of these shelters will explode the shell or bomb, and the other receive the burst. The horse-lines have been changed and pits dug for all drivers and detachments and traversed for possible enfilade bursts. The men are working on a shelter for our basement room with tins of earth piled up. Tins are fearfully scarce, as hundreds have been requisitioned for the defence of H.M.S. *Sumana* and other things. We have, we believe, sheltered the probable zones with what tins we have. Thus the doorway and window are unprotected because the upper back room would stop all except howitzer fire, and the enemy's howitzer is south of Kut. Similarly from a lucky shell bursting through the wall of the first-floor room and roof of our present one, we have had three rows of tins—all we could get—arranged in front of the wall upstairs. I have calculated that any burst entering higher than this would get the opposite upstairs wall and pass out into the street.

Tudway and Square-Peg have accused me of being cold-blooded over the affair. But I intended to be nothing if not practical, and the next morning discovered that any shell of average intentions, in fact one falling ten feet shorter than the very one that had plugged into my bedroom wall up above, would have no difficulty in going through the mess roof and so through the mess cupboard—a large receptacle into the wall—into our so-called impregnable bedroom which was to be the emergency shelter for all hands. My bed was just beyond the cupboard the other side of the three-foot wall. So this evening when Tudway went to the cupboard for the jam and meat and bread he found a solid wall of tins filled with earth. This he considered a master-stroke. The provisions, as he explained, would have been directly in the line of fire !

Moreover, I have had removed a score or two of loose bricks which were wedged in the best Damocletian style between the joists and the ceiling. For last night I dreamed one fell on my head. Why my head is always in the line of trouble I can't say.

Talking of dreams, that is the second nasty one in a few days. The previous time I dreamed I was being hung. That was probably due to a button that I had sewn on to the neck of my pyjama jacket by the uncertain light of dubbin oil !

10 *p.m.*—There is heavy and continuous firing downstream. I respectfully suggest a variation of Watts's " Hope "—that popular picture. A junior sub asleep in a barricaded corner of a room in Kut beside a four-ounce slice of bread, listening in his dreams to distant guns.

I must now make one of the most important entries of the whole siege. General Smith gave me a *Punch*. I mean that having finished with a copy of *Punch*, sent to him by aeroplane, he has passed it on to me.

Shakespeare, Thackeray, and Punch. In the flesh, what friends those three would have been !

" If," writes an unborn Teufeldrockh, " I were not a German, I would like to be Punch."

" If," replies Punch, with a dignified bow, " you were not a German, you could aspire."

For what duellist but that great English gentleman Punch has the seeing eye, the delicate wrist, the merciful smile ?

March 26*th*.—I am in Indian khaki again, for summer has come to Kut. It is even getting unpleasantly warm.

The massaging has decreased the rheumatics if anything, although I am very much weaker and can't walk 400 yards without getting blown. It is worth while to avoid the chaff bread, and I stick to an occasional egg and rice-husk and soup.

How fit I was when I started on this front ! Square-Peg

was seedy yesterday and in pain. I gave him some essence of ginger tabloids, and later on opium, which relieved him somewhat.

It is rumoured that the 6-inch guns from home have at last reached Gorringe. The enemy is now completely out-classed in artillery.

Tudway took me with him on board the *Sumana* to see the effects of the recent bombardment. By a miracle one shell missed the main steam-pipes and carried away part of the bridge and cabin and funnel. Tudway is a keen officer, and has all the delightful insouciance of his service. We went over the whole boat and the barges. He was all on the alert, in his quiet way, to gather any suggestions for further protecting his alumnus. We sat in his dismantled cabin and talked of the sea, or rather he did, and I mentally annotated him with my own dreams. The sea, the sea, so vast, so great, so deep, so far away! As the hart panteth after the water-brooks so pant we Englishmen after thee, O Sea, even after thee, wild and lonely as thou art, and after thy waters briny as tears. Mighty, untamed, eternal! We, thy children, love thee. Alone, thou art free!

Turkish snipers followed us up, and we had to run the gauntlet on the way to the shore over the waters of the flood. I bought three small fish yesterday here, but some one's native servant was killed last evening by a stray shell while fishing, so for the future it's all off. On one occasion, Tudway and I tried to net some, but both the Turks and the fish were against us.

This siege is a perfect device for leaving a man to his own plaguings. A book is now almost as great a luxury as bread. I am even driven to re-robing and criticizing some of our early endeared legacies. Let us begin with the poet's notion of service—admittedly of a bygone day.

The Soldier's Dream.

By the other Campbell.

Our bugles sang truce for the night-cloud had lowered—
Delightful arrangement that, one must admit. A truce is, after all, more fun than a night attack. And perhaps the cloud was a big one and it looked like rain!

I

And the Sentinel stars set their watch in the sky—
    Much better ! But that does away with the rain theory.
And thousands had sunk on the ground overpowered—
    Bad-fitting word. Sounds like avoirdupois. But it
    must have referred to gas fumes, otherwise the line
    certainly reflects on the condition of the men. This
    climate could be called " overpowering."
The weary to sleep and the wounded to die—
    That scouts the gas theory ! As a matter of fact it's
    the last thing the weary have a chance to do, and the
    wounded certainly take weeks to die. Look at Cockie !
While reposing one night on my pallet of straw—
    Fancy Tommy " reposing " ! Campbell, may I in-
    form you that Thomas neither poses nor reposes, which
    suggests the soft, rounded limbs of a Grecian maiden on
    a bed of rose-leaves. Tommy likes his mouth open, and
    often prefers to lie on his stomach with his legs wide
    apart. Reposing ! My hat ! What an awful swank
    the man was with his knocking off work because of the
    night-cloud, and what with his reposing on a pallet of
    straw. Why he didn't go in for a convertible four-legged
    wheelbarrow bedstead puzzles me. Tommy lies on the
    " good 'ole dirt " if it's hot, and otherwise screws himself
    up into his blanket, head and all. I hear Graoul asking
    his pal, " O, Halgie, koindly porse erlong may pallet
    hof straarw hat wance."
        " Roight yer hare ! 'Ere, Toenails, pallit-er strore is
    forwerd—hand the quilt halso."
At the dead of night a sweet vision I saw,
And thrice ere the morning I dreamed it again—
    Kindly eliminate " dreamed " and substitute " saw,"
    then re-read it. Don't laugh ! Why shouldn't he
    " see " it the second and even the third time also ?
    Tommy sees lots of things—at times.
I dreamed from the battlefield's dreadful array
Far, far, I had roamed on a desolate track.
It was springtime and summer arose on the way—
To the home of my fathers that welcomed me back—
    Tommy wouldn't dream of dreaming such a thing.
    As for the " home of my fathers," the shape of the idea
    would give him a fit. " Bit o' skirt more like it."

Stay, stay with us, thou art weary and worn ;
And fain was the war beaten soldier to stay—
But sorrow returned with the dawning of morn
And the voice in my dreaming ear melted away—
"D'ye 'ear this, Spud?" says Tommy Toenails.
"The voice in 'is dreeamin' hear melted."
"Bit o' wax, more like," says Spud.
"I say a flea an' charnce it," adds Tooting Tom.
"Hand," says Spud, "wen 'e hawoke 'e got anuther stomikful o' sorrer. Marrid man, too. Gawd 'elp 'im.
We pass on. Let us take that dear little hymn lots of us learned at our mother's knee—
"There is a green hill far away
Without a city wall."
How I used to wonder what a green hill could possibly want *with* a city wall. Ah! the dear doubts of childhood! I shall be told that "without" meant "beyond." Another doubt was about "Llewellyn and his Dog." How the siege has helped us to join hands with childhood once more. Surely I haven't thought of the lines for many years. They run—
"The gallant hound the wolf had slain,
To save Llewellyn's heir."
I remember we had to write a composition on the poem, and having decided that it was the wolf that had killed the hound—just as one says, "The scanty bone the beggar picked"—I had to square matters so as to explain how the hound died a second time at the hands of Llewellyn. It's all misty now, but I at least remember propounding the theory that the Welsh chieftain, in his terror, must have mistaken the wolf for the hound, and consequently did *him* in for murdering the lost child. It was this incident, I believe, that induced my parents to select for me a career at the Bar.
That incident recalls another one later on. At school we had a delightful master who hated using chalk. He informed us that we were to write an essay on—
"Beneath the rule of men entirely great
The pen is mightier than the sword."
One promising fellow misheard the last word as "saw." He was rather an authority on saws, and treated

us to a delightful treatise on saws in general, band-saws, hand-saws, rip-saws, fret-saws, and circular saws. As far as I remember, the drift of his argument was that a pen could merely write, whereas a saw could cut a piece of wood.

Once more, " Eheu ! *Fugaces postumi——* "

I wonder where that lad is now. I should think he must be a large saw-miller somewhere—possibly asleep on a " pallet of straw " in France, and seeing " visions " of his beloved saws. Why not ! God bless him. I've forgotten his name and even what he was like.

Well, well, these frivolities must come to an end for it's ten o'clock. I had intended to set out more details of our starvation methods, but we talk enough of it and I'm sick of the subject. Besides, what is happiness but a big digression ?

March 27th.—The day's bulletin is that the Churches in England are praying for us. How we hope they pray hard. There is, we understand, to be a last forward movement of all arms to the relief of Kut. The position down below seems to have developed into something like that in France, as the Turkish forces are dug deep and well flanked with impassable swamps. It is difficult to force such a position against the clock, but we easily outnumber the enemy, so it is said, and then our heavy guns may do a great deal.

The water of the floods is now all over the *maidan* around our old first line, in fact in front of our present first line is a great lake some feet deep, and possibly eight feet above the dry base of our trench. The large *bund* or wall we have made is excellent. The enemy has had to withdraw still further back, and in places he is 1500 yards off. In this way the floods have saved us. There is little chance of an attack through the water. It may be doubted whether our men could have stood the strain in their present condition if the enemy had maintained his original proximity of from 50 to 150 yards. I remember a listening post at C Redoubt something like ten yards from the first line of the enemy.

Over the river all around Woolpress and beyond, and also reaching southward, are shining sheets of water with ever-diminishing green patches between. During the last flood of a few days back the water percolated into Woolpress, which,

of course, is on the bank of the river, and wrought great
havoc in the trenches and among the men there.

It must be an awfully lonely and desolated existence over
there at Woolpress, a siege within a siege. The post is a
mere sequence of mud houses, all adjoined, five yards or so
from the water and forming a segment of a circle on the river
about 250 yards frontage, its first line being the arc extending
150 yards inland at its farthest. They have first and
second line trenches, and barbed wire, and since the heavy
floods, a *bund*. So that it is now practically an island. The
Turkish lines reach all round it in larger arcs also resting on
the river-bank. They have not even the chance of buying
stores as we have, and never come over, nor is it permitted
for any to cross. The communication is by motor-boat or
almost always by the *Sumana*. Tudway has the nerve of
Beelzebub, and delights most of all in his moonlight trips. It
would, of course, be certain destruction for him to cross in
the daytime. At the beginning of the siege there was tele-
phonic communication, but the wire was rotten and broke
continually. We have helio now, and some sort of understanding for emergency signalling by lights. Our river-front
guns are all registered on the enemy's lines around the place,
and on one or two occasions we have gone to gun-fire, thus
preventing any Turkish reserves getting up. From this side
of the river a section of the 82nd R.F.A.'s guns can enfilade
the enemy's northern lines around Woolpress.

We get news of the place by the drafts that now and then
reinforce the post on relief. The story goes that the other
day a party of Turks peered over their trenches and cried
aloud to our Mussulman soldiers not to fight against their
brother followers of Mahomet, but to go over to them who
had plenty of food. This sort of thing had gone on quite a
time when the officer on picket duty got about a dozen sepoys
to fire a volley at the Turks just by way of exchanging compli-
ments. The Turks replied, and general fire ensued. That
highly intuitional body over here, Headquarters, believing that
Woolpress was being attacked by all the spare Turks in the
Ottoman Empire, gave our artillery enthusiastic orders, and
Woolpress began to think they took some part in the siege
after all, in fact that they belonged to us. And although it
was a storm in a teapot, no doubt for those in the teapot it

was highly interesting. It is even said that senior officers struggled out from beneath spider-webbed blankets where they had hoped to complete their hibernation until the siege was over, to see the reason for this turn of events. Woolpress are a gallant little band, no doubt, and there have been times when no insurance company on earth would have looked twice at any one of them, although a philanthropic society might have stretched a point for those certified able to swim ; for a red Turkish crescent ringed them in and grew ever closer to them, and once the river took sides and offered to drown them. But that was months ago.

Woolpress, too, has its advantages. They have been practically never shelled and rarely bombed. On the contrary, when we are getting bombarded or any particular show is on, they all take front seats on their river-bank in absolute security and observe our emotions. I well remember that gala day of March 1st, when enemy guns of both sides took part in that very well conducted " command matinée " performance for the entertainment of the gods. The whole crowd of Woolpress was seated early, orchestral stalls for field officers, subalterns in specially erected boxes, and the rank and file everywhere else. I was, of course, very much on the stage, being stuck up there shooting my guns, while the Turks cut patterns round me with all the artistry of Turkish artillery. The heavy gunners on the observation post farther along, that well-battered remnant that is the despair of the Sultan's artillery observers, also attracted considerable attention from an audience particularly sporting. I felt that the Woolpressers were making and taking huge bets as to what time my wee sandbag arrangement with contents would go by the board. Opera glasses were there by the dozen. But Jove, Trenchion, and Shraptune, the sporting gods that had decreed the performance, naturally objected to such small fry sharing the entertainment, and sent Fritz along with bombs. This considerably thinned the box plan, from which many adjourned for afternoon tea, while those more deeply in debt remained taking still larger bets on their own immediate existence.

This is my birthday. We have raised a small quantity of rum with which we three shall notch the year to-night. Why doesn't one feel older ? Life lies immediately behind us like the wake of a ship, but *we* don't change—only the distance behind us changes (and a few of us are a stone lighter !).

9.30 *p.m.*—I returned from my round with a copy of *The Field* from General Smith. There was an excellent article on Pan-Germanism, and another that brought to Kut the brown wintry heather, the smell of the peat streams, the pheasants, and the free rolling moors of Yorkshire. And that led me to contrast the present flooded aspect of this dreary stretch of God's ancient mud with the frilled hedges and those gay wild banners of English springtime.

Speaking for myself on this my thirtieth birthday, I never felt so restful and free from the gnawings of ambition. For better fellows have fallen, and promising careers have closed, and disastrous ones terminated before amends could be made ; while I have lots of credit in hand, for I have had many lucky narrow shaves.

CHAPTER VI

THE LAST DAYS OF KUT—SICKNESS—DEATH—SURRENDER

MARCH 28th.—It is a quiet day. On the right bank there is some movement of the enemy downstream. Convoys of camels and mules trekked from Shamrun camp over the Shat-el-hai to the Turkish depôts below.

We are all eagerly awaiting news of our preparation for the big show, and there is much debating as to what would be the best plan of attack.

3 *p.m.*—There is considerable Turkish activity all around, and reinforcements are probably being pushed down below, for the enemy knows quite well that we are on our last legs and that a big attempt will be made to relieve us.

The river is gradually falling, and one 4·7 has been towed back into position, but the other is still under-water.

A bombardment is proceeding downstream, probably the shelling of Sunaiyat, the formidable position of the enemy on the left bank, a series of trenches on a tiny front of 400 yards between a marsh and a river. In this position the enemy is so deep down and has such excellent cover that the place has so far baffled every attempt to take it. Not the least difficulty is that the intervening ground, which every storming party must cross, is wet as a bog. This has, of course, been worked by the Turks. On the right bank Gorringe seems to have pushed on almost level of Sunaiyat, and, with a little more success, enfilade of the Sunaiyat position should be possible.

According to rumour, the plan of attack roughly may be as follows :—

One division will probably have the task of holding Sunaiyat forces while the other two divisions push up through Beit Aessa, whence our 6-inch guns should enfilade the Sunaiyat position. The line of advance would probably make for Dujaila Redoubt which would be taken on by our big guns and the bridge at O destroyed to prevent escape of the enemy to other bank. One division would then have a large part of the Turkish force hemmed in on the Essin ridge right bank, and the other division crossing into Kut by a bridge to be erected by us would swing around past the Fort to prevent the remaining enemy forces on the left bank from getting away. It will be either a dismal failure or brilliant success, and much at this belated hour must depend upon the floods.

March 29th.—A beautiful day and quite hot. We have been unmolested except for some shells on the Fort. I have finished " Septimus," by W. Locke. Septimus is a delightful chap, and would make much fun for us if he were here.

Then we played chess, and I visited Pas Nip on my way around the trenches. He returned and lunched with us. I have managed to get a tin of gooseberry jam at ten rupees, one tin of milk twelve rupees, 1½ lbs. of atta for fifteen rupees.

I held another inspection of the native drivers among whom scurvy has increased. They still refuse to eat horse-flesh.

Don Juan has turned from a dark black to a burned brown. That, possibly, is his way of turning grey! I gather him some grass every possible day.

March 30th.—It has been a day of the most perfect tranquillity, and as I couldn't sleep for this confounded backache I was up for the dawn. I climbed up to the observation post and looked around on a lovely earth. I mean it. The very wretchedness and misery of the floods, and the broken palm grove, and the disfigured earth, were all woven into the most bewitching harmony by sheets of silver and bars of golden sunlight. It was hard to realize it was a scene of war, that those receding terraces were trenches filled with armed Turks. I am beginning to think that, after all, the Garden of Eden could have been very beautiful—at any rate in the dawn, for then it is a country of long shadows and persuasive lights. This morning the drooping palm fronds patterned the water and the wide plain. There was gold and green in every patch of grass. As for the rest of the earth, it was all a wonderful and faithful mirror, for in the lucent waters of the ever-growing flood one saw the moving images of clouds and wild fowl.

Down below there was not a breath, but high above a gentle breeze from the west caught some fleecy islets of the sky and washed them out into the great blue sea. To-night the geography of the sky has changed. There are no islets, there is no movement. But across the whole western quarter of the sky the clouds have formed an ethereal beach of white-ribbed sands that reach around the world, and form the shores of a wide dark ocean that is lit by flashing stars.

To-night I should like to be Peter Pan in an obedient cutter and sail there far and wide. Jolly runs I could have, and how very easy to find my way about safely with all those splendid lights and beacons. And being Peter Pan I should know them all.

An ominous buzz recalls me to things nearer at hand. The room has been invaded by mosquitoes. Already the flies are an abominable nuisance in the daytime, and cockroaches are plentiful.

Last night the *Sumana* was strafed again, and Tudway has been toiling all the evening at her defences.

This morning I paid the men and did some office work, and brought the war diary up to date. After that I found time to try a longer walk around our first line, but felt too seedy to go into the Fort. I heard that the sickness is rapidly increasing, and the condition of the troops is so bad that the chief dread of the whole routine is the marching to and from the trenches. This being so, regiments are now allowed to remain out there permanently. In one Indian regiment man after man has simply sunk down in his tracks and died through want of food. And an extraordinary number of soldiers wretchedly ill won't report sick, partly through a horror of entering the crowded and unhappy hospitals, and also from a sense of duty. Among the men there is, of course, a good deal of ragging and general barracking about our not being relieved, but their spirit and patience and trust in their general is truly magnificent. No soldier, I truly believe, could wish for a more splendid loyalty from his rank and file than these men, the European troops, at any rate, feel and show in a hundred ways for their "Alphonse." They get little news but of disappointments, still they go about their duties with a step unsteady and painfully slow, and at every fresh misfortune they joke and smile.

We miss very much all communication with the outside

world. The generals get a few letters and papers by aeroplane, but no one else. The other day, however, our mess bombardier received one from an enterprising brother who directed the letter to General Townshend, and enclosed the letter to his brother inside. He tells me his brother is a seaman in a Royal Indian Mail boat, and is a very up-to-date sort of chap. I should just think so !

March 31st.—The weather has broken and once more the steady downpour has made Kut into a mild sort of Venice. We have no gondolas it is true, but if our *bund* goes we can make shift with rafts.

The *Sumana* got badly shelled last evening. One shell went through the awning and crashed through the main stop-valve over the boiler, missing the funnel and boiler by an inch or two. That would have been irreparable. As it is things are quite serious with her. Great volumes of steam escaped, no doubt to the huge delight of the Turkish gunners. Great consternation prevailed at headquarters, and Tudway was immediately reminded—much to his disgust—of the " example set by Beresford on the Nile when he repaired his boiler under fire." Tudway is not the sort of fellow who needs any example.

I went on board this morning and saw the damage done. The old boat has simply been shot through and through. We drew up a scheme for using shields of gun wagons spread out over the awning to lend additional protection. As we sprinted over the planks back to the shore, the Turks at Snipers' Nest were evidently waiting for us, and a hail of bullets flew by. We found cover by some millstones, and after a few minutes' rest took to our heels for the remaining stretch. We are hoping to get a valve up from below by aeroplane.

Native rations, except for meal, have ceased altogether. This may induce them to eat horse. There is nothing against it now as they have the full permission of the Chief Mullahs in India. The horses are on 4 lbs. of bran and 12 lbs. of grass cut by fatigue parties off the *maidan*. It keeps them going, and that is all. The young animals are merely drawing on their constitution.

I am deeply sorry to hear that poor Woods has gone. He was the subaltern I have mentioned before as having got the Military Cross for bravery at the Fort on December 24th, when he lost his arm. He was a jovial fellow, and a very good sort.

We have had many a gossip together at the hospital. He died from jaundice. It is very, very unfortunate, as his arm was quite well, and he was back on light duty. The truth is our condition is so low that anything carries us off. We are all very glad he died happily.

April 1st.—A terrific thunderstorm swamped everything last night. The place was alive with electricity, and flashings kept me awake for hours.

Most of our heavy bombardment trenches are full of water, and I have had fatigue parties on all day baling them out and shifting the horses.

A rumour has it that the Russians are in the Pushtikus, the distant range just to the eastward. I consider this a pathetic rumour, and I'm more interested in what Shackleton is doing at the South Pole.

To-night we had a meagre portion of fish which one of my drivers caught in the river. We pay him well and he buys atta for himself and his pals.

Square-Peg sleeps most of the day, and represents the three of us in collecting a daily account of Cockie's doings. There is no one, I am given to understand, sorrier that Cockie was hit than General "G. B.," who happens to be next door to him. The hospital, I was yesterday informed by an inmate slow to anger and of great mercy, consists of two factions, those that do not love Cockie and those who can't hear him. I hope he doesn't mind my writing this. I have sent him fish and fowl, and for my pains he sent me back inquiries as to why I hadn't done so before. Bah! Cockie can be *so* rude if you don't always do sufficient homage—and then I'm so forgetful in these matters. Not a man in the garrison has risen to-day to an April fool's joke—not one!

April 2nd.—We tried some green weed or other the Sepoys gathered on the *maidan.* Boiled and eaten with a little salad oil that Tudway fished out from heaven knows where, it seemed quite palatable. After all, as he says, all we want is something of a gluey nature to keep our souls stuck on to us.

A delightful little mess is ours. There is none cheerier in Kut. Picture a long bare wooden table, the other end piled up with war diaries, books, papers, pipes, and empty bottles, revolvers and field-glasses, we three at this end. Tudway is much senior to me, but insists that I preside. So I have the camp armchair, and he the other, which has very short legs so that he often seems to be talking under the table. It has also paralysis in the right arm, so that it is necessary to be very careful in leaning that way. Now and then, usually once a night, Tudway forgets, or perhaps he likes doing it, for he simply bowls over sideways, and by dint of repeated practice can now do so while clutching at the bread or joint en route. Sometimes he does it in the middle of a sentence, which he nevertheless completes leisurely on the floor as becomes an imperturbable sailor.

Square-Peg opposite has a high wooden chair, and is getting up a pose for the Woolsack, which I understand he will one day adorn.

My position is strategically a difficult one, for the other two acting in conjunction can at a pinch remove the victuals beyond my reach towards the other end of the table, and my rum—when we do raise a peg—is in constant danger until consumed. Square-Peg, whose pseudonym has nothing whatever to do with a drink, is extraordinarily forgetful in this way at times, and has been known in the course of an excellent story to drink all my rum and half of Tudway's. But I've an excellent memory, and the next rum night—possibly weeks after—Square-Peg goes short.

I am carver and taster, both useful functions in a siege. Tudway likes it thin, but with Square-Peg it is necessary to cut it thick. After the third helping Square-Peg has to carve for himself. We inaugurated that last week. If by accident the horse is extra tough, and Square-Peg gets splashed, he gets four helpings, but Tudway does not, for he can take cover under the table.

As regards the vegetables, " Sparrow-grass " and potato meal or beetroot and rice, I divide, and we all cut cards for first pick. There is always plenty of horse, but vegetables are a great delicacy. Tudway and I conspire to do Square-Peg out of his greens so as to keep him up to the scratch in procuring or in " pinching " vegetables from the garden of which he is C.O. It works admirably, and I am only sorry his small pockets necessitate his making several trips. On wet days we have " encore " in the vegetables, for then he wears a top coat with big pockets. He refuses to do so on fine days as he says it looks suspicious. If we have an issue of a spoonful of sugar I barter it for milk, and the date juice, when we get it, is measured out with a spoon.

For pudding we have kabobs, fried flour and fat, two each, and we cut for choice. An excellent idea which we have lately followed is to get the fat off a horse—there is very little now, poor things—and render it into dripping, which is quite excellent. I have sometimes waited for hours to get this from the butchery. While we had sardines our bombardier produced a savoury with toast, but that is long ago. Instead we have coffee, which is mostly ground-up roots, plus liquorice powder, if you're not careful in buying. The date juice goes into the coffee, but Square-Peg complains that he can't "feel it that way," so he drinks his like a liqueur. I prefer bad tea, as the coffee is generally atrocious, but Tudway likes it for the sake of "the smell." I provide the tobacco out of the funds, and sometimes have been diligent enough to make cigarettes, which are better than those the Arabs make, by screwing up the paper like a lollipop, pouring the tobacco in and twisting the top end up. The latter cigarettes require great art in smoking. One has to lie back in one's chair and point the cigarette to the roof so as to prevent the baccy emptying out of the cigarette into one's coffee.

This is the hour sacred to us. We exchange rumours or invent them. We pool all our gossip into a common heap which becomes the altar of another day's hope. We avoid all matters of misfortune or suffering. We have mutually and tacitly barred the subject of Home. But when the smoke cloud above the remains of our sorry banquet grows dense from the pipes of three excellent smokers, we lapse into silence, and see in the moving mists sweet fantasies far away. If we were Germans we would, I have no doubt, sing "Home, Sweet Home" in parts, and shake hands, and shed tears in unison. But we are merely Englishmen, and if anyone were to sing five notes of that song he would get slung out for making a brutal assault on our hearts. So instead we merely smoke on and on, and the jackals' chorus grows less and less as memories drift about among the wisps and wraiths of this strange fog-land. We are glad we are here. We have no tears to give, but although we know it not, in the heart of us each is a prayer.

April 3rd.—It is four months to-day since the Sixth

Division on its last legs entered Kut-el-Amara, expecting relief to be here in three weeks, a month, possibly six weeks.

Inscrutable are the ways of Allah !

This afternoon a fierce thunderstorm broke over Kut, and hailstones larger than pigeons' eggs rattled upon us with the sharp music of musketry. One should be quite sufficient to knock a fellow out if it got him bare-headed. Afterwards it turned to rain, which we fear may delay the next battle for Kut. We hear that the enemy is making every effort to hold up the relieving force down below, or delay us, for the short time beyond which the garrison cannot now hold out.

I am feeling very seedy again to-day, what with this enteritis and rheumatics and jaundice. So is Tudway, to whom I have given various opium pills and camphoradine. I am, however, lucky so far to have escaped the severe form of enteritis which many others have had. It is a deadly and horrible thing enough, accompanied by violent pains in the abdomen, and vomiting. To be sure I have had the former for so many weeks that I am used to it, and we often say we can scarcely remember the time when we hadn't these infernal pains. " A brandy flip, my dear fellow, is the one and only for it," our medical friend says, and smiles. Ho ! for a brandy flip. In the Arctic circle the two seasons are light and dark, and in India dry and wet, and in Kut when one has stomach ache and when one hasn't.

It is said that a certain cavalry regiment has at last unanimously rescinded the rule that it is bad form for any officer of the regiment not to be fit. Most of us have been put down for sick leave at once when the relief occurs. The India list is the most cheerful phrase one hears. Tudway has asked me to go downstream with him on the *Sumana*, and proposes a grand progression down to Basra and to pass H.M.S. *Clio*, his parent boat, when we get there. I am quite intoxicated with the notion. And truly the sight of the *Sumana* ripped and torn through and through by shell and bullet, with her shotted funnel and her smashed cabins and her twisted bridge, and her white ensign that soiled and tattered bunting, the finest flag in all the world, still fluttering in the stern—would be a sight for the gods. But then I've had nothing whatever to do with the *Sumana*, so I must prefer to be ashore. I see it all exactly, her grey dirty form with the black patches where shells have shifted her paint, and near the path of that Windy Lizzie that crashed through the bridge, the redoubtable countenance of our friend Tudway, the youthful commander and preserver of this eloquent trophy. The *Clio*, of course, salutes her diminutive sister, and ah, those terrible and honest cheers ! An awful moment for Tudway I admit. . . . But at twelve o'clock that night he will have indigenous metamorphosis !

"Tudway ! " I exclaim, "you no longer have the inches of a god. Can't you stand up ? "

"Donsh wansh stansh up. If you'd hads many cockstailsh I've had couldn't either."

Perhaps !

April 4th.—A heavy bombardment downstream continued for hours this morning. The rain has ceased and the soaken earth is steaming under a bright hot sun.

Reports from the hospital are to the effect that Cockie's temperament "has increased, is increasing, and ought to be diminished." His delusions include a notion that he still commands the column. To dispel the latter delusion it is necessary for one to cancel quite a number of his orders.

Dorking has evolved quite a number of literary ideas since my leaving the battery. He has read the letters of " Dorothy to Temple " which I recommended to him, and quite enjoyed them. In fact he says he would not have minded marrying Dorothy himself. Now I wonder what Dorothy would have had to say about Dorking—I wonder.

I hear on very reliable authority that the plane, our own plane, dropped yesterday a packet which was supposed to be a stop-valve for the *Sumana*. The valve, however, went off on the *maidan*, and in fact proved to be a three-pound bomb. To-day another plane dropped another supposed valve which turned out to be a gear-box for an L boat.

Very facetious of them, I'm sure, but Tudway calls it an indifferent joke.

A mild artillery duel wound up the day's events.

April 5th.—To-day we have had a strenuous Shikar after food. We raised a half-pound of dirty dates which we boiled into jam ; also two rupees worth of chupattis and hard, white, mealy flat-jacks—they are eight in number, a two-pound tin of barley which will make an exciting porridge.

We visited the officers' hospital which is full again to over-flowing with dysentery, jaundice, and malaria cases. The doctors have put me on diet of one egg and cup of milk daily, which commodities are only procurable on special certificates, and rarely. The mess bombardier draws these.

"I 'ear, sir, that this 'ere milk is sometimes 'uman and sometimes donkey's. I 'ope as you won't drink it, sir."

"To save one's life, bombardier, one may have to eat anything," I told him. Then I heard him in sad conference with the mess cook.

"Gawd! It's 'ot 'uman milk, Bill. An' 'e ain't 'ad no milk for ages. It'll knock 'im hover like 'ot punch."

"Wen you live in Kut," said Bill, "you 'ave to do az Gawd's hancient people do."

10 *p.m.*—Cheerful news at last! Early this morning Gorringe bombarded and smashed through the Turkish lines above Hannay, and five lines of trenches have been taken. He is consolidating his position before advancing on Essin. It does not seem clear on which bank this success was.

At 8 p.m. this evening the heavy firing recommenced. Square-Peg and I restrained our enthusiasm by a long game of chess. The news has cheered up every one immeasurably. It is the most hopeful night for months.

April 6th.—Downstream a terrific bombardment went on intermittently for hours. We are on six ounces of bread to-day and are almost on to our emergency rations, which can be made to spin out for three days.

The *Sumana* is going over to Woolpress to bring over reliefs. I had arranged with Tudway to have a starlight excursion there and see something of these strangers, but headquarters disapproved.

Green cress has been issued from the gardens, and every effort is made to save every crumb. The sick and those in hospital are worst off, as hospital comforts like cornflour and Mellins' Food have long since gone.

It is a beautiful day, but the river came up during the night and beat all previous records of the siege by two inches. How very close the relieving force has driven things. Altogether the situation, as Punch said of the man dangling from the drag rope of a balloon, is most interesting.

I have made inventories of ammunition and wagons, lines

K

and horse-lines of the 6th D.A.C., as I am officially returned to my battery pending the relief of Kut. I hope to enter on the next page that the siege has been lifted.

April 7th.—There is a lull in the operations downstream. How we hate lulls. A lull is a divine leg-pull. The word " lull " has an odious sound !

Gunner Graoul has returned to me from the battery apropos of my re-transfer to my original battery, and Amir Bux has returned to duty. There are a good many things to fix up in the ammunition column, so I am remaining in my comfortable billet here unless wanted for urgent duty at the battery—pending relief. I am so weak that my legs collapsed on the ladder, and I find a long staff better than a walking-stick.

We killed one of our two emergency fowls, which we boiled, and I found the broth delicious. Graoul called it " 'en brorth."

The river has risen seriously and is now a good three feet deep all over the plain in front of the *bunds*. General Gorringe has had hard work to bund the river down below and has evidently met with flood difficulties already.

There is an ominous whisper about a " wireless " which is not being made known.

Other and wilder rumours, obviously untrue, are in quick circulation. The men, poor fellows, are keenly on edge for news. There are many merely remaining alive to hear that Kut is saved. They all know the end is now in sight and the coma of the past months is over. We are like restless bees in swarming time.

April 8th.—A quiet day ! Some few shells wandered into the town and a steady stream of sniping indicated that the enemy had probably withdrawn many men for reinforcements downstream. Woolpress is a complete island. In fact a part of it had to be abandoned yesterday, and last night the *Sumana* brought a large part of its garrison back. As a last resort one regiment will remain there to hold the Woolpress buildings only.

From my old observation post to-day, which I climbed with great difficulty, I looked on a very changed scene. The whole country is a series of huge lakes with tiny green patches between. The enemy has had to abandon his lines around

Woolpress. In front of our first line tiny waves on this tiny ocean lap against our preserving *bunds*. In fact, Kut is an island!

3 *p.m.*—Gorringe has wired to say " all's well." " Advance continues ! "

Once more with Micawber it is permitted to us to hope.

April 9th.—Shells, expletives, and suspense fell into Kut in unusual quantities. We are on the edge of a volcano. Who could keep a diary while sitting on the edge of a volcano ? The gods, those humorous birds, have just flown over Kut on a tour of inspection. We can almost—as John Bright did not say—hear the *flapping* of their wings.

April 10th.—Poor Don Juan has taken his last hedge ! I have hitherto managed to extend his reprieve, but to-day the order came. I gathered him a last feed of grass myself. He salaamed most vigorously as I had taught him. The chargers have been kept to the last. His companions stood by him trembling as the quick shot despatched one after another. Not so he ! now and then he stamped, but otherwise stood perfectly still. I asked the N.C.O. to be careful that his first bullet was effective and to tell me when it was over. I kissed Don on the cheek " good-bye." He turned to watch me go. Shortly after they brought me his black tail, as I asked for a souvenir. Strange as it may seem we ate his heart and kidneys for dinner, as they are now reserved for owners. I am sure he would have preferred that I, rather than another, should do so.

He carried me faithfully, and died like a sahib. In the garrison I had no better friend. Being so he shall have this entry to himself.

April 11th.—Two paramount budgets of especial interest and importance reached us first thing this morning. One was that Cockie was annoyed with us for eating our own fowl, the other being from Sir Percy Lake to the effect that Gorringe cannot possibly be present here for the 15th, but will have great pleasure in doing so by the 21st instant. With the help of God and the strength derived from having eaten the hen, we hope to survive the first budget. To this end Square-Peg and Tudway and I immediately slaughtered the second hen and sent a polite message of this information to Cockie with a promise to reserve for him the head and feet. Tudway has been in shrieks of laughter all day, and mounted guard over the hen himself. To be sure I intended to reserve for him half of my portion, but the others voted this treachery, as they think Cockie has done very well lately with hospital rations of fish and eggs. Cockie still consumes slabs of horse, the size of a slab being about that of the ordinary Nelson's 7*d*. edition.

The news from Sir Percy Lake is serious enough. Our men are now dying by the score and their condition is reduced to the last degree, many being scarce able to walk. It is not merely rations that they require, but sick comforts.

General Townshend has issued these communiqués to the troops—

Kut-el-Amara,
April 10th, 1916.

"The result of the attack of the Relief Force on the Turks entrenched in the Sannaiyat position is that the Relief Force has not as yet won its way through, but is entrenched close up to the Turks in places some 200 to 300 yards distant. General Gorringe wired me last night that he was consolidating his position, as close to the enemy's trenches as he can get, with the intention of attacking again. He had had some difficulty with the flood which he had remedied. I have no other details. However, you will see that I must not run any risk over the date calculated to which our rations would last, namely April 15th, as you will all understand well that digging means delay, though General Gorringe does not say so. I am compelled, therefore, to make an appeal to you all to make a determined effort to eke out our scanty means, so that I can hold out for certain till our comrades arrive, and I know I shall not appeal to you in vain.

"I have, then, to reduce the rations to five ounces of meal for all ranks, British and Indian. In this way I can hold out till April 21st if it becomes necessary. I do not think it will become necessary, but it is my duty to take all precautions in my power. I am very sorry I can no longer favour the Indian soldiers in the matter of meal, but there is no possibility of doing so now. It must be remembered that there is plenty of horseflesh which they have been authorized by their religious leaders to eat.

"In my communiqué to you on January 26th I told you

that our duty stood out plain and simple : it was to stand here
and hold up the Turkish advance on the Tigris, working heart
and soul together; and I expressed the hope that we would make
this defence to be remembered in history as a glorious one,
and I asked you in this connection to remember the defence
of Plevna, which was longer than that even of Ladysmith.

"Well, you have nobly carried out your mission, you have
nobly answered the trust and appeal I put to you. The whole
British Empire, let me tell you, is ringing now with our defence
of Kut. You will all be proud to say one day, ' I was one of
the garrison of Kut,' and as for Plevna and Ladysmith, we
have beaten them also. Whatever happens now, we have
done our duty. In my report of the defence of this place,
which has now been telegraphed to headquarters, I said that
it was not possible in dispatches to mention every one, but I
could safely say that every individual in this force had done
his duty to his King and Country. I was absolutely calm
and confident, as I told you on January 26th, of the ultimate
result, and I am confident now, I ask you all, comrades of all
ranks, British and Indian, to help me now in this food question."

(Sd.) CHARLES TOWNSHEND,
Major-General,
Commanding the Garrison at Kut.

This *communiqué* is a breezy one ! But we all know our
General has a difficult task in communicating these repeated
disappointments. The native troops are beginning to recall
that the G.O.C. months ago passed his word for early relief.
To a British Tommy this was what he calls " 'opeful buck,"
but to the Sepoy it is a promise.

Kut-el-Amara,
April 11th, 1916.

"General Sir Percy Lake, the Army Commander,
wired me yesterday evening to say : ' There can be no doubt
that Gorringe can in time force his way through to Kut. In
consequence of yesterday's failure, however, it is certainly
doubtful if he can reach you by April 15th.' This is in answer
to a telegram from me yesterday morning to say that, as it
appeared to me doubtful that General Gorringe would be
here by the 15th, I had reluctantly still further reduced the

rations so as to hold on till April 21st.   I hope the Indian officers will help me now in my great need in using common-sense talk with the Indian soldiers to eat horseflesh, as the Arabs of the town are doing."

(Sd.) CHARLES TOWNSHEND,
Major-General,
Commanding the Garrison at Kut.

April 12th.—This entry I am making with my eyes almost shut.   I have had a miraculously narrow shave, and got a nasty shock and contusion since the last entry.   At about 3 p.m. shells began to k-r-r-ump into the town, and the fire steadily thickened.   I had just finished the war diary, and was sitting up on my bed restlessly awake with stomach pains, and Square-Peg was fast asleep by the other wall, when a high-velocity shell crashed into the room and burst.   I was completely dazed by the concussion, which drove me against the wall.   In fact, I was half stunned, as I was directly in line for the back-lash of the burst.   I wasn't certain I wasn't hit, and my back felt queer.   The room was so dark with dust and the dense yellow fumes that stank horribly that I couldn't see an inch.   We were half smothered in *débris*.   The walls and roof in part collapsed, letting fall dozens of bricks which had propped up some huge beams on the ceiling.

Square-Peg, who was groping about, assured me he wasn't hit, and hurrahed when he heard I was alive.   However, on trying to rise, I found myself partly paralysed in my back, my spine in severe pain, and I could hardly see at all.   He helped me out of the yellow gases, for I couldn't walk alone. I lay down in the mess, and after drinking some water felt better.   But I am horribly shaken and suffer acute pain in whatever position I lie.   In fact, last night I couldn't sleep, for every movement awoke me.

It proved to be a segment shell that had burst inside the room, and dozens of pieces were buried deep all round the walls and on the floor.

There is no luck like good luck.   Tudway says it was an intended punishment for the affair of the fowl, which, never-theless, we ate completely.

We are sleeping in the mess until the wreckage is cleared up.   Major Aylen, commanding the officers' hospital, visited

RECENT PHOTO OF AUTHOR'S LAST BILLET IN KUT
(ABOVE LITTLE ARAB BOY). THE SHELL DEMOLISHED
THE UPPER STORY

me, and, although there is no incision, says there is a contusion over the spine from a blow. Either a brick must have hit me, or when I was flung violently back I struck the broken bed. I am writing this in bed.

The shelling continued last evening until late, and began again early this morning. I have been severely shaken, and it was as much as I could manage, even with assistance, to get on the verandah to my old room to see how it was the shell got in. For a time I could find no sign of its entry, but in getting my servant to remove the tins of earth I saw the shell-hole. There was no doubt the two tins had been removed, and the culprit had replaced them after the shell came. We were terribly angry, and had the whole crowd of men-servants and bearers and orderlies up about it at once. The orders had been strict. I had myself made a practice of going around the place every morning. Yesterday morning they were all right. They all said they knew nothing of it, but this afternoon I discovered that a syce from the lines had gone up to the room for my saddlery about an hour before the affair and moved the tins. He was in the next room when the shell entered, and hastily replacing the tins, he bolted in fright. I threatened him with a court-martial for removing defences, etc., at which he got in an awful funk, so I let him go. He shifted them, he said, to look for a tin of saddle soap, which I don't believe, as the wooden frieze was missing. He probably had come after the firewood.

In the night we had another thunderstorm. This will assist the floods, against which Gorringe is building at a fever rate.

According to general opinion, the suspense now occasioned by this last news from Sir Percy Lake is the most severe trial of the siege. We are all rather glad than otherwise that the state of our rations must precipitate the crisis one way or the other soon. The casualties on our behalf are appalling. An extraordinary sequence of fortunate factors, such as the discovery of the mill, has enabled us to hold out months longer than ever we could have dreamed possible—and we are in as great a state of uncertainty as ever. It is true that we all try to avoid the selfish point of view of requiring Kut to be relieved at all costs. The military situation is the only one to be considered, and to that end every other consideration must be sacrificed. If it is necessary that Kut should be sacrificed to the military end, none of His Majesty's forces could be more ready for sacrifice than the Sixth Division. But when one thinks of the past months and the neglect to face the obvious military situation after Ctesiphon, one feels that the sufferings of the troops in Kut and the heavy loss of life downstream could easily have been avoided. There yet remains for us the hope that unnecessary as these sacrifices may have been, they will at least not have been made in vain.

To a soldier war may be sheer fatalism, but to a general it should be snatching victory from the knees of the gods.

Later.—General Hoghton, commanding the 17th Brigade, entered hospital yesterday suffering from acute enteritis and dysentery. Early this morning, to the universal sorrow of the garrison, he died. It is said that the wild green grass stuff was partly the cause, and also abstinence from horse-flesh, which a digestion ravaged by the siege could not stand. He was a most genial and kind general, and always cheerful. I saw quite a lot of him in the "fort" days. I was sorry to be unable to attend his funeral. A great number were present. There was no funeral party, but from the verandah I heard the piercing bugle notes of the soldier's requiem. The Last Post came thrilling and sharp from the silence of the palm grove, and was no doubt heard in the Turkish lines. A brave soldier in a soldier's grave, amidst a goodly number !

8 *p.m.*—It has been a cool, breezy day, and the floods have subsided one inch. We hope the heavy rains that fell in the night won't bring them up again.

Tudway brought a rumour that good news had been received, but could not be published just yet. Has Sunnaiyat fallen ? That is the question in every one's mouth. I have given my rations to the others and stuck to barley for two days. They aren't much to give, certainly—merely two small slices of bread. My shell-shock and bruise have affected my digestion, and all my nerves are in constant trembling, and my legs and arms jump and twitch.

It is a damp evening, and although I have been up only three or four hours to-day I shall get back to bed presently. At any rate it is much better than being in hospital, and one can do minor duties. Tudway is an awful brick at his job, and he is very seedy indeed.

A month or two ago three or four of men who were also at the siege of Ladysmith had a dinner. They say that the conditions there were infinitely less severe than they are here. There was only one hostile siege-gun that reached into the town ; the hillsides and higher slopes were not under fire ; they had some provisions, no floods, and their enemies did not include Arabs.

April 13*th.*—More rain ! We hear that Gorringe is awaiting the arrival of another British division, the *seventh* in number, according to rumour, that has come into this infernal problem. Even the Twenty-first April isn't so certain now, and that must be the last day. There is practically nothing to eat. However, we are prepared for anything. Even an order for the whole garrison to undergo a fasting cure for six weeks wouldn't startle us.

The death of General Hoghton seems to have impressed every one with the ruthless passage of the God of the Siege. They are aware, a little more plainly than before, how undeviating is the course of that Relentless Spirit. Somehow one expects generals should be spared. Two others have recovered from sharp attacks of sickness, and one has been wounded.

It has been said that the soldier becomes callous. It would be more true to say that he merely becomes indifferent. But an exceptional phase of death removes the blinds from many disused windows of his mind, and he sees all too well. Such an event is the loss of this kind-hearted general, and it has given to many a higher altitude in point of view. There is the point of view of the trench and dug-out, of the hospital, of the observation post, on a roof top. There is that of an aeroplane. There is the standpoint of the overhead stars that see us as a flashing sphere. Tommy does not borrow the vantage point of a god from way beyond the farthest star, the most distant sun, to behold the universe, that gaily lighted ship of destiny travelling forward through the Seas of Time. But he has at any rate reached very far. This morning I was visited by some of my old section at the battery, and talked a time to the men, and I gave them some Arab tobacco. I find they have thought a good deal about things in general, and one was induced, to the amusement of the others, to give us what he considered a " bird's hye view " of our immediate future, which certainly didn't seem too bright. He saw Kut, a tiny spot under famine and fire, completely surrounded by hordes of the enemy, beyond them the menacing waters and fatal floods, beyond the floods the God-forsaken country of murderous Arabs,—and beyond that great and stretching continents of desert reaching thousands of miles away and ending in those strangely silent and unknown shores or losing themselves in the heart of Asia.

But fortune has smiled on us quite a deal, too. We found the grain stores at Woolpress, and the Flying Corps rigged up the mill-crusher discovered lying there. Then a large store of oil for the river steamers was utilized for fuel and lighting for all duty, and the Sappers and Flying Corps artificers made our bombs out of various charges for the howitzers and 4·7's. The aeroplanes brought us the detonators. Then the subsidence of the floods brought up the grass with which we bribed the animals to exist a little longer, while we ate their grain— and them.

The ammunition has lasted wonderfully well. We have over half of the original lot still in hand.

In truth, when one thinks how the Fighting Sixth fought its way across Mesopotamia, battling with fire and floods, thirst and heat, right up to the gate of Baghdad, and then was let down by want of supports, one has to extract thankfulness from the thought that Chance left it to the same division, alone and unreinforced, to stem the result of the turned tide. This it has done from December 1st at Um-al-Tabul until now, April 13th, a temporal avenue through sickness and death.

One is informed that if Kut had not been held, the position of the Turks would have been consolidated, and the tactical and strategical usefulness of its position with the enemy. These are the most cheerful thoughts possible in the garrison when one feels extra weary and sick.

It is not too much to say that almost no one has any misgiving as to the future. In this tiny horse-shoe panorama on the Tigris, where the destiny of Kut has pursued its dramatic evolution for the last four and a half months, the garrison awaits the ultimate development of the drama with a feeling merely of wide curiosity. Will the last scene be Tragedy, or will the people be allowed to leave the theatre feeling " comfortable," that it all came right in the end ?

Alas ! whatever the play is, it cannot be Comedy. And

when one remembers the large-hearted general who has gone, and whom some few medical comforts in time might have saved, one is made aware of the stern conditions of victory!

The enemy provoked an artillery duel this afternoon, and quite a number of shells fell in the town. Rain has stopped Gorringe's attack. Every possible disposition has been made for the entry of our relieving force or co-operation with their arriving on the other bank. We can only wait.

We brought about a delightful coup this afternoon in the purchase of 2½ lbs. of bad rice for five rupees. Tudway and Square-Peg go hungry now. I don't feel the last decrease in bread so much as they, as I am too seedy to eat it, and sometimes I can scarcely see. However, I am better to-day. Some one has placed a bradawl in the dessert dish! It forms the second and last course. It is " not to be eaten " in large letters, and " may be used for making another hole in your belt." The fish have left Kut. I wonder that even the birds don't fly away. . . .

Outside in the street, beneath my window, a decrepit Arab beggar, in a deep passionate voice, asks for alms for the love of Allah and Mahomet. It is often the first sound I hear in the morning. Later in the day the Arab children make their appearance in groups, begging and wailing piteously. Once the babes in their mothers' arms used to cry the whole day long, but the unfortunates are probably long since gone. The Arab population has been dying by the hundreds, and they look dreadfully shrunken and gaunt. A few escaped, but were shot by the Turks. They have had everything possible done for them.

It is the hour of the *muezzin*, the most peaceful of the day, for at that ancient call of prayer even the wailing and begging ceases. From the mosque near by, whose open doorway faces Mecca, I hear the high thrilling notes quivering and trembling with all the passion of the East, the high-pitched semi-tone cadences sailing afar out and cutting ever greater ripples on the bosom of the still night air like growing circles from a stone dropped into a placid pool. It is truly wonderful this immemorial custom of calling the Followers of Mahomet. The volume of sound echoing from the minaret is thrown by the *muezzin* further and further. With extraordinary power his voice rises and falls, describing circles, arcs, and strangely winding parabolas out of the still silences of evening. It is but an appeal. He calls the world to prayer. It is more potent than the appeal of bells. In the *muezzin* the Mussulman hears the voice of Allah.

Now the *muezzin* is finished, and everything is so very still. I wonder if they are praying for the relief—as hard as their fellow religionists in the rest of Turkey are praying for the fall—of Kut. The odds, I fear, are against us.

I must sleep ! I cannot remain awake five minutes longer. God in His wisdom made sleep the great possession. For the first essential to man is a gift of humour, and the second is the capacity for sleep. Sleep and forgetfulness ! How many warriors on this dreadful planet at this fearful hour would willingly drink of Lethe and wake up on their respective battlefields when the war is over ?

Eheu ! I see the dark forms asleep on the snows of Russia, in the trenches of France, on the mountains of Italy, on the decks swept by the night winds of the North Sea. Who of them would not wish it ?

> " Nox ruit, et fuscis tellurem amplectitur alis."

" Night descends and folds the earth in her dusky wings ! "

April 14th.—Heavy firing began downstream just before the dawn. It continued till about 8 a.m.

The floods are spreading. A little rain fell during the night. Around Kut everything is extraordinarily quiet. I was very seedy during the night with violent pains and nausea, possibly the result of attempting to eat a little liver for dinner. I don't remember feeling worse. I took some opium pills at once, and Graoul came in early this morning with some hot water, which I drank. Have had two eggs sent from the hospital, and am ordered to eat nothing beside the yolk and a half cup of milk. About midday I felt quite bright again, and wrote some letters with one eye more or less closed. One's stomach these days has become an awful snob and simply won't look at anything. How fit I was until these wretched floods !

A report says that we must be fed by aeroplanes, but it seems that it will take three days in which to carry one day's provisions.

I imagine *Punch* will have something to say on this. We

shall be represented as fielding for loaves and cakes and fishes and whisky bottles, Mellins' Food, and some of us charging towards the Tigris under fire from the opposite bank and endeavouring to recover our balance on the edge as we watch the priceless articles falling into the water.

The coming of the Turkish armada down the Shat-el-hai is evidently postponed. They are possibly frightened of John Bull on the water, even if it is only the river.

The Catholic padre and Square-Peg are playing chess. The Pope in other lands is probably entering in his diary that he has had a tiring day and that Kut must fall. Not because God has forgotten it, but because the garrison has no provisions.

Equally well advised is our mess bombardier, who has invented certain rhymes which he repeats over his cooking as no soothsayer ever did.

> "Hashes to hashes! Bust ter bust!
> If Gorringe cawn't 'elp us the Lord Gawd must!"

April 15th.—This was the day beyond which we were assured it was impossible to go. We are evidently out for records.

The floods are steady. They can scarcely fall. Will the Turk attack to-day? Will Gorringe?

There is a tide in the affairs of Kut
That taken at the flood will let through Gorringe—
Omitted, all the voyage of the survivors is bound on donkeys or on
    camels.
On such a full sea we are now afloat
And we must chance the Tigris at the curves or down go Kut
    debentures!

Shelling now is a regular thing on and off the whole day. The Arabs are preparing to flee.

Last night the thunder bellowed her despair, or rather ours, according to Kipling, and Square-Peg talked horribly in his sleep, and was putting up a masterly defence in his best English against some Arab hordes—women were in it—who had him at bay somewhere in the gardens. Having lulled them into inattention he shot clean off the bed and out of the door, when he pulled up and said something sheepishly. Of course I pretended to be asleep; and after examining my face carefully he lay down again. Square-Peg is quite touchy about his nightmares. I heard him say " Damn " softly once or twice under his breath, and then fall asleep again. This time he was in an attack, and behaved shockingly, tossing about the bed in a most ghastly manner. Suddenly it dawned on me that he was taking cover. He knew the road to the door too well not to manage an advance or retire at the double. I think it must have been the former, because he hesitated a second this time before he moved, but I gave such a terrific roar that he immediately collapsed on the bed and swore horribly.

" Don't do it again," I said. " If you do, I'll put a bucket in your way. I swear it."

" What the devil do you mean ? "

" Mean ! Why, don't go after cigarettes with such enthusiasm again, that's all. Have one of these."

Then he called me names, at which I laughed the more.

" They are nothing to what your wife will call you, Square-Peg, if you carry on in that fashion when you are married ! "

That set him thinking. The only thing to be said for him is that during a nightmare he doesn't snore.

April 16th.—It is a beautiful summer day full of spiciness. It was impossible to lie in bed, so I got up, imagining I was leaving aches and pains in my sleeping-bag. A distinct scent of green grass and the balmy air filled me with thoughts of England ! It was good to be out and to find myself walking again.

After breakfast I crawled out with Tudway on board the *Sumana*, and saw the excellent repair our sappers had effected in the main stop-valve. I make myself walk. We discussed her defences and I worked out the number of gun shields that would be necessary if they were utilized to cover all her deck. The plan was partly adopted. Then we lazied an hour or two in her smashed cabin, getting a hot sniping on our return. Afterwards, I played chess with Square-Peg and Father Tim.

Pars Nip came to tiffin. God has endowed him with two things—a perpetual appetite and a short memory, for he comes to tiffin very often without his bread.

Moreover, on any subject under the sun Pars Nip will dogmatize with all the splendid audacity of youth, with all youth's magnificent indifference to authority. With the smallest amount of encouragement he has politically the makings of a magnificent catastrophe ; otherwise he is normal.

We speculated on the treatment we should receive if captured. The Turk is said to be off the civilized map, but every one seems to think we should be done first rate, and some believe that he would be so bucked at capturing a whole army and five real live generals that we should be offered the Sultan's Palace of Sweet Waters on the Bosphorus and a special seraglio.

An evening communiqué said that Gorringe had captured the enemy's pickets, at Sunnaiyat, presumably, and was ready for a further advance, the results of which are expected by the morning.

For the first time aeroplanes to-day made several early trips, carrying some 150 lbs. of atta each trip. One lot fell into the Turkish lines. Kut apparently is not the easy mark it seems, for at different times quite a few parcels, detonators, money, and medicines have got the other bank or the enemy's lines here. In fact, one wonders why the Turks, instead of shooting at our fliers, don't encourage them. They do some very fair ranging with shrapnel at our planes. The whole garrison is indulging in such calculations as this: If a man and a half eats a slice and a half in a day and a half, how many trips of the planes are necessary before the Turks get more of the rations than we ? By going hard all day they cannot supply us with one day's provisions, even on these fractional rations.

But we *are* grateful. When we saw the first sack come tumbling down we felt much as Elijah may have done when the ravens ministered to his wants. Of course no aeroplane has landed in Kut during the siege. That would mean very probable disaster, so close are we to the enemy's lines.

To-night at dinner (?) we were without salt again. This is the third or fourth day of an affliction a hundred times worse than having no sugar. I can recommend all doubters to try dispensing with this necessary commodity for a few days in the preparation and eating of food, and to note the result.

Square-Peg and Tudway eat no bread at all for tiffin ; just meat. The utmost effort gives them a spoonful of rice every other day for dinner or boiled cress. But we go through the form of dinner, and that helps a lot. Some messes of different mind have almost dispensed with the regular meal, and merely negotiate their rations at any old time. It is just possible they miss a lot. For some of us think that the decencies and conventionalities of life go a long way. In diluted quantities they themselves supply motive power to life's wearily knocking engine. They use energy gathered from past events and help us to carry on through gaping periods of our life when nothing seems worth while ; and when we are indifferent or impatient with destiny, they are the pace-makers of existence. " A rich man," says the future philoso-pher, " may afford to dispense with dressing for dinner, but a poor man certainly cannot."

Now there are, of course, quite a few things said beneath our nightly cloud of tobacco smoke that do not appear in this diary. It would be sacrilege in some cases, and in others, why, one never knows who may come across one's diary. Con-fession is the salt of life, but suppression the sugar. And does not Maeterlinck tell us that the reservoirs of thought are higher than those of speech, and the reservoirs of silence higher still ? But so far I have not heard that this has been quoted in a court of law. And to show that we are not totally devoid of artistic intentions I must record a sample of our mental gymnastics this evening. We were tilting at a few enthusi-astic sentences of Robert Chambers' books.

" We are informed," I began, " that this interesting youth was sitting disconsolately awaiting his beloved, his well-shaped head in his hands. Any remarks ? "

" Prig," said Tudway. " What business has a fellow to have a well-shaped head ? Besides, where else could he put it except in his hands ? "

" Don't be catty," said Square-Peg, " he wasn't in the navy. Why shouldn't he have a well-shaped head ? "

" Probably he hadn't," I suggested mischievously. " We merely have the novelist's word for that, you know." At which they both called me an ass.

" If he did have such a head, I don't see why he shouldn't put it in his hands as well as anywhere else ? " ventured the senior service.

" Possibly as he was in love he was hanging on to his head, having already lost his heart." This from the future K.C.

" But if his heart was in his mouth, how——" I was shouted down.

Then we all thought hard.

" What is the point, Curly ? " This to me.

" Yes ! What's the matter with the sentence after all ? " added S.-P.

" Well, I can't quite say. You see she came along the corridor at midnight, we are told, and saw him, his well-shaped, etc. One doesn't like the excellent shape of his head being shoved in there. The fact, after all, was that his head was in his hands, and she surprised him, sorrowing in solitude."

" But if his head was well-shaped, why not say so ? " said the truthful Tudway.

" Yes," nodded S.-P., " that may have been essential. If his head hadn't been well-shaped she mightn't have gushed all over him."

" Hang it," I broke in desperately, " I don't care if it was well-shaped or not. The word doesn't fit. Any other word or none. You see it suggests—er—something outside the matter in hand, she may as well have said his mathematical——"

They considered me beaten, and laughed horribly.

" The next is, ' her superb young figure straightened confronting the sea.' Any remarks ? "

" She was playing to the gallery, of course," said S.-P., " or else she stood on a thistle."

" Don't talk rot ! I'm with Curly there. ' Superb ' swanks it too much. There's nothing superb in the world except a destroyer at thirty knots."

" Or the action of a blood filly going through her first pacings," I prompted. This raised a yell.

" The next is, ' her skirts swung high above the delicate contour of ankle and limb.' Any remarks ? "

" That's naughty," said Square-Peg. " Besides, it doesn't say which limb."

" There's no doubt about the limb," I said, " unless her arm was meant, in which case her skirts—— " But an awful roar interrupted me.

" Cut out ' limb ' and substitute ' leg,' " suggested Tudway.

" Worse and worse. If ' limb ' suggests anatomy, leg suggests—— "

L

" The Empire," they both screamed, and after the immoderate laughter had ceased I declared I wouldn't go on.

We refilled our pipes, but Tudway grew horribly silent. After a long time we chaffed him about the *Sumana*, and offered him a kabob for his thoughts.

" Ah ! " he said, " it was that limb. It recalled—— " Then he stopped and actually reddened ; and nothing would induce him to go on.

That set us all thinking.

We both retired to bed, and with one eye I finished the story. It is quite a good one, and tells you many other things about the call of the rain. That reminded me of an evening years ago in faraway New Zealand, when in the heart of the great silences I looked through my tent door and saw the rain on the wild river and great forests and distant mountains. . . .

Well, I read with my half-shut eyes by the flickering dubbin tin that gave a small and ever-dwindling light, and although my eyes burned and jumped I read through to the end. And in the end Robert Chambers married them after all—those two young and ardent spirits, and together, no doubt, they looked at the night waves, and the snow on the wintry trees and at the distant stars, and heard the whisper of sweetness ineffable, the inarticulate music of the call of the rain.

And facing the last page was a bold advertisement and the picture of " Our extra guest folding bedstead—folds quite flat when not in use ! "

That also was a human note, and how real ! It invites us to view the deserted stage, the drabs of colour with grey torn canvas, the ghostly framework of the scenes, the tinsel robes and stifled flowers.

" Folds quite flat when not in use "—which will be quite often, as we have not many friends. . . .

> and a tiny little boy
> With hey ho, the wind and the rain !
> A foolish thing was but a toy
> For the rain it raineth every day. . . .

It's awfully late. Only millions of starlings are abroad. I wonder if Tudway is dreaming of the limb !

April 18th.—A terrific bombardment continued downstream from last night until early this morning. We have since heard that the Third Lahore Division, under General Keary, after a

magnificent struggle, has taken the lines of Beit Aissa, and that
Turkish hordes are counter-attacking in successive waves.
Our casualties are very heavy. The large pontoons which the
Turks dragged overland for a ferry downstream are now in
position. Tudway was recently to have led a river attack
at night in H.M.S. *Sumana* and to have pierced or blown up
the bridge. The scheme, however, was cancelled.

Arabs continue to wait around the butchery for horse
bladders on which to float downstream. They are shot at
by the Turks, who want them to stay on here and eat our food,
or else they are killed by hostile Arabs. Every night they go
down, and a little later one hears their cries from the darkness.
There are rumours that the Arab Sheik and his son, who are
here with us and are badly wanted by the Turks, are to escape
secretly to-night. These people know the Turk and the
treatment they are likely to get for having associated with us.

For three or four days our heavy sea-planes have brought
us food, dropping each day from one half to a ton of flour and
sugar in the town and as often as not into the Tigris or Turkish
lines. We are grateful to our brother officers downstream for
this, and realize the difficulty of getting a correct " drop "
always. I for one don't consider this at all a possible *soulage-
ment*, as even with their best effort our tiny four-ounce ration
cannot be nearly kept up. In fact, one ounce would be nearer
the mark. Money is also dropped, and many coins dented in
the fall go as souvenirs at double value.

April 24th.—I have been compelled to abandon keeping
my diary owing to excruciating pain in my spine from the shell
contusion. What is wrong I can't make out, but sometimes
the tiniest movement sends a sharp thrill of keenest pain
through one's whole being. I think I must have struck the
wall forcibly and affected the vertebræ. After lying in one
position for any little time this particular spot in my spine
aches with a most ravaging pulsation of neuralgia, and I find it
difficult to sit upright for many minutes. On these occasions
if I lie still my arms and legs shoot out at intervals with a sort
of reflex action, and sometimes repeat the performance several
times.

But for being much easier to-day I thank God. I have
even walked a little with a stick, and the twitching is much
less violent and less often. My eyes, however, are still dim, and

I find it difficult to see very distinctly. To complete the list of my infirmities of the flesh the enteritis, which has continued in a mild form for three weeks, has got worse, and I find emmatine the only thing that has done any good. Here, again, I have much to be thankful for, in that I have not had the severe form as so many others have, or else with other troubles I should be on unskateable ice. My legs are shockingly thin, less than my arms were, and I can fold my skin round my legs. In fact, I might think of applying my remarks on the poor fellow at the hospital to myself. The daily egg and ounce of milk stopped days ago. We have paid Rupees 30 for a tin of milk which I have with some rice my very good friend Major Aylen sends me from the officers' hospital. He now wishes me to enter hospital, but I prefer being an out-patient. The atmosphere there is both siegy and sick.

The bombardment of the 22nd downstream appears to have been a tremendous attempt by Gorringe to get through at Sannaiyat. It failed. Our comrades gave their lives freely for us and they fought in the mud feet deep trying to get at their enemy. As they fell wounded they were drowned.

What an appalling price we are costing ! A calm seems to be stealing over the garrison. It is the reaction from suspense extended infinitely far, and we know that we have done all possible to carry our resistance to the last possible day. These words are not so self-righteous as they look when one considers the gallant effort to walk and to carry out the simplest routine by men dying and doomed. There are men, with cholera staring from their faces, moving along at a crawl with the help of a long stick ; men resting against the wall of the trench every ten yards. One wills hard to do the simplest thing. From our men the siege has demanded even more than from us. We have now drifted very near the weir and within a few days must know our fate. A few say it appears already. There is, between us and that, however, only the habit, now strong within us, of refusing to believe that Kut can fall. And yet if Gorringe has not yet got Sunnaiyat, how can he cross these successions of defences in a few days ?

April 25th.—I am making a great effort to write further in this diary. Last night there happened one of those gallant episodes that confirm our pride of race.

A relief ship, *Julna* by name, had been fitted out down-stream and loaded with every available comfort for us, and provisions for several weeks. She was heavily protected and commanded by Lieut. Cowley, R.N.R., the famous local celebrity who knows every yard of the Tigris. He with two other officers and some men of the Royal Navy volunteered to outdo the Mountjoy episode. The Turkish gunners were engaged by our artillery down below, and under cover of dark-ness the *Julna* left. The Turks, no doubt, knew, or soon found out, what the show was. She came along gallantly, drawing a heavy fire, and surmounted all difficulties until reaching Megasis ferry, where, fouling a heavy cable, she swung on to a sandbank. Here the Turkish guns confronted her at a few yards' range. Her officers were killed, Lieut. Cowley captured, and she was taken within sight of our men waiting to unload her by the Fort, and of the sad little group of the garrison who beheld her from the roof-tops of Kut. She lies there now. It appears that this tragic but obvious end of so glorious an enter-prise is a last hope. We have scarcely rations for to-morrow. It now remains for us to submit ourselves as best we can to the workings of the Inexorable Law.

April 27th.—Last night we destroyed surplus ammunition. To-day General Townshend, Colonel Parr (G.S.O.I.), and Captain Morland have gone upstream to interview the Turkish Commander-in-Chief. There is a hum of inquiries. One says it is parole and marching out with the honours of war. Another talks of the Turks requiring our guns as the price of the garrison. To-day it is a changed Kut. It is armistice. No sound of fire breaks the hush of expectations. The river-front, grass-grown from long disuse, and the landing-stage likewise, for it has been certain death to go on that fire-swept zone, to-day swarm with people walking and talking. The Turks on the opposite bank do the same. It is strange. I walked a little with a stick. Hope has made one almost strong. This afternoon I went over the river to Woolpress village, where the tiny garrison has been the whole siege, and many of them have not once visited Kut. The defences are excellent. They have also had to fight floods. A little hockey ground and mess overlooking the river safe from bullets suggested Woolpress as a peaceful spot, notwithstanding its liability to instant isolation from Kut.

April 28th.—General Townshend has issued this *communiqué*, and its joyous effect on the whole garrison is indescribable. With the tragic side that the relieving forces cannot get through in time we are acquainted as with the fact that we have actually eaten our iron emergency rations, but General Townshend has given out a strong probability that we are to be released and sent back to India on parole, not to fight against Turkey again.

This *communiqué* is as follows :—

Kut-el-Amara,
April 28th, 1916.

" It became clear, after General Gorringe's second repulse on April 22nd at Sannaiyat, of which I was informed by the Army Commander by wire, that the Relief Force could not win its way through in anything like time to relieve us, our limit of resistance as regards food being April 29th. It is hard to believe that the large forces comprising the Relief Force now could not fight their way to Kut, but there is the fact staring us in the face. I was then ordered to open negotiations for the surrender of Kut, in the words of the Army Commander's telegram, ' the onus not lying on yourself. You are in the position of having conducted a gallant and successful defence and you will be in a position to get better terms than any emissary of ours . . . the Admiral, who had been in consultation with the Army Commander, considers that you with your prestige are likely to get the best terms. . . . We can, of course, supply food as you may arrange.'

" Those considerations alone, namely, that I can help my comrades of all ranks to the end, have decided me to overcome my bodily illness and the anguish of mind which I am suffering now, and I have interviewed the Turkish General-in-Chief yesterday, who is full of admiration at ' an heroic defence of five months,' as he put it. Negotiations are still in progress, but I hope to be able to announce your departure for India on parole not to serve against the Turks, since the Turkish Commander-in-Chief says he thinks it will be allowed, and has wired to Constantinople to ask for this, and the *Julna*, which is lying with food for us at Megasis now, may be permitted to come to us.

" Whatever has happened, my comrades, you can only be

proud of yourselves. We have done our duty to King and Empire, the whole world knows we have done our duty.

" I ask you to stand by me with your ready and splendid discipline, shown throughout, in the next few days for the expedition of all service I demand of you. We may possibly go into camp, I hope between the Fort and town along the shore whence we can easily embark.

" The following message has been received from the Army Commander : ' The C.-in-C. has desired me to convey to you and your brave and devoted troops his appreciation of the manner in which you together have undergone the suffering and hardships of the siege, which he knows has been due to the high spirit of devotion to duty in which you have met the call of your Sovereign and Empire. The C.-in-C.'s sentiments are shared by myself, General Gorringe, and all the troops of the Tigris column. We can only express extreme disappointment and regret that our effort to relieve you should not have been crowned with success.'

Copy of a telegram from Captain Nunn, C.M.G., R.N.

" ' We, the officers and men of the Royal Navy who have been associated with the Tigris Corps, and many of us so often worked with you and your gallant troops, desire to express our heartfelt regret at our inability to join hands with you and your comrades in Kut.' "

(Sd.) C. V. F. TOWNSHEND,
Major-General,
Commanding 6th Division and Forces at Kut.

A great arrangement. We are a sick army, a skeleton army rocking with cholera and disease. Instead of the lot of captivity in this terrible land, with the Turks who have never had any *bandobast* for anything, and merely barbaric food themselves, the garrison may see India again and have a welcome there. Whatever our end, there is no denying the great fighting qualities of the Sixth Poona Division. More than its glorious career, its stupendous efforts in vain to overtake the tragic destiny decreed by the gods for the mistake of others, must make it famous in arms.

The fact that the communiqué does not state for absolute

certainty the condition of parole does not detract so much from the spirit of the garrison, such faith have they in the G.O.C., and General Townshend's prestige with the Turks is held sufficient to get this condition. Besides, they say a general must always leave a big margin, and when he states probability he means certainty. I cannot imagine a greater change than this that has come over all to-day.

Dying men laugh and talk of Bombay and news of home. The sepoy sees again his village and feels the shade of the banyan. "Not to bear arms against Turkey." That still leaves Germany and all the rest. Others say they knew all along it had to come like this, that in high heaven the gods that had forsaken the Sixth Division at the zenith of its conquest and decreed for it tasks too Herculean, would now crown its career with an honourable return. Except on the two occasions when we expected to debouch, I doubt if the heart of Kut ever beat higher.

Later.—Two junior officers visited the Turkish headquarters' camp. General Townshend did not go.

They brought back news that Enver Pasha had refused parole and demands unconditional surrender. Destruction of our ammunition, spare rifles, and kit, proceeds apace. I have just destroyed my two saddles, field-glasses, revolver, and much else. Detonations are heard all along the trenches. Kut falls to-morrow. This news on top of these few short hours of hope seems incredible, and the silence with which the garrison received it is too magnificent for reference.

Later, 4.30 *p.m.*—At lunch Tudway informed me in his quiet way that he contemplated running the gauntlet downstream in the *Sumana* to-night in the hope of saving his ship from the Turks. He has communicated with his S.N.O. at Basrah. He invited me to come with him. I felt very complimented and after some consideration I agreed. Tudway knew his ship, the river, and the likely stoppages. He had counted the risk of cables. The current would help us and the Turkish guns were all still, no doubt, pointing downstream against other possible *Julnas*. In two hours we should be down. We left things at this and Tudway went to make inquiries.

He has just returned in a resigned frame of mind. The project was absolutely private and not known to headquarters, who, however, sent anticipatory orders to Tudway that the

Sumana was under no circumstance to be damaged but kept intact in Kut.

The surrender was unconditional, and we were destroying everything. The *Sumana*, however, was a most valuable asset for inducing Turks to give us transport. One learnt subsequently, however, that the G.O.C. had retained it for his own use on a Turkish promise to allow him to go down-stream to see Sir Percy Lake the Army Commander.

Whether this was actually so I cannot say. We have considered the chance of getting downstream by night on a ship's lifebelt, the current doing several knots and quite enough to carry one down. There was, of course, the considerable chance of capture by the devilish Arabs or being seen by the Turks. The chief question, however, was whether we could stay in the water six or seven hours. In our present health we decided it out of question, even if we had covered ourself with oil.

9 *p.m.*—Our little mess had its last talk. We sat and smoked, divided the remnants of tobacco and tin of atta, and awaited news. I am told to come into hospital, but a later report says there is no room.

April 29th.—General Townshend has issued a last communique holding out hope that he will go home and arrange the exchange on parole. It is, however, a very slender hope.

Kut-el-Amara,
April 29th, 1916.

" *Communiqué.* 1. The G.O.C. has sent the following letter to the Turkish Commander-in-Chief :

' YOUR EXCELLENCY,

Hunger forces me to lay down our arms, and I am ready to surrender to you my brave soldiers who have done their duty, as you have affirmed when you said, " Your gallant troops will be our most sincere and precious guests." Be generous, then, they have done their duty, you have seen them in the Battle of Ctesiphon, you have seen them during the retirement, and you have seen them during the Siege of Kut for the last five months, in which time I have played the strategical rôle of blocking your counter-offensive and allowed time for our reinforcements to arrive in Iraq. You have seen how they have done their duty, and I am certain that the military history of this war will affirm this in a decisive manner. I send two of my officers, Captain Morland and Major Gilchrist, to arrange details.

I am ready to put Kut into your hands at once and go into your camp as soon as you can arrange details, but I pray you to expedite the arrival of food.

I propose that your Chief Medical Officer should visit my hospitals with my P.M.O. He will be able to see for himself the state of many of my troops—there are some without arms and legs, some with scurvy. I do not suppose you wish to take these into captivity, and in fact the better course would be to let the wounded and sick go to India.

The Chief of the Imperial General Staff, London, wires me that the exchange of prisoners of war is permitted. An equal number of Turks in Egypt and India would be liberated in exchange for the same number of my combatants.

Accept my highest regards.

(Sd.) GENERAL TOWNSHEND,
Major-General,
Commanding the 6th Division and the Force at Kut.'

' 2. I would add to the above that there is strong ground for hoping that the Turks will eventually agree to all being exchanged. I have received notification from the Turkish Commander-in-Chief to say I can start for Constantinople. Having arrived there, I shall petition to be allowed to go to London on parole, and see the Secretary of State for War and get you exchanged at once. In this way I hope to be of great assistance to you all. I thank you from the bottom of my heart for your devotion and your discipline and bravery, and may we all meet in better times.

(Sd.) CHARLES TOWNSHEND,
Major-General,
Commanding the 6th Division and the Force at Kut.' "

No orders have been issued about the entry of the Turks. Some sort of formality in handing over is talked of. We have demolished everything. I have just met the brigade armourer, a most valuable N.C.O., who has the history of every gun in the brigade. He looked many years older, and said he had just helped to blow up the last gun. One breech-block of the howitzers which we demolished by lyddite in the bore travelled over Kut far on to the *maidan*.

* *

May 7th.—I am lying in a very shaky condition in the overcrowded officers' hospital in Kut. This is due to temperature of a 104° from malaria, also dysentery, and mild enteritis, apart from my bruise. Many ages seem to have passed since my last entry. We had understood that the Turks would make a formal entrance into Kut. Instead, some time after lunch, I heard wild yelling in the streets. Arabs armed with dozens of crescent flags danced and cheered some Turkish horsemen that rode along a street known as Regent Street. Then, suddenly, wild yells and scuffling came from the wall upstairs on our tiny roof, and over this wall separating the adjoining houses I saw crowds of wild bearded men in the most unkempt condition conceivable, armed with rifles and bayonets. With loud shouts and cries they passed over our kit, yelling out "Kirich" (sword). One seized mine and tried to open my kit. They were very excited. At the same moment our front door was knocked in, and Square-Peg's effects were similarly wanted. Looting of the mess and of our mess servants followed. They seized the bombardier's coat which was hanging on a nail. He objected, and got hammered with rifle butts until I intervened. It looked like a general scuffle. I went outside and found a diminutive officer who spoke German, was extraordinarily polite, and evidently much elated. He came in and restored some small degree of order by requesting his men, in fact he pleaded with them rather than ordered them. I took my sword from the Turkish soldier and handed it to this officer. At this he was most moved. Square-Peg went into the hospital near by for orders. There, also, it seemed events had taken unexpected turns, and looting had begun. We were ordered in at once.

While he was away I had kept the officer with me, and we went about the street stopping similar scenes. When we returned a few moments later we heard our bombardier had been unmercifully beaten by Turks for trying to retain his boots. The Turkish officers did not mind much when this was reported. We got some sepoys to carry our kit, or rather the remains of it, and as I left the tiny courtyard the last thing I saw was poor Don Juan's black tail hanging on a nail on the post in the sun to dry. I wanted it for a souvenir of a trusty friend, but there was not a second to be lost. In the street the Arabs were all hostile to us. Turks full of loot raced up and down. We met officers whose rings had been taken and pockets emptied.

The padre's wrist-watch and personal effects were taken. In hospital, Square-Peg and I lay on our valises on the ground of the tiny yard, as the hospital was overflowing and officers kept still arriving. Sir Charles Melliss came shortly after. He had a bed beside mine near the doorway, and I thought looked very ill. His little white dog was beside him and all around him were sick and dying officers. Nothing I can say could measure my gratitude and admiration for Major Aylen, the C.O. officers' hospital. While living on the hardest and most severe of diet himself he has gone from minute to minute with only one thought—for his charge. He is everywhere, and in adversity his industry, patience, and hopefulness are all we have left. If I am to be fortunate enough to survive this ordeal I shall have him to thank.

Tudway turned up as arranged for the evening meal. We pooled our flour and had *Chuppatis*, one-fourth of which we gave to Holmes my orderly. We lay on blankets on the ground and smoked the lime-leaves, and Tudway said good-bye. After leaving us in the morning he had returned to the *Sumana* to find a party of Turks had been sent over to seize her, taking everything on board, including the whole of his kit. His men had been put off. Remonstrations were useless. At the last moment the G.O.C. was not permitted to go downstream, and so we lost the *Sumana* intact to the Turks. Naturally her able and devoted commander felt sore about this. He announced his intention to go upstream with some other brigade, and I said good-bye to a very pleasant companion.

The hospital had already been looted several times by Turks. The night was hot. One heard the moans of the enteritis patients and the tramp of troops all night long.

In the early dawn some Turkish troops entered past the sentry, whom they ignored. I had slept in my boots and hidden all my loose kit, but they commenced to seize what they wanted from others. One took General Melliss' boots from under his bed and another his shoes, and made off, notwithstanding the general's loud protests. Sir Charles jumped out of the bed and followed them. A scuffle ensued in the street. The general reappeared, and put on his cap and jacket showing his rank and decorations, and then returned to the fray. The soldier, however, seized him by the throat, and the general, in a highly indignant frame of mind, and looking very dishevelled, returned and got leave to go to General Townshend, which he did in his socks. While he was gone more Turks swarmed in and robbed patients who were too ill to move, taking shoes, razors, mirrors, knives, and anything they fancied.

Our C.O., Major Aylen, in a tremendous rage seized the sentry and pointed to his red-cross badge and the flag of the hospital. Although his not knowing a word of the language made things worse, there could be no mistaking his meaning as he pointed to the looters and our red-cross flag. A group of Turks, some junior officers, stood looking on, merely interested spectators. Half an hour later a Turkish officer appeared from headquarters in a frenzy. He had evidently been severely reprimanded. He kicked the sentry and struck him repeatedly in the face. After this for some hours looting was less frequent, but later recommenced.

Square-Peg's interpreter was next found on the roof of the hospital. He was kicked down head foremost, and dragged off to be hung. This was the unfortunate man who had brought us vegetables and supplies from the Arabs. Officially interpreter to Square-Peg who was fire-brigade officer, he had asked us about escaping, and hoped to disguise himself as a Eurasian from the Volunteer Battery. A Baghdadi by nationality he said he had lived in Calcutta. He had been with our force, and was no doubt betrayed by the pro-Turk Arabs in the town. Sassoon, our other interpreter and a well-known figure in Kut, has also, I hear, been hung with his legs broken, for he had been so thrashed and tortured that he jumped off the roof to kill himself. The friendly Sheik and family have met a similar fate. One now sees the Turk at close quarters.

To crown all, the disastrous news has come that, despite most elaborate assurances to the effect that the garrison would be conveyed upstream in barges, the men have been ordered to march to Baghdad with kit through this fearful heat. They have no rations except the coarse black Turkish biscuit. Officers have not been allowed to accompany them and their guards are mostly Kurdish rank and file, the most barbarous savages in this country. In some cases there are no Turkish officers, but merely Turkish sergeants or privates in charge of our prisoners. We are all many stages past indignation. The Turkish promises at the surrender were too much relied upon. General Townshend, we hear, has already left for Constantinople by a special steamer and car, and is permitted to travel *en prince*. I can believe already the prophecy of the reverend father that surrender would mean a trail of dead. Most of our troops left Kut on the 29th or next day for Shamrun, ten miles up-river. We had eaten our last rations on the 28th, and supplies were expected immediately from our captors. However, they sent us nothing for four days, and only black biscuit then. Everything must be bought from the Arab bazar—after the Turks have taken what they want. Some stores and letters have gone upstream from down below, but so far nothing has arrived for the lonely hospital here filled with wounded and sick and dying. Nothing, except for a few gifts Major Aylen brought us from the hospital ship and a few cigars from the padre.

May 9th.—The Turkish authorities seem determined not to send any British officer back if it can be helped. More than one who was rejected by the Turkish medical officer as not sufficiently ill to warrant exchange has succumbed. A poor fellow in the next ward who has been groaning for days died yesterday. One is not likely to recover on Turkish biscuits at this stage. I was ordered by Colonel Brown-Mason, our P.M.O., to translate for the Turkish doctor who knew German and a little French. This I did for several officers, but we were all rejected, although about six of us had been told we were certain to go. Four were selected in all, by no means the worse of the cases, while men with legs in splints, smashed thighs, and shot backs, one of whom could not sit or stand up, were rejected. Kut was deserted and lone. General Aylmer, we heard, had retired to Amarah. We expect to leave every day for Baghdad. How the men

GENERAL TOWNSHEND A PRISONER, WITH KHALIL PACHA, OUR CAPTOR (RIGHT), AT BAGHDAD AFTER KUT FELL.

have fared we don't know, but from time to time terrible stories reach us.

**
* **

June 1st.—I am writing from Baghdad in what is supposed to be the hospital, but is actually an empty house commanded by a Turkish dug-out cavalry captain, quite a well-meaning old fellow, but not much use to any one sick, and very strict. After many false alarms we were moved from Kut in a hospital boat, which proved to be the ill-fated *Julna*. I was carried on a stretcher which the Turks tried to loot as I passed. On my way I saw looting on every side. Our Indian troops lay like rows of skeletons. Their food and boots were taken from them by their own guards. A few cases of looting have been admonished, but no general measures taken. On more than one occasion the officer whose aid was requested merely asked the Turkish Askar to return the loot. Our kit was searched, and I lost my tiny camera and some excellent photos taken of Aziziyeh on the evacuation, showing our army retreating and the Turkish army advancing. Other photos were of the field artillery in action at Ummal Tabul, and some excellent ones of interesting corners in Kut, dug-outs, battery positions, shelters, and our inner life below—rare photos that, unfortunately, can never be replaced.

We were packed on the deck of the *Julna,* which had been captured practically intact, one engine working perfectly and one screw. Every yard had a bullet hole. We called this the Death Ship, as on it were all the remnants of the sick. Men were dying as they came aboard. Brigadier-General G. B. Smith was senior officer, but Colonel Brown-Mason, P.M.O., was in charge. We carried a few sentries. As we moved upstream past the palm grove, scene after scene in a tussle of five months became again vivid. Then the Turkish crescent, floating from the Serai in place of our Union Jack, was shut out from our eyes by the bend of the river, and we realized a little more that Kut and the siege were back history, and we prisoners in a relentless captivity. . . .

PART II

THE TREK.   KASTAMUNI

CHAPTER VII

THE voyage was a sad and long one. There was mildewed and rotten bread that no one could touch. It was worse than the biscuits. Other things like eggs and milk we had to buy at huge prices. At Baghailah Arabs came within a yard of our boat, and danced in ecstasy, gibing at us, and drawing their fingers across their throats indicating what they thought we deserved or were in for. That did not trouble us much. But we tingled with anger and shame at seeing on the other bank a sad little column of British troops who had marched up from Kut being driven by a wild crowd of Kurdish horsemen who brandished sticks and what looked like whips. The eyes of our men stared from white faces drawn long with the suffering of a too tardy death, and they held out their hands towards our boat. As they dragged one foot after another some fell, and those with the rearguard came in for blows from cudgels and sticks. I saw one Kurd strike a British soldier who was limping along. He reeled under the blows. We shouted out, and if ever men felt like murdering their guards we did. But that procedure was useless. We prevailed on the Turk in charge of our boat to stop and take some of the men. It seemed that half their number were a few miles ahead and the rest strewed the road to Kut. Some have been thrashed to death, some killed, and some robbed of their kit and left to be tortured by the Arabs. I have been told by a sergeant that he saw one of the *Sumana* crew killed instantly by a blow on the head from a stirrup iron swung by a Kurdish horseman for stopping by a road a few seconds. Men were dying of cholera and dysentery and often fell out from sheer weakness. But the remorseless Kurd, worse than the Turk, knows no excuse.

Every now and then we stopped to bury our dead. The awful disease, enteritis, a form of cholera, attacked the whole garrison with greater vigour after Kut fell, and the change of food no doubt helped this. It showed also that before surrender the garrison had drawn on its last ounce of strength. A man turned green and foamed at the mouth. His eyes became sightless and the most terrible moans conceivable came from his inner being, a wild, terrible retching sort of vomiting moan. They died, one and all, with terrible suddenness. One night several Indians were missing. Others reported that these have fallen overboard or jumped overboard to end their wretchedness. But more than one was probably trying to escape. Some officers played bridge and one or two chess.

In a cot close by the wasted form of a well-known major still balanced between life and death. He was a big man, but nevertheless now weighs less than a child of ten.

Then Lieutenant Tozer succumbed to enteritis after a terrible ordeal of some days. The groans of this poor fellow as he lay unconscious hour after hour stirred one to the heart. Periodical violent vomiting succeeded, and one morning the changed and drawn face was still and the tired eyes of a ghastly green were closed. We held a tiny service below Ctesiphon, Arabs waiting around and casting longing eyes on the blanket that enclosed him. But we buried him deep, and a sheik promised to see his grave was respected. General Smith, Major Thomson, and I attended his funeral. He was a very popular and good fellow. We realized as we stood around his grave that the remorseless hand of death overshadowed us too. I think we were ready to fight the symptoms when they should appear and ready to die quietly if it had to be. We were still cheerful but a little quieter.

The voyage up to Baghdad lasted almost two weeks, owing to our running short of petrol. A tin of this turned up here and there and the ship simply went on until this was done.

Messages and countless orders were sent. We waited day after day moored to the bank some miles from Baghdad. The death rate was increasing. This ship seems stricken. Then we were told we had to walk to Baghdad. Very few of us could have got there. Fortunately our resistance prevailed, although had we been the rank and file I am convinced this order would have been carried out. Finally the engineer in charge of the boat set off on a donkey for Baghdad, his legs doing a dangling jig from side to side. We were now within ten miles or so of Baghdad and the green date palms of the city were before us. Some days afterwards the Mejidieh came and took us in tow, but we made very slow headway against the current and had to tie up once more at night. Waterways worked by a horse running up and down on an incline and hauling over a wheel a rope attached to a large skin receptacle of water was the new irrigation scheme in this district. We passed more palm groves within high walls, and tried to think of Haroun-al-Rashid. Then minarets and the domes of mosques appeared, and we swung into view of a fine river-front of buildings less dilapidated than we had seen for many months. In going round the corner against the rapid current we had to make about eight attempts, each time resulting in our getting swung round, and to avoid the sandbanks we had to return. Assisted by men on shore with ropes we managed this at length and drew near the bank. It was about eight o'clock at night. We passed within a few feet of crowds of fezzed figures on the verandah cafés that stood on piles in the river on the right bank. We heard their carousals, and I remember the red line of their flaming pipes as they cried together yelling and cheering in exultation. Then we drew alongside the left bank near what we called the Water Tower. We were very hungry and ill, and alongside our dead on board many others were dying. The only visitors we had were disreputable Arabs and Turks who, as the night grew darker, swarmed on board and looted or thieved. I define loot as open theft under threat of violence, by a captor from a captive.

In the morning we were subjected to more looting, and if one left one's kit a second it disappeared. Having to carry some of our kit as best we could, the rest was imperilled. I lost my haversack with all my knives and plates and razor and toilet kit and scanty supply of medicine like chlorodyne and quinine, of which the Turks had none. We were left in the sun in rows still without food and under the eyes of a curious crowd. We bought a few things from women hawkers.

This same major who lies here dying in this house in Baghdad was, so soon as we disembarked, left lying uncovered from the sun on a stretcher apparently unconscious and covered by thousands of flies, in fact, black with them. Now and then a wasted arm rose a few inches as if to brush them off but fell back inadequate to the task. One wondered if he were dead. Our protests as we realized he had been left there hours before we arrived were more than vehement. One of our orderlies was finally allowed to remove him under cover from the fierce sun and to give him water. One saw British soldiers in a similar state dying of enteritis with a green ooze issuing from their lips, their mouths fixed open, in and out of which flies walked like bees entering and issuing from a hive. We were thankful to leave the ill-fated *Julna*, and personally I felt very grateful to Col. Brown-Mason, the P.M.O., our eternal friend Major Aylen (O.C. officers' hospital) and General G. B. Smith who, in the periods of long waiting, was most cheerful and encouraging.

We were split up into parties of sick in various hospitals so called. Two officers accompanied me and the sentry. We were told it was one minute's walk. Lieutenant Richardson, who had a shot back and could not stand for many seconds, had to walk. Lieutenant Forbes and I took his arms to assist him, and like three drunken men lurched forward through the bazaar. Poor Richardson collapsed several times on the way and finally fainted. It was at least a mile off, and our sentry lost his way. He was quite a decent fellow and did not object to some Armenian women who ran out with lemonade. We got a stretcher and at last arrived.

I am in a long room filled with bug and flea infested beds. Twice a day at hours impossible to conjecture a Turk brings in youghut, a curdled milk, in a bucket which we found most uninviting but have since learnt to take, and some rice and pilaf. We have been here some days, and through talking German to the son of the old cavalry commandant, I have actually been allowed to get dressed and go to the adjacent shops to buy castor oil with some of my remaining coins.

The American Consul has visited us. He is a kind man, and regrets that he has not any money left, as he gave all he could get to the first column, but he helped us with our luggage and sent along a few comforts such as tobacco and quinine. I

OUR PRISON, BAGHDAD, AS IMPROVED AFTER BRITISH OCCUPATION

heard that all the money at the fall of Kut was distributed among the garrison, and about three or four gold liras were to have reached me. They did not, however. I have only eighty piastres left, the balance of changing fifty rupees. At night it is very hot and we sleep on the roofs, as does all Baghdad. Major Cotton has grown worse. On arrival here he was taken to some contagious disease hospital by mistake, and met no one who knew who he was or who could speak for him, days after he came here. His sufferings and mental anguish had been terrible away from us all. Major Aylen gave him a tablespoonful of champagne brought up secretly from the camp by another party. After this the poor fellow became more coherent and quite restful. Late that night he begged me to take him on to the balcony. Notwithstanding the pain of my back I managed to get him on the verandah. He could not have weighed more than five stone. He said he was very grateful to feel the gentle movement of a breeze. Next morning he was dead. Details of other similar cases I won't write about.

May 26th.—Cavalry Barracks, Baghdad. I have been here some days, having decided that one could not hope to recover in an empty house, and so after a week or more there resolved on a supreme effort. We were sent to these Turkish barracks near the north gate on the *maidan.* It was no great distance but took much effort to get there. We left in the late afternoon, but owing to mistakes of the sentries, who took us to several wrong places, and to the fact that the Turkish sergeants at the barracks did not approve of our papers, we still wandered about after dark. He sent us back. This was repeated several times. We wandered round the place in the dark huddled up like sheep on the foul and stenching *maidan* by our postas who awaited the Commandant.

Towards 10 p.m., in the dark we got up from the mud pool, which reeked of the dead horses therein and the rubbish of the city. Sick, hungry and cold we plodded up the steps to empty rooms, our means of existence being only what remained to us, that is to say, what the various parties had not looted. This meant two or three tins of milk, a little bad tea, and possibly raisins.

The chief columns of officers have already left for Mosul. Daily I practise walking on the wall, a space that offers opportunity for a good promenade.   I want to see how much I can do.   Altogether I feel a little better but the dysentery has left me very weak, and after a half-mile have to sit down. I have contrived to send my British orderly to the town where, with the money I have raised by selling some of my kit, he has bought on occasion small pieces of meat or fish, a few vegetables, and even a small fowl which we shared among six sick people.   We stewed the fowl to rags and drank the soup.

I have been allowed by special leave to visit General Smith in hospital.   He had asked me during the last days of Kut to do A.D.C. again to him in captivity.   This was an excellent chance for which I was most grateful, as it seemed doubtful whether I would last the trek.   But I have no money and can't get any, and am averse to travelling on my general's supply, as money now is one's chance of life.   I told him frankly that I am doubtful about being fit enough to carry on very efficiently for him, but as he is to travel in a carriage over the desert for all those hundreds of miles I could do a certain amount, and I hoped to be of use in knowing something of French and German.   However, in my woebegone condition I was promptly turned down.   I recognize now that I am in for the ordeal of the survival of the fittest with a heavy handicap. We hear sometimes terrible accounts of the hardships undergone over these hundreds of miles of foodless and often waterless land, to struggle over which is an achievement even for a strong man.   But for one thing, we should be too dismayed to start—that is the hope and will strong within us to survive. One recognizes this show has become a competition between a man and a merciless fate.   I believe I shall get through.

Major Middlemas and Lieutenant Greenwood shared my room and we slept on our blankets on the floor.

Later.—We have been allowed three times into the town and wandered through a bazaar full of bootshops and cafés. Gunner Holmes sticks faithfully to me.   He is lucky to have escaped the lot of the others.   Shortly after our arrival we saw what even the oldest soldiers amongst us regarded as the most awful spectacle of their lives—the sight of a column of British soldiers under Turk and Arab guards entering Baghdad after the march from Kut.   They were literally walking corpses, some doubled with the pains of cholera, some limping from blows received *en route*. They were pressed on by their guards. Some had lost their boots and shoes or had parted with them for food. Some fell, but under the coercion of loud shouts or a Turkish heel got up and lurched forward again.

We heard from hospital of the awful sufferings of the men here who were quite unnecessarily confined in a bare baked-up field near the station. Indians and British were all mixed up, a deliberate effort of the Turk to encourage strife between the Mussulman prisoners and the others. For some days, mad with thirst, they struggled around a tiny foul pool into which the sick crawled and collapsed. It became stirred up with mud but the men, poor fellows, drank it.

They have no cover from the sun except a few wretched sticks propped on poles.

Baghdad is a very old city. But from its grimy and ill-kept streets and from its dust-smothered houses, the glamour of its ancient romance seems very far off. One minaret of Byzantine design we passed on our way to the town. There is nothing else to tell one of its glorious past, in fact it is said that all Baghdad was on the other bank. It is merely a drab, dull succession of buildings formed of the sun-baked mud of the desert. On the river, however, especially at sunset when the dirt and dust are obscured and only the pipes of the Baghdadis and Arabs blaze in the dusk, it is decidedly picturesque.

All the sick, even if only partly able to walk, start on the desert trek for Mosul in a few days. We have heard so much of waterless marches and barren lands crossed only by the nastiest Arabs, that one has the resistless desire to try one's chance. To move is to live ; to stay here is to die.

Later.—I have made a small tour of some antique shops in the bazaar with a delightful youth named Lacy of the Hants. He has just left school and is as slender and green as the young willow, and yet he has contrived to keep his manners intact, to await quietly his turn and to prefer dignified acquiescence to selfishness. We found quite an amount of silver work and even china, some of which we heard had found its way here during the war from an old caravan route from China.

I have corrupted my first sentry by giving him a drink, swallowed a horrible cognac, the immediate effects of which were promising, and learned two Turkish words. One is

" yok," which means " there is not," and the other is " yesak,"
which means forbidden !

Mosul, June 14th.—Nearly three weeks ago at Baghdad
the convalescent and sick who were able to move at all were
given several false starts, and then without notice marched in
the fierce heat to the railway station nearly two miles off.   We
then lay down in the road until evening when the train was found
to be unable to start.   We bought some bread and at intervals
managed leave from our guards to get water.   In the early morning we left by train for Samarra, the rail head eighty miles off, a
tiny village on the scorching plain.   Dust storms enveloped
us as we marched to quarters which were on the ground inside
a serai.   A few branches interwoven overhead afforded most
inadequate shelter.   Here we met some other officers who had
been left behind from previous columns.   Feverish preparations filled the interval while we awaited donkeys which were
to transport us.   One heard that previous columns had bought
the few available stores, and that the Arabs had learned
to put up prices.   The novelty for the Turk of white prisoners
was wearing off, and altogether we seemed in for a rough time.
We were allowed to go down to the river near by to bathe under
escort.   On one occasion our padre quoted " By the waters of
Babylon we sat down and wept when we thought of thee,
O Zion."   We realized we were the Third Captivity.   In
fact he might have selected another psalm.

About a quarter of the donkeys turned up.   Our senior
officer objected ; but ultimately we had to start with what we
could get, a half donkey for one's kit and one-third for oneself.   We had to walk in turns, and from the size and condition
of the donkeys a collapse was soon inevitable.   Major Middlemas
and I piled our kit on a large donkey, whom we called the
Cynic, from the cut of his head and from his eye and his
perpetual sneer, no doubt brought about by a disgust of the
Turk's hopeless *bandobast.*   He went at his own pace.

The sun was setting on the desert as our column of about
forty British officers, a number of native officers, and some
sick men whom we took as orderlies, wound slowly over the
scorching sand.   Dust from the forward column blinded us,
and one was frequently almost ridden down by others pressing
on.   A riding animal I shared with Lieutenant Lee-Bennett,
who feeling ill collapsed after doing a mile or two, and so he

rode most of the time. He had been very ill, whereas I was recovering, and although racked with pain I managed to keep going by holding on to a strap. At intervals in the hot night we halted. I shall never forget the impressiveness of this scene. Our long shadows reached far over the plain. For the most part we were silent men, and determination to get as far as possible was in every one's heart, but it was an absolute gamble. Here and there friends walked beside a donkey and held a sick man up. I felt an inner conviction I would manage all right, and this kept me up in many a doubtful moment later. Here and there an Indian Mussulman soldier fell out for a few seconds, and with his forehead in the desert dust paid his devotion to Allah. More than one of our guards did so likewise. A glorious sky of red sailing clouds stretched above us, and there came over me the battle picture of Détaille's "Dream," a procession of soldier spirits marching across the sky with banners streaming, while down on the plain below, among stacks of piled rifles, men lay sleeping among the dead. Some Arab set up his chant and the rhythm then fitted in exactly with that of Beethoven's funeral march. I was sorry for having had to start without some of my friends. Lieutenant Lacy of the Hants was too ill. He has drawn very much on his youth. I have been much struck with his quiet manly self-possession.

It was a feverish night, and as it wore on we found our strength giving out. To fall out was to be neglected and lost. One pressed on as in a sort of nightmare. Now and then a donkey fell or refused to budge and our orderlies had to be carried also. This meant casting kit. At last we reached the camping place, but there was no water. After an hour or two of broken sleep we were aroused by shouts of "Haidee" (hurry) "Yallah" (get on). Now our donkeys had been requisitioned from Arabs at Samarra, and Turkish payment is generally nothing. These Arabs followed us in the night. In the morning most of the donkeys were missing. We had had to sleep where we were ordered and could not guard them ourselves. This meant a fruitless search, and after much labour the Cynic only was recovered from another convoy. Our riding animal was gone so I had to walk. It was an awful march once the sun had got up. In the distance a few sand-stone hills appeared. Our tongues were swollen and our throats on fire as we at last staggered on to the river. The donkeys bolted into the water, and some fell in with their packs on them. After a rest of two hours we went on again over stony defiles. I had to fall out several times and then had some luck in buying from an Arab a ride on his tiny donkey, whom I called Peter Pan, a small thing not two feet high but awfully game. We pulled each other up the hills, and hours afterwards tumbled into Te Krit, a hostile Arab village which treated our men abominally.

We slept in a Serai stable place and rested two days, purchasing what food we could. On the river front was a camp of our soldiers dying from enteritis and dysentery. Medicine that had been left in charge of a native assistant surgeon had been sold to the Turks and the money kept by him. Many and loud were the complaints of our men against him. This man I understand is to be dealt with. He was an absolute traitor, in fact, murderer. The Turks had no medicine, and what this man sold had been carefully preserved and given to the camp by a previous column. The ration for the men (who had no money) was indigestible bread, and they were only allowed to crawl to the muddy river which made dysentery worse. The Arabs were particularly bad, and it wasn't safe to go outside the door without a guard. While defending my bundle of scanty clothes on the donkey from a big Arab, his friends made off with my spare haversack of utensils, and I lost this haversack also with my water-bottle.

From here the trek became a daily affair. Men fell out and died or were left in some village. Donkeys collapsed and kit had to be abandoned. From out of the darkness one heard moaning cries of " Marghaya, Sahib " " Marghaya " (dying) from our Indian friends who could go no farther. One looked into the night and saw the Arab fires, and knew the fate of him who fell out.

Turkish troops passing our column in the night seized our water-bottles and rugs or anything they could get without making too much disturbance, and although I have no doubt this was against orders, still no one seems concerned to see Turkish orders carried out. We made bivouac tents of our rugs by the river at which we fetched up each night. The country became a sand-grassy waste. Here and there were a few goats or sheep herded by the river. The rest was desert.

At Khan Khernina, a stopping place on the Tigris, we prepared for the long waterless march of which we had heard so much. We bought waterskins, cast spare kit, and with our dates, chupattis, and the bones of our last meal for stew, for we could afford meat only once a week as our small pay from Baghdad was almost finished, we pressed on.   It was a terrible march for sick men.   Hour after hour we kept going, our thirst increasing and our water evaporating from the skins.   I had no donkey but borrowed one here and there from my brother officers. We all tried to help our orderlies also.

Later, I coaxed on a small beast that had collapsed and had been left to die.   Gunner Holmes and I had to chastise him along and he required pushing.   After a time we got him to go a little better and tried making him walk behind our water-bottles strung on the donkey ahead that carried now three officers' kits.   Every one asked why we bothered.   That night, however, when other donkeys were giving out and the halting place drew near, our donkey revived and made off at a great rate expecting to end up with his usual draught of water.   It was this beast that helped us to negotiate the worst patch.

The night of the first great waterless march we rested on the *maidan*, a hilly bare spot near some salt springs, and had a most entertaining time of it.   Dust storms revolved around us and donkeys stamped over our heads as they stampeded. Kit, men, and beasts became indistinguishable.   Nightmare followed nightmare in quick succession, and shortly after, while it was still dark, we were hurried on.   The thing was to get in the lead of the column and, having the use of a donkey for the first hour, I left with the leading file alongside Fauad Bey, our half-Turk, half-Arab Commander.   This meant getting ready early.   He was a rough sort but his chief sins were ignorance and faulty judgment and inability to make any sort of *bandobast*.   With proper orders much of our sorrows could have been obviated.   The waterless march continued through dust and heat.   Donkey after donkey collapsed.   Our last drop of water was evaporating, so we drank it.   At last, after some hours, we looked down over a depression and the cry " mai," " mai " (water), came from our guards ahead—they, too, wanted water.

The Tigris lay far below.   The cry was taken up in Hindu-stani " pani," " pani."   It travelled down the column giving

hope to the faltering. The village was still three miles off.
Then a thunderstorm with heavy rain broke over us. The
beautiful water soaked on to our skin. We loved it.

An hour or so afterwards we reached Shergat, that in old
times was Asshur—the Assyrian capital of the 13th century,
B.C. The excavations enabled us to see something of the
life of that ancient town. There seemed much Roman work
there, too. In the first hour we drank and drank and drank
again, and then got into the river, sick men and all, to let
the glorious element caress us once again. Then we settled
down for sleep among donkeys, drivers, and Turks, the bearers
flourishing pots all round us. The better rooms on the balcony
and first floor were for senior officers. I was feeling very
weakened and could not sleep for pain in my spine, but hoped
to get through as the waterless march was over.

Malaria returned the second night, and with a temperature
of 105° I heard we were off. I felt appallingly unsteady and my
head throbbed to every movement of the donkey, as it does
in such cases. I was lucky to have any donkey at all, because
some of the native orderlies having lost their own donkeys clean
shaved most of the others, thus erasing the letters that had
been cut out of the hair of the animal. Wild and high raged
many a conflict over donkeys. I found mine had been re-
branded and was claimed by another. At the last moment I
managed to get a tiny animal from an Arab water-carrier
for my last money.

Once again we filed out to the setting sun past Bedouin
camps. We crossed some heavy water-courses, and more than
one humorous event occurred thereat. To see a colonel
seated on a diminutive donkey that stuck midstream, refusing
to budge either forward or backward while the water gradually
climbed up the angry colonel's breeches, was quite entertaining. In such cases a fat Turk or Arab would seize the
animal's nose while the others pushed the beast or the colonel
from behind. I remember that on one such occasion a very
" bobbery " major rode a donkey that had conceived an
affection for mine, and always followed my little beast. So when
we stuck midstream the major's beast stopped also, and, less
lucky than I, his animal happened to have stopped on some
quicksand so that when finally my beast was got to move
the major's could not. The whole four of us were equally

put out. I suggested later that we should exchange donkeys, but as I had only a slight lien on my animal the major disagreed.

A detailed account of our many wanderings would spoil the perspective of this diary. We went on through the nights and through the days ; through duststorms and heat, by night passing the fires of Arabs who awaited the stragglers, sometimes camping by Bedouin tents or pebbly watercourses, always following the trail of dead, for every mile or so one saw mounds of our dead soldiers by the wayside. We left Hammamali, a village of sulphur-baths, on the 14th June, and stumbling over rocky ground for some hours we reached far-famed Mosul, and with great delight saw again a few trees. Then appeared the mounds of Nineveh and the mounds of the palace of the great King Sardanapalus. But even the shades of Sargon, Shalmaneser and Sennacherib scarcely interested us. In the foreground we saw a great tomb which we were told was John the Baptist's ! And Alexander's great battlefield of Arbela lay on the eastern plain.

The impression of life in Mosul is bad. We have some rooms in an appalling dirty barracks among gangs of Kurds in chains. Every day or so one of these is hung. Down below in the basement our men are dying wholesale. They are the survivors of previous columns. We have been compulsory guests of a Turkish officers' club. They charged us three times as much as the town did, and generally neglected us. General Melliss, however, told us to-day to go to the town. We quoted his high authority freely and went to a most excellent little Italian restaurant. The proprietor was from Naples, and we had some conversation of his old haunts. He did us very well and quite reasonably, actually cashing a cheque or two for us.

Nisibin, June 26th.—After many false rumours of wagons and carts for transport and the usual half-dozen false starts we left Mosul on June 20th. Early in the morning before starting I slipped out in the confusion of preparing the columns and did the round of Mosul absolutely unattended. With the little Turkish I had picked up and French here and there, I visited the bank quarter to try to raise some money by cheque. There was no chance of this, but I succeeded in changing the notes I had for smaller. The notes were not accepted in the

bazaar, and one was charged for paper change. I had not
the fortune of meeting one likely person or I should not have
returned, but to attempt to escape without help in such a
place with the desert all around was too hopeless. I saw
merely bazaar and squabbling Arabs.

On the 20th a few tiny donkeys were given us for riding
animals, about enough to allow one officer out of six a ride
one hour in three. Some donkeys were on three legs, some so
poor and sick they could scarcely move. For transport we
were shown a set of a dozen untrained, wild and unharnessed
camels, altogether the most savage and nasty brutes I have
ever seen. They were unapproachable and snapped and
gyrated and then trotted away. If a kit were fixed on they
proceeded to brush it off. One or two had a rotten saddle-
tree without any girths, bridles or head-straps there were none,
only a piece of rotten rag or rope being around the animals'
heads. We had, however, already laid in a stock of the best
rope we could get, and having first fitted this into the jaws of
the brutes, proceeded to fix on our kit. I was very amused
at the efforts of the Turks to help us. They tied the kit
actually on one camel's neck, and our Indian bearers went one
better by tying it on to his legs. However, finally we got
most of our kit on board, and then the fun started. First
one and then another got loose, as the servants were too
weak to hold them. Soon the road was a procession of fleeing
camels dropping bundle after bundle in their headlong flight. .

This pantomime went on for hours. It was awfully hot.
We took a long time to get them refitted. An hour later,
blinded with perspiration and dust and in the last stage of
exhaustion, we set out again, having done only about four
miles of this terrible trek of which we had heard so much and
which was now said to be worse than the other we had just
finished. We plodded on. Presently loud shouts of consternation broke from the rear, and we saw a gigantic camel laden
up with well-roped valises, firewood, and stores topped with
rugs, and a fowl or two. He simply charged through the
procession, brushing every bit of kit off the other camels as
he passed and setting off two or three along with him. One
camel followed him with a helpless bearer seated on the top
of the stores, the head-rope gone. His shouts as he was borne
toward the wrong part of the horizon would have been funny

if it had not meant disaster for his sahib. We rested an hour or two and then went on in two columns, one of which got lost and did several miles too much, joining us before the dawn in time to start again. The camel pantomime continued. I walked or borrowed a ride from an Arab. My endurance was to me the marvellous thing.

I was almost two stone underweight, and very unwell from the long bout of colitis, my digestion quite out of gear, weak from want of nourishment and my shell-bruise, not to mention continual pain from my eyes. Yet with all the exertion and sleepless nights, so fascinating was movement after long inaction that I managed to go along quite well, and at times felt my legs swinging rhythmically along in the night and believed it possible to be well one day again. One donkey I managed to get for my baggage and that of my fellow voyager, Lieutenant Stapleton, I.A.R., who was an official " of important dimensions " in the I.C.S., and although not much *au fait* with knots and donkeys, made a most excellent purchasing officer, as his Arabic was so doubtful that the Arabs, being at a loss to know his wants, had to produce all their possessions, and in this way we ended up more than once in having a goat's head when he had set out to describe the more expensive chicken. He was keen on ologies, and we called him the Ologist. One tried to extract humour out of our incongruous situations, but getting tired of being humorous we ended by examining things from the resigned angle of the fatalist.

Each day before the dawn broke we were up, and after a breakfast of tea, black bread, a small piece of cheese and two figs, or generally only raisins, we prepared to leave. Then the camel pantomime started afresh, and it was no uncommon sight to see half our convoy of camels bolting headlong in the wrong direction before a crowd of galloping gendarmes and Turks, their uplifted tails disappearing over a sand-ridge against the rising sun and their kit distributed at intervals on the plain.

On this trek we lost the sense of time. Sometimes we marched by day, but generally in the evening and well on into the night. But for us time was not. I knew two seasons only : when we walked and when we did not. I did not always sleep. We have had to rely on provisions we brought with us and live chiefly on raisins. Sometimes one was on foot, sometimes one rode, and a broken-down wagon or two offered a fraction of a seat to any one that collapsed up to the number of six. But so many from one cause or another got sick or footsore that the extra had to hang on to the wagon.

Our Commandant, Fauad Bey, has been in a most obstreperous and belligerent mood for days. He allowed our senior officer, Colonel Cummings, to remain and fish at the latter's request at the first camp out of Mosul on the understanding that he would follow with his escort the same night. The colonel turned up some days later, and whatever misunderstanding there was, Fauad considered his kindness abused, and made the whole column suffer with regulations and restrictions. At Demir Kapu we finished the most strenuous march I have ever done. It was a dry, waterless stretch of forty kilometres over parched ground with not even salt springs *en route*. Again and again we had nothing left but the will to go on. My donkey collapsed, and with difficulty I got him to a swamp of foul slime in which, besides many bones, were the half-picked skeletons of two donkeys that had apparently been drowned in their attempt to get water.

So dry and thirsty were the animals that most of them rushed into the slimy pool up to their backs and then subsided, kit and all, into the mud. We extricated them, and having drunk our fill also of slime, we set out for the last few miles. This water was green and filled with germs, but one's experience had pretty well inoculated one by this time. Our thirst was not to be denied. One's soul was hot within one and one's tongue dry and hard. With our limit of transport there was no alternative, and most of us had had no money wherewith to buy " mussocks " (waterskins). The column reached out for miles. Even our guard were quite done.

At length we reached Demir Kapu (iron gates), where a cool translucent stream runs through some rocks, and we drank and bathed, and some having slept began to fish. At our next halting-place a dust-storm descended on our camp in the night. I have been in dust-storms in various places, but this was of a new order. With a roar like thunder a deluge of sand fell upon us, travelling terrifically fast. It tore down bivouacs, carried off tents and valises, pulled up picketing pegs, and rolled even heavy pots hundreds of yards off, where they were buried in the sand and many lost. We could not stand against it any more than against an incoming tide. It lasted for some minutes. One buried one's head and lay with all one's weight on one's kit. I understand how people are often suffocated in these storms, as even this was quite long enough. My chief loss was my topee, for which I looked long in the dark and even walked along the river to within a few yards of an Arab village to see if it had been carried down. The next day my improvised headgear of a towel proved inadequate, and I went down with an awful attack of sunstroke. Our medical officer allowed me to ride some of the way in the ambulance cart, as my temperature, he said, was quite high. Thanks to his kindness and attention and wet cloths I picked up enough to walk a little. I arrived at Nisibin feeling very ill and feverish.

I am writing under an old Roman stone bridge. Nisibin was once the outpost of the Roman Empire, and ruins of an ancient university life are found on the plain and along the wall. It is frightfully hot. There is little food in the bazaar and prices are the highest yet met, a handful of raisins being about half a crown.

I set out yesterday for the hospital to recover a topee, as I heard a British officer had died there. After many wanderings through tiny streets and dark quarters and backyards and many redirections, I was led through a doorway of matting hanging from the mud-brick wall into a courtyard, where through an opening in the wall I saw a sight that staggered the imagination.

A bare strip of filthy ground ran down to the river some two hundred yards off. Along the wall, protected by only a few scanty leaves and loose grass flung over some tatti work of branches through which the fierce sun streamed with unabated violence, I saw some human forms which no eye but one acquainted with the phenomenon of the trek could possibly recognize as British soldiery. They were wasted to wreathes of skin hanging upon a bone frame. For the most part they were stark naked except for a rag around their loins, their garments having been sold to buy food, bread, milk, and medicine. Their eyes were white with the death hue. Their sunken cheeks were covered with the unshaven growth of weeks. One had just died and two or three corpses just been removed, the Turkish attendant no doubt having heard of the approach of an officers' column. But the corpses had lain there for days. Some of the men were too weak to move. The result of the collection of filth and the unsanitary state in the centre of which these men lay in a climate like this can be imagined. Water was not regularly supplied to them, and those unable to walk had to crawl to the river for water. One could see their tracks through the dirt and grime. Three or four hard black biscuits lay near the dead man. Other forms near by I thought dead, but they moved unconsciously again. One saw the bee-hive phenomenon of flies which swarmed by the million going in and out of living men's open mouths. I was discovered talking to the men by a Turk and "haideed" off to the Turkish officer. Having assured them of doing all in my power, and having given them the two or three poor useless little coins I could spare, I went to the Turk, having got the topee of Lieutenant O'Donoghoe, who had died under conditions little better, with no doctor, no medicine, and no food but "chorba" (vegetable soup, practically water). He had lingered in this awfully lonely place for weeks and no transport had been offered him.

I talked long to the Turk, who understood some French, and told him how this sort of thing was destroying the name of Turkey and how for these things the day of reckoning must come. He was more moved by the latter than the former, knowing that in Turkey officials may be sacrificed for any caprice of another person. An Armenian was there also, and I much despised him for expressing horror to me of *les barbares* when the Turk was outside, but obviously siding with him when together. He then showed me the place of the men in order to point out that I was wrong in not understanding that Turkish kindness was proportionate to their mercy. He was angry, however, when I tried to take him towards " the " place, and more so when he heard that I had actually been allowed to go. The case was taken up by our padre, Rev. H. Spooner, and Father Mullan. What men could move, came along with us. We have raised a subscription of some £60 for the men. Then we heaped large curses on the Commandant and vowed vengeance. The men's lot altered for the better, and we promised to press Turkish authority to send transport. The great pity is that General Melliss, who had achieved miracles *en route* in alleviating the sufferings of our men, did not stop at Nisibin, the real state of the worst quarters having been withheld from him.

Nisibin is halfway on the second trek, and the column is getting decidedly weaker. At night, when the remorseless sun is gone, we wander up and down our tiny front between the sentries smoking what Arab tobacco we can get and casting many an anxious glance towards the western horizon over which far, far away lies Ras-el-Ain, the railway terminus. Between this and that there are many marches throughout long nights and days. Shall we reach it ?

. . . . .

Ras-el-Ain, July 4th.—I am thankful to Providence that I am lucky enough to write this heading. At last we are arrived in the wretched village, but as I write I hear a loco-motive puffing and puffing. We are on the railhead. No sailor after being tossed amid shipwreck in a frantic ocean ever felt happier to be in port than do we, to realize the long march is done. There are other marches ahead over mountains, but they are short, we hear. The desert is crossed.

We left Nisibin on June 29th at 6.30 p.m. with some very unsatisfactory donkeys, taking with us all the sick we could. One or two of these had slipped out from hospital unawares, and joined us as we passed on. They begged to be allowed to come, saying they preferred dying on the desert to going back to the terrors of Nisibin. We put them up on every available donkey, and some in our hospital cart, and our orderlies helped the rest along. For the most part they did well, although, as the trek wore on, one after another collapsed, and those that did not die at once we left in the most congenial camp we could. The first two nights were bad. The donkeys went stubbornly, as they invariably did, before getting into the swing of the trek.

The pace of the column was coming down to about two miles and often less an hour. The local Arabs seemed wilder, and we had to keep together, as one party of Turks had been recently massacred outright.

We were reinforced with vigilant gendarmes. For the stragglers it was certain death at the Arabs' hands. The tail of the column was an awful place. Sometimes one got here when one's donkey collapsed or kit fell off, or when one felt too seedy to sit on one's donkey, or too tired to walk fast when it was one's relay to walk. Four of us shared one donkey, Stapleton and I and our orderlies. At the rear of the column the mounted gendarmes, Turk and Arab, galloped about, exhorting the sick and dying to hurry, almost riding them down and driving them on with blows of sticks and their rifle butts. We, of course, stopped this when we could. One night I got badly left, and the column was miles off. My donkey and orderly had collapsed at the same time, and Stapleton was not available on this occasion, in fact he was probably ill himself. A small band of us we were, and more than once I was practically knocked over by the impetuous horsemen.

The padre was awfully good and diligent in assisting men, but, nevertheless, from out the night one heard the high Indian wail, "murghaya, sahib," "dying, sahib, dying." For the most part British soldiers stayed with their friends until they were dead. I saw some of the finest examples history could produce of the British soldier's self-sacrifice for and fidelity to his friend. It was a grim reality for the sick of the column. For those well, and many were comparatively so, it was quite a different thing. I shall never forget one soldier who could go no farther. He fell resignedly on to the ground, the stump of a cigarette in his mouth, and with a tiredness born of long suffering, buried his head in his arms to shut out the disappearing column and smoked on. Night was around us and Arab fires near. We were a half-mile behind the column. I was quite exhausted. One sick soldier was hanging on to a strap of my donkey. My orderly on another. His feet were all blood, as his boots had been taken from him. A soldier went to the sick man behind, but I did not see him again. Shortly after, on the same awful night, I saw another man crawling on all fours over the desert in the dark quite alone. He said he hoped to reach the next halt, and get his promised ride for half an hour, and by that time he might go on again to the next place. We picked him up, and I gave him my strap. Another sick orderly held him up. He was all bone, and could scarcely lurch along. We eventually got him to the halt, and gave him a place in a cart.

At another place we came across a British soldier whose suffering had been so acute that he had gone out of his mind and lost his memory. He had been left in a cave, and had evidently eaten nothing for days, but had crawled down to the water. He was delirious and jabbering, and thought he was a dog. We carried him along in the cart to the next camp.

On another occasion our donkey bolted, and we were left with no transport whatever, even for our blankets or water. By the greatest good luck I hired a donkey for some of my kit from a passing convoy, and the Arab followed me up for days, getting all he could out of me. Our Commandant finally thrashed him for charging too much, and gave us the donkey henceforth for nothing. But it disappeared the same night, and was probably stolen. I thought hard things of the Commandant.

The column grew weak and slower, and at the end we had to use three carts to move the sick on in relays.

The march to Tel Ermen was the worst. We were raided by Turkish troops on the march, and lost our boots and lots more. Above us the famous old town of Mardin lay perched up on its altitude, a high-walled and ramparted city of the Ancients looking over a waste of desert and enjoying a secluded life. We wondered how many treks like ours it had seen.

We left more and more of the men and orderlies behind. The last stage was terribly trying, and we were doing forced marches by night and day. We were done to a turn. Only the driving power of one's will made one press on to the magic word " Ras-el-Ain." The future is doubtful enough. But we are at least here. To-morrow we may leave for Aleppo or Konia, no one knows which, least of all the Turk.

We found here most of the doctors, including Fritz and Murphy, living in a wretched little mud-building on rotten and stale eggs brought from Aleppo.

The Hindoos, less favoured than the Mohammedan prisoners, are to remain here. We saw their gaunt skeletons at work carrying baskets of gravel in constructing the railway for the Turks back over the desert they had crossed. This outlook seemed to me sufficiently appalling. They had very little food. The British soldier was to move on. We were glad he was spared this.

I have just visited secretly a German N.C.O. camp of mechanical transport close by. They gave me coffee and biscuits, and, in exchange for a khaki jacket and jodpurs, some tins of bully, a bag of coffee, and some cheese. They were on the point of giving me some more, but I had to go. They told me a lot about Germany, and of the German victory at Kattegat, of which I saw a description in a cutting just received by one of them. We believed, nevertheless, the German had in reality been well hammered on the sea. The Germans couldn't understand my incredulity, and said they didn't see why they shouldn't do on the sea what they had done on the land. Verdun, they said, would be taken in two weeks. They admitted the French defence was a surprise.

Lord Kitchener's death at sea I didn't believe.

Nevertheless, one feels one has reached partial civilization to be able to speak of France and the fleet, even to a German.

We were huddled together near some stagnant water in the village for some hours without cover in the heat of the day. Then the sun went down behind the tiny collection of mud huts. Our future was in doubt. We smoked for the most part in silence, and watched the shadows lengthening towards the Eastern desert over which we had managed to survive. I can only record the dreadful aspect of the lot of those unfortunate prisoners destined to remain here until the end of the war.

.   .   .   .   .

I feel dreadfully ill and weak. The last spurt has drained our remaining vitality.

CHAPTER VIII

BY RAIL AND TREK OVER THE TAURUS TO ANGORA—THE LAST TREK TO KASTAMUNI

En Route.

SUDDENLY, some time after sunset, we were just preparing to settle down by the station for the night when a train drew up. With some other subalterns I found a small place for a bed in a truck. There was a space of four feet by two for each of us. We stuffed our legs anywhere and slept. The train started and we awoke. The doors of the truck were open. We watched the desert go by, thankful beyond expression, mystified at this extraordinary change, the conveyance of dying men without their own effort. The terrible bumps and the state of the trucks were nothing. It was a train.

Some time in the early morning we crossed the Euphrates, near where stood the site of ancient Jarabolis. The archæologist of the party told of the excavations here, and, somewhere to the north, of Karkemish the Hittite capital in the twilight of history.

About 10 a.m. we arrived at Mouslemie, the junction of Aleppo, some half-hour off by train from that city, whither were sent most of the sick rank and file that had accompanied us, including all our servants. Only one batman for four officers was allowed us. To my dismay I had to part with poor Graoul, otherwise Holmes, to whom I gave half my rations the Germans had given me and my last kron. I found afterwards more than one had " wangled " an extra servant. Padre Spooner asked me to share with him and a subaltern nicknamed Hummerbug, in order to keep a sick servant he had with him. This meant we had to move our own luggage.

The prospect was appalling, as I was too sick and weak to walk far without sitting down.

We had no food and no money, not having been paid since Mosul. Father Mullan, our kind Catholic padre, gave me a piastre. With it I bought a piece of bread, and shared it with another subaltern. Other officers were too poor to pay the small debts they owed.

At five we stopped near a German train bound for Ras-el-Ain. A trooper aboard it was trying to buy gold signet rings at a tenth of their value. He showed us several he had got from other unfortunates. He advised our getting supplies at once, as at the mountain stop there was nothing to be had.

An hour later we proved it true enough. The place was called Islahie—merely a station with two or three new houses where a German Staff dwelt, and some skin and brushwood shelters where sick British soldiers lay—all under the shadow of wooded heights. An awful Turkish brute followed me as I tried to drag our kits over the country to the camping place. Cholera was supposed to be raging here, and we were kept apart from the others. Excellent water was brought us in a water-cart. I missed my orderly Graoul. The padre and a subaltern nicknamed Hummerbug and I now messed together. His servant I afterwards found was too sick to do much.

We boiled the German ration, and I had some soup—besides which we had the coffee. Some real tobacco had turned up, and I remember sitting beside the fire smoking disconsolately and missing Graoul. Graoul, too, would be lost without me. Why, he had no sense of humour whatever!

I sat smoking, I say, disconsolately until the long shadows lengthened along the hills of the Taurus and climbed higher and higher upon the mountain sides. The last twilight left little coppery patterns on the crest of the dark glens. The white-washed houses on the lower slope reminded me forcibly of Scotland. I felt I might hear the tinkle of a bell and expect at any moment to see a brawny Scotch shepherd with his shaggy dogs at his heels take the cottage path from the height above. We made a jugga and slept. The next morning early we came across a German Flying Corps officer, who informed us he was engaged to some one in England, and proceeded to help us. We raked up sardines, a little milk, and small change. Also he promised to speak to a German colonel arriving that day, about the way we were being hustled.

We had a better breakfast, and being allowed to see the now isolated patients, I went among the men's quarters and found them in a shocking state. About thirty had died there. They had money which had been given them by the Red Cross people at Aleppo. In the course of the day the German colonel turned up and walked into Fauad in true Prussian style, the result being that carts were provided for us—four to a cart, with kit, and, happy to the point of shouting, we clambered into them. Two officers having to walk an inquiry was made as to who had taken a cart for two only instead of for four. Although they were asked they admitted nothing until a tally of each cart being taken it was found that two officers had bagged one cart to themselves so that they could lie stretched out. This meant others walking. Without carts we must have left half our number behind.

The Turkish method of driving a cart is to gallop 200 yards and then crawl. At 2 a.m. we stopped three-quarters of the way up and, without unpacking our valises, slept on the ground. Before dawn we were away again, and every one had to walk except those crippled with sprained ankles and so on. I found it a most dreadful climb in my condition. I was trembling through weakness, and the well-belaboured mules went at a very fast walk up the steep gradient, so that I had to hustle to keep up. Deep ravines fell away from the road, but the hills were not high enough to grow the mountain fir. Other scrub and dwarf pines grew thickly. We walked for two and a half hours, the perspiration dripping from our clothes. I was in acute pain for some of the time with ravages of old complaints. There were plenty of clear, running streams from springs, and at each of these we soused our hands and heads in the cool water. We walked up the steep inclines. Near the top the wretched drivers galloped away to prevent our getting in, but I caught a belated one after going a mile farther, while some still toddled away astern. The driver tried to turn me out, but his mules required most of his attention, so I stayed up.

The whole trip was to be about twenty-four miles. These mountains were being pierced by tunnels, as yet only recently begun from the western slope, a switchback ride being nothing to it. Without brakes of any kind, but only trusting to the collars and pole chain of the mules, the drivers, with loud shouts, galloped their animals down; now and again a wheel going over the edge of the ravine or the pole fetching up in the cutting, or in the back of some fellow sitting in the rear of the cart ahead. The carts were the usual four-wheeled, groggy thing we had got used to. Several times our cart got away, we tipping another cart over into a hole, and on another occasion we raced to pass another at awful speed before reaching a narrow corner. We did it by inches, but hit the corner, the second cart getting its pole into the kit I sat on, and hoisting me feet uppermost into the air. One collision happened, injuring a mule, smashing a cart, and just missing Colonel Cummings, who said things in English to all whom it might concern. As it was, his servant was sent flying over the *khud*.

We arrived at the village of Hassan Beyli at 8.30 a.m. It nestled in a pretty little wooded valley among orchards clustering on the adjoining slopes. As we passed through the main street I noticed that all the houses were closed with shutters. We learned that their Armenian tenants had been butchered *à la Turque*. We waited in the sun, and were moved here and there, each time dragging our kits with us. I was waiting beside mine in a stony field when suddenly I felt extremely dizzy and faint with a feeling of nausea. I had to abandon my kit, and I plodded over to some shelter, where I lay down, and a cold perspiration broke out all over my body, and I experienced the pains and vomitings of the enteritis attack in Kut. At this moment the English padre appeared, and suggested that to think one's self well is to be well. Here I said something distressing, so he said. I am sure he meant well. I had not felt so wretchedly sick since Kut fell, and the doctor told me that evening that the chlorodyne I had taken possibly prevented a collapse. We were on the verge of cholera. In the evening after a sleep I gathered some sticks and carried a little water, while the padre was meditating. Then while our orderly made the stew and coffee I strolled away to the stream and bathed. I dallied there quite a long time.

In the half light we had " dinner." The padre returned from his soliloquy in a most obviously exemplary and virtuous mood. Oh, to be able to accumulate virtue on such an occasion like a shilling gas meter, and without warning, turn it on, even if an hour after it has all gone. I suggest taps affixed to the person with little black letters on ivory thereon to the effect : "HUMILITY," "BALM," "PRECEPT," "PATIENCE," "MARTYRDOM," "ADVICE—On—Off." Hammerbug annotated him. I encouraged both. I liked it.

We slept that night until about 1 a.m., and in the darkness loaded up the carts and pushed off. All had to walk in turn to give the orderly a lift also. We drove through a pleasing country of green foot-hills covered by wandering pine and beech. In taking short cuts from road to road to catch up to the carts as we walked, we came across many Armenian homes smashed in and corpses half-covered with soil or flung down a hollow, where the Turk had passed. About six o'clock we met a great crowd of Armenian and Greek peasants, with old men and old grey-haired women and children carrying small bundles or articles of cooking, all herded together *en route* for somewhere. They were guarded by askars (soldiers). In this way they are moved from place to place, their number dwindling until all have gone. At a tiny coffee-place here we had coffee and lebon and then walked the remaining miles into Marmourie as the carts had been ordered not to wait for us. It was a long and hurried walk.

The country here looked quite pleasing to the eye. Fine terraces, fringing woods that lined the slopes of moderate hills and overlooking green valleys and splashing water-falls, seemed to ask for a hydro and golf links. We reached Marmourie about 8 o'clock, passing some Turkish soldiers *en route* over the Taurus, as also small ammunition transport. Every bit of their ammunition for Mesopotamia has, it seems, to go over these hills, as the other road, via Diabecca, is crossed and occupied by the Russian troops. Near the top of the Taurus we passed fittings for an aeroplane in huge cases that had come all the way from Germany. These were for service in Palestine obviously. Through some difference among the Turkish officers we were not allowed to sit in the shade at Marmourie while we awaited our train, but were made to sit along a dirty wall in the fierce sun for hours like so many convicts. We waited there in the sweltering heat, date the 8th July, from 8 a.m. until 1 p.m., drinking lebon every half-hour, which we got from a shop near by.

The train accommodation was small carriages, and the trucks were reserved for luggage. Only the orderlies were allowed in them, so we sat packed upright, and couldn't sleep a wink. The stations along this line were larger and busier than those east of the Taurus. Only once since getting into the train at Ras-el-Ain had Fauad Bey, our Turkish Commandant, helped us in the way of food. On that occasion he issued a ration of bread to every one. Here we persuaded him to send a wire to Adana to have lunch ready for us, Adana being a large town near Taurus. When we arrived at Adana at 4.30 there was great excitement on the thronged platform. Gorgeously-attired police and other petty officials buzzed about. It appeared that some Turkish officer was passing through. We jumped off and ran along on the edge of the platform, when we were told we were too wild and unkempt-looking to be seen by the high Turkish official. " Damn the high Turkish official," said we, " we want yesterday's lunch." Yes ! the lunch was there all ready, but they couldn't allow us in ! Moreover, we were not allowed to fill our bottles. If we had been fit I verily believe we would have taken our lunch. I was hauled back. But, getting through my train on the other side and the cordon of Turks, I got inside the enclosure unperceived, filled the bottles, brought a loaf of bread, and caught our train as it left. No ! escape was useless that way. Soldiers thronged around every station. We went on our doleful way until 9 p.m., when we were pulled up short by a German coffee-shop, to which we were not permitted to go. This was Gulek bei Tarsus of St. Paul's memory.

After hauling our kits some distance we were pushed into a square tent. We fell down and slept at once. It was an awful jamb. My head was half outside the tent, and people kept walking over it as if it were a cushion. Now I don't mind sleeping in the horse lines a bit. But then horses are so sensible. They know a head when they see it. People were going in and out of the tent all night long, but I'm glad to say I got a fair amount of sleep. One or two unfortunate fellows had fever. Before the dawn I was up, and went among the thick settlement of huts to the stream, which I was threatened by the Turk sentry not to cross, but I walked over before the Turk could say anything, and started talking to some Germans there. Even to talk to a German is a passport in this benighted land, so thoroughly do they override their allies. I had a splendid dip, while others looked enviously at me from the other side. Recrossing I made the acquaintance of a spectacled German doing Y.M.C.A. work among his own troops here. He was a Biblical research student, and journeyed frequently to Tarsus, some twelve miles off. This was called Gulek bei Tarsus. Tarsus one could see in the distance. I thought of St. Paul and Cleopatra, and hoped Tarsus had more trees about it than this sandy plain, for their sakes. The German seemed a very decent sort. We discussed Berlin. He had been a visitor there once from Southern Germany. He asked if we were short of money. When we started in motor-lorries some hours later at 10 a.m. he came to my lorry and flung in a bag of several liras from Red Cross Funds. This came to about half a lira a piece. We thanked him sincerely, and he wished us good luck.

He had told me in the morning to come to his quarters, but I had no opportunity. Cholera was raging there, and the Germans had a pumping water-distillery, from which I got some extra water. I learned later that many of our troops were working at a tunnel on the slope of the Anti-Taurus mountain here, and were dying like sheep. We saw nothing of them, nor were we allowed to inquire.

The *bandobast* for this mountain was German, and we were hustled off with commendable dispatch. At 9.45 a dozen motor lorries drew up. At 10 we were off. They were absolutely run by German officers and men. We swayed and bounced about, quite reconciled to that, and thanking God it wasn't a case of " leg it " again. These mountains are much more barren than the others, being largely, on their eastern slopes, white clay or lime-stone ravines and crags, with a few shrubs here and there growing out of the stony ground. They are also much wider. We passed some desolate Armenian villages and tore along to the upper heights. At 11.30 we stopped at a ruined mill by a fall to cool the hot engines, and there had a drink and a piece of bread, also a slab of baked meat, chiefly fat. It was a wild spot, great rocky crags falling across the road. Another hour and we arrived at Park Taurus, a German military halfway house, forty kilos from Gulek, and thirty-two from Bozanti, whither we were going.

Park Taurus is situated on a small plateau leading down into three or four valleys surrounded by hills of crumpled granite dotted with pines. The valleys are now dry, but in winter must be filled with racing torrents. It is absolutely German, and evidently erected during the last eighteen months. The enclosures easily accommodate over a hundred motor lorries, besides which they have huge electrically-lighted store sheds and depôt, where they accumulate stores *en route*.

We were turned loose at 1.30 p.m. in a field where stood a huge, empty tent. The Germans here were not so well disposed towards us, and would not help us at all. Some N.C.Os. who wanted to do a deal were hustled away. The first arrivals bought out an Arab's tiny shop of honey and raisins and potatoes, and there was little else to go round. After a solid sleep, for our rest the previous night had been very broken, we made a very bad meal. Our application to bathe in an adjoining pool was not allowed. Then we all sat around the side of the hill and smoked while once more night floated down upon the world. The motors that had been passing all day were now housed, and there was an appreciable calm broken by falling streams and tumbling brooks. Pale yellow stars burned passionately over the pine tops; and once again here there was something in the far-away spot that recalled the mountain forests of Thüringen. There was less forest and more rock, but it served as another span in that bridge we are all constructing back to old times—the bridge that must span Kut and the trek. . . .

At 4.15 the next morning, before it was light, we were in the motors and away again. There followed, as usual, a wild scramble and fearful scrumming around the lines, as we were not awakened until five minutes before leaving. This journey was decidedly bumpy, and we had to grip hard to stick inside the four walls of the thing at times. The country became wilder and rockier with only a few boulder pines climbing up the heights. Along the face of these limestone bluffs one observed a queer phenomenon of splashed yellow rocks, seemingly spilled from some gigantic cauldron, dried and hung out like blanketings in the morning sun. Then there were caves and water-worn caverns, said to have been once the homes of the Hittites. Many Turkish and others worked on the road, and dishevelled troops passed us *en route* for the Mosul or Palestine front, via Aleppo.

At last, two great tall upstretching tongues of rock, almost meeting, filled the mouth of the converging valley, and rendered any attempt to cross into that valley by any other way than between them almost impossible, except for an Alpiner. These were the famous Cilician Gates through which passed Alexander in the fourth century, B.C., on his way to Syria. Darius had lain in waiting somewhere near Islahie on the other side of the Anti-Taurus mountains, and when Alexander had got safely down between the seacoast and the Anti-Taurus, Darius and his army scampered over the mountains, probably, the very way we had come, and cut Alexander off from his communications. But Alexander turned on the Persian king and smashed him at Tarsus. Five hundred years before that, Shalmanaser II., the great Assyrian king, had crossed and recrossed this very pass on his way to and from his victories. After Alexander, the hordes of Barbarossa, and in fact, every ancient army on its way east had had to pass through them.

Some old Hittite inscription was on the outer face of the rock, and on either side of the road a Roman altar cut out of the flat rock by the roadside testified to the military importance conceded to this Gate by Roman Generals, locking the way to the Orient. In those days the pathway was a few feet wide only, and now cannot be more than five yards. Heavy blasting, however, widened the way along which we came.

A few miles further on we reached the rail-head again at Bozanti from where they were tunnelling the Taurus. Here we saw many British soldiers at work. They were mostly from the Dardanelles and some of them seemed quite fit, but the tunnelling was heavy work, and they said that the men from Kut there could not stand it—and had died.

For some hours we were shoved in a stable with billions of flies. Many officers were very indignant at being put alongside horses. Being a field artilleryman it didn't worry me in the least after what we had gone through. We bought a few stores and a German presented me with a bottle of beer, as he found I spoke German !

At 8 p.m. that night we left, packed in a train, all very

o

tired and weak. There were in the train some German
N.C.Os. and men all on their way back to Berlin, and in a
highly hilarious state at the prospect. Some of them were
the nasty sort, and they all told us of the English naval
disaster off the Skager Rack in which we had lost ten large
ships and so on. We knew this was an untruth and suspected
it was a fine victory for us, especially as the Boches ran back
to Kiel.

We travelled all night fearfully cramped up in carriages.
I managed to get two or three hours of restless sleep among
moving boots and feet on the floor, with my knees by my nose
and some one's boots in my face. At 12 noon we arrived at
Cognia or Konia, the Iconium of St. Paul, a large town with
a real hotel to which only a few of us were allowed to go,
and a plentiful array of shops. After the usual dozen moves
up and down the station, each time entailing carrying our
beds and kits, we were taken to a restaurant where our notes
were refused, but ultimately taken at a large discount. How
we carry on without money is really extraordinary! One
simply does not eat, but gets weaker and weaker. Acute
diarrhœa has broken out again with many of us, for we are
still on nuts and sour bread and water. That night, the
12th July, we slept in the station yard.

The next morning we were aroused at an unearthly hour,
and then did not leave until quite 11.15 a.m., the intervening
hours being employed by waiting in a queue to get water or
being moved first this way and then that. No Turk as yet
seems to know his own mind or any one else's apparently.
The country around Konia is very flat and more or less bare.
The Hindoo native officers remain in Konia, which should be
a good spot for them, and quite healthy. Konia appears to
be absolutely rebuilt and quite new. Two hours out of Konia
our engine broke down. We waited four hours for another
engine from Konia. I found a German doctor travelling on
our train, and from him I got some colitis and cholera powders.
He also was quite polite and anxious to help one. Then we
passed Kala Hissar, a lonely town on the plain with a fort
perched high up on a hill. Here a good many Russian, French,
and British prisoners are said to be placed, but we saw nothing
of any of them. We travelled all night over the plain, and
it was another wretched night for sleep, as we had to take

it in turns sleeping on the floor. We had by this time lost
a lot of our veneer of desert sunburn, and the pallor of sickness stared out from our faces. Father Tim, our excellent
Catholic padre, told me this evening that I had appeared
twenty years older during the last few days. At 11, forenoon,
on the 13th, we arrived at Eski Chehir, a large town on the
junction of lines to Constantinople and Angora. Here, again,
the want of a servant made the immediate present a tragedy
of vile proportions. Thus we would get the order to move
at once, no one knowing where. Everything had to be moved
with you. So you gathered up water-bottle, haversack,
blankets and coat, and dragged your valise over lines and
other obstacles indefinitely. Then you sat on them until
you had to take them back, crossing trains and piles of luggage
and stores, a *posta* or Turkish guard at your heels with a rifle
shouting, " Yallah " or " Haidee Git." We dropped Captain
Booth accidentally on the way from Konia. He was asleep
in a carriage which was taken off near Kala Hissar. Great
excitement prevailed as to whether he would take the branch
line to Smyrna and try to escape, but he turned up again
later. In the meantime, Fauad Bey thrashed every Turkish
official within reach.

At Eski Chehir we were allowed into an hotel restaurant
place near the station and forbidden to go outside. We saw
one or two Greek maidens, well on towards their prime, wel-
coming us with smiles, but although the first of Eve's daughters
seen for a long time, one's heart did not flutter much. We
were so whacked that we wanted a meal and a bed on which
to sleep, sleep, sleep. So we fell to discussing what we would
do at Constantinople, whither both Fauad Bey and some
Germans at Konia had assured us we were being taken. The
prospect of seeing this famous city and especially of seeing
Europe again, and of having ambassadors and consuls to take
a friendly interest in us, cheered up our tired and sad hearts.
But by this time we knew the Turk well enough to doubt
all things. In the meanwhile we were shut up. We had a
decent meal or two at terrible prices, so we ate sparingly.
Some of the senior officers had wandered too far away at Konia
so Fauad said, and it was " Yesak "—forbidden. In fact,
just before leaving Konia he would not allow them to recross
for a final meal, but I bolted around the station over a fence,

and on his seeing me I humbly pretended I wanted to ask his permission. To my surprise, he asked me if the colonel and all had returned, and on my reassuring him he took me to a restaurant and demanded meat and rolls and soup and cheese. None appearing to be ready he created such a storm in the place that the people evidently produced their own meal. Moreover, he paid and would not take any money from me ; but then I have never quarrelled much with him, and he knows he is to leave us and wants a good report. I observe he is very nervous whenever I talk to a German, and asks me to talk in French if at all. French he understands a little.

At 10 p.m. the same day, as we arrived in Eski Chehir, we were again packed frightfully close into carriages, and left for where we did not know, but half expected to awake beholding the minarets of Stambul. The Mohammedan native officers had all been dropped at Eski Chehir, where from all accounts they were to be done quite well. However, after starting it proved that our destination was Angora. Our hopes fell below zero. I clambered out of the carriage and, worming my way into the luggage car, slept full length on a blanket, or almost full length. Presently, other officers filled the place up. I determined to sleep that night, and drinking half a bottle of local cognac I had luckily procured for a debt, I gave the other to the orderlies and slept. It was an uphill climb, and we went very slowly. With the dawn we met a startling rumour that some prisoners, having attempted an escape, we were all being sent on to Kastamuni, a lonely town on the edge of the hills, fringing the Black Sea, and 150 miles distant from Angora—150 miles that had to be trekked ! This was just the last edge. One wondered whether the journey would ever end or whether our kind protecting gods would get tired of fathering our shattered and siege-battered systems to the terminus.

If our health had been so good as even at the beginning of the trek it would all have seemed very funny no doubt. But people's nerves were shattered and ragged and tempers raw, and our digestions quite gone.

The train climbed a gradient plain, treeless and lifeless, until 10 a.m., when we arrived at Angora, a dilapidated old town on undulating country. The station seemed the only decent building in it.   We seemed to be at the end of creation. Everything was so quiet and sleepy.   It is indeed a branch line and one sees no Germans or Europeans.   We were hustled at once into two deep and marched half a mile to a wretched low little eating restaurant place with some sleeping rooms upstairs.   Our luggage came in afterwards.   Mine had been looted, I found, quite considerably, two or three times since the Aleppo change, but I don't know where.   The hotel promised us a gay time, as we saw battalions of bugs skirmishing on the walls.   We had marched up at a smart pace and I felt like collapsing at every step.   Then we were left in the sun for hours outside the place, with the result that I was soon pouring with the perspiration of fever.   Then ague succeeded.   A Turk took my temperature as 102°, and left me.

Six hours afterwards I got a bed on a landing and fell into it, my temperature being over 103°.

There is no tea or coffee except the black smoky stuff. The senior officers and those first to arrive, including the padre and Hummerbug, went to another hotel somewhat better, taking the one orderly with them, so I lost the only servant who ever did a thing.   No one else cared for the sick or took any notice.   I had a tiny bowl of rice soup.   The rest of the fatty fare I avoided.   The next morning three-quarters of us had collapsed.   Colitis and fever were all around, and the Turkish doctor inoculated those who were well enough to be done, for cholera, of which Angora was full. During the night a fearful itching broke out all over my body, the most maddening itching imaginable.   Spots and a red flush followed.   I thought I was in for scarlet fever or something.   It proved to be " hives," however, and others had it at the same time in less degree.   Reports from the hotel were that most of them were in bed sick also.   It seemed as though we had forced ourselves on to the railways' end by will power, and then, that being over, had collapsed.

July 20th.—We are still in Angora, and are not allowed to go outside the door, while for the first day or so they objected to one's going downstairs.   Sending out for supplies is also forbidden, and we are thus forced to leave ourselves to the mercy of the hotel-keeper, who, by the way he behaves, I should say is a Young Turk.   Hives leaves one a mass of swellings that itch like a million chilblains, and is due, I hear, to the impoverished nature of the blood and general want of nourishment.

The time here is no rosy one, and although more comfortable than in Mosul, the trek being mostly behind us, still one's vitality is even worse.

Two days after we arrived another party that had been waylaid at Kala Hissar came along with several officers I knew, and some I didn't, Colonel Peacock amongst them. He and I and another made tea between us, and then they were moved to dingy quarters up the road, and the surplus fellows without rooms were sent also. Trembling with weakness and fever I stumbled into my clothes and found I could scarcely walk ; but the Turks were demonstratively insistent, and, carrying a few things, I assisted an orderly to carry my bed and kit. We hauled it upstairs, and then another Turkish officer turned up and ordered me back as being sick. Leaving my luggage I toddled back, but that kindly-hearted cavalry giant, Captain Kirkwood, followed me with it, for which I was more grateful than I can say.

We are still without money. One day some of those fit enough were taken to a café near by, but as they had no money " nothing happened," as they expressed it on returning. Anyway we are running up a bill here, and unless they pay us before leaving, the hotel walla will get nothing. I have a few spoonfuls of fatty rice, and lebon, and marrow soup daily. Stapleton and another officer share my room.

There is no news, except a reported Russian shove through Roumania. It is also rumoured that we may move in a day or two. A Turkish doctor has been round, and has ordered me milk, etc., with medicine. I've sent frequently for both, but neither has come so far—four days since.

And these bugs are the " Devil's own." I suggest the Inns of Court Officers' Training Corps should have a bug rampant as their crest.

Except the Bible, one has no books. I have now finished the Psalms and Proverbs to-day, and am going on. They say the second phase of the Titanic struggle (or Teutonic struggle) is beginning in France. I wish nothing better than to be fit again and in it.

July 22nd.—Oh ! This wretched confined bug-eaten little

café! They would not let us go to hospital, where one might have got milk. They had no carts, they said, no medicine, no room . . ., and cholera was there, etc., etc. To-day the doctor brought us black draughts for colitis, which we have chanced taking, and it has already done us some good. I am bitten red with bugs, and can feel at any moment several on me at once. The bed is full. I must try to sleep and forget them, as it is no use brushing them off. Temperature 100°.

July 23rd.—We left Angora to-day in carts. Feeling a little steadier, and the hospital being so inhospitable, I decided to try and keep going with the same column, trusting my luck once again. From the money they paid us I promptly kept a lira, and left the hotel-keeper's account partly unpaid. We promised him the money when we could cash cheques or get our remittances. With some of the cash I got the interpreter to buy two tins of milk and a little sugar and tea for the journey. We did not, however, get clear of the hotel-keeper and Commandant of Angora so easily. There was a riotous scene, yelling and screaming, shaking of fists in one's face, because we hadn't paid, when the Turks themselves had not paid us since Mosul! What an awful brute that Commandant of Angora was! A vicious, spiteful, selfish, callous savage. We let him know it, too, by the time we had finished with him. For instance, a lot of us were very ill and without money, and although there were rooms full of parcels sent us from home when Kut fell, he wouldn't even look to see. We saw some marked for several officers through a clink in the door, but he wouldn't shift himself an inch to see about anything. So we had malaria without quinine, and drank wheat-coffee when tea was lying in our parcels inside.

I am glad to have left that vile café.

We went on all day very cramped, in the same carts, and that night slept in a stable full of bugs and fleas. I bought some lebon and slept. At 4 a.m. we were away again through hills and bare, treeless heights all day. The horses galloped and walked, and one's back bounced on the side of the narrow carts, which at the bottom were about two feet six inches wide, with sides sloping outwards. There were the usual upsets, and boltings, racing, and collisions. Twice our cart jambed another over the edge of a cliff, and we got rammed. There is nothing to eat except bread. It was an extra weary day. For fourteen hours we jolted and jerked onwards, and then a pretty little green village hove in sight. We saw geese and ducks and fowls, which meant eggs, and a running stream, and brushwood for fires. But we were driven on and past this into the night. An hour and a half later we reached a filthy Arab enclosure, inside which we were driven. There was scarcely room for us to lie. One could not get water or firewood or anything. There was no Turkish officer to appeal to. We were all under the orders of a choush or sergeant. The colonel was very indignant, but the choush seemed afraid we might escape unless we were shut up. The place swarmed with mosquitoes and fleas. This choush was taking no risks. It was only after a long delay, when I found a Greek youth who knew a little German, that arrangements were made for one or two of us to go to a spring and get water. We had some tea and tried to sleep. That, however, was out of the question. For the last dozen miles one of the occupants of our cart was taken suddenly ill and had to lie down, so we had to break our backs under the driver's seat while the vehicle galloped and jolted. To any one except those in our condition this would have been merely inconvenience. It was an exceptionally beautiful sunset, with pink-limbed baby clouds resting on the rolling summits of soft grassy hills.

July 25th.—We were up at 6 a.m. The horses were very done, but their drivers goaded or thrashed them with thick sticks and made them gallop, and there were no brakes to help them. To pull up they ran into the bank, or into another cart. We had, on the previous day, passed through hilly country dotted with villages and fairly well cropped. Everywhere we saw grazing the herds of Angora goats with their gaily-dressed goatherd standing over them blowing his pipes. The Angora goat is a most beautifully fleeced animal with twisted horns and snow-white curly locks of fleece. The animals are kept for their wool as well as milk, and often supply the chief means of the people's subsistence in these parts. Besides milk, butter, and cheese, and sometimes the meat, the wool is woven into various garments, and the hide, laced with string, forms their shoes. These goatherds are very picturesquely dressed with coloured jackets and caps, and a bright red-striped kummerbund, in which is stuck the eternal Turkish knife. The arms and legs are criss-crossed with coloured cord.

The hills here and there are covered with herds, and at the head of these moving white dots moves their picturesque goatherd, blowing quaint sounds from his pipes. We passed lots of these fellows marching as impressed recruits between Turkish soldiers, and shoved on to fight in the forlorn hope.

We have left the peak El Divan far behind. It is 4900 feet, so we must have climbed some 3000 feet above Angora. The country has now changed again to the more barren higher hills. A thunder shower surprised us on the top of one, but it cleared the air immensely. Then our cart broke down, and they repaired the pole with a pine tree growing near.

My wonder at these carts increases daily. Rattling and loosely bolted and wobbling, they appear to be on the point of breaking down every minute. Sometimes three of the tyres of our cart simultaneously were almost off, and the pole hung between the body of the cart and the tree often quite detached. If the wheel slips off they bash it on with a rock or lump of wood, and, like Turkey itself, it just goes on.

At 3 p.m. we reached the small town of Changrai, the only place of any importance between Angora and Kastamuni. We were frightfully done, but luck ordained it that we were bivouacked by a stream and under some trees quite close to the town.

Changrai is a pleasant little town with ten mosques on the steep hillside, heights all round, and many green orchards all about. We got honey, apples, and apricots, fairly cheap. I saw the Angora goat at close quarters. He is a classy little fellow, small, and prettily shaped, with fine bright eyes and carrying the most spotless silken white fleece in the world.

July 26*th*.—We left Changrai about 9 a.m. I had managed to change to another broken cart which would support me. It was more comfortable, and I travelled alone with the choush, enjoying my own thoughts and amusing myself by watching the antics of the goats or weaving romance around the feet of every goatherd. I could stretch my limbs, and I thanked God I was left to enjoy the peace of the mountain heights alone with a pipe. My cart being broken we were far in the rear of the column. At the hills I drove, and so escaped walking, the driver, a huge fellow, walking to watch his cart, and perhaps not unduly strain his repairs. As for me, my weight had fallen from ten stone twelve pounds to considerably under nine stone, so this came in convenient just now. In the afternoon we followed a track fringed by deep precipices crossed only by goat tracks. We camped in a gully near a village, to which we were not permitted to go. A few loaves arrived for us. We were very hungry in this spot, and the cold night sharpened up one's craving for food. We made some cocoa and soup, and after a spot of cognac like nothing quite else on earth we slept—for a time—until we discovered we were on ant-hills. I have since decided to back a squadron of red ants on the war-path against two battalions of Angora bugs. It was very cold, but the ants kept us moving.

July 27th.—We made an early start just after the dawn. We went down, down, down for 2000 feet, and then gradually up again over hills and gullies. We passed some well-worn Hittite caves, like watch-keepers of the valley below. These quaint people that sprinted about among primæval dews, and about whom so little is known, must have had a queer life of it in those high detached and lonely caves. They selected inaccessible places, like the eyrie of the eagle.

We rested at midday from eleven till one. Two goats were killed, but as we had no money we did without. The note is of no value in the country, and of little value in the town. No change can be got for any, however big the note is. Two of our officers we had to leave behind at Changrai sick with fever. We subscribed some cash for them. I was glad to be able to keep going still, although I often felt fearfully nauseous and weak, with a thundering headache, at which time the cart generally started some of its gymnastic tricks. Malaria was still on me.

The big climb now lay ahead of us. We pushed on. The scenery became much more interesting. The forest thickened, and instead of chestnut and beech appeared the *pinus insignis* and the mountain fir. We went up and up. Again I was reminded of Thüringen in Germany, and this time it was much more like it. The road grew steeper, the ravines larger, and the courses of winter's mountain torrents were now dry rocky boulder paths. The mountain fir with its drooping branches stood erect in marshalled battalions on the mountain slopes

in the valleys, the tops swaying to the eternal music of the
mountains. We quenched our thirst at excellent falls and
springs on the way. It grew from chilly to very cold. Our
blood was in a very poor condition, and the biting wind bit
clean through one. We were now at the last climb of (Mount)
El Ghaz Dagh, 5481 feet high, the ridge of which we were to
cross being 4500. At five o'clock other horses gave out, and
ours were taken, so I cramped up in another vehicle with the
choush, from whom I understood by signs that we had in our
turn invested Kut. Our heavy guns will soon shake it to
pieces if we do invest it.

It was slow work to the top of the peak, but once over we
descended rapidly in the face of an icy wind for two hours.
Tiny log-built hamlets lay clustered up together for warmth
on the sides of the valleys. We followed the main valley until
the stream widened at a saw-mill. There we lit fires and made
ourselves warm and cooked some soup. We slept inside dark
empty rooms in the mill, and here struck a new pest. They
were swarms of lice and fleas, and we did a *shikar* for them
most of the night. I arose early feeling a rhythm of returning
health. The cold bracing air of the mountains had undoubtedly done me a lot of good, and I felt stronger, although
colitis and malaria still troubled me, and everything we ate
was followed by sharp abdominal pains—a legacy of the siege.
I washed in the icy stream by the light of dawn. What a
magnificent morning it was ! The last mists of night floated
away, and left the terraces of bronze-green firs shimmering
in the morning sun and climbing up to the blue of heaven on
the white sheets of El Ghaz Dagh. This would make an
excellent trout stream. My last tin of milk and sugar which
had kept me going so far was finished. My own cart had
appeared in the night, and I left in it at 7 a.m. After a few
miles of fern-edged brooks that tumbled along quite New
Zealandy, we reached the plain again, and followed a road
among scantily cropped stretches until three o'clock, when
my driver pointed away to the right and said the one word,
"*Kastamuni!*" Turning around I beheld far away in a treeless
basin a reddish-brown patch which proved to be the clay tiles
of houses. In the distance it appeared as a brown-carpeted
dip sunk down beneath the almost treeless grassy plain. This,
then, was my first glimpse of our immediate bourne.

We were divided into two columns outside the town—
evidently intended for different houses. I now learnt that in
previous columns the officers of British regiments, including
the R.F.A., my own regiment, had gone to Yozgard, due east
from Angora. This was rather bad luck in a way, as among
them were most of the officers I knew best.

We strolled down into a town larger than Changrai, with
plentiful minarets arising above the brown roofs. The houses
line the sides of the basin, which is merely the broadening out
of a fertile little valley watered by a small stream that in the
town is crossed by an interesting looking old stone bridge.
In the background and overlooking the town is a picturesquely
situated fort, now in ruins.

We were rattled through the town, the people all gazing
at us very interestedly. The shops, we observed, actually had
in them such things as local tobacco (dreadful stuff, but better
than nothing), sugar, and rice, and even sardines. We walked
behind the carts that climbed and climbed to the further side
of the town, which was the Greek Christian quarter, and on
passing a long row of dirty houses saw some of the other officers
on the look-out, including Square-Peg. There were two groups
of houses, Upper and Lower. We were to occupy a new house,
the highest of all, attached to the Upper House. We swarmed
into a front door down along an alley flanked by a wall, and
found ourselves in what appeared a decent house for Turkey.
On going upstairs I found a landing, off which led four doors.
I opened one of them, and found myself inside a small room
fourteen feet by ten feet, containing two beds, and, on going
to the windows, saw a glorious view of the whole of Kastamuni and of the valley reaching out to the blue ranges in
the distance, beyond which lay, somewhere near by, the Black
Sea. A fresh breeze, seemingly straight from the hidden sea,
drifted towards me as I stood by the open window. That
decided me. I slung my things down and fell on the bed
nearest the window, thanking God that the trek was done. I
am now writing at the corner facing the same hills. It seems
that here we must rest until we have done with these chains.
Our brother officers had put the Turks up to preparing a meal
for us. Heavens! how we ate! There was white bread,
boiled eggs, honey, butter, fresh milk. We ate and drank
and drank and drank. There was a hot competition now for

bedrooms, and as mine had to be shared, I was fortunate enough to get a quiet stable companion to share with me.

We were not allowed out of the house until 7.30, when we were taken to a large two-storied Upper House—Mektub they called it, as it had previously been a school, and there a large room had been turned into a restaurant, and was run by a Turkish caterer. He gave us soup, and what we called toad-in-the-cucumber, or tomato as it happened, rice *pilau*, and a fried meat dish all heavily reeking with fat. A coffee shop was opened, which ran extra supplies of butter and honey, and also cognac, *mastik* (the Turkish drink tasting of aniseed), and local thin German beer at 5s. a bottle. We got back after a lengthy wait, which we beguiled by comparing our experiences with those of other officers, and then hastened to bed. A few celebrated our arrival by a carousal, but I slept. Oh! the ecstasy of that night with the breeze playing over one's face—sleep that would not be broken at any unearthly hour by a "*Yallah*" for donkeys or by dust-storms or by a stampede.

At intervals in the night I awoke startled. Once I imagined I had fallen asleep on my donkey again, that we were pressing on in darkness over the desert, and, again, that an order had been given to move. But each time I found myself in bed beneath the cool night wind laden with scents of the mountains and the sea, and heard above the deep silence the sound of splashing water from some spring below. And I thought how very life-like was the trek that had led we knew not whither, and how, as in life also, we had craved for a sight beforehand into the future for a glimpse at our destiny. But one sees now the greater wisdom of God's plan that denied us a vision into the future which might have lessened our motive power and removed the need for trust or hope, but which demanded of us instead the virtue of patience to await the evolution of God's ways. And now more than that priceless perfect gift of being able to say honestly, "Thy will be done," would I desire to achieve the patience to overcome the difficult stretches of any road, patience to wait and await. We are told that whatever sorrow one has, it must exist in one's mind *only* at the present. In this sense only the Present can be sorrow, and it is often a joy. But carrying us on from Present to Present, from Sorrowful Present to Happy Present, be it near or far, there is the Stream of Time, which the Divine Giver has placed by us all. To await, then, is merely to make a friend of this Stream of Time, the Happy Carrier, and pray for the patience to endure until . . .

July 29th.—No words could describe my unbounded joy at receiving to-day news from the outside world. There was a postcard from friends in Camberley, saying that our defence has at last been understood, and asking what one wanted. It was such a cheery word. There was also a tiny letter three and three-quarter lines in length, which came many thousands of miles congratulating us on the siege, and announcing that parcels had already left for me. We hear they cannot arrive for months. There is yet, however, no word from my dear mother, or from home. I am now practically without socks, shirt, vests, or anything else, my boots in ribbons, and with one blanket.

We are to get seven liras a month, and our board and lodging costs nine liras at the least, as we have to pay an unjustified rent. What with tobacco and medicine, not to mention English food with which we must reinforce this Oriental provender, it will be at least fourteen liras and possibly eighteen a month.

July 30th.—The intervening hours we have slept. One eats and then goes back to bed. We are all still extraordinarily done. To-day we visited the Turkish bath. One enters a large dilapidated vestibule with tiny sitting-up beds about four feet long arranged around the room. One undresses and wraps oneself up in a towel and shuffles in clogs into other rooms where hot water pours from a jet. Here one douses oneself, and then sweats heavily. A bucketful of cold water completes the bath, and then arrayed in clean towels we retreat to the bed, and over a cigarette and black coffee (awful stuff) watch the spiders in the great dome of the roof, or by counting the dozen layers of clothes with which the Turks hide their iniquities. We lie at full length, letting our legs stick out, feet beyond the beds, or cock them up on the nearest wall.

All the people here seem well disposed towards us. They know we represent cash to them. At least they think so.

After the bath we were allowed to visit the bazaar for a few moments under the charge of a *posta*. There was an awful climb back to our house, to which we shall no doubt get accustomed in time.

We have written four postcards home, chiefly about what to send us. I am anxious to hear from my parents and sisters. Their letters must have been returned, and I suppose they have had anxious times, not hearing from me for so long or knowing whether I was still alive. The cheerful four-lined letter I received from Camberley must have been written after newspaper announcement of the fall of Kut.

CHAPTER IX

JULY 31*st.*—Yesterday was two months since leaving Baghdad, a journey I shall always associate with sorrow and fortitude. It was already a trail of dead and dying from other columns, and we freshened it up with contributions of our own. But time flies. It is already three months since we left Kut. During that time I cannot recall one Turkish promise that they have kept. This is a performance, but for us to have so far survived it and also their indifference, is an achievement.

After a time we hope news will leak through, but at present there is none. We are to be allowed a German-inspired daily written in French and published in Stamboul, called the *Hillal*. According to it fighting still proceeds in France in the same old zone, while in Mesopotamia the front is near Amara—which one doubts. It is almost two years since the war started. Great movements in the national life of most European nations seem to be merging into international. With peace, I believe fresh and wonderful Gulf Streams will circulate in the new political world that must arise.

August 1*st.*—I have met Haig of the 24th, whom I knew at Hyderabad, and whom I saw last in the retirement. We have so far almost no liberty, not being allowed to go even to the second part of the house. But we understand this will change very soon. Once a week we are permitted to go to the Turkish bath, and once a week to the bazaar, where the prices are exorbitant. Butter or honey is 30 piastres an oke, or 2s. 6d. a pound, sugar 40 to 50 piastres, or 4s. 6d. a pound, and tea, bad tea at that, 10s. a pound. There is little else to be had, and clothing is a fictitious price. However, one's credit in the bazaar is practically unlimited. The shop-keepers prefer to trust us rather than their own people, and take cheques rather than paper money. Medicines are more or less unprocurable.

5 *p.m.*—Turned in with rising fever. Several officers in our house have been down with it already, and I hoped I was to have escaped. A strong physical reaction has set in with many of our column, and all sorts of sicknesses are going about. For one thing, we have practically starved for half a year, and now these fatty foods of the Turks rather try one's weakened digestion. We negotiate huge quantities of fresh milk and lebon.

August 2nd.—Lieut. Locke died in the Turkish hospital last night, and, as a result, a scare started among the Turkish officials. One of their doctors came around to see all those in bed, and I was ordered, much against my will, to the Turkish hospital. They don't understand malaria at all, or that, for colitis, the only thing to do is to diet. And, from what we hear, the last place for diet is a Turkish hospital. However, one is in the hands of these interpreters, and for the most part they are lying, frightened, Greek or Armenian knaves. Ours required me to leave everything—even mere requisites—and set out for the hospital a "few moments away. Extraordinarily weak, I shambled off and followed him on a considerable trek, for a sick man, all around the town. Then he bolted for his dinner, leaving me in charge of the soldier, who, poor chap, couldn't read his papers. On arriving at the place we were refused admittance, and there was no one there to read the admission paper. A wait of hours I spent by sitting out on the roadside in the hot sun, near a café; a delightful occupation for a man shivering with ague and with a temperature of 103°. Then I discovered a patient who spoke some French, and he got the only Turkish orderly there to show me a bed. I was taken to the bed whereon poor Locke had just died from enteritis and dysentery. They had not even removed the sheets. How I loathed the Turks at that moment. However, I was so tired that I got into bed. In the same room were three Turkish civilians, and two British officers I found next door.

No one appeared. I had left my room in the morning, but by night I had only succeeded in getting some water. By

P

evening the ague had gone, and I wanted some nourishment, and set to prowl around the place to get it. I had plenty of violent scenes, but did not succeed in finding the pantry. I began to believe that I had come to a huge automatic healing establishment where by a series of Christian Scientific brain waves one imagined oneself fed and convalescent. I heard that Locke had been left unattended in his house, after request, four or five days before he was even inspected by the Turkish doctor, and then, on his moving to this hospital, had a reception similar to mine. He died the same evening as he entered.

After my unsuccessful shikar for food through the great building I returned in no amiable mood, and it was then that the humorous gods held high council, and, remembering my opinion on Angora bugs, provided a little joke for themselves afresh. These new bugs were for shock tactics. There was no artillery preparation or demonstration from flank battalions, but suddenly I was awakened from a doze by bitings in fifty places. Leaping out of bed I gathered them up in threes and fours. Tearing my clothes off I caught the rear files before they could get to cover. Undismayed, they renewed the attack as soon as I again tried to sleep. This became too ridiculous. Finally, my language attracted a crowd of laughing Turks, and one informed me in French that the hospital was famous for bugs. The pillow and mattress I discovered to be their first line, but their reserve lines were in the wooden frieze. " Ye gods ! " I thought, " this is too much. Here am I starving and curing myself and doing my best to smile over it when I'm expected to put up a regular hunt ! " I slung the mattress away and, seizing some clothes from a wardrobe outside, with the orderly hanging on to me the while, remade the bed. Still on they came. I decided that if I were Napoleon I would change the Turkish crescent to a bug passant, with that half-comical grin the lions passant have, the near fore paw in the air and face screwed around at you. I collapsed towards dawn with sheer irritation. But in my sleep on they came, on from every wall, from every point of the horizon, from the sky, from beyond the confines of the universe—I myself was becoming a bug—when I awoke with a roar, and saw the Turkish orderly standing beside me grinning. I gave him cigarettes for appreciating a situation

I no longer could myself, and he taught me some more Turkish " Zorari yok " (never mind), and " Yawash " (gently).

I awaited the dawn with an increasing hunger, having now devoured about a handful of lump sugar I had put into my pocket as an emergency ration. The hours crawled by until eleven, when the visiting doctor came.

Now, by this time I had begun to find out a thing or two about the Turk. Unless you ask, he never does anything; if you do, he merely promises he will. Your only chance is to be demonstrative and impress him. This fellow was a robust, bouncing, overfed, callous, perpetual-smile-sort-of-fellow. Waiting until he wished me good morning, I leaped clean out of bed, with a frightful roar that brought a dozen people into the room, and showed him pints of blood—mine and the bugs'—all over the wall, bed, mattress, etc., etc. Then I cursed the place in German, in English, and terrible French, and applied my word, " fenner," vigorously, ending up my objecting to my treatment with gestures, etc., etc. For the first minute or two he laughed, and then he sat down and mopped his forehead and explained he came only once a day, and without an order from him it might have been risky to give me any food, etc. He wrote out a beautiful diet sheet, and sent me some medicine for the colitis. This did me good, certainly, but I waited all day for the milk and cornflour and soup. At five o'clock one small cup of the weakest imaginable tea arrived. Nothing else. It now appeared that an order by the doctor on one day did not take effect until the following day, as they had to send out for supplies. I was really terribly ravenous. That evening, about 8 p.m., when two orderlies brought round a trench table filled with loaves of bread and plates of soup, I waited until they were gone a second and seized a loaf, which I plunged in the soup, and returned to my bed, where I devoured most of it. The other Turks in the room, I believe, informed the orderly, who searched for the remainder of the loaf in my bag ; but we had a wrestle for it, and while he sent out for a posta, I finished it. Later he appeared, laughing, and took some more cigarettes.

The situation developed along these lines until the next morning, when the doctor came again. This time I was coldly indignant, and showed him a letter of complaint to the American Ambassador at Stamboul, and requiring to be sent back to my house. The result was he put me on an enormous diet at once of bread and buffalo meat that would have killed any Englishman, certainly a siege-battered, starved, feverish, colitis-stricken sick man. I distributed my rations among the two officers next door, one of whom was a most congenial person, named Fox—an officer I didn't know in Kut, as he had been in Woolpress most of the time. We had long discussions on Turks and bugs. The next morning another doctor came, and, seeing my diet sheet full, evidently thought the Turkish commissariat couldn't stand this, and discharged me from hospital.

The medicine had done me some good, but otherwise I was weaker on leaving the hospital than entering it. Fox and I trekked back. How glad we were to get out of it ! I had expected an interesting girl in a purdah to look after me, and all kinds of delicacies. One learns apace in these days. On the way we passed Captain Martin, I.M.S., recently arrived, and he sympathized with us, and promised us that in future he would look after us all. I was very glad to regain my room once more. Another small party of relicts had arrived from Angora, amongst whom were Blind Hookey, who was at the Christmas dinner in Kut, and Young Lacy, whom I had left at Samarra. He had had great luck. When he was quit of the fever he had managed to join a small party and was driven the whole way. Our column, including as it did the native officers, and travelling in the wake of the whole division, seems to have had probably the worst time of any, and certainly one saw most of the tragedy of the trek. Our whole house is now pretty full.

August 7th.—Malaria returned. The ague was more severe this time. Quinine we have at last procured in small quantities at the rate of five piastres a cachet, which means that one's malaria medicine bill will be fifteen shillings daily. A cold snap in the weather has sent several others here down with malaria. Kastamuni is said to have a cold winter, so we hope to get this fever quite out of our system. It is raining steadily—the first rain since arriving here.

We have no books as yet, but it is to be hoped the Turks will allow them to come through later on. I have finished the Bible—a complete reading now since Baghdad. What a

vigorous teacher is St. Paul. No mundane considerations
seemed to prevent his putting the true value on this transient
existence, and from that probably sprang the facility with
which he decided always for the Lord.

August 17th.—The mornings continue fine and sunny, but
in the afternoons a sharp, shadowy wind springs up, and the
evenings are quite cold. We are anxiously awaiting the
parcels waylaid in Stamboul. The fever has largely gone,
but muscular rheumatism has taken its place. No one hears
from or is allowed to write to Yozgad or Kara Hissa.

The Turks here seem to have already settled on their plan
of campaign, which is to make us get into debt at huge prices,
which already are increasing. I am, however, assuming a
sublime indifference to money matters. The financial anxiety
of the trek was enough, and I have a long score to pay off
against the Turk in this respect, so once in his debt he will
have to facilitate our getting our money from home, or else
receive cheques.

August 22nd.—On the 18th I attempted a long walk,
permission having been obtained for a party of us to go.
The direction led me over hills towards some pine woods—a
considerable climb for those in our condition. An extraordinary phenomenon common to almost all Kut people,
young and old—but more especially to the young who had
starved on account of enteritis troubles—is their sudden
huge girth expansion. One's figure protrudes like any
Turk's. The fatty foods and weak state of the stomach are
said to be the cause of this.

Still, with fixed determination, the walk party pushed
on, blowing and perspiring. One remembered one's duty
to get fit. At the pine woods one longed to be alone for an
hour—a forgotten pleasure—but we were marshalled like
geese. It is a pleasant spot of young pines and pleasantly
murmuring grassy glades, strewn in places with pine needles,
that gave additional exercise by making one fight for a foot-
hold. Through the opening in the pine wood one saw the
mountainous horizon that ringed us round. Kastamuni
was out of sight somewhere beneath us.

The next day I actually turned out to rugger for our
house, as left wing three-quarter. The delight after all one's
sickness in feeling one's legs really attempting to run was

so encouraging that one Brabazon and I, for dinner, divided a bottle of German beer. This is to become a custom. We played three spells of ten minutes each, and quite enough too—with a ball stuffed with wool, as we had no bladder. Kastamuni is totally hilly, and the footer ground over a mile away, is uneven and stony, but the best we can get. Correct collaring is barred, but we go croppers just the same. On Sunday we went bazaaring, and were allowed to attend church at 6.30, when we sang hymns from memory. The text was : " You are sons of God." We hope to make a little chapel here, by and by.

Hailstones as large as hazel nuts, but not so large as in Kut, made merry music yesterday over the town. The streets then become drains and gutters, as they are intended to. Besides being an economy, it cleans the streets.

What a quaint town this is ! All water is drawn from springs or wells. There are no lights of any kind, except, possibly, some faint glimmer burning from a police station. There are no trams or much vehicular traffic, donkeys being the chief transit. In the early morning one hears the ancient Biblical solid-wheeled oxen cart groaning on its turning axle beneath the weight of a huge tree trunk brought in for firewood. At night the distant tinkling of bells sometimes reaches one as the goats come back. And, later still, over the sheets of darkness in deep, pulsing waves, like the voice of a dark and mysteriously moving spirit, floats the muezzin, which is taken up from mosque to mosque until the whole town echoes with the cry.

I have had some rough chessmen made out of bits of wood, and am settling down to discipline my mind again to some sort of methodical thinking. One feels that some such effort as this stands between us and oblivion.

September 1st.—I am feeling very much better than I have since those awful floods came in Kut that left me legacies of rheumatics, and Heaven knows what else. We play rugger three times weekly, and eat huge teas. One of us makes cakes, another carpenters, another makes jam, and yet another has started tailoring. My present hobby is to get fit and clean my windows and " bazaar." I am putting on flesh, or rather, fat, and must be now a half stone more in weight. But my digestion is still weak, nerves bad, and a periodical pain from my spine.

We have been to a Greek dentist (?) The awful stuff we ate in Kut played havoc with my teeth, which were in rather good condition before. This fellow proposes to crown about half of the back ones, is willing to accept a cheque, and talks frequently in French. These are his distinguishing qualities. He seems everything. Moreover, he will take a live nerve out and think nothing of it. Sometimes he pretends to kill it by pushing in small supplies of something or other which the nerve likes so much that it fattens on it, with the result that it grows so rapidly that soon one's whole body exists as an appendix of the particular nerve! The Turks looted his rooms lately. He has now, in consequence, only a rickety, straight-backed kitchen chair, two bottles, a wheel and string, and about four picks, with which he is very adept, using both ends of each. Altogether the Greeks here are a most disappointing, shifty lot. Poor Greece! where Pericles once lived, and which now exports currants—as they say.

Roumania is in the war at last. Turkey is pretty well on her last legs ; but then, like her carts and donkeys, she always seems good for another few yards. With returning fitness I begin to hate, loathe, detest, and abhor this soul-smothering life. The way the Turk *in authority* treats us, his ignorance of his own mind, his partiality for intrigue and roguery and robbery, as also the way he runs his country, proves him unworthy of Empire. The brains and finance of this country are absolutely Greek or Armenian. The Turk holds the sword, and arrears of mismanagement he puts right by a periodical massacre. He is barbarously ignorant and misinformed. The most worthy fellow is the common soldier, who has some idea of manliness and of service, but the officer and official is a double-edged scoundrel, a smiling, dishonest, lubricous sneak, and totally untrustworthy, also a bad soldier.

The Armenian I would describe as the Jew of Turkey, hence his unpopularity. He hoards money, is indifferent to the military needs or other aspect of the development of the country, except the financial one, and is not without treachery. The Greek is also more able and better educated than the Turk. With the Armenian he does the penmanship of Turkey. He supplies surveyors, artisans, architects ; but he, too, cannot go straight. In fact, I would rather trust a Turkish soldier than any Greek or Armenian. Hundreds of years of oppression have dried up their springs of independent action, and the Armenian goes about in constant fear of massacre ; the Greek just escapes it. They have no thought whatever of throwing off their yoke or leaving the country, although they have nothing in common with their oppressors, and their religious divergence is as wide as it can well be. They hate the Turk, yet choose to suffer. Even among the children we see the tyranny of the Turk. A diversion of ours is to watch the children playing near here. Tiny Turkish boys maltreat and bully big Greek boys and girls, who dare not retaliate.

The explanation of the sorry state of Greece and of the Greeks and Armenians here I believe to be the utter selfishness of the people and their want of public-spirited men. But, if only because they are less unenlightened than their oppressors, reform should be possible to them, and although on looking at the Greeks of the land from Aleppo to Kastamuni, they seem an indifferent lot, still they have in them the seeds of culture and the ardent wish for civilization. On this, then, I believe we can build. The Turk is an interesting study. He is half child and half savage. His predilection and habits are like those of a child. He takes offence at small things, like a child. Like a child, he responds to small favours. And Germany is the last country to take the Turk successfully under her wing. England, I believe, alone could do it. We could utilize the Turkish talent for soldiering and practical affairs, removing from their midst these over-corrupt officials and Government, whom they detest. We should win their confidence by applying rigid and accessible justice between them and the Greek and Armenian, who would find unswerving adherence to law and order unavoidable. Religious toleration we could grant, and I believe that within a few years, Turkey would settle comfortably under our influence, and learn to trust us. But as it is, the country is rotten, the habits rotten, and so many wretched corrupt Turks are in authority, that one feels inclined to sweep them all away.

October 1st.—Loud shouting and cheering and wild stampede towards the restaurant dining-room announced that another mail had come. We all go quite mad on these occasions, and charge past postas, knocking over chairs or each other, and crowd around the table while the letters are given out.

I have heard again from home, written before Kut fell. I wonder what sort of a time they picture me having. Kut still seems to have been kept dark from everybody, and especially so the trek ; but I shall always remember the great thoughtfulness and affection of our friends reaching out to our lonely life across thousands of miles of sea and land. With these letters I am among the heath of Camberley, the hills of New Zealand, and the 'buses of London, once again.

The commandant or kaimakam (colonel) is a foolish and babyish fellow, and also a rogue ; but I, for one, believe he has less vice in him than the other junior officer, Sheriff Bey, who is a dangerous and treacherous villain. The old kaimakam does rake up a smile when we try to be happy, and although the Tartar is often apparent, he has, on occasion, given us such a privilege as a special walk.

We are trying to erect some structure of habits wherein to dwell until God's good time allows us to get away from here. Thus we make cakes twice a week. This will last a little longer until prices become too outrageous. Which makes two events. Church and bazaar and Turkish bath make three more, total of five altogether, and these, scarcely incidents in another's life, but episodes in ours, punctuate the vacuum of time in which we roll. At 6.30 a.m. there is *chota haziri*, tea and toast, for which we have made private arrangements.

Then one smokes or sleeps again. At 9 we have breakfast of eggs and milk and butter and bread. With a posta at our heels we return to our own house, 150 yards away. Then some sleep, some play cards, some merely sit on a chair. Others of us write diaries or re-read an old book. We have lunch of fatty foods and smoke and sleep. We have tea (our own *bandobast* again) after which there may be a walk. We all set off under a guard, and are trying to get farther afield. Once a week a long walk is allowed. On returning some of us change, even if it is to put aside one torn shirt for another or a spare jacket. But in these times I jealously guard every conventional cable that anchors one to the decent life. There is a tendency to allow the coma to steal over one's personality. This, I think, one should combat. Dinner over, we have to wait in the *mektub*, a boresome hour. We attempt bridge or chess. Back again in our room we smoke awhile and sleep. It may read nicely, but in truth, it is a sorry existence. Still, day by day, the structure grows, and who knows, in a few months we may have a palace like the pleasure dome of Kubla Khan !

The extraordinary thing is that one is so secluded. One seems on the other side of creation's wall—in the backwash of the waters. But we all know it only seems so. The stream of Time flows on, sweeping along with it great events in the changing scene from which we here are far removed. I have ever been of a restless nature, and I am told this may operate as a rest cure. One hundred and fifty miles from the nearest railway, and that far from anywhere, locked in by mountains bordering the Black Sea, cut off from papers and books and news, in a town that but awakes and sleeps, with no public institutions or even a picture theatre, one has left for a hobby only the delivery of direct interrogatories to oneself, and the supplying of answers thereto. I believe this is a supreme test of character, and may prove a strength to some and a ruination to others.

Sometimes an event overtakes us. For instance, I have been placed in " gaol " for a short time, and the incident was so funny I must set it down.

One day, while I was filling in notes of this diary, I observed one of the flimsy untied curtains was ablaze. How it started I can only conjecture. Either it blew on to the hot cigarette ash tray, or a hot part of a cigarette must have fallen down near the bed and caught in the curtain. These local cigarettes are wretched things and burn furiously, the head often falling off so that it is a common thing to find one's clothes alight. I ripped the curtain down and stamped it out. The two beds had caught, and the room filled with smoke. I stamped out the fire and doused the bed with water. As it still smouldered I flung it out of the door. And then they came, Turks, choushs, postas, Sheriff Bey, the kaimakam himself, and I began to expect the Sultan. They were very angry, a fire having occurred in the Gurkhas' quarters a few days previously. They persisted in saying I tried to burn the house down and to set fire to Kastamuni. That afternoon a sort of court-martial was made of it, and I was arraigned before the Turkish Commandant, thinking it a delightful joke. Their serious faces amused me. I told them it was an accident, that I was sorry, that I would pay the damage, and after a debate of ordinary budget length, the kaimakam decided to let me off on my paying a lira. (The curtain would have cost about ten piastres, and the bed was only singed.) Then Sheriff Bey stormed and protested for more punishment, and I was sent under an escort after handing over all my smokes and matches, to a dirty iron-barred cellar room in a house used by the kaimakam as an office. It was full of paper, and there was no bed or chair. I had no supplies at all. When I was left in peace I took a copy of Robert Louis Stevenson's " Virginibus Puerisque " from my pocket, and sitting in a corner started to read. Presently I became aware of an eye watching me through the crack. In fact, I was just on the point of lighting up from a spare cigarette case and matches in my hip pocket. The eye changed. Still reading, I observed several peering and whispering, so taking a pencil and paper from my pocket I went through the form of writing a letter to our Foreign Minister via the American Ambassador, complaining of my treatment. Then pointing to the eye, I called for the interpreter, informing him that I wanted this letter to be shown to the kaimakam, and that even if he didn't send it I should take care that our Government took the matter up and dealt with those responsible when I was free. The result was he bolted from the room, and in ten minutes reappeared with a posta, and said I was free. Sheriff Bey met me at the top of the road, and proceeded to harangue me about wanting to frighten me only.

Bluff is the only thing, and their ignorance one's only chance. Since then, however, the kaimakam has treated me with extraordinary respect, so much so, that I have successfully refused to obey his order to pay for what I have not had, *i.e.* food in the *mektub* for all the time I was sick. The best way to treat these Turks is to be distantly polite. Much annoyance and trouble has been caused through some officers chumming up to them, plying them with drinks, and conducting them by the arm here and there. The next day there's a row about some point of pay or privilege, and the Turk thinks himself snubbed. The net result is that the Turk, being our captor, is in much the better position to hit back. This he does vigorously, with insulting titles and notices that make life a great burden. Some of their notices posted up in the *mektub* are screamingly funny. The following are actual samples, with spelling corrected—

1. "English imprisoned officers cannot only please themselves by disobeying the Turkish posta who have the order of them. Neither can they go past the posta or outside the door. In which case the posta can beat them with the stick or rough handle the officer or officers concerned."

2. "English officers ought to pay their money willingly. Why do they have the trick of deceiving the peasants and poor Turkish subjects, which is dishonest?

(Sd.) "TEUFIK,
"Kaimakam."

3. "Officers cannot talk to any one except themselves, strong punishments will pursue swiftly. What is the use of pouring dirty water into the street? Surely they need not chivvy 'bints' in the bazaar, and officers educated in London could know better. When officers go for a walk in charge of a posta they shall not go to the front or the posta gets behind in which case the posta has orders to shoot or remonstrate with the culprit. Let every one pay the price in the bazaar and let them pay all their money to Usnu, the contractor, who is not a robber.

(Sd.) "TEUFIK,
"Kaimakam."

4. "It has been taken to my notice that English officers never stop kicking up a shinty (shindy) in their rooms. Cards will be stopped. Let us not play cards or kick up any more shindy. You shall behave civilized."

5. "In future great supplies of liquor and cognac will not be drunk by our order as the floor of the school will go through. In which case the officers concerned cannot hold Turkish authorities responsible if they meet death. Also punishment must be given. Officers will be always tidy the room. Why choose the pig-stye? This is also a punishable affair.

(Sd.) "TEUFIK,
"Commandant."

6. " Officers are allowed the bath and bazaar and footer. Why not go about properly dressed. Surely no hat or in the hand is not properly dressed. Sticks are forbidden and officers cannot walk with sticks. It is forbidden to get drunk or sing as the noise stops the sleep of neighbours. If a fire starts it goes. Therefore don't smoke in bedrooms for God sake.

(Sd.) " TEUFIK,
" Commandant,
" British Prisoners' Camp."

And so on. The explanation of these extraordinary documents is that some of the postas (bluebottles we call them) being old dug-outs, can't keep up with us when we walk, and trail out behind. The people in the town do us down at every turn, and we have to argue and bargain to get anything. In fact, we enjoy it. As regards the noise, some of us have a sing-song on every other Saturday in the *mektub*, and the Turks fear our applause may be too much for the floor. Regarding the "binks" we, not having spoken to the gentler sex from periods ranging to two years, have taught some Greek dreadnoughts to wish us good morning. The fire episode was, of course, due to me. Their Captain, Sheriff Bey, is the source of most of the trouble, and he stirs up the old kaimakam. Sheriff Bey is captain of the guard, and is at once treacherous and spiteful. To be sure he had for a time captured the ear of a few of our officers who were misled by his lubricity and perpetual smiles. He fawns upon them, defaming his own country, which he predicts will be finished in a few weeks, and has decided to leave Turkey after the war. I loathed the man more than ever on hearing him speak of his country so. They say he is spying on the kaimakam in order to get his command.

On arriving here we all hoped to get away within a few weeks, as there was rumour of an advance in the West. At present, however, the indications are, at any rate, for a winter campaign.

CHAPTER X

*F*EBRUARY 1st, 1917.—Four months have gone. As I write the earth is white with feet of snow. It is a white world, the roofs no longer brown, the trees no longer green, for even those few trees, like pines that have not shed their verdure, have donned the white raiment of winter's carnival. Snow! This pure and godly element, silent and secretive, the *avant-courrier* of the Ultimate, of Things doomed, one day to be reclaimed by the once again triumphant elements when, from the dome of the universe, the last white great snow sheets shall fall, fall, fall—and this universe, once again locked in the ice-grip of the Snow God, shall drive forward mysteriously on its lonely way—lonely for it shall have been separated from Life, and the Spirit, Man, will have gone.

As I look out on the undulating expanse terraced down to me from the mountain horizon to the northward, I am for a minute tempted to believe that the Great Snow Deluge has really come, and I alone am awake to behold it. But looking still closer I see tiny windows peeping out from their white frames, and I know the bees within that human hive are having their winter sleep. With an effort I trace among the smothered definition of the buildings, the snowed-up roads and alleys, and rising above it all I see, scattered over the town, the white upright minarets of the mosques. Kastamuni in winter-time is a picturesque Turkish town, and has a character all its own. The streets are deserted, but on the hill-path white-mottled figures move slowly upwards. It is the hour of prayer, and the *muezzin* has just begun to swell out in icy circles from the minarets, reaching out to the hearts of the prayerful, and calling them to communion with Allah. *La*

WINTER

illa ha, illa la. There is but one God, and that is God. From
how many thousands of mosques, and for how many millions of
the followers of the prophet does the *muezzin* cry at this hour?

And so I, too, find my silence unlocked after all these months
and am at last persuaded to throw off the coma that has
been stealing over us body and soul, that has buried beneath
its snow-drift our intentions one by one, and I am tempted
to jot down a few more notes to my reminiscences.

Sometimes, as the other day, we are allowed to take down
the bob-sleighs we have made to a hill about a mile away,
and pretend we are schoolboys again. After snowballing the
starters and getting snowballed ourselves, we shot down the
slope or over the bank, as the case occurred, and once or
twice we collided, but no one got seriously hurt. The hard
toiling uphill again, pulling the sleigh, proved how unfit we
were. On the way home we religiously snowballed every
fowl we passed, and the roads are full of them. The days
are dreadfully dreary, and it is only these events that seem
to lighten the monotonous gloom. Firewood is very scarce
and expensive, and only on rare occasions do we have a fire
worth anything. If we do by chance have wood it is often
wet, and the wretched tin stoves choke the place with smoke.
I half decided to have a stove in my bedroom, but, besides
that being fearfully small, the trouble is to get wood, which
comes in tiny donkey loads at fictitious prices. So we lie
in bed under the clothes, and with the intense cold sleep
steals over us. There is the same difficulty in getting kerosene, now five shillings a bottle, and what one gets either
goes out, or splutters until you kick it out. We hibernate,
therefore. Once or twice it has been so cold that I have gone
down to the kitchen and sat by the smoke heap there. This
is very popular these days.

Letters are turning up more regularly. I am delighted
to have at last heard from home and several friends all over
the world, including the brilliant author of " Problems of
Philosophy." He has very kindly sent me some books and
recommends me to see Schiller on "Grumps." I also heard
from Wallace, from whom I have not heard for years and
years, and to whom I wrote in Kut along with people in the
neglected recesses of my memory, but the letter, of course,
was never sent. It must be eleven years since he and I sat

on the golden sand of a green-vestured island in that silvery sea around Auckland—smoking our pipes as we lay on our backs, and filling in with a wish what we wanted to complete the scene. I remember wanting the suitable girl, but he wanted books and debate. In between are my world travels, and Cambridge, and Germany, and now I've been running about in a war, and he, since a professor in Princetown, writes to condole with me at being out of the war so early! He ought to congratulate me on my luck in staying in it so long. But then, of course, he can't know anything about Kut yet.

It seems I have been reported dead in Kut, and again on the trek, and in England they are only just hearing to the contrary. What an unnecessary suspense for one's people! Mine have been magnificent, even throughout the long period of tragic rumour.

About my other friends at Cambridge, and in the regiment, and in France, I never hear a word.

Parcels have arrived, thank Heaven, from several friends. Sir Thomas Mackenzie has been a perfect trump, and the most wonderful and thoughtful parcels from a very kind heart in Australia. The first three or four have arrived. My dear old friends, the Pallisers, remember me faithfully. And Lord Grey, not forgetting the lonely subaltern in the middle of Asia who once held forth on Imperial affairs sketched out by the cloistered lawns of the Cam, has sent me kind messages and a fortnightly parcel. One's emotions of thankfulness and gratitude are infinite. I feel it is my duty to buck up every ounce possible when one of the busiest and most over-worked men in England, in indifferent health, too, finds time to think of a worthless subaltern like me. My Camberley friends also have sent me some parcels, and some wonderful letters. These momentous things happen only once in a while, but when they do they tell us that somewhere beyond these snow-bound mountains are English hearts that are glad we are come through so far, which means they know we have tried and are chiefly sorry we are chained because we can't try again.

Some few books have also arrived from time to time, but only old ones are allowed through, though sometimes we manage to conceal one or two. This, however, is very difficult, as all parcels have to be opened before the Turkish authorities. We have formed a library, and the indefatigable librarian, Herepath, who catalogues the books and *shikars* every one a moment overdue, caused us infinite delight months ago by placing in the library most of Kipling's works which he had miraculously brought through with him from Kut. We devour anything in the reading line, especially now, as bridge has fallen off.

None of the many books sent to me have turned up so far, and have probably been intercepted at Constantinople, whither even those that do arrive here have to be sent back for censorship.

No games outside except an occasional soccer match are played now as the ground is too hard. One highly interesting tournament was, however, recently completed. Eight soccer teams participated, and we ran two bookies on the field. I have not played since Christmas Day when, in getting down to a forward rush, I had several giants on top of me and twisted my knee badly. Just before this, however, as left three-quarter in a match against the Lower House I scored one of the hardest tries since I was a boy. One can't run much these days, but I did it diving for the line as a nailed fist left four ruddy tracks from my neck down my back. Even then we lost the match by two goals to a goal and a try. I came to the conclusion that my conceit was excusable.

Christmas passed quietly enough. We consumed a tremendous amount of cognac and mastik, and anything else going, regardless of price, and for a few hours we quite took charge of things. There was a concert of sorts with a few banjo items and a farce at the end which was more ridiculous than funny, but it served as well.

On Christmas Eve we eluded the postas, and about midnight, while trying to correct my bearings for the house, for I had somehow got downhill, I saw a figure of him we call the Admiral (a naval paymaster), who evidently having wearied of trying to discipline his legs had given it up and was crawling vigorously on all fours in the dark. The sight of this white figure crawling mysteriously along in the darkness, believing himself unobserved, made me shout with laughter. The Admiral put on a huge spurt when he heard it !

But the feature of Christmas was the children's party we

Q

gave by special leave of the kaimakam. For days we had been cooking tartlets and cakes and macaroons. They knew it was on, and before breakfast a big crowd of children and mothers had accumulated near our alley-way. We took our long table and spread upon it " our events," as we called them, including apples and special quantities of milk and nuts. The poor little wretches are half-starved. For weeks previously we had given them bits of bread, so that each one of us had an " adopted " nipper. But besides our little pals—mostly Greek, but some Turks—dozens of youngsters from far and wide had turned up, some in their mothers' arms. Sam Mayo, an ex-sergeant-major, took charge and formed them into column of route, mothers and all. He did splendidly. There was much crying and yelling, but he got them in order and then made them file past. I don't think we had laughed so much for many months. Each one of us soon found himself administering milk to a monthling in one arm with half a dozen brats into one's pockets or wrestling with one's legs at the same time. Once there was a stampede set up by a " Young Turk Party " (boys of eight and upwards), and we each had to grab all the mites by a leg or an arm and hold them up out of harm's way. One or two got a bit squashed as it was. The supreme joke was when Sam was proudly showing us how to coax a tiny infant to eat a macaroon ; it got so enthusiastic as to bite a half inch of his thumb nearly off. " The little devil nipped like a mongoose," yelled Sam, upsetting his second youngster into the sweet rock that stuck *en bloc* to its head. We enjoyed ourselves as much as they. The postas, with one or two exceptions, helped us. The poor little wretches ate and drank as if they hadn't for a week at least. Then we had a scramble among the larger children for the nuts and surplus, and when the fights had subsided gave them some piastre notes. Altogether it was a great show and made us very happy.

The people, we hear, couldn't understand at first how war veterans could worry about children. But you require to be a prisoner of war with no privilege of speaking to any one, adult or child, to understand the meaning of children. The after result was that for days and days a huge swarm of youngsters followed us everywhere we went yelling " Backsheesh " and " Ekmek " (bread) and " Chocolate."

Shortly after Christmas an Armenian turned up with a violin of sorts. I had been on the look-out for one for months. He wanted a fictitious price, and it wasn't a good one but fairly loud. The strings were on the wrong pegs, and such strings surely never existed before on any violin. The bow wanted some hair restorer badly. I tuned it up and powdered the few remaining hairs well on a lump of gummy resin, probably off a pine-tree, and then, by the smoking stove of a Turkish fire, I began to play—the first time for years and years. The room was empty but every one came up from below to see what on earth had happened. I found I had forgotten everything. After a half-hour bits of Beethoven, Raff, Dvorak and Vieuxtemps came back to me, but they wanted waltzes and marches. The end of it was they persuaded me to buy the thing. I practised assiduously for two or three hours a day for weeks and then the bow began to collapse and the strings gave out.

It was now dreadfully cold in one's room, but we managed to have some cheery evenings. Banjos made of hide stretched over tins purchased at the bazaar did quite well for an accompaniment. One of our number, Lieutenant Munro, has shown a deal of skill in cabinet making, and has turned out a 'cello which is the queerest thing in the whole world, looking rather like a dough roll squeezed considerably in the middle by a small boy until its waist threatens to go altogether. But it makes a noise. My violin is improving wonderfully, and I have found some bad strings in an Armenian shop.

In other words, my violin has grown to a band composed of two violins, a 'cello, a cracked flute, a clarionet, and banjos. The Admiral plays a little, and having unearthed another fiddle has come in as second violin. Major Davis plays the violin a little, and we are going to fossick others out. Drums are under construction, and another 'cello is to follow. Remains the music. As none has ever been seen in Kastamuni probably since the town existed, nor can be obtained anywhere or is allowed through, we have to write our own. This involves composition. There was luckily a volume of Prout's Harmony that turned up at Christmas, so one or two with leisure hours are working at it hard. We have had five practices. I never could have believed I would endure such an offensive noise, let alone help to make it! " Dreaming " and

"Destiny" and "The Girl on the Film" were the first things we attempted. It was a thin stream of trickling melody followed by the weirdest of side noises!

How dreadfully cold it is, and how interminably long the winter seems! Malaria and colds have pursued us. Our boots have collapsed everywhere, and the few pairs in the bazaar cost over eight liras. Here, again, we have fallen back on ourselves, and two officers started repairing in an institution called the "Snob's Shop." They are now quite good at it, and turn out really fine work. The only leather obtainable, however, is rotten local stuff.

Other prices have risen steadily. The wretched tea available is about two liras a pound, and there is little of that. Sugar is ten shillings a pound, coffee dearer than tea, meat two shillings a pound, and wood works out at about three-pence a stick. The wonder is how all these people live. Many are pinched and haggard, and funeral processions in the snow are more frequent. The Turkish contractor at the *mektub* has been playing the extortionate *rôle*, and for weeks we have threatened to strike and had meeting after meeting. The net result has been to get the Turks' backs up against us, and it seems evident enough that the military authorities are in the financial swim with the fleecers. We have almost decided to mess ourselves—the chief objection to this being that every obstacle will be put in our way and prices will go up accordingly in the bazaar.

The other day we were allowed our permitted long walk and took the direction of the pine woods, away up the long ascent. We trod in young snow a few inches deep. It was a glorious walk with the tiny bronze pines peeping through the white sheets that stretched from horizon to horizon over hill and valley. We climbed until on a patch of upland from which the sun had ousted the snow, thousands of tiny crocuses invited us to stop and listen to their premature whispers of spring. But since then winter seems to have fastened on us another clutch of unmistakable proprietorship. On our way back we stopped at our cemetery, which has gradually grown larger since we came. Last November the survivors of the unfortunate yacht *Nida* reached us. She had struck a mine near Alexandretta and lost half her crew. The commander had a terribly rough trip here, and the disaster seemed to have preyed upon his mind. He died in the hospital here, poor fellow. Recently we buried a gunner orderly arrived from Angora. He had belonged to the 82nd R.F.A., and came with the last batch allowed us by the authorities as the result of continuous applications. The reports they brought of the men were simply terrible. Hundreds of them seem to have perished in the cold. The sick were allowed to die without any attention whatever. A daily loaf of bread and one blanket, and often no medical care at all, had accounted for hundreds. Whole regiments are wiped out. Father Tim and the Reverend Wright, who were recently ordered to Kara Hissah for the other officers, managed to get a line back to us to the effect that the reports about the men were true. Rumours are in the air that General Townshend has gone home on parole and is arranging for us to be exchanged or go to a neutral country. One can't hope for that. We have heard in the bazaar that Kut once more is in our hands. Thank God !

May 1st.—At last the winter has gone, but it went slowly and fought a strenuous rearguard action up to quite recently. How jolly it is to have dismantled those wretched tin stoves and be able to write and read in one's room once more. Walks have been resumed, and lead us even further and further afield. Many changes have overtaken us—changes seemingly insignificant and yet to us very momentous. We started to run our own mess in February, the Turks taking away all our Turkish and Greek servants and making us rely on our own orderlies. They prove themselves more childish and more babyish every week. An inquiry was held into affairs here, and the old kaimakam was thrown out, but Sheriff Bey, the worst of all, lied his way into remaining. Our new kaimakam is a more decent fellow, speaks German, and has lived in Berlin for four years. We have had him up to dinner, and it fell to me to do all the talking to him about Berlin. He means well, and has done all he can to help us, but he is so dreadfully afraid of Sheriff Bey and his own restrictions.

The band has made great strides. I'm now first violin and leader of the " Orchestra." We have five violins, two 'cellos and a double bass, besides the drums, two clarionettes, flute, and banjo, and the Human Crochet has made commendable progress in writing out our music from bits of anything we got through the post, piano solos, and many we have

had to write from memory.   We perform on Saturday evenings
alternately at either house.   Sometimes we sound almost like
a seaside band at Home ! ! !   I long for the old Queen's Hall
Concerts again.   To attend even those, I would willingly
forget the London Symphony or Nikisch's at the Gewandhaus
in Leipsig.   The band is almost the only live thing here.   One
pines for music.   Every evening I can get (so to speak) with
my violin beyond these forests and mountains.   My window
overlooks the town and I have quite an audience of Turkish
heads listening.   I am told the sound carries as far as the
muezzin.   These people have not heard any music in their
lives, and think my crude efforts quite divine.   Books arrive
slowly.   Swinburne has never come.   But we have Shakespeare and some of Thackeray and a lot of cheap stuff.

With the advent of spring we all responded to the call and
took fresh hope and formed new resolves.   Amongst them I
started a fortnightly paper called *Smoke*, the Kastamuni
Punch and *Tatler*.   In a rash moment I finally consented to
the " General's " request, the General being Captain Kirkwood, our Mess-President.   So far it has been a decided
success.   Our artist was an officer from the Lower House
whose handy pen finished the cartoon and illustrated the serial
and verse.   The paper was not wholly given to ragging and
joking, but in a serious corner we discussed aspects of Kut
and the Trek and Kastamuni and the war.   We also ran fictitious
notes from Kara Hissa, Yozgad, Brusa (where the generals are),
and " Eve " of the *Tatler* finally came to live in Kastamuni to
cheer us up with a certain famous chaperone called " The
Destroyer."   The most popular article amongst our own mess
was the current one called " The Oblong Table," at which we
all sat—King Arthur, Sir John Happy Tight, Sir Saundontius
the Good, Sir Sulphurous Blears, Sir Bedevere le Géant, Sir
Leslie Bec de Canard, Sir Cliftus Smallkake, Sir Samuel
Longbow, Sir Carol le Filbert, Sir Richard Oldlace, Sir Pompous
Oldass, Sir Lancelot the Bard, Sir Galahad the Silent, and Sir
Rufus Appletree.   And we lived well up to the best traditions
of the Round Table, and conversations and jests and challenges
flew to and fro.   But altogether it is rather a sweat, as I have
to do the whole thing, and then it has to be copied out again
by some one with a decent caligraphy.   Great care has to be
taken to keep it out of the Turks' hands.

I have also worked on a further constitutional study of the possible Society of Nations or International Body, following out constitutional developments and tendencies as revealed by the war since my pre-war work " The Place of International Law in Jurisprudence."

And so what with the band and *Smoke* and this diary and bits of French and my law work, I have plenty to do.   I am only wondering how long it will be before these, too, follow the rest of our enterprises to oblivion.   It is true that one's springs of action seem almost run out, and that with leading this dreary existence the iron of Kastamuni has already eaten into the souls of many.   The psychology of a captive is an extraordinary one.

At night-time, when the last tremors of the muezzin have died away and all is still, we sometimes fancy we can hear the echoes of those great events that are rearranging the world, the crashing of nations in mortal combat, the battle cries of men fighting for their faith, the death cries of the fallen, above all, the cannon cacophany of the fire deluge.

And from here in the backwater of the world, without news or knowledge, our hearts go out to our countrymen on the other front, and we pray to God that we may soon be amongst them again.

CHAPTER XI

SMOKE was the Kastamuni *Punch*, which I edited. Its existence became known to the Turks, who tried by every means to discover it. When I escaped from the prison in Stamboul, I had it around my waist. Unwilling to risk its capture in my subsequent adventures, I entrusted it to some one in Stamboul, from where it was safely recovered after the entry of the British troops. The photos are of the original copy and the extracts perpetrated by me.

* * *

(1) Letter from " Eve," whom to cheer our loneliness we transported to live amongst us in Kastamuni.

> 201, Curzon Street,
> Mayfair,
> May 28th, '17.

DEAR MR. SMOKE,

Such wonderful news for you. I'm to leave for Kastamuni in two days. Think of it, my dear. For Kastamuni and all of you. Almost *too* wonderful, isn't it ? You know by the time the third edition of *Smoke* arrived home it became quite well known that you were incorporated with the *Tatler*, and, of course, you and I are naturally expected to become awfully interested in each other. Also by a marvellous bit of planning on the part of Providence at the same time Mrs. Huntingdon-East received such an extraordinarily warm-hearted letter from a Mr. Carol Manrow of Kastamuni (do you know him ?), begging her to visit Kastamuni and prescribe for his (little Carol's, if you please) loneliness, and also—but I mustn't tell you too much, must I ?

LETTER FROM "EVE," PHOTOGRAPHED FROM "SMOKE," THE KASTAMUNI "PUNCH"

Oh, and we just love *Smoke*. Well, you know, the next day I met the Destroyer at tea, *i.e.* Mrs. H. E., because she's always under full sail, or whatever you call it. She has persuaded my friends to make me go with her. But, my dear, I was only too *delighted* to go, and I do so want to see all the dear things in that wonderful little place. Oh, I'm so glad you are incorporated with the *Tatler*, and that I am to tattle for you. The Women War Workers' Association has arranged for the Destroyer to look after me. Can you imagine that ? But I shan't stretch my reins until I am safe with you all, and then we shall see what pace is to be set in Kastamuni.

I'm to send news to the *Tatler* as ever, and a column for you on local gossip or fashionable intelligence. The last sounds the best. Our spare time you must make interesting for us, and as we are to have *carte blanche* from our funny old enemies, we can promise you a terrific time. And such news I've got for you—just *too* exciting.

We leave in two days via Boulogne, Paris, Berne, Vienna, Constanti, and Ineboli—and the Sultan has offered the Destroyer the use of his private yacht, *Abdul Hamid Secundus*. We *screamed* when we got his wire. So nice of him, and he hopes to find us " chic." Just fancy the Destroyer being chic. And we are to remain with you all until you go away. Isn't that splendid ?

Thank you so much for your long wire. So *thoughtful* of you, but, my dear, I'm not a bit shy, and I've not forgotten you. In fact, 1 have tried to dream about you quite often. Please try to believe this. We are to have the Vali's old house, whatever that means. The Destroyer is a dear old thing, and, of course, I leave all the arrangements to her. She sends a message. " Give the dear things my love, and tell them to pray that the weather will be good and the Black Sea smooth."

Well, I must away to pack. Such appalling weather here, and we have no potatoes. But no one cares the tiniest bit, as the news is dreadfully good. The one drawback is that the war will be over before we have finished the wonderful time we shall all have in Kastamuni.

Bye-bye, dear Mr. Smoke.

Yours with love,

EVE.

* * *

(2) Advertisement of Kuttites Klearout Kompany, Unlimited.

KASTAMUNI KUTTITES KLEAROUT KOMPANY, UNLIMITED

OBJECT, To defray the expenses of constructing, furnishing,
and equipping

The " HOMEWARD BOUND " Airship.

PROPOSED CAPITAL, £2000 (Turkish).

Consisting of 1000 Fully-Paid Preference and 1000 Ordinary
Shares.

TERMS, Preference Fully Paid, Ordinary Five per cent. on
allotment.

Balance after the War.

CONDITIONS, The investment in twenty shares will carry
the privilege of one seat in the " Homeward Bound," to
leave Kastamuni at some date unknown.

N.B.—In the event of having to jettison ballast from the
airship, Preference Shareholders will not be rated as ballast
until Ordinary Shareholders have been thrown overboard.

ADVANTAGES, On the back of every coupon will be found a
policy of insurance with the Credit Ottoman Insurance
Company covering risks against (1) Recapture, (2)
Collision, (3) Fire, (4) Cherif Bey, (5) Drowning,
(6) Falling Overboard, (7) Landing in Enemy Country.

Last date of Application for Shares, May 10th, 1917.

Original Allottees : (Katronides) The Rt. Hon. Marquis-de-
Quinine ; (Cloulourides) Vicomte-de-Moular and five
Field Officers.

Bankers : Kastamuni Providential Banking Co., Ltd.

Secretary : A. Fludd,
47.8.9 *Smoke* Offices.

* * *

KASTAMUNI KUTTITES KLEAROUT KOMPANY
(AN ESCAPE ADVERTISEMENT FROM "SMOKE")

(3) SATIRE'S MY WEAPON, BUT I'M TOO DISCREET
TO RUN AMOK AND TILT AT ALL I MEET

THE WINGS OF A DOVE (Leading Article)

Had I the wings of a dove, far, far would I fly—away from this dove-cot—from the Mekhteb and memories of Huznu—from the Turkish bath fond joy of earlier days, away from the chapel that has so often seen me, but now to see me no more, from the bazaar where in days of yore I visited Ekki Bachouk's, from the postas and Turkish female delights untasted—from the band—ah, band of memories—most of all from the Oblong Table—in short, from the Flesh and the Devil far, far would I fly.

Ah, those wings. I feel them already upon me. Like a bird I feel also my capacity for flight. Wings that lie closely to my shoulders, white pinions the outer ribs in stiff strong rows, beside them smaller ones lighter than air, stronger than steel, folding like a fan, opening like an umbrella, locked and fast. Wings flinging arced shadows, wings with which to issue some early morn from my window, to cleave the air, to mount up, up, up above these mosques, the river, the town, until Kastamuni shall appear a wee pattern of dusky patch-work crossed by a silver thread and dotted with woolly smoke. Wings to lift me so high that even that shall disappear—and beyond the ranges will gleam the sea. Ah, the sea. How I long for thee also. Since when have I walked within range of thy tossing spray, thou sea skirting the crimson battlefields of Europe. Thee would I follow until in the last light of even I beheld once more " that isle set in a silver sea—— "

Oh, for the wings of a dove. Far, far would I fly. Oh, to be a dove. I, too, would stop to pluck an olive leaf, and on it would scratch with my beak, *Mene, Mene, Tekel, Upharsin,* and then having reached Potsdam, would I drop it at the Kaiser's feet as he strolls about the palace grounds of Sans-souci. Sans-souci, forsooth!

Then would he not conquer the world any more, but wring the necks of all his eagles.

And then on to other isles and scenes, whence the voices are calling——

Oh, for the wings, those free white wings of a dove.

* * *

(4) A Prophecy as to the Fate of Turkey.

THE DEATH OF COCK TURKEY

(With apologies to Cock Robin)

" Who killed Cock Turkey ? "
  " I," said Bull Jack,
  " With my usual knack—
I killed Cock Turkey."

" Who helped to do it ? "
  " I," said old Bruno,
  " With my little U know—
I helped to do it."

" Who saw him die ? "
  " I," said her ally,
  With perfectly dry eye—
" I saw him die."

" Who'll have his feathers ? "
  " I," said the Lion,
  " With my usual try-on,
I'll have his feathers."

" Who'll dig his grave ? "
  " I," said the vulture,
  An eagle plus culture—
" I'll dig his grave."

" Who'll grow on his grave ? "
  " I," said the Lily,
  She spoke quite shrilly—
" I'll grow on his grave."

" Who'll write his epitaph ? "
  " I," said the Armenian,
  With the help of the Athenian—
" I'll write his epitaph."

" Who's heir-apparent ? "
   " I," said Uncle Sam,
   " I guess that I am
The heir-apparent."

" Who'll toll the knell ? "
   " I," said the Kangaroo,
   " With the help of the Emu,
I'll toll the knell."

And the Things of the Earth danced in ecstasy—
   When they heard of the death of the Cock Turkey—
      When they heard of the death of the Cock Turkey.
PACIFIC BILLOW.
April, 1917.

*_**

(5) Breach of Promise Case.

KING'S BENCH DIVISION

Mr. Justice Owes-Leigh.

Sonia *alias* the Fair Girl *v.* Bimbashi Stew-Hot.

Damages for Breach of Promise.

Counsel for plaintiff, Mr. Wm. Sykes, K.C., of Dukes. The defendant defended himself, and was assisted, where necessary, by the learned judge.

Mr. Sykes, on traversing the Statement of Claim, alleged that the plaintiff had been wrongfully deceived by certain overtures and advances on the part of the defendant in that he had, on many occasions, smiled at her, gesticulated towards her, called her " choke guzelle," winked, and even kissed his fingers at her when the postas were not looking. Moreover, written evidence of a formal declaration of affection and willingness to marry was in possession of the plaintiff. For these reasons, submitted Mr. Sykes, an offer of the contract of matrimony had been made by the defendant and accepted by the plaintiff. The defendant was unwilling to fulfil—or at least hung fire—plaintiff estimated her damages at piastres 500.

The defendant, who was evidently a humorist, was understood to demur.

Mr. Sykes then called his chief witness, the plaintiff, the Fair Girl herself. Her appearance caused a great sensation in the court. There came a dream in daisy-patterned chintz, the pattering of small red-stockinged feet, and a dainty whiff of garlic streamed over the court as the fragile and closely-hooded damsel clambered into the witness-box. Then, and not till then, she threw back her veil, and the whole court beheld, or rather heard, a tone poem of superlative beauty—a song without words. Her striking looks affected the public queerly, who fell to digging one another in the ribs, and the learned judge had twice to threaten to clear the court.

She answered her counsel's questions firmly and sweetly. The defendant then put her through the following cross-examination, by the help of an interpreter.

" Sonia, do you love me ? " (Violent nods.)

" How can you love me when I haven't talked to you ? "

" You tried to kiss me."

" Who stopped me ? "

" The postas."

" Do you want to marry everybody who kisses you ? "

" Certainly not. Some kiss for fun, and some for love."

" How could I marry you when I am already married ? " The learned judge here intervened to the effect that in Turkey a man might have several wives.

A question was now put by defendant to the witness with reference to other affections, but was disallowed. Plaintiff was now required to produce the written evidence, but counsel for plaintiff, springing to his feet, opposed this proceeding as violating the religious law of the plaintiff's sect. He was over-ruled by the learned judge, and the witness produced from her stocking a piece of crumpled paper. All eyes were turned on the defendant, and it seemed now improbable that he could win his case. However, after some delay, and much to the embarrassment of plaintiff's counsel, and to the amusement of the rest of the court, the paper was found to be an old laundry list of the defendant, which he may or may not have dropped accidentally.

At this point a startling revelation was made in Mr. Sykes' re-examination of plaintiff to the effect that witness had been twice actually kissed by the defendant, and a collar stud of his, retained in plaintiff's possession, was produced in court.

The defendant, who had hitherto conducted an able defence, was considerably put out by the last fact, and applied to the learned judge for special permission further to question the plaintiff. This being given, the Bimbashi severely taxed the witness as to her means of support, and several times the learned judge had to intervene on plaintiff's behalf. The questions were satisfactorily answered, and the witness left the box.

Mr. Sykes summed up in a manner so scathing that the Bimbashi was heard to interrupt the court by saying that he wished both Mr. Sykes and he himself had never been born. Counsel was well into his final peroration, when he chanced to refer to the plaintiff's "rosy innocence," which, on being interpreted to the Fair Girl, caused her to burst out laughing. On being admonished by the learned judge, she inquired of Mr. Justice Owes-Leigh whether the picture of her counsel, Mr. Sykes, talking of innocence, was not too funny even for a Turk. This caused a counter-sentiment in favour of the Bimbashi, and closed the case for the plaintiff.

The defendant, a man of mischievous disposition, and inclined to be humorous, opened his defence by reciting Wordsworth's "We are Seven," and had got well into Mrs. Hemans' "The Graves of a Household," when the learned judge asked what this had to do with the case.

"Nothing, my lord. I am merely making an impression." Upon which the learned judge dropped on him like a chimney, and Mr. Sykes suggested the defendant had tried to make an impression on the Fair Girl.

Unabashed, the defendant proceeded with his case, which was—

(1) That he had said or done nothing to encourage the plaintiff.

(2) If he had done so he had not meant it.

(3) If he had meant to do so he had had no idea——

"You are wasting the time of this court," thundered the learned judge, and demanded the line of defence.

"I have no defence, my lord."

"Then why on earth are you fighting the case?"

"I'm not fighting anybody. I am willing to marry her on certain conditions."

The elucidation of these conditions necessitated the

clearance of the court, and for some time the case was heard *in camera*. However, it is generally known that the learned judge himself re-examined both parties, as a result of which the Fair Girl admitted to being secretly in love with a gendarme, and flatly declined to marry the defendant. The case was dismissed without costs on either side. Counsel for plaintiff explained that the officers of Kastamuni had subscribed the amount of plaintiff's court costs. A question by the Bimbashi as to whether plaintiff's counsel had received his professional costs from the Fair Girl was disallowed by the learned judge. Counsel for plaintiff, who became greatly heated, was distinctly heard by some to say something about "a jealous counsel," but the remark evidently did not reach the ears of Mr. Justice Owes-Leigh.

The court rose, and the Fair Girl, whose nerve possibly failed at the last moment, went out on her counsel's arm.

* * *

(6) Knights of the Oblong Table.

THE OBLONG TABLE

KNIGHTS AT MESS (Subject: Pooling of Parcels)

KING ARTHUR (*a three-parcel wallah with designs on Sir Saundontius the Good, a fourteen-parcel wallah*): Gentlemen, I propose that in future all parcels are pooled in the mess. (*Loud protests and uproar.*)

SIR SAMUEL LONGBOW: No, I'm against that. Fancy dividing two tins of sardines amongst fourteen.

SIR CLIFTUS SMALLKAKE: Well, I'll tell you this much, I shan't give mine up. One cake wouldn't feed two knights.

SIR SULPHUROUS BLEARS: Blank your blankety blank. I'm for pooling the blankety blanks, blank it.

SIR EDWARD LE FUMEUR: I've a chicken, that means a bone each.

SIR POMPOUS OLDASS TO SIR S. BLEARS: How many parcels have you received?

SIR SULPH. BLEARS: None, you blank-headed blankety blank.

SIR LESLIE BEC DE CANARD: Very good idea. I've got flea powders and thirst quenchers. Pool 'em, with pleasure.

"KING ARTHUR'S KNIGHTS OF THE OBLONG TABLE" IN OUR MESS. THE HILLS OF KASTAMUNI IN THE DISTANCE!

MERMAID READING "SMOKE"

Sir Rufus Appletree : I've had no parcels. Even if I had I would have pooled them. (*Laughter and exclamations.*)

Sir Shinytop Stewartus (*who sits next King A. and knows that in any case Royalty appropriates*) : Hear, hear, let's pool them.

Sir Carol Cœur de Lion : I'm not afraid of speaking my mind. I'm against it, as I don't approve of socialism or cheap parcels.

Sir Saundontius the Good (*fourteen-parcel wallah, and feeling under the circumstances that he had better go no further than timidly venturing to agree with the last speaker*) : I hardly think so, Sir King, Old Thing. One tin of jam would last me for a week, but the mess scarcely one minute. (*Storm grows wilder, the only voices for the affirmative being those who up to date have received no parcels.*)

King Arthur (*much annoyed, and seeing a way of retreat, in a whisper to Sir Shinytop*) : Pass the word it's only a ramp against Saundontius. (*The murmur grows to one of general accord and cry of " Pool 'em."*)

Sir Saundontius (*an excellent thought-reader, aside to Sir Sulph. Blears*) : Pass the word the ramp is only an excuse of King A. to get his point. Ramp or no ramp, the vote will count.

King Arthur (*not a good thought-reader, and believing all well*) : Gentlemen, the vote ! Who's for pooling them ? (*Votes for, six, including Sir Saundontius (who has counted) ; votes against, eight.*)

* * *

(7)   PARCEL DAY
            (*Accele-rato, con moto, mysterioso*)

There's a murmur in the air—in the air—
      There are ninety parcels there
      Full of jams, anchovies rare
      For the prisoners de guerre—
            Bless their souls.

Hark ! I hear him read the list—read the list—
      Six for you—I do insist—
      One for me is rather triste—
      Though size counts too I wist—
            Bless our souls.

R

At the room we breathless wait—breathless wait—
   You must not risk being late,
   It might change your parcel's fate,
   So on our boldness do not prate.
      Bless our souls.

All is o'er, they have them fast—have them fast—
   There's some jam that will not last,
   Some tongue for a repast—
   Quenchers, shirts, and tea ! avast !
      Bless *their* souls.

* *

(8)   LETTERS COME

(*Adagio*)

Letters come. Letters go.
Winter's gone. Gone the snow.
   Gone the footer and toboggan,
   Gone our erstwhile trick of hoggin,
   And the price prevents our groggin,
      Life is so.

Rumours come. Rumours go.
What's the truth ?—we don't know.
   In Kastamuni our hearts are breaking
   And we fear the rude awaking
   When from her tracks we'll be making,
      Love is so.

* *

(9) " Die Nacht "—an inversion of " Der Tag," a one-act
play of 1914.

DIE NACHT

(*A New Version of " Der Tag," all about Billy Primus,*
June, 1917.)

Scene I (and only).

(*Large room used as smoker-library with tall windows over-*
looking the waters of Wandsee. The Kaiser in the
uniform of the Death's Head Hussars, seated behind a
table-desk. A shaded lamp throws the sharp silhouette

of his features upon the wall, leaving him mostly in shadow and the rest of the room in the light. He presses a bell. Enters ZIMMERMAN, *Foreign Minister.*)

KAISER (*motioning Z. to be seated*) : Before Talaat arrives let me know briefly how the matter stands.

ZIM. : Turkey desires peace at once, but gives the last possible date as three months. An immediate loan of 10,000,000 liras on mutual security is demanded.

KAISER : Is Enver in with this, or is it a feeler only ?

Z. : I assure your Majesty, it requires urgent attention. The whole of Turkey is behind it, led by the few vested and private interests that remain. You remember my saying that as soon as the private interests are hit the Turks will murmur.

KAISER : What hold have they on the public ?

Z. : According to Talaat, and privately confirmed, the wealthy classes are heading the general dissatisfaction at the famine prices and daily loss of territory. It is an ultimatum.

KAISER : What course do you propose for extending the three months ?

Z. : I suggest the situation would concern the War Minister.

KAISER (*ringing*, HINDENBURG *appears*) : The day, my general, is nearer than we thought. Turkey pulls out in three months. How will the map lie then ?

H. : With Russia merely held, or, if necessary, by retiring to our system of railways and carrying on with smaller forces on our Eastern Front, we can intensify our shortened line in the West and hold it against all odds until the autumn. This is providing Holland remains neutral and the Turkish campaign is pushed.

KAISER : What is your opinion of the news from Turkey ?

H. : Palestine and Syria will go during the summer. Possibly Russia will get astride the Baghdad Railway from their Eastern push.

KAISER : Our connection to Constantinople ?

H. : We can keep open for three or four months, when the Western wastage will necessitate withdrawal of Mackensen's forces and further concentration. Say four months, providing Turkish wastages are replaced and she remains firm.

KAISER *to* Z. : To what extent can you trust Turkey for three months ?

Z. : If the line is not cut she can be kept in by our military dispositions, so my reports say. The Turkish forces are kept in the out-field and German troops are fought nearer to the Capital. Their staff is still wholly German, and reports give no ground for uneasiness, except, of course, non-military riots. In which case comes in our " Remedy " among the Ultimate Provisions drawn up by your Majesty. We can seize and garrison Stamboul within twenty-four hours.

KAISER (*turning over papers*) : Hindenburg, is your opinion still unaltered about our last stand there ? Remember, it is of the greatest consequence to the whole issue. For how long can we hold Stamboul ?

H. (*drawing himself up proudly*) : Your Majesty, our plans are perfect. On the dispositions made I will undertake to hold Constantinople behind the Tchataldja lines and a south trench for three years against the world.

KAISER : There is nothing overlooked ? (*Rings, and* BETHMAN-HOLLWEG *appears.*)

H. : Nothing. With our shore batteries we could outrange any gun ashore or afloat, and as a submarine base it would be excellent. Ammunition and food would last that time.

KAISER (*dreamily*) : Three years. It would astonish posterity.

BETH.-HOLLWEG : Magnificent, my Emperor, but more than necessary.

KAISER : You mean England would be sickened out long before then ?

B.-H. : If the rest of the war-map could remain as it is, · it wouldn't be worth her while to insist on unconditional terms. But gallery play in Stamboul is useless once our line gives in the West.

KAISER (*to* HINDENBURG) : If we sacrifice the Roumanian line and hold one across Austria instead, make a stand in Constantinople, and concentrate all our forces on the Western Front, how long can we go on for ?

H. : To the autumn of 1918, when it will all collapse like a house of cards.

KAISER (*to* B.-H.) : The siege of Constantinople then would not be mere gallery play, Herr Chancellor ?

"DIE NACHT," AN INVERSION OF "DER TAG," WRITTEN JUNE, 1917, PROPHESYING THE DOOM OF GERMANY IN AUTUMN OF 1918.—"SMOKE"

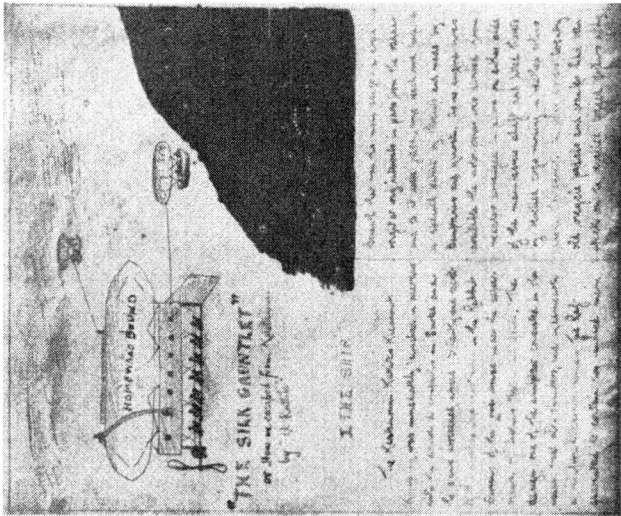

AN ESCAPE STORY FROM "SMOKE," THE AIRSHIP ENTERING THE BLACK SEA

B.-H. : There is yet a more serious factor. We can crush or sacrifice Turkey in revolution, but before a revolution in Germany your Majesty's guns will melt like butter in the sun.

KAISER : Have you not quietened the National Liberals by nominally conceding the constitutional point of veto, and in assembling and proroguing the Reichstag ?

B.-H. : It's not that. Neither is it the Socialists or the Left Centre. It's the agrarian classes of the Out Provinces. They already imagine that disaster has overtaken their absorption by Prussia, and thought towards decentralization must not be trusted too far. As they had least to win so they have most to lose in a war of taxation and attrition. Moreover, they fear the aftermath of fearful reprisals if the enemy carries war into Germany.

KAISER : But my army, surely it can maintain its supremacy ?

B.-H. : We cannot spare troops to garrison railways, and once the seed is sown lines will be cut, communications interrupted, and the army—excepting the Prussians—which is sick of fighting, will dissolve. I speak, your Majesty, from a near view of facts. Three months may be short, but when Turkey goes the terms will be harder.

KAISER : Turkey may go. Constantinople will not go. (*Rings.*)

B.-H. : The time to negotiate is now. We shall not succeed in sickening England out, and if we wait until we are right back before we ask peace, our enemies will push. (*Enter* VON KAPELLAR.)

KAISER : Von Kapellar, First Sailor of the World, you are our present hope. You have three months within which to paralyse British shipping completely—there must not remain one ship afloat. Everything comes back to this.

VON K. : My Emperor, in that time I can dismember, but I cannot annihilate. Every submarine must consult opportunity. Their chief boats are convoyed. If necessary, the American and Japanese destroyer flotillas will be used against us. It would take a year before we got at her throat. Besides, she is building.

KAISER : It must be done. It shall be. We are working against a time-table. With England cut off, and Turkey remaining in, Germany is consolidated. Von Tirpitz was right, after all. It is our chief weapon of parley. You must smash every ship and redouble our submarine tactics ten times from to-night—from this minute. I see it all plainly and all will be well.

(VON KAPELLAR *withdraws.* KAISER *motions to the Chancellor, who disappears through the door, to reappear immediately conducting* TALAAT PASHA.)

B.-H. : I present to your Majesty our friend and Embassy from Turkey—Talaat Pasha.

(*The* KAISER *rises to his full height, silent and immovable, for ten awful seconds. And during those ten seconds the heart of* TALAAT, *humped violently, as he beheld, at last, beyond the bowed heads of these grim men, the famous figure, strangely terrible, of the Great War Lord standing there dark and silent as Fate in the lamp shadow—the War Lord that had carpeted the earth with blood.* TALAAT, *not being used to these things, bows low. The* KAISER *advances and takes him cordially by the two hands.*)

KAISER : Welcome, faithful friend of the Fatherland in peace and war, and soon in victory. You see, I have just been reviewing my sinews of war. A magnificent piece of news has just arrived. We have smashed the Mistress of the Seas. It but remains to sweep away the fragments. (*Enter* VON KAPELLAR.) I will introduce to you Baron Von Kapellar, the hero of the hour.

(*Introduces them to* TALAAT, *and after a few moments' conversation they withdraw, and* TALAAT *is left alone with the* KAISER, *who smokes.*)

KAISER : Your arrival, my friend Talaat, has been the precursor of most wonderful news. I am happy to be able to tell the distinguished leader of our brave and faithful ally that the end of the war is a matter of a few weeks only. In four days we have sunk seventy-two large boats. There is a panic in England, and we have been touched about terms of peace.

TALAAT : Oh, that is good. My mission was for ten millions now, and to say we can't stand the strain for more than three months.

KAISER : The strain ? My generals will see to that. We are at England's throat. You must press every ounce—her terms depend on these blows. We could have peace to-night, but the peace we want requires manœuvring for. You remain firm, do you not ? (TALAAT *nods meekly*.) Our submarines are supreme, and every day the position improves.

TALAAT : There are riots in Constantinople.

KAISER : I will arrange for sufficient policing of the place. Now do not misunderstand me. The case for Turkey is everything or nothing, and without Germany it will be nothing. You are to dine with the Chancellor and me to-night. Is there any question you would like to ask ?

TALAAT : What is your plan of retirement in the West ?

KAISER : To fall back to a line we can hold for years—to prove to our enemies that at the rate of their advance it will take them two years to get into Germany, which extra effort will not mean so much gain to them more than they have at present—but the expenditure of millions of lives and double their war debt. That being so, we win. And now (*rising*) it is my royal wish to distinguish this occasion by conferring on you a Grand Duchy of the Fatherland. I have one vacant. The revenues have accumulated since the war. We will speak further of this at dinner.

(*The* KAISER, *smiling at* TALAAT, *shakes him by the hand. As the Chancellor reappears for* TALAAT, *the latter, pale with excitement, bows himself out of the royal presence.*)

(*The* KAISER *falls dejectedly into his chair and rings again.* PROFESSOR ADAM LASSOON *enters—the arch-spy, Press gagger, and confidential friend.*)

KAISER : Well, Adam. What news ?

L. : There has been much public comment on the fact that the Reichstag has even made it possible to demand changes in the Constitution so openly. This has been dealt with. There is also a growing tendency towards isolation. Men sit in cafés and talk. The world is against us, and even the entrance of Hayti has a bad moral effect. They hear the hordes already thundering at our gates for vengeance. This also has been dealt with and articles prescribed for it.

KAISER : Be extra vigilant about the provinces, and make a submarine boom.

(LASSOON *disappears.*)

(KAISER, *now alone and smoking hard, walks to the window. He looks out on the lake in silence. The moonlight*

*streams in across the room. As he watches, a black
sailing cloud obscures the moon, and the* KAISER, *turning
down the lights, sinks back dreamily in his chair. The
smoke from his cigar floats up in thick clouds as he rests
his haggard face in one hand. He sleeps. Past the
smothered light the mists grow thicker and in them
suddenly appears a form, a spectre—it is the* SHADE OF
BISMARCK. *With fearful voice it speaks.*)

THE SHADE : It is true, Wilhelm. You have need for the
pilot, nicht wahr ? The glorious empire I gave is on the brink
of an abyss. Colonies, commerce, shipping, armies, friends—
all are gone. The isolation of England has ended in the
isolation of Germany. The very cement with which I bound
State by State to Prussia is crumbling to dust. Germany is
sliding—soon she will be an avalanche charging to her doom.
Even now there is barely time to avert the catastrophe. You
dropped me. This is my revenge.

KAISER (*awakes with a start, and the* SHADE *flees*) : What a
fearful dream (*quotes*)—
  " There is a tide in the affair of Nations,
    Which, taken at the flood, leads God knows where."
On such a full sea are we now afloat, and we must take the
current when it serves or, like our submarines, go to the
bottom. I'll ring for wine. . . .
      (*Rings as the curtain falls.*)
                    Written in June, 1917.

* *

(10) Ballad by a bombardier on night of Fall of Kut.

THE FALL OF KUT
April 29th, 1916

Crack me the last bottle of date-juice
  And hand me some leaves of the lime—
For to-day falls Kut-el-Amarah,
  And for us, God knows, it's time.

We're only a siege-battered army,
  And most of us bones and skin ;
And we thought that our troubles were over ;
  But we find they only begin.

BALLAD OF THE FALL OF KUT. ("SMOKE")
THIS SKETCH AS ALL OTHERS WAS DONE BY LIEUT. GALLOWAY

"THE SONG OF THE RAIN"

Photo from "Smoke"

For five months the might of the Turk
  Tried to take this tiny Kut.
Now he says that we are devils—
  And we know that he can loot.

We thrashed him at Shaiba and Kurna,
  At Amarah we bluffed him to flight,
At Essin we grappled and threw him—
  How we swore when he left in the night !

That gave us Kut-el-Amarah
  Where runs in the Shat-el-Hai.
'Tis the key to Mesopotamia,
  And surrounded by Arab canaille.

We were now a conquering army,
  And we fought well and ate well and drank ;
And though he'd retreated to Baghdad,
  We followed for military swank.

The march was a long one and thirsty,
  Still we thought of the Baghdad goal—
Till the Turk barred our way at Ctesiphon,
  Thrice our force and entrenched like a mole.

But Townshend saw it all swiftly—
  To him were all our wins due.
" I'll not fight without reinforcements—
  There's my communications, too."

Now, it's a trick they have in the Army,
  To ask you " What's absurd ? "
So unsupported, Charlie T.
  He took them—at their word.

" It's a risk, and I'm not for it ;
  But if fight it's got to be,
We'll fight like the Sixth Division,"
  Quoth our General, Charlie T.

We found his flank and joined battle,
   And held with a frontal attack.
Stormed his first line—he vacated his second,
   Was reinforced, and we had to fall back.

A third of our force on the field ;
   But the Turk had suffered much more.
We knew that the game was up,
   So retired with the honours of war.

Then came the wild hordes of Islam,
   Hot-footed upon our track.
They caught us at Um-al-Tabul,
   But in the open we flung them back.

Mars surely was in his chariot,
   And smiled at Townshend then ;
And Charles made good to the God of War,
   And snatched from the grave dead men.

We hurled him back and held him,
   And got our transport through—
It was a glorious gunner's show—
   But that's 'twixt me and you.

For forty hours we marched on,
   The nights were fearfully cold.
Men hungered and fainting, and men
   That slept as they walked, I'm told.

But Townshend got us to Kut,
   And the remnants stumbled in.
And Hunger and Death stared from our eyes,
   But we counted it all a win.

We dug down deep and quickly—
   Next day they were all around,
And our planes flew away to the southward.
   We were alone and battle bound.

We fought them from the trenches—
  We came to blows in the Fort.
We fought them and we fought the floods—
  And then the food ran short.

Relief had been expected
  In two weeks, or four, at the most.
So we starved, or we died by the hundred ;
  But we stuck each man to his post.

All this time the enemy, vengeful,
  That ringed us tightly round,
Swept us with shell and rifle fire
  That followed us underground.

Our front line gazed into the blue,
  Where Formless Things rode by,
And followed the wake of sound and heard
  Them burst in the old Serai.

Or sometimes it was the Hospital,
  And sometimes anywhere,
And later came planes that bombed us—
  'Twas only luck served you there.

So the months went by, and we ate husks,
  Chupatties, and mule, and weeds.
We'd Divisional Orders for breakfast,
  And ribs of the silent steeds.

And still the Relief kept coming—
  The Staff nominated the day.
Twenty times they fixed it for certain,
  And each time explained the delay.

So we swallowed disappointments,
  Tommy only groused his share ;
But one sad day the floods came,
  And Destiny seemed unfair.

The trenches filled with water,
  And the plain showed scarce a sod,
And we slithered and waded, or murmured—
  " On top, for the love of God ! "

And many's the unfortunate devil
  Fell to the sniper's shot
Through " chancing his arm " in the open ;
  But the others heeded it not.

Once again, on that waste of waters,
  I gaze from the gun-pit floor,
Where Tanks and I kept vigil
  Through each hour of the twenty-four.

I see the maidan silvered
  With waters in the dawn—
Dark lines of distant parapets.
  Fresh earth against the morn,

With files of khaki turbans
  Moving forward to relief—
I see the busy shovel,
  Hear the cursings underneath.

Farther still, beyond the sand-hills,
  The trenches of our foe,
Seeming silent and deserted—
  But I know that they're below

In lines on lines encircling
  Us, north, south, east, and west—
And if my glasses tell me true,
  They're reinforcing for the test.

'Tis moonlight, and they're sleeping,
  The detachments of my guns—
Here, just behind the limber,
  These best of England's sons.

For the dug-outs are now flooded,
　　Washed by this muddy sea—
The gun-wheels half in water,
　　The breech-blocks scarcely free.

And parapets and sandbags,
　　Our trenches fallen, too—
There's room for ammunition,
　　But not for me or you.

Once more, from the mouth of my dug-out,
　　I smoke the leaves of the lime—
Sort the destinies of my shells,
　　" Percussion" and also " time."

There's a light in the telephone dug-out—
　　I think I'll have a peep,
For I'm half expecting a message—
　　Maybe the Bombardier's asleep.

Asleep ! in the arms of Hunger ;
　　But I'll report him not,
Though I " rounded" him well for his slackness,
　　And returned to my watery lot.

Past sheets of wintry moonlight
　　I see the drooping palm,
And the ribboned edge of the Tigris,
　　Dreaming of Eden's calm.

Hard by, in ghastly stillness,
　　His four feet toward the moon,
I see the corpse of a stricken horse,
　　Death-knelled by the shrapnel-tune.

A broken wagon there yonder—
　　A topee adrift in the flood—
Its owner was strafed in the trenches,
　　There's the case of the shell in the mud.

I hear the belated mule-carts
   A-rumbling on to the Fort
Under the cover of night—
   For so their provisions were brought.

I hear the jackals' chorus,
   Athirst for expected prey,
Where the Arab tribes lie sleeping,
   Patiently awaiting "the day."

Enough ! these things are over,
   The moon is on the wane,
And the palm-fronds' festooned shadows
   I ne'er shall see again.

For Kut at last is fallen,
   And more men have to die—
Our flag is down, and the Crescent
   Waves o'er the old Serai.

God grant to us, now captives—
   Who at Death's gate boldly dare
Boast we haven't succumbed to battle—
   Grant us this fervent prayer—

That in our future cheerless,
   We yet shall know o'er Kut
Our avengers see the Union Jack—
   Tramp the Crescent underfoot.

To that, then, drink from this date-juice,
   And fill up your pipe with the lime.
We have fought till the Great Gong sounded—
   Till the Referee called out—" Time ! "

SPARKLING MOSELLE.

* * *

(11)   THE SILK GAUNTLET

OR, HOW WE ESCAPED FROM KASTAMUNI

By "A Kuttite."

I. THE SHIP.

The Kastamuni Kuttites Klearout Kompany was immediately launched in accordance with the advertised prospectus in *Smoke*, and the plans proceeded apace. Silently and secretly the airship was constructed in the Rabbit Warrens of the Lower House under the supervision of Captains Tipton and Wells. The design, one of the simplest, consisted in the usual vast air-chambers, and underneath a reinforced carrier named the Raft guaranteed to contain two hundred men. Beneath that ran the main shaft—a street tube bought at long intervals in parts from the bazaar, and to it were fitted some beechwood propellers, a special patent by Parsnip, and made by Bamptarius and Munrati. As no engine was available, the motor power was derived from treadles arranged in pairs on either side of the main-screw shaft, and fitted thereto by bevelled cogs turning in teethed collars along the screw. In other words, twenty old bicycle pedals and cranks had been stuck on to bevelled cogged collars along the shaft, and when pedalled vigorously by twenty stalwart officers, it was calculated by the designers that a speed of at least thirty knots would be attained. A secret trial was out of the question, but so great was the faith of every one in the abilities of our members of the R.F.C. that parole was recalled in small batches so as not to occasion suspicion. Then one day an excited whisper spread from mouth to mouth. Although officers lounged about as usual, and even played footer, or smoked and read, the hearts of all beat high with hope, and in every eye was the old look one remembers on the evening of our intended debouch from Kut. The whisper was, "Tonight's the night."

II. THE ESCAPE.

There was no moon—only a faint starlight that seemed to intensify the darkness. At 2 a.m. strange figures, some hatless, all bootless, and some in pyjamas, flitted swiftly and noiselessly through the empty streets. The rendezvous was the large stone mosque in the grassy plot to the right flank beneath Mr. Smoke's window, which had been selected as the most suitable place for fitting the " Homeward Bound " together. At this rendezvous the committee had been working on it since midnight, and when the others arrived the "airship" rode proudly in the air tethered to the minaret by a cable. I am now writing on board, and the blue sea is far beneath us. . . .

In order to picture our embarkation, cast your mind back to the sketch in a previous issue of *Smoke* of a " Homeward Bound " model riding anchored to the minaret, and dark figures with monkey-like spasmodic movements crawling along a rope ladder to the airship. Stores and water were quickly got on board. There was a committee for everything, and nothing had been forgotten. The organization was wonderful. The bandsmen were privileged to bring their instruments. In fifteen minutes we were all aboard, and even with the extra weight she still strained upwards at the ropes.

The first fatigue took their places at the treadles, and the propellers whirred. Crack ! A shot rang sharply through the night—another and another ! It was the alarm being given to Kastamuni. In thirty seconds it had grown to a fusillade. Lights flashed here and there in the town, but the " Homeward Bound " was in darkness. . . .

" Cast off," shouted our Commander Tipton, and as the ropes were cut the "ship" leaped to a height of 10,000 feet. "Ye gods ! " " Heavens ! " "What's happened?" were heard on all sides. What a leap at the heavens it was. We fell sprawling, clutching at anything, but the caution we had previously received saved us, and for the most part we held the guard-ropes. You see, we had expected something, but scarcely that. Yet the plans were perfect. The 10,000 feet had been calculated to a pound of gas. " It's all right," yelled out Tipton, no doubt accustomed to these stunts. The fatigue party had been jerked half off their seats and couldn't pedal as her bow tilted upwards. That was righted with the air valves, and in a few seconds she brought up at dead level. Then the fatigues started pedalling hard, and we waited— waited. A cheer burst out as the " Homeward Bound " slowly started forward, her pace increasing every second.

Then, overcome with joy, the band seized their instruments and struck up an air. Away down in Kastamuni the people awakened out of their sleep by the alarm, heard a soft whirring high up in the sky, and then the strains of " Destiny Waltz " came floating down to their astonished ears. This changed to " Rule Britannia " and " God Save the King."

Bullets pished-pished past us, but as we got further away we lit up, and all they probably saw was a light or two in the sky, moving like stars towards the hills.

III. THE FLIGHT.

We now proceeded to make ourselves comfortable on the raft. We rigged up sleeping corners, a reading corner, a band corner, and storeroom—although many stores were suspended from the airship by dangling ropes. Not the least feature about the appointments was the coffee-shop and bar, presided over by Sir Bedevere le Geant, King Arthur's henchman and mastik drawer. The Oblong Table as the chief promoters, with Mr. Smoke, of the scheme, rigged up an oblong table of sorts, and kept up the old order of things, King Arthur being in great form. Sir Shinytop regaled us all with humorous lamentations for his lost love in Kastamuni. The consumption of *mastik* was limited to ten per man per night. Oh, the sensation of those first starry hours of freedom, the exquisite sensation of easy movement (it wasn't my fatigue) on a glorious early summer's night, the thrill of joy after months of confinements, the speeding on towards liberty ! If you have been a prisoner of war you will know the meaning of this. It was exactly the reverse sensation to that we had on going upstream as captives after Kut. So we drank, drank, drank mastik after mastik and thanked the gods.

But I must hasten to repair an omission and say something about the " Homeward Bound." Tipton was commander and aeronaut wallah, assisted by Lieut. Nicholson, R.N., navigating officer. Captain Wells " repairs," and Sir Lancelot le Fumeur as international lawyer in case of complications, Lieut. Wulley, M.A. (Maiden Aunt), as Intelligence Officer, had a little crow's-nest on top to which he pluckily scrambled by a ladder. In an ingenious manner he had drawn maps all around him on the silk cover of the ship. Major Syer had Supply, and Captain Reyne did Sergeant-Major of Fatigues, as he got more

s

work out of the boys who went on in two-hour spells. The " Admiral," our pilot, had much time to spare, and started a book with Fludd and Hunger on the various risks uncovered, also betting on where we should land and when. The tiny bridge was forward in the bows, with a glass window that looked out ahead. Some of the orderlies were on the after-part of the raft and others on a trailer just below. Away astern, and towed by a long tow-rope, was the dinghy, a con-trivance of King Arthur's by which punishments were inflicted, the boat being hauled alongside, and after the delinquent being placed therein, let out astern. The first offender was Sir Pompous for *lèse majesté*, and as he drifted past he yelled— *quelle politesse!* Sir Sulphurous followed for " language," and Brabby for promoting a fight between two small game-cocks he had smuggled on board, thus drawing a crowd and tilting the " airship " at a dangerous angle. Hummerbug came next for regretting the kaimakam was not with him. Most mysterious of all was a buoyant canoe called the cradle, also in tow, that floated high over the " Homeward Bound." Great secrecy was maintained about this, but rumour had it that Sir Lancelot le Fumeur and Sir Carol le Filbert had worked this project for exploiting a new model in the London music halls—in other words, that Sonia the Fair Girl was in the cradle. In support of this theory it may be mentioned that during the first night of the voyage each of these knights was missing for a time, and could nowhere be found. We averaged about twenty knots and soon passed over the dark passage 7000 feet below us that stood for the ranges we had so long beheld as the horizon of our imprisonment. Less than three hours after leaving, as the dawn was breaking, we saw far beneath us a silver feathery line.

" Gentlemen," said our genial commander, " Turkey is behind you—behold the sea." A small wiry figure came scrambling down the observation ladder in breathless excite-ment. " It is the Black Sea," he said, and every one laughed, and Le Fumeur, who sat writing in the corner, swore he would shove that into *Smoke* if he was hung for it. By the way, he promised us a last edition of *Smoke en voyage*. It appeared yesterday, but all in good time. We kept on this course for an hour, and the mist prevented us seeing any shipping. In the distance we had seen a few white dots—possibly Sinope.

"Head wind springing up. Storm ahead, sir," reported the pilot to the commander. "Clap on pace," yelled old Tipton. "Stick her at it, half-hour fatigues, band strike up, emergency guard-ropes out, lash everything quick."

The wildest scrimmage took place. Sleepers were trodden on, mastik bottles upset, and people sent sprawling as the "first twenty," all fit as fleas, sprang to take a relief. How those fellows pedalled. The propellers screamed a higher note, and for a moment we swept along ; but a second later, as the tide of wind caught us, our pace slackened more and more until we remained almost stationary. The wind whistled through us, and the canvas screens on the raft reported like cannon shots. Every one had hold of something, except the band, who were in a sheltered corner. We played ragtime and poppies to some purpose, but when we struck up the "Marche aux Flambeaux" a miraculous thing happened. Scarcely had we done ten bars when we bounded ahead as if we had cut a tow-rope holding us back. We did ten knots in the teeth of the gale. The fatigue pedalled six revolutions of a leg to every note of the Marche, and The Crochet set the pace. The whole ship cheered, and a solitary shout came from far behind. This was from dear old Pompous in the dinghy, whom every one had forgotten. We beheld the latter being twirled round and round like a spinner, but now that we moved its occupant shouted with glee to find himself on an even keel. This kept on for two hours, and as man after man gave out or got cramp another replaced him at the pedals. "Storm approaching, portbow," yelled the pilot. "Emergency holds every man. Prepare to mount," our commander yelled in a cavalry voice. The band instruments were secured. We held tight. A lull had succeeded the heavy wind, and somehow the sea was much nearer.

"More speed, more speed, keep her head to it," was the order.

Suddenly, without a second's warning, an avalanche of wind swept down on us, and the shock of impact seemed to hurl us a mile back. "Stick it, boys," yelled Captain Reyne. "Splendid, splendid. Try a bit more, kick it in."

Stuff got swept overboard. We held like grim death. The ship plunged and reared like a mad horse as we were hurled from side to side, and the deck took every imaginable angle. But Nicholson somehow managed to keep her nose to it. Something snapped, and there was a wild beating and creaking. The next moment the repair party, headed by Captain Wells, all on life-lines, got to work, and one or two who fell off were fished back. Then the propeller went, and a violent controversy was waged between Parsnip and Bamptarius on the matter. But a new one was fitted by Bamptarius with extraordinary skill and daring. It was just in time. The ship was bearing round, and once beam on she would have gone smash. I remember looking astern the while and seeing the dinghy playing high jinks and whizzing like a ball. Then came the hail and lightning that played over the steel ribs in an awful fashion. Something else gave on top, and there was a wild fluttering of canvas.

"Hold tight," yelled Tipton. It happened the second time, and this time much worse.

A man astride of a bullet couldn't have gone up faster than we did. Something to do with exploding a gas charge—a secret stunt of Tipton's own. We found ourselves gliding along smoothly and evenly with incredible swiftness, possibly doing eighty knots. The relief from the storm-tossing to the thrill of racing smoothly was wonderful. Have you ever while yachting beaten up in the teeth of a heavy gale round a headland and had the sea sweeping over you and the boat dancing and leaping like a mad thing, and then suddenly found yourself gliding down a smooth channel with the wind behind you ? Then you will know what this was.

"Why on earth did not you do it before ? " we all demanded.

Tipton laughed. "To lend colour to our enterprise, of course, and then we have now left one emergency charge only."

Our first thought was to have the dinghy alongside and rescue Sir Pompous. We found him very white. "Thank God you are alive," we said.

"Seems so ! " he answered sarcastically, a favourite phrase of his.

"Fearful time, wasn't it ? "

"No. I liked it, of course."

With that King Arthur clapped him on the shoulder and poured half a bottle of mastik down his throat and shirt. Sir Lancelot gingerly climbed along the ladder with a reviver for Lieutenant Wully, expecting to see that officer in a faint, instead of which he was quite cheery with an empty bottle of mastik protruding from his pocket.

" How the devil did you stick on ? "

" Stick on ? Oh, eashy ! "

" What's this ? " asked Le Fumeur, producing the empty mastik bottle from the pocket of our Intelligence Officer.

" Ohsh, thaths noshing. Nerve resthorah. Keep oush cold, verish draftish ere. Donst shay anyshing to boysh. Don't wansh go dingsh."

Sir Lancelot helped him down, and he slept.

IV. Lost.

The wind fell and the sun came out. The ship was put to rights and, scarcely knowing where we were, we headed due north. It seemed about midday. We had a full ration and dosed away in a pleasant sunshine to the steady creaking of some stay or rippling flutter of some loose ribbon in the air-chambers above. We smoked and dreamed of home. A little later our Intelligence Officer, now at his post again, assured us he could tell from the birds beneath us that we were near land.

" What land ? " we all asked.

" I'll tell you at tea-time," he said. At tea-time he re-appeared. " Through a break in the mists below us I'm sure I saw a town," he said, " white dots on green."

" Possibly sheep," said one.

" Or sea birds on a green sea," ventured another.

" Rot," replied he. " It is not green ; why, it is the Black Sea."

Two hours later, as the twilight fell around us, we saw, as in a flash through a rent veil, the twinkling of a myriad lights. Some one suggested fire-flies. " A mirage," said an orderly from the stern raft.

Without doubt it was a town. Great excitement prevailed.

Our navigating officer believed it to be Odessa.

" I believe it's Constanty," declared Wully, and as the lights grew nearer he became more insistent. " The sea is beyond and around the lights, it must be Constanty." And half an hour later, " I tell you I can see mosques and minarets ; besides, I know Constanty. I am absolutely—— "

Boom ! A dull billowy wave of sound reached us.

" That proves it," he said ; " we are being fired at."

On this a council was held, and it was decided to steer due N.W. We ran before a strong southerly wind that until now had been on our port beam. We did about sixty knots, and by fifty hoped to have reached Russian territory. But to be quite sure we kept on until midnight, when we descended to what we considered was 5000 feet. Suddenly a cry from the pilot brought every one to his feet. There, not a 1000 feet below us—a mere 300 yards—were the white-crested, creeping waves towards which we were rushing. . . . " Hold on." Boom ! Swish ! Our second barrel of gas was exploded and we rushed up and up. But once there the " Homeward Bound " began to sink again.

" Pedal, pedal, or we are lost," shouted Tipton. And they *did* pedal. But we still sank slowly. . . . .

" Lighten ship," he roared, as the repair party tackled a huge rent in the side of the bag. Things were slung overboard wholesale and the dinghy cut adrift. The ship then steadied and gently rose, but not before a large volume of the *Mastik* was hurled overboard by Blind Hookey.

" My poems, my precious poems," shouted Mr. Belton, as he leaped to save them. He slipped, beat the air, and had not Mr. *Smoke* seized him by the coat tails and twirled himself around a stanchion he had followed *Mastik* into the abyss of mist and cold grey sea. The gas generator was set going and we gradually rose to 10,000 feet once more.

" Gentlemen," said our commander coolly, " we have been under way twenty-four hours, and I beg to report we are lost at sea."

Lost, lost, lost, the words echoed. A ringing cheer was our only answer.

* * *

(12)   FROM MY BEDROOM WINDOW

Spring has come. The tree I told you of is thick with leaves. And so when as now the evening wind blows, a changed music falls on my ear. Instead of the soft swish of branches is the lisp of the young leaves, stirring in delight as they listen to the story about the winter dreams of the old tree. Birds are back once more, Old Jim Crow, the jackdaws that awoke me early last summer, and a little fellow like a wagtail who in his own fashion is accompanying the lyrics of a thrush in the mosque garden close by. One and all they have the look of adventurers thick upon them. "Happy to meet, Sorry to part, Happy to meet again," is the leit-motif of their song. Perhaps like birds we shall ourselves soon return to English woods.

A great window is this of mine with its view from the garden across the town to the distant hills. Now, to appreciate a view fully, it is imperative that you shall have spent just previously some considerable time in trenches and dugouts and gun-pits. No, it is not a view either, but rather a stage. In the background is the drop-scene of mountainous hills, dotted with villages and scored with paths and gullies. It is a scene shadowed with forests and sprayed by the advancing sunlight, or sometimes by this light misty rain. Other drop-scenes are the mists that advance or retreat with the rain, and sometimes a thunder blanket shuts off the stage just outside the town. For the curtain there is the mantle of night—when there is no moon.

An extraordinary stage. Let us look at it more closely. I can promise you no set drama, but great entertainment if you are the sort of fellow to enjoy sitting on a bit of a hill above a winding river in the country—with a pipe and some field-glasses wherewith to watch the affairs of the world around you. No man-made drama, no plot, no prompter, and not a cue. The players stray on to and off the stage, and suggestion can do lots.

In the fowlyard below two cocks have renewed their battle for the right to crow last. "Seems so," says Sir Pompous beneath my window, as he watches them intently. The youngest pullet, coy and not uncoquettish, withdraws from the scene of combat to arrange her feathers in the far corner. She, in any case, will have to abide by the decision of the contest.

Cynically the old hens condescend to a dull interest only, contrasting this sorry affair with the strenuous and gory combats that waged over *them* in *their* day, when their hearts, too, were young. Love's young dream long since awakened to matter of factness and steady routine. But for an example of love still dreaming observe the cocks themselves—the

younger lamenting his lack of experience, but game; the elder
no doubt regretting that his Virgil is not at hand to adorn
further Georgics with the account of his strenuous endeavours
—to point anew that old moral in the Battle of the Bulls.

A mate has joined the chirruping wagtail with many a
ship and twist of her small head. The cock-bird, prepared to
earn his amours, indulges in risky flights round the twigs and
back again, landing suddenly beside her with a little joyful
chirp. "In the spring a brighter crimson comes upon the
robin's breast—in the spring the wanton lapwing gets himself
another crest."

"The call of Spring," as Pacific Roller says in another
column, "announcing that the season of love is at hand and
inviting youth to put on his gayest apparel."

There has just appeared in the foreground of our stage the
wee bear Alphonse, delightful little fellow except when he
makes that awful noise—and why shouldn't he? 'Tis time,
he thinks, that he was on the warpath alongside his dam, for
it grows dark and the call of the wild rings out for him in
clarion notes, challenging him to fulfil his destiny. Manfully
the little fellow is trying to do so, roaring lustily and making
commendable attempts to stand on his hind legs and reach a
bough. As he thrusts his way through some *débris* I can see
his woodcraft is coming on apace.

The first drops of rain are falling, and as they swish on to
him his wee heart, I've no doubt, throbs restlessly for
freedom once again. Freedom. Poor little lad, I sympathize
with him. Different from the cocks or the wagtail he, if he
could speak, would agree with me on this point at least. But
one thing he doesn't know, and that is the future, nor how
close the hand of Fate is to him even now. For it is as good
as decided to poison him for being in disposition incompatible
with all of us—to wit, that he is a bear and roars. As a matter
of fact, five grains of strychnine were given to him last night
and he survived.

And what could augur better for the normality of the
Knights of the Oblong Table than to say that some cheered
and all felt glad when, to-day, we saw Alphonse still going
strong, apparently overdosed. The iron of Kastamuni, that
rumour says has entered into more than one soul (and rusted,
too, withal in others), cannot have bitten so very deep into

King Arthur's Knights. And Alphonse the bear, innocent of our design or of the attitude of Destiny, stands on his hind legs like a wee man and chuckles. Is all this drama a tragedy, or comedy, or what ?

Please note there has been a duel over an *affaire de cœur*, a love episode, a captive, with a great Fate of uncertain mood flinging a dark shadow at the end. . . .

Past the column of grey smoke thickly climbing through the raining mist, a black speck moves down a white path. It is a labourer returning from his fields beyond the town. To the west is the smothered glow of the setting sun. In the central background of the stage above the high lights, observe a wee, grey coil of smoke twisting upwards from the shining speck in the gully. I know the hut well, although never has it appeared larger than the tiniest button. There is a romance of an old man and woman, a son at the war, and a pretty girl within, if you look closely!! Behind the house a long track winds uphill to the pass. But the last light has left the hills and I see only the dark patches of forest. Look carefully, and, if I mistake not, you will see an advancing pair of darkly burning orbs. They are the eyes of another Alphonse, luckier, let us believe, on the warpath, traversing his domains, the dusky fastnesses of the wild glens. . . .

The sun has set and the rain falls more thickly on the hills. Through the gossamer of moving mist fond fancies steal to me. And so the last scene before this slowly falling curtain sings of the Past.

What play does not ? It is the song of the rain. Would you like to hear it ? . . .

***

THE SONG OF THE RAIN

Oh, I'm longing for the homeland way past the setting sun—
I'm yearning for old faces and for more sober fun ;
  But sometimes, as at even, my heart with pleasure fills,
  While it drifts back to England—when the rain is on the
    hills.

Oh, I'm tired of the Orient, I want the old, old lanes.
I want the Dear Old Country—her pleasures and her pains.
 I want the white-frilled hedgerows—the heather and the
  rills
 That lift me back to England now the rain is on the hills.

Night's mantle softly falling o'er Kastamuni town,
The last dim colours flying, dark grey and dusky brown.
 I hear the goatherd piping to the flock his good-night trills,
 And my heart hies back to England—for the rain is on the
  hills.

Below me in its basin the old town dreams away—
I see the first light flicker that ends another day.
 The distant bugles dying—the muezzin floats and stills
 My heart to pray for England—when the rain is on the hills.

Oh, I'm longing for the homeland, my homefolk and my pals,
I know that some have fallen 'mid the bullets' madrigals ;
 But a memory's in her woodlands—a love no distance
  kills—
 And to-night my heart's in England—for the rain is on the
  hills.

PACIFIC ROLLER.

CHAPTER XII

SPRING—PLOTS TO ESCAPE—BETRAYAL—ESCAPE OF OTHERS—
I AM SENT TO STAMBOUL FOR HOSPITAL

IN this diary, notwithstanding it has been written in
the greatest secrecy and kept hidden, I have nevertheless refrained from including any mention of a
subject that in my latter days in Kastamuni engaged almost
all my attention, *i.e.* escape. Besides being an unnecessary
risk, it would have been unfair to those concerned. I am
adding a note from Brusa.

. . . .

After our first winter in Kastamuni, the warmth of April
stirred our blood to respond to the call of spring. I decided
to try every human device to get away.

The Turks asked us to give our parole not to escape. A
keen controversy sprang up in our midst. From the point of
view of some officers it meant a few more privileges and less
punishment, and escape was almost impossible anyway they
said.

Some senior officers were for giving orders forbidding the
whole camp individually to escape. Others, including myself,
considered this a private matter for the person concerned. I
refused my parole, and was down in a black list of the Turks.
It meant extra convoy and less privileges, but we asked for,
and were given, no facilities for escaping than what we could
make.

In the town some months before I had got to know a
Russian " runner," Kantimaroff by name, who was interned
in Kastamuni, but secretly in touch with the Russians. For
a heavy bribe he got me news of the Black Sea coast only
some forty kilometres to the north. So careful was I with

Kantimaroff that outside the Turkish baths I spoke to him only once, and then in a shop.

It would take many chapters to set down all the many changes of programme of increased and diminishing hope according as the octroi posts between us and the ranges were changed, or as the Black Sea patrol scoured this coast for fishing-boats. Sometimes vigilance was so increased as to terrify any one against helping us at all. This took months.

At last, by great good fortune, I discovered a Greek outlaw, on whose head the Turks had put a price. He was in hiding, and wanted to get away to Russia. He was in need of money, and, provided he did not run too much risk, would meet us at the Black Sea's edge, and take us with him.

Kantimaroff, who was practically free in Kastamuni, sent him again and again to the coast, or said he did. The scheme looked rosy enough. The main road to Ineboli was heavily guarded, as was that to Samsun.

But between them was a track over the mountains known only to a few. It led to a sacked village halfway to the coast. Here, formerly, the Greek had lived. It was within ten miles of the sea, and in case the coast were too crowded one might rendezvous here in caves.

The boat problem was the most serious. All these had been collected or destroyed by the German and Turkish authorities, and only a few licensed ones were allowed at all. They were simply not to be had for any money. The nearest coast of Russia lay only 250 miles away.

The Greek, however, after collecting a considerable amount of money for his trips to and from the coast, announced that he had bought a boat, tested it, and buried it in the sand near a creek. There were oars, but no sail. It was while waiting for the return of the Greek on this occasion that Captain Ellis of the Duke of Cornwall's Light Infantry asked to accompany me, and Lieutenant Sweet of the Gurkhas also decided to come. We had every detail ready, our kit and disguises and stores and compass, and wanted to start that night. But Kantimaroff said he could not agree to this. Suspicion might fall on him. He must be given a few days to perfect his schemes. It was now June, and the moon was rising too early. A later rising about 11 p.m., while leaving us obscured in getting out of the town, would enable us to negotiate the hills and rocky detours we proposed to make, as quickly as possible. So we decided to wait. In the meantime I reserved for myself the supreme luxury of breaking bounds to test the feasibility of this part of our programme. Just after dinner, when the other officers were settling down to bridge, and before the postas had put on their all-important " night " bearing, for at night they were extra vigilant, I side-tracked the sentry downstairs and hid in the woodshed. After waiting half an hour for exchange of guard I got a tiny window open and hopped out into our back-yard. I had to wait another hour before I could close it behind me. Then I went through the yard, over a roof-top and a high wall, and found myself half stunned at the bottom of the wall on a side street, with some sleepy Turks near by going to prayer.

The mischievous feeling of a schoolboy breaking bounds for the first time was nothing to mine, although I had been out on previous occasions. This time I felt that the first step of the escape was feasible. I wandered around the town in a fez and old clothes, shuffling a pair of dilapidated shoes *a la Turque*, and coughing steadily. This because I had disguised my face with a scarf as if I had a severe cold in the head. I found out where the postas were, and where not, and after more than one narrow squeak got back over the wall with the greatest difficulty, pulling a part of it down in doing so. Some days later, as the plan was being held up, it was necessary for me to get out again. This time I slipped out in the afternoon in uniform with a basket of purchases, ostensibly from the bazaar. Now, sometimes our postas lagged behind us in the town so that an officer walking apparently alone was no un-common sight. It worked beautifully. On being seen alone with the purchases I imagined our own postas would think I had outdistanced or lost my posta, and on this occasion I merely walked boldly past all our sentries and into the front door of our house. They were suspicious the second time. Not a word of all this I said to any one. Experience was dearly bought and precious.

Two days before we were to start I heard that somehow or other Kantimaroff had been approached by a party from the Lower House, and anxious to reap a double harvest, he had, it appeared, taken money from them and divulged about the boat. At this time any intercourse between the houses was difficult, and I endeavoured to communicate with Keeling, who was organizing the other escape. Ellis was less watched than I was and asked the other party not to touch Kantimaroff who was, it appeared, heavily suspected. We agreed to give each other notice of our " bunk," so as to arrange to go the same night. So soon as one party got away the other would have little chance.

I now met Vicomte d'Arici, the Italian songster that had lately come to Kastamuni, and who resided with the Italian interned. I met him secretly in the castle above our house, and he helped me with information considerably. I found also that he was a political prisoner, and had done an amount of political work before the war, and knew people I knew in Berlin and on the Continent. He was a light-hearted and plucky fellow, and except that it wouldn't suit him, would have come himself. He told me to beware of Kantimaroff, who was on the point of betraying us to the Turks. The Greek seemed straight enough, and wanted to see us.

Later I took Ellis, and we·both had a night " rehearsal." Being two helped matters at the wall. We improved our disguise, and even gave lights to unsuspecting Turks.

On the way back, however, we took a wrong corner and ran into the arms of a sentry who challenged us. Ellis tried to answer in Turkish, which was fatal. The sentry was obdurate. He had hold of us lightly by the sleeve. Pushing some liras into his hand we disengaged ourselves and took to our heels, scrambled over the wall, and got back into bed by inches ahead of the search party.

The next morning, to our secret amusement, and the wonder of the camp, a certain major, who had given his parole, and who used to walk about proudly without any postas at all, was suspected by the Turks with having been " out at night." The variations of the rumour were highly interesting. Who were the two out ? Every one good humouredly accused every one else, and quite a number of officers decided to get out as it now appeared that it could be done.

I supplied the other escape party with particulars of the brigands with Cowi Bey in the valleys between us and the sea. If one could get to them the chances were that for a ransom they would assist one across the Black Sea with the extreme chance of getting knocked on the head for one's boots.

I was now secretly informed by d'Arici that I was heavily suspected. This made inter-communication between houses most difficult. Sweet who was in the Lower House decided to start with the other party, and Captain Ellis and Lieutenant Taylor, I.A.R., who were in my house, to come with me. We got everything ready, and on an evening in the third week in July, we waited in our room ready to start with all our disguises and equipment ready. At the last moment I got an urgent message that Kantimaroff's house was picketed by police, and the Greek had run away in fright to a house near by. We made one more desperate effort to go and join him and make our plans after getting out. I sent urgent messages to Lieutenant Keeling through our trusty Sergeant Britain not to try to see Kantimaroff openly, as he was suspected. However, that day he and two members of the other party went up to the Russians in the street, with the consequence that I got a chit on a paper bag saying the Greek had fled, and he was in danger of his life and that, for the money we had given him, he could not do more than give us all the information he had. The same night a posta was delegated to watch me, and every half-hour he came to my bed. We waited for an opportunity. None came. And our escape, which had offered a most excellent chance of success, went "phut" accordingly.

The other party duly informed us that they intended to start. Three weeks afterwards they did. The posta had just left me about eleven, when we heard a shot. Some excitement occurred down below, and postas swarmed up to our house to see if I was there. Search parties were out all night.

We were all confined to our house. Next day I heard that at the last minute the escape was nearly nipped in the bud at the start. This was prevented by our old Bombardier Prosser, who did servant down there. One of the party forgot his watch, and actually sent the bombardier, who was showing them out, back for it. A posta accosted him. He knocked the posta down, and rushing up to his room, shaved his moustache off and got into bed. They had him out and listened to his heart to see, as they did on such occasions, if it was still beating quickly. This would have meant he had just been out.

We remained under "bund" without incident. Hourly

reports came that the other party had been captured. But they didn't return. The following notice appeared posted up next day and signed by the commandant.

"*Possession of the offensives have been taken. Other officers are requested not to escape, and will be surely shot in bunking. Officers offensive in this fashion, giving their parole, are informed they must be fired at in any case. All are requested to be happy. Do not take rotten advantage of your old postas for God sake. This is final notice before shooting. Let the special one note.*"

I was voted the special one in my house.

We heard a rumour that the party while trying to avoid the bandits in making for the coast had actually struck the main band, and after getting away, tried to pass off as Germans. They were discovered. I have no wonder—and a letter written by an officer, amateur at Turkish, was taken.

Clumsy as the start was, they have done well, and we all wish them the very best of luck.

So the days dragged on and the nights stood still. Once more summer was over. Once more it seemed we were entering the long stretch of autumn that led into the terrors of winter, with its cold, and scarcity of food that our slender means could not negotiate. But through the nights and days always, always, there was the same range of hills dividing us from the sea. In the first days of September there suddenly appeared in Kastamuni a tall Turkish Mir Ali (full colonel), named Zia Bey, the inspecting officer of the Government. He came to hear our complaints. His visit last year had been hailed with great glee, but we had since learned that these events were shorn of possibilities of increase of liberty. He came, no doubt, to inquire about the escape. We were still heavily under "bund," and so he visited each house. He had a pleasant appearance, was very quiet, and extraordinarily polite, but he did nothing. We stood around his chair while our spokesman told of our petty troubles, the large ones we knew it useless to recount, so we asked for fresh air and money and leave for our British servants to go to the pump without a posta as they were few and we were often thirsty. He noted our points, but promised nothing except one or two.

I heard him ask which was I, and I could see I was still under heavy suspicion about escaping, although my eyelids were so swollen that I could not see at all out of one eye, and only indifferently out of the other. But I was not so blind that I could not see that Zia was the polite type of lazy Turk that in the heart of him has fear. I said nothing of the scheme that evolved itself as we all sat together. It was fatal to hand over one's embassy to another. When he had gone I wrote a letter to him.

My assets were that I had really been very ill from the effects of a shell contusion in my spine for a very long time. Of this I could show nothing except in two places, the vertebræ were parted and irregular, and one had since grown nearer. If one could refer to anything so damnable as captivity being blighted, I might say that bruise has blighted mine. Of the untold hours that I lie awake waiting, waiting, for the roof, sky, and earth to stop pulsating to the pulsation in my spine, no one can ever know. But the eye trouble, originally strain from shell-shock and from grit, is now only bad conjunctivitis, although it looks awfully serious. As first violin of our band my bandaged eye, and, later, my absence, had been conspicuous enough to the Turks. Moreover, I had recently received word from the late Lord Grey and a letter from some friends at the Foreign Office. In one letter a kind inquiry existed about my health, noting the special treatment our enemy prisoners were getting in cases like mine in London, and saying medicine and glasses were being sent me to save my eyes in the meantime. On this I made my case without threatening the Turk, but indicating that they had become aware of my case in London. That I had been so neglected my eyes were imperilled, and that whatever had happened in the past the inspecting officer, at all events, now had the opportunity of giving me in Stamboul the treatment that the Turks got in our best hospitals.

I terrified my interpreter into giving this application to Zia Bey himself, as I could not trust Sheriff Bey. This I did by showing him another letter to be delivered by another source that night to Zia Bey, showing that as had happened in previous cases applications were not allowed to reach him. Ananias, as we called him, took my letter to Zia Bey. The next morning I was summoned to the office. They led me down. Several fat Turks stuck oily thumbs into my eyes. The local doctor had to say what my complaint was, and

T

although they admitted that under him my eyes had got worse, and he would not accept further responsibility, they allowed him to say what the trouble was. It developed into a hot discussion. I refused, point blank, to be diagnosed by a doctor who wasn't a specialist. Had they no specialists? Finally they produced a file of letters to me and extracts and bad reports on " qatcheor " (escaping). They asked me if I was willing to go to Angora for examination. Now I loathed this place above all, but it was *en route* to Constantinople. Here I made the most important move of my captivity. Lieutenant Greenwood, with a smashed shoulder from football, aggravated by an old wound in Kut, was a dead certainty to go. I refused unless I could go with him. They agreed.

On my return the whole camp was discussing " Mousley." How the devil had he worked it ! What a fool he was to go to Angora ! Others said I was going to escape *en route* or at Constantinople. I was told I was leaving the next day.

Oh, the delicious whirl of life again as I felt the first un-loosening of the chains. Only three officers at long intervals have gone over the mountains from our camp to Constantinople. Here in this basin by the Black Sea, buried from the world, and far away from the great issue, one has been left alone with one's inactivity, one's interrupted career, the unaccepted portion of one's sacrifice, and has too much time for morbidity. But now, to-day, the sun shines on Kastamuni as it never did. The postas are more than kind. The castle alone is green. I may be off to an indifferent fate, but I am off. Munro our lightning carpenter has justified his reputation.

" A box, righto ! This cupboard just it. Oh yes, about twenty minutes." So he did. He kicked the lid off, closed the sides, braced the back, and altered the hinges, and as we looked there appeared the box good and strong. I have packed a heavy accumulation of stores as belated parcels have recently started to arrive in exciting quantities.

I have given away all my spare kit to my former companion. In fact, with my good joy, I couldn't auction anything. Every one has been very kind and given me odds and ends for the journey, and the doctor has sent up special packages of emergencies *en route*. I am told I am to leave at dawn, but we are still under bund, and I can neither visit the other houses nor see Greenwood to make a *bandobast* for the journey. It will mean our carrying two of some things and nothing of others. The Round Table gave me a very lively dinner. My box is ready with all my worldly possessions, including my manuscript packed in below. I tried to get a false bottom made to my box, but with the wood this is not possible in time, although I expect a search, but rely on their previous permission given to me to work at these.

Angora.—We arrived here last night on foot in a battered, lame, halting and blind condition in the dark. I must set down how our gay cavalcade that left Kastamuni early on September 3rd dwindled away to this. After my last entry I did not leave the following morning, but waited in terrible tension lest they should cancel the arrangement. But the delay was the worst. One horse had just had a foal, and a substitute could not be found. Another horse had gone sick and had no shoes. The arabana or wagon was to cost us twenty liras. This we refused to pay out of our funds, but told them to cut it out of our pay. As a matter of fact, and by a miracle, we got off paying, as, of course, we ought. They found an old vehicle in some yard and put the commandant's bodyguard on to it. They nailed up the wheels, put on a cover, and in the early dawn Ananias, the interpreter, burst into my room screaming " Haidee." This was the day after my last entry. Sergeant Britain, our very estimable N.C.O., and another took my box and kettles downhill to the commandant. Here I was made to sign my pay sheet. Then, suddenly, Sheriff Bey entered the room, closed the door and demanded to see all in my pockets. I had to produce them. He took from me my private papers, including addresses, dates of remittances received, numbers of cheques cashed, and private accounts. Also my manuscript music in part. Then, tragedy of tragedies, he demanded on my word of honour if I had anything else written. One was by this time fairly sick of giving one's word on nothing, but there was no way out. I told him, however, that I had had permission to work on my book, and on a law study, that I had given much time and thought to this, that they knew in England I was working at it, and that I would show him all I had if he promised to give it me back on my assurance that it contained nothing against the Turk or of military or political importance. His glee on receiving a large book of manuscript was unbounded. The interpreter read parts of this to him, anecdotes of captivity, of the campaign and other selections on problems of the new International State or Society. He assured me on his sworn word of honour I should have them back at once after the censor had seen them if they contained no plans of Turkish Forts, and in any case on the signing of peace. (I subsequently heard my book was found torn up in his office.) In vain I begged for them. He felt that at last he had me at a disadvantage. I appealed to Zia Bey. He was all politeness, and gave orders my name should be carefully and legibly written on the book. But my heart sank as I thought of the fate of such things on former occasions, and of the many many hours I had worked at it.

Our kit was put on board the wagon, a place made with our rugs for Greenwood to rest his broken shoulder, and an orderly named Mathews, who was being sent back to Angora for breaking barracks repeatedly, was to do servant for us. This was untold luxury compared with our trip to Kastamuni eighteen months before, but I was terribly depressed over my book and parts of this diary. Valuable or worthless, it stood in any case for a part of my life, and I felt as though something very close to me had been snatched away. For many months here and there I had written this. It was a history written among dying men, not of them, but of many things, and such that I can never reproduce. On many a night in winter, by a black smoky oil light bought with money saved from my tobacco or mastik money, I had worked with the flickering wick near my bandaged eyes, my two worn blankets wrapped around my legs and feet, stockings around my head and neck to keep out the paralysing cold. Outside was three feet of snow, and sleet and wind from the Russian waste blew icily over the Black Sea straight to my window. Ours was the highest and coldest house in camp, and faced the north high on the bluff above the town. And so I wrote and re-wrote until often only my writing hand remained unfrozen.

Before leaving Kastamuni we had to wait two or three hours for the gendarmes that were to accompany us. I was not allowed to visit the two shops to rectify my accounts, so carefully did they watch any one leaving lest any communication should be set up for those left behind. I went to the Lower House to say good-bye to some friends, including Square Peg, at work on law. His friend, whom we called the Count (Horwood), was most sympathetic over my book, and took me to the bar to have a last bottle of beer (so-called) that had arrived. This beer, to me so long estranged, was so good that I bucked up to a degree, and decided, as I have always tried to do since in moments of catastrophe, to merely suspend judgment and my grief. At the time it is too much deliberately not to care or to try to diminish the size of the catastrophe.

At last we were rushed off, crowds of people following us, and small boys wanting tips, and many peasants whose faces one knew were honestly grieved to lose us, and possibly our money as well. Last of all Sonia, our Sonia, who had on occasion had quite an amount to do with me, and had danced to my fiddle and carried notes for me, and decoyed the postas from my rendezvous in the castle, followed us for miles with her basket, crying bitterly. She was a case-hardened daughter of Eve, a wild little untamed savage, but pretty and entrancing and very daring. She waved to me, and threw many kisses with lightning rapidity when the gendarmes were not looking, then followed the river bank to her destiny, and we rounded a bend towards ours.

The first time in one and a half years of restriction, that seemed one and a half centuries, we wound up the eastern road back on to the plateau, and the brown roofs of " Kastamuni the Terrible " fell beneath the brow.

It was a beautifully soft morning. Our cavalcade scattered themselves out on the flanks to scour for brigands. Besides the *arabanchi* (driver), there was our excellent sentry Mustapha and his *choush*, a sergeant, from the Lower House, who was reported rather treacherous, also a wretched little officer cadet fellow named Ali, and about three or four *askars* and eight gendarmes mounted. We halted for lunch among some trees in a delightful glade between two hamlets. In the evening we walked to get over the jolting of the springless cart, which bumped and bounced over every rut. My travelling companion had a bad time on occasions with his fracture, although it was better than we had hoped. We reached the region of pines and ravines, and in the dusk pulled up at a grimy and dirty Serai a few miles short of the old sawmill where we had stopped on our way out.

We were bundled into a tiny room filled with smoke and

all sorts of travellers. We emptied this room after much argument, and allowed in two or three of our postas only. This was my first scrap with Ali. He was afraid, as Zia Bey had arrived at the Serai just after. Zia was off to Angora, but travelling in luxury in a landau. We had a good supper after paying huge amounts for water and firewood, and to the owner of the wretched *khan* or shed. The place teemed with fleas and bugs. In the early dawn we had breakfast of Cambridge sausage, biscuits, tea, and jam, from our parcels. My travelling companion likewise had a large box full of stores just arrived, and I should think ours was the best supplied caravan that ever crossed that mountain.

We walked along beside the wagon up the incline. The horses were so poor that they could scarcely pull the empty wagon. The route led among pine woods and waterfalls alongside a sparkling brook. I exchanged a few words with Zia, who was also walking, but he soon passed us. He had seen service in the Dardanelles and at Sivas.

Slowly we climbed, sometimes walking, sometimes riding. The great forests of fir with tiny log houses perched among the heights on every clearance, were above us as we started. By three o'clock we were on the summit above them. Al Ghaz Dhag, a fine peak, lay alongside us wreathed in mists. We were kept together, and quite an army of gendarmes convoyed us. Recently the brigands who swarmed in these hills had robbed the mails and repeatedly held up passengers for tribute.

My eyes became troublesome, and Greenwood's arm inflamed. However, we made a good halt and lunch in the summit among pines, and here met our old good Commandant, Fatteh Bey, who was storming against Enver Pasha and Sheriff Bey. He had had some difference at last with Sheriff Bey, whom he was too weak to restrain. This led to Fatteh's getting removed to Eski Chehir. He had had so many contradictory orders to go that at last he set off without them. While he was away the escape occurred, and he was interrupted at Changrai and ordered to return. Sheriff, the nominal commandant when the affair occurred, accused Fatteh of conniving. He caused Fatteh's kit to be searched secretly at Changrai, and a letter, really innocent, was found from an officer in Kastamuni to a friend at another camp. So Fatteh got in disgrace, and was now pensioned off. It was all worked by Sheriff. Fatteh told us he wanted to leave Turkey and go to England to live. Every now and then he produced a Cook's English-Turkish. He has already learned the money quite well !

That night we reached another wretched *khan*, and slept on the roof. We smoked a little while the drivers slept, and the gates being well secured we could not escape. Ali became obstreperous and obstinate, and wished to show his authority even in the matter of our walking or riding or getting firewood or procuring water to wash. He wants us to get it from the place where we must, of course, pay for it. But these have been wonderful days of movement, a voyage of rediscovery of the world, a passing from sleep to dreamland, from death to life.

We find very many old landmarks that we now remember perfectly to have seen on our outward trip—a lonely cabin, a path over the mountain, a deserted mill, a desolate Armenian house. Thus in moments of tragedy can the eye collect vivid impressions of things so commonplace that they are usually missed. A very hot day of trekking, followed with frequent collapsing of the horses, and more frequently of the harness, which was tied with string or rope. Periodically came a louder crash from our groaning wheels, which wobbled dreadfully, sometimes so ominously as to threaten to tip us out altogether. We were at an angle certainly of forty degrees off the perpendicular quite often, and Greenwood, being a sapper, developed a trick of making elaborate calculations as to how many more fractions we might go over, and what the momentum of our boxes packed behind our heads would be in a general roll. We were hemmed in by the ribs of the wagon's cover, and in case of accident could not move a foot. Once we actually did go over, but only tipped on to the side of the bluff, and luckily not the other way. We kept Ali in cigarettes, and gave him more than one tin of food. Fatteh and another very fat Turkish officer who accompanied him lived, I verily believe, on the same onion and melon from Kastamuni to Changrai. They ate bread and olives.

I was not altogether free from suspense lest I should be held up in Angora and not allowed to proceed to Constantinople, and I had asked Ali if Zia's letter to the medical officer at Angora really existed. He said we would both go to

Constantinople, but this in the lying way of appearing pleasant the Turk has. As we had been quite good friends, I asked Fatteh in German to have a look for me. He got the letter, and said aloud that it was for us to go to Stamboul. I asked him again that night, and he admitted it was only for examination in Angora, and did not mention Stamboul! However, I saw the line. There was no need to pretend, as my eyes were really bad. More than once I had to be completely blindfolded, and sometimes lie down in the roadside.

We passed the Hittite caves in the cliffside near Kosah river, and then reached Changrai, the halfway village. Here we were taken into another serai in the town, an empty room with hanging doors and broken windows. We ate hard, and drank bad *raki* hard, and slept hard. We stayed there all the next day. Here I hid a section of my papers I had not shown to Sheriff. When he pronounced his intention with regard to my book, I slung the rest of my kit back into the box in a great rage, and, of course, over the other parts of the book he had not yet seen. These I expected to lose here. I now forestalled a search by getting them sewn into some old rugs. Fatteh promised to do all sorts of things for us, but I had the usual doubts. He wishes us well, but is a Turk.

We saw the wretched little bazaar, and heard that the whole of Kastamuni camp was to be moved to some lonely barracks outside the town, so as to prevent more escapes. On the morning of our departure we walked out slowly about a mile over the fields to these barracks which lay en route. They stood alone in the plain beside what in winter was a stream, a four-sided great building of many rooms enclosing possibly an acre of ground with a pump of bad water in the centre. The rooms, or rather divisions, were large, enclosed on two sides only, and strewed with filth and litter. Sheep and goats ran from corridor to room as we went the round. Windows were broken, and doors long since burned. The building itself was fairly solid, as these go in Turkey, but altogether the change from Kastamuni to this would be a serious one for the worse. I tried very hard to get some cryptic word back to our friends in Kastamuni, so that they might put up every objection. (This I heard later never reached them, and they were told excellent quarters were awaiting them in Changrai.)

My resolution to leave this part of the country increased, and I prepared to risk much, even life itself, for a change. From Changrai on our voyage was much more uncomfortable. It lay through the region of dry arid land, stony and dusty tracks, or bare rocky defiles. The horses collapsed, our guard got sick, and was reduced to Ali the *choush*, and Mustapha the guard. The gendarmes had turned back on emerging from the passes. Escape from here was hopeless, so barren was the land. We hoped brigands might surprise us. We hatched schemes for knocking Ali on the head and wrecking the wagon. With one good friend something might have been possible, but as it was I was half blind, in fact in the last month my eyes had become very much worse, and my companion walked with pain. So we went on. Ali, or rather Peter Pan, as we called him, with a huge revolver and tin sword grew more overbearing as the trek wore on. When we were most weary he pressed on. The fellow was congenitally a fool, and often after passing a decent camping place with shade and water, stopped on a burned-up patch. At night he stuck us into some vile *khan*. However, one way and another we got through. At Changrai I doctored the wheel, which was nearly off, and decided by pocketing the rivet to stop the caravan when necessary. This I did more than once. However, two marches off Angora, in the middle of some ruined and sacked villages, two wheels had got so bad that they came off, the wagon nearly going over a *khud*. They fixed it up with sticks and rope, and then a few miles farther the spokes fell out, two or three at a time. Just here Mustapha, who had walked the whole way, collapsed with acute ague and malaria, and shook violently on the ground. This simple soldier had come along pluckily, and often did sentry duty at night as well, after eating his bread ration that he carried. We admired him, and although tired and in pain with over-walking ourselves, we got out at once to give him a lift. Imagine our feelings when the malignant Peter Pan broke into a terrible rage, bullied, and struck his soldier for daring to ride, kicked him into going on, and took our seat himself. We had a general row, and Peter Pan struck the *arabunchi*. It was he and the *choush* against us three, but Mustapha, the patient soul of the Turkish peasant, and the best thing we had found in this country, was too good a soldier not to submit. He was fond of us, and even cursed his officer. He said he wished their officers were like ours, who considered their men a little, but no word of rebellion escaped him, and so collapsing every few moments he staggered on. Then Peter Pan half drew his sword on Greenwood and jostled him, a cripple. This was too much. I seized his arm, and in a most impressive rage told him if he drew it I would disarm him. He was speechless. It was a most colossal row. Then we sat down and refused to go, unless we could get our seats. "We are invalids, special cases *en route* for hospital. You have no right to sneak our seats." His defence was that he was to be an officer by and by, and if his man could ride, he could. The *choush* sided with him, and we had to follow, while he rode. But I showed him some letters, and swore to report him to Zia Bey, who was not far ahead. He then showed his teeth, and said his secret orders were to *shikar* us, and give no liberty, as I was a dangerous person whom they couldn't catch. Anyway I took good care the wagon went phut again soon, although he proposed to go on still a distance, dragging the broken wheel. Finally the whole show crashed, and he had to get out. Another driving *arabana* of much the same quality was commandeered, and we were wanted to move without our kit. This we wouldn't do, and smoked cigarette after cigarette on the road like disobedient school-boys. Finally the kit was put up, and we had to walk. The *choush* then became very ill with what he thought was cholera, but what was evidently cold in the stomach and malaria. He was rather a coward. He asked me for medicine and prescription. I told him castor oil was a good thing, and gave him enough of this and some ginger to put him out of any future arguments. Peter Pan then had to capitulate, for he was all that was left. We walked side by side, and more than once made off as if we were escaping after water. Then he let us drive a spell, at least I drove, and the *choush* lay huddled up frightfully ill in the back of the wagon. His rifle lay resting on our knees, and if there had been five per cent. of chance I believe we would have risked everything. But we were pretty rocky by now.

Eventually we had to deposit the *choush* by the roadside near a *khan*. The wagon couldn't get up the hills, and so, on foot, blundering on in the dark without a guard, and almost too weak to go a step further, we at last staggered into Angora.

Here we were shown into a *gasthof* of sorts where men and women, Turks and Jews, and mongrel Armenians all seemed mixed up in one living-room. Eventually we got rid of Peter Pan, who went to his wife.

I squared the proprietor. Mustapha, who had come along in some conveyance, was most accommodating. So when Ali returned the next morning he found us in the hotel next door, we two with Mathews our servant in one small room which I had got emptied, and Mustapha asleep outside. He said I had to go to a medical board at once, and Greenwood was for Stamboul that night.

I found several dignified Turks around a table who proposed to examine my eyes and spine. Before they did so I asked leave to tell them something. This I did in German and indifferent Turkish, but I told them certain things about their politics that made them stare, also about the responsibility of medical boards to whom a sick officer after eighteen months' neglect had been sent in a wretched conveyance 150 miles over mountains in a Turkish cart. I refused to stay in Angora, and said I wanted a diagnosis in Constantinople. It was a long competition between their disinclination to send to the capital one who had seen so much of Turkish maltreatment, and their fear. I won. In fact, I made myself such a nuisance that they had to do so. But I am certain it was only a parade of arguments that won. The Turk can't grant a straight-out request to a prisoner. But there are ways of getting him not to object to a certain thing happening.

We went to the Military Commandant of Angora for a servant, as we are in no condition to move our boxes. He is the same evil-looking old villain we remember of old. He literally spat at us and roared. I roared also, and when he ordered me out of the room I walked the other way, being blindfolded. He caught my arm rudely, but had scarcely touched it than I sprang up as if electrocuted, almost upsetting him. I told him that it was merely surprise, as Zia Bey told us no one in Turkey must touch a British officer. He snapped and snarled like a dog. We got out. I reappeared to ask him if he could let us have any of our parcels that were *en route* to Kastamuni. We were quite polite. But he barked that there were none. Oh yes, pardon ! there were. We had seen them. He screamed that he had finished the interview.

We withdrew with chuckles. To-night we had the usual appalling scenes about leaving. Eventually we got to the station, and after a score of interviews and running about the station against orders, I managed to get two seats in a carriage with Fatteh, our old commandant. One had to browbeat the officials, who said they had no orders for us unless we paid. Our boxes must come on by a slow train. Finally, weak to exhaustion, but elated at heart, we got into the stifling carriage.

En Route.—It is night, and delicious music of a train that is carrying me away, away, is in my ears. We drank two bottles of beer and a small bottle of Julienne, which we got from an Armenian at the station. I met there my excellent former acting-sergeant-major, Sergeant Graves. He looked well, and said the survivors were now more or less free, but these good times came only after all the terrible deaths and complaints. There were, besides himself, six survivors of my battery. I spoke to some of the men. Their sufferings last winter had been awful in the Taurus, and even here at No. 12, Angora. They had lived in holes in the ground, without kit or cover, working from sunrise to sunset on the roads. Their food was a mixture of wheat and water, and sometimes bones. One called it Chorba. At the end of their meagre reserve strength they fell ill. Some were then thrashed. Others were left to die, and in some cases did not receive even bread-and-soup rations unless their friends earned this for them by working overtime. Here also the deaths had been so numerous that the survivors kept themselves going by the dead men's parcels which a German commandant caused to be distributed now and then. The stories of the men having been compelled to eat various kinds of vermin found on them was verified beyond shadow of doubt. This was the Turkish method of keeping down typhus. It was, however, impossible for our poor lads, in the appalling conditions under which they lived, to keep themselves clean. There had been several mutinies, and often unsuccessful escapes, also with disastrous consequences. I heard a ghastly rumour of some sick British soldiers suspected of having cholera being deliberately murdered with a dark serum with which they were inoculated, and from which almost no one was known to recover, death usually following within two or three hours. I cannot vouch for this being true, so record the fact as it stands. There are very many Turkish officers who would scorn to do this. On the other hand, there is the class of official like the *Vali*, promoted to Angora *Vilayet*, when his predecessor refused to countenance a wholesale massacre of Armenians in 1916. This enterprising gentleman picked his troops, and then, firing half the Armenian quarter, drove the other half into it. I heard the most terrible stories of fanatical Turks bursting in upon a family at their evening meal. The men and old women and children were first killed. The young and prettiest girls were promised life, but were spared only for a night or two. One heard of cases where a busy *Askar* in the middle of the carnage maimed a girl to prevent her getting away.

We thought Angora was very changed. So were several of the Armenian villages a few marches out of Angora where we had bought milk and fruit on our outward journey. They were now deserted. Weeds grew above the walls and in the burned floors. Here and there a vine or vegetable told of the swift and terrible change. Still Armenians go about in Angora, having daily affairs with the Turks. A consuming fire of black impotent hate is in their hearts. And because it is impotent the Armenian has by destiny become treacherous. Fatteh and I talked German on many things ; and after whistling the " Merry Widow " out of tune for another hour, he fell asleep.

We reached Eski Chehir in early morning and found our Choush quite willing to be reasonable, if we did him well. We went to the hotel opposite, had a meal, slept, and then walked to the town with our guard. Some loud and rather disreputable women, Armenian and Jewish Levantines, I think, were in the hotel. They were in some theatrical show, or had been. Greenwood and I described them as performing women. We travelled on again that night with Fatteh Bey and our guard. Fatteh promised many things for us in Constantinople, but being pensioned off, seemed doubtful of his ground.

The carriages were packed with travellers, including a great number of children with mothers. They carried household effects. One heard they were Armenians or Greeks whose husbands were dead, and they were off to some new town. We heard a confirmation that the big terminus station of the Baghdad line on the Asiatic side of Constantinople, Haidah Pacha. had been blown up two or three days previously.

After a pleasant run round Ismid Gulf we got to Ismid, a large town with railway works. There in the silvery waters of the Marmora we beheld Principo, Halki, and the other islands, their bronze green shimmering in the bright sunshine. A few sails were on the sea, the sea, the sea ! Never shall I forget the thrill we both had as, for the first time, after ages in tiny mud dug-outs, flat plains, and a taunting confinement behind a high range, we saw, a few yards off us, the sparkling drops glistening as they fell from the tiny waves of the Marmora.

The sky darkened as we stopped at a place called Kadakeuy. We now heard Haidah Pacha was in ruins, as a well-directed plot had arranged that a huge consignment of petrol should be fired. The flames prevented a train-load of ammunition from being removed. This went off, playing havoc all around. Missiles had been thrown into the adjoining districts.

After some delay we got our scanty kit on a ferry. The boxes had not arrived. They contained our all. From the paddle steamer we beheld a thunderstorm burst over Stamboul. The minarets stood out above the streaks of yellow and electric blue. Altogether I thought it a most impressive and magnificent city, with all the beauty and passion and mystery of Turner. From the close quarters of Galata bridge it appeared less delightful. We said good-bye to Fatteh. It was now nearly sunset. Our Choush, who had been quite pleasant hitherto, grew obstreperous. We were bandied about from barracks to barracks, deserted empty buildings that made a tired and sick traveller faint. He wouldn't allow us to get any food. We drew nourishment from the strange sights and a few pleasant ones, such as the dainty progression of Turkish ladies. They were sombrely but prettily apparelled from head to foot in the prescribed Mussalman dress, an overmantle from the forehead thrown back and hanging over the shoulders as a cape. For the most part their carriage was excellent. The better-looking ones were more or less unveiled.

As it grew dark we grew hungrier. We were tired and sick, and in pain, hungry, cold, and thirsty. In this state to have to sit hour after hour in an *arabana*, with the fees amounting up to the last paper notes in one's pocket, while one's guard goes off to drink or gets lost, left in his absence to the unkind caprice of a passing soldier, is the lot of a prisoner of war. Some time after dark we halted at an Armenian church, now our new commandant's office. The locality was called Psamatia. Here was more delay. A doll-faced and heavily-scented Turkish subaltern at last appeared, and after administering ridiculous questions, left us to some vicious-looking postas, who led us away. Our *arabana* took us on another half-mile, and stopped at a tall, gloomy building behind heavy, tall iron railings. We crossed a tiny yard behind them about forty feet by fifteen. The gate was double locked and guarded by sentries. We groped in the dark, up flights of stairs, through the empty house, and reached a room where was an iron bedstead and a filthy mattress. Here we were left.

After a moment or two some white-faced pyjamad figures came to us, and proved to be Russian prisoners from Sala-kamish, prisoners already for three years ! One, Roussine by name, we liked better than the rest. We drank their tea, almost water, but it was hot, and we talked of news. Roussine was inclined to be Bolshevist, and as Russia was now collapsing, we held decided opinions on it. We ate some raisins brought all the way from Kastamuni, and I remember well with what solemnity on this sad night of disillusionment, I regarded those raisins. This, then, was the Stamboul of rest and peace, of clean sheets, of fresh flowers, medical attention, and delightfully prepared meals handed to me by some Byronian Stamboulie ! A garret empty save for rats and bugs ! No food, no water, only the selfsame raisins. We still said we were glad to have left Kastamuni, but, all the same, they made us almost homesick for that we had left behind.

This was the first night. Others were precisely similar. No one came, no one cared. The third day we got black bread. Water that had flowed intermittently from a single pipe now ceased. The commandant had been once to see us in the dark. I complained to him. He was one of the worst type of Turks I have met, a sullen, ignorant, hopeless brute. He said *peckee* (very good) once or twice and withdrew, his tin sword clinking down the ghosty stairs.

We wondered how long this would last.

PART III

STAMBOUL AND BRUSA

CHAPTER XIII

SENTRIES stood on the stairway to keep us from talking to some Russian soldiers herded like animals down below. We had not noticed them the first night, as they had been on fatigue. On occasion one might go downstairs to walk on the tiny stone courtyard. From near our room the stairs led upwards to a large garret from where one looked over Stamboul. The view of the city from here was excellent. The many minarets flanking an expansive sea stood out against the sun. One idea was predominant—the idea that seldom if ever left us—Escape! The walls were high. Guards marched ceaselessly to and fro below.

Among the prisoner officers was a sea captain. Greenwood and I consorted with him. Our plan was through the local restaurant, a wretched hovel, whither we were allowed once about every three days for a meal of Kariwannah (vegetable soup). We offered heavy bribes for oars. It meant going over the high roofs with the hope finally of getting down, seizing a boat, and trying the Bosphorus disguised, getting out to the Black Sea before the dawn, or trying a long walk to Rumania on the chance of something turning up *en route*. But a few days after we arrived some Rumanian prisoners escaped from a working party. All boats were drawn up, and only the heavy ones allowed on the seashore. Guards were redoubled. Our hopes diminished.

We watched from our desolate room all day long to get acquainted with the movement of ships and trains. The

Balkan Express passed near our house, but every point was guarded. We were somewhat weak and ill, but waited for our chance. Money was a hindrance. This deterred us more than the fact that the train was heavily guarded and closely searched, and ran through Bulgaria, where prison life was even worse—or Austria, if one chanced to get there. After some ten days, we were sent to hospital, guarded by a Turkish soldier, without any papers, and were told we weren't wanted, as it was not a prisoners' hospital. At one of these Greenwood remained, but he was placed by mistake in an infectious disease ward, and when, in addition, a junior subaltern proposed the most serious alternative operations, he made himself such a nuisance that he was sent back to the prison camp. In the meantime I wrote letters in French and German and English, which I gave to passers-by or threw into the road, and more than one I gave to German soldiers, who were sympathetic with us. I wrote Bach Pasha himself, quoting extracts from Conventions and Parliament on reciprocity of prisoners' treatment.

The net result was the appearance, late one night, of our commandant, livid with rage and excitement. Roussine and I were playing chess by a flickering oil light, and my eyes were bandaged. He strode up and dashed the chessmen violently to the ground, and kept on touching his sword. I am afraid his wrath was nothing to mine. I intended to impress him with the fact that we were not schoolboys, and in vigorous manner demanded why he hadn't visited us, or given us bread or water, or allowed us our boxes. Was this the hospital? Was he the commandant? Was it not a whole week since, as he rode by, we besought him through the railings for bread? I was overwrought with pain and endurance, and came very close to physical remonstration. We literally shouted him down. This brought the Russians around. Before they had been cowed down, now they lamented loudly too. All the while the doll subaltern stood by the commandant, obeying his orders, but the sickest and sorriest object one could wish to see. Most of all, I demanded leave to see the commandant when necessary, in order to get an application read.

We were then allowed once daily to the restaurant for half an hour. Hospital attention seemed out of the question.

We made one more attempt, when the Chief of Haidah Pasha Hospital sent for us, but the Choush took us to the wrong hospital, through ignorance, and we were not allowed to explain. We gave up hope of treatment. Then Ramazan commenced, and the commandant did not appear for days together. I was now watched, especially for letters. An amusing incident concerned a letter I sent after this to Bach Pasha, and one to the Dutch Minister. We had been so well watched that all communication seemed impossible with the outside world. For example, in the restaurant our plates were searched, and our seats also after we had left. We were not permitted to speak in any language our interpreter did not know—generally Turkish only. I had contrived to leave more than one letter in the street. If directed officially in German, I thought it probable that it would be sent on. Bach Pasha, the German General in charge of prisoners, did not, however, prove sufficiently enthusiastic to reply. I quoted conventions and parliamentary extracts for his benefit in case we got freed. He now evidently rang the commandant up, who merely came round and ordered me not to be allowed to speak to any one. Our bread ration ceasing the following day, I wrote another letter. As I paced up and down the tiny courtyard, waiting for a German soldier to pass, the postas followed every movement. I managed, however, to have more than one conversation with Germans by pretence of declaiming aloud from a book as I walked. The difficulties were that the sentry would see a letter thrown on the path, also that no German was allowed to approach the bars if I was near them. I had managed to talk to one private from Wilmersdorf, a suburb of Berlin, a homesick lad who hated the Turks and enjoyed outwitting them. Besides, I said the letter was for his officer. I told him not to approach until I was seized. Seeing some other privates approaching in the distance, I beckoned to them with my right hand with some cigarettes, and rushed towards them. Half a dozen Turks seized my hand and the cigarettes before I had gone five yards, in order to interrupt me from communicating to the Germans approaching. They did not notice, however, that as I waved my right hand, I had placed a letter on the bars. The German from Wilmersdorf, who, instructed by me, had waited close by, dropped some cigarettes in. The postas rushed up. I

saw a certain cell if the letter was still there ; but it had gone.
The Russians, who had breathlessly watched the show from
on top, cheered loudly.   It was great fun seeing our lad
return an hour later, on the opposite side of the road, and hear
him shouting, ostensibly to his companion, "Richtig.
Gegeben." I had said certain things, and results could safely
be expected.

Nothing happened the next day until about 8.30. By
the glimmer of a fat candle the Russians and I were playing
chess with some pieces I had had sent out from home.   My
eyes were bandaged up, and I had to peer over the board to
play.   We were deep in a game, trying to forget our wretched
pains and hunger, when loud stamps, followed by increasing
roars, approached the room.   The door was kicked open, and
our commandant, his face black with hate and rage, strode
up to us, struck the board with his fist, and knocked things
off the table.   The only way to impress a Turk is with rage
or fear.   He had hardly struck the board when I started up,
knocking and kicking the bench and chairs yards away.   I
rushed to the door, shut it violently, and cannoned into the
fighting wax doll of a subaltern who accompanied him.
Being bandaged up I had a good excuse for going within an
inch of the commandant's head.   I told him things in Turkish
and French, and more in English.   We threatened him,
showed him some official letters from England I had kept, and
told him that answers were already on their way to England
about his treatment of our men, and that he was in for it, whatever happened.   It appeared that some kind of inquiry had
been made about our ability to write letters, rather than
about our cause of complaint.   However, he had at least to
realize that we weren't children, to be starved to death without
a protest.   He had evidently been well reprimanded for my
having contrived to write letters.   In fact, my letters had
become quite a propaganda.

Russians flocked into the room, and, once started, they
also developed considerable horse-power, although the poor
brutes were too much kicked to say much.

The commandant ended up by mopping his head and
ordering me to go to gaol.   But he subsided later, and after
waiting an hour in the cold, quite triumphant, I was allowed
to remain in my quarters.   The next day we got one loaf and

some water, and were allowed to go to a filthy eating-shop " to have hoof soup ! '' Instead I ordered eggs at an enormous price, and, having eaten them, left it to the posta to carry on, for we were months behind in our pay, and were not allowed to cash cheques or get our Embassy moneys.   This led to a wordy scene in the street, and while the row was on I got another letter off to the Dutch Minister by exchanging matchboxes with a Greek.   In it were my last lira note and a letter.   That night the commandant came again, and with dignity almost too terrible even to be laughed at, pointed to me with his tin sword, and ordered me to be taken away.   I felt relieved. Change is good for the soul.

We filed through the moonlight, a solemn little procession of my few goods and blanket.   A posta, who had received from me heavy bribes—an awful scamp—took this oppor-tunity of jostling me along, to ingratiate his commandant. I arrived at the garrison, the camp office of the commandant, who, however, lived on the Asiatic side.

I was shown into a small empty room.   The door was locked behind me, but after some time, fearing I would escape from the window, they unlocked it.   I was not allowed out of the room for the first day.   Repeated remonstrations with the posta resulted in nothing but the information that I had to call the Choush if I wanted anything.   Late that night they pushed in a filthy straw mattress, ages old.   Bugs fell from it as it was carried in.   It swarmed with them. Being by now fairly accustomed to them, I tried to sleep. Their voracity, however, proved too much.   I was not allowed to push it out of the door, so I put it out of the window into the street.   A posta was below, and reported this.   Another posta reappeared, and I gave him cigarettes for him to keep it.   He tried to sleep on it, and loud roars of laughter kept me awake all night.   They, also, had tried in vain.

A low-class Armenian was now allowed to buy me food. He retained half the price for himself.   The fellow was an absolute bounder and coward, a hypocrite at heart and a treacherous cur at all times.   I can safely say he spied not only to save his skin, but at any time there seemed money in it.

I heard tick-tacking in Morse from the men's quarters in the same quadrangle.   Quite an amount I made out.   They wanted money, money.   I tried to buzz a message or two back on the violin. Staccato notes are quite effective in their way. I had no access to the commandant. The room was small, but the light from the window was so intense that my eyes could not stand it. I hung most of my clothes upon it. When I did not sleep, I planned and planned escape. It all seemed futile, but nevertheless one went on. I wanted, at any rate, to get outside. Five days after, a Turk drove up in a carriage to see the commandant. He seemed a man of note, and I saw the commandant bow graciously to him, and make as to kiss his hand. Giving them time to get into conversation, I forced my way past the old posta, and kicked into pieces a door of what had once been a bathroom. One had got tired of being days without water or convenience. Three or four soldiers came in, but I made as if to bolt out the back way, and then sprinted upstairs, back as if to my room, passed it, and, in a wild, dishevelled state, burst in on the commandant. I gave my reason to the distinguished guest, and altogether the commandant was badly rattled, for I showed a letter from an important quarter in England about our treatment, and he appeared very disturbed. I made a horrible scene by refusing to leave the room, and eventually got leave to go out for a walk around the thirty yards' beat of the yard for half an hour a day. Here, for the first time, I managed secretly to get direct speech with our men, most of whom were either totally or partially disabled. They had been collected for exchange. On each occasion, months apart, they had got as far as the station, some even on to the train, but the train so far had never gone. They had not been paid for months. A Turkish subaltern had stolen some of their pay and faked a receipt.

Their parcels had been opened, and a one-armed sergeant, who spoke up, had been assaulted by the guard. We were almost the first officers to arrive at Psamatia, and the first the men had seen for years. From them I heard details of the fall of Baghdad.

I got a letter into the Kivas' pocket about all this for the Dutch Minister, Monsieur Villebois. A few days after this a fat, beefy figure entered the door and said, " Bleiben sie ruhig." It was our new commandant, Gelal Bey. I had at least effected some good result by getting the old rascal kicked out. I can honestly say that his own postas loathed him, and said he put their soup money in his pocket. Matters improved

BAGHDAD CAPTURED AT LAST. GENERAL MAUDE'S ENTRY

to a degree. Some order was possible, and a minimum of freedom. Gelal was a straight Turk, from what I saw of him, and certainly more fair. The men's complaints were heard and some were allowed a daily walk, although it was obvious my reputation was quite terrible. A raging toothache I had had for a fortnight was now mercifully righted. The other commandant had not allowed a visit to a dentist. Before this I had been fairly sick of my room, and even went so far as to try to burn the whole show down with a large box of matches which I stuffed in a rat-hole ; but the fire went out, probably, I should think, extinguished by bugs.

It was before this new commandant arrived that I commenced arrangements for sending news to England. A Sergeant Mandel, who had lost one arm at the shoulder, was to be exchanged, and I arranged for him to take it, as I thought him a likely person for exchange, but I wanted to run no risks. He was strongly for having it put in a crutch, or sewn into the sole of his boot ; but as I anticipated a search of every particle of kit, I adopted my own plan. With my scanty money I bought candles. Having written my letter quite small and as carefully as I could with my bunged-up eyes, I rolled it up tightly in a small cylindrical shape, and making a paper mould around it, filled up the interstices with dripped fat, thus making a candle with the letter inside. This was to preserve it. I shaved it down, pushed it in a water-bottle, and ran the other candles boiling into it, thus filling the bottle two inches from the bottom. I shook it, and found it firm. The bottle was then filled up with strong tea. This was because it was not transparent, and cold tea was a usual drink—when one could get it.

I hoped this would answer, and that they would not suspect anything. Nothing rattled, and inside the water-bottle was quite dark.

One letter was to Lord Islington, and contained, besides a *précis* of information I had been asked to send from the senior officer of the prison camp, a statement by me of the condition of the men, and their treatment since the trek. I gave some information on the high cost of living, and the great difficulty of keeping oneself alive without cashing many cheques at a worthless exchange.

I had heard of a convention recently signed between

England and Turkey at Berne about prisoners, and quoted some glaring cases of maltreatment which, as one of the original arrivals in Stamboul from provincial camps, I was in a position to know about. I sent also a few other matters of information about the state of Turkey. I prefaced all my letters with a statement, "I alone am responsible for statements therein, which are unknown to the bearer of the packet." I did this in case the letter was found.

I had scarcely got it away when I was sent to Harbiay Hospital for treatment. I had now left Kastamuni some ten weeks without receiving any medical treatment, except for one visit to a place called Tash Kushla, where a doctor examined my eyes, and said I was to be exchanged. Even in spite of my distrust, gradually a gleam of hope found its way into my mind, and grew to huge dimensions. I was afterwards coldly informed, however, that his actual written report was merely that Turkish eye treatment was preferable to German, and I was not to be allowed to go to German specialists !

At Harbiay I was put in a room with a half-mad Russian, who had been shot in the head, and some poor old Russian grey-headed men—sailors, I think—who smoked and cried most of the night. Here I had no food for thirty-six hours, and then only watery soup. We were not allowed to leave the room, and the postas were unusually brutal. The director of the hospital, who had been most kind to me at our first interview, offered to send me diet and books, and even medicine, and to attend to me himself—all of which I doubted. After about four days I was sent to a Turk, and an old savage he was, who said if God willed I would get right. Then a German doctor examined me, but was most aggressive and rude, and seemingly angry at being asked to diagnose an Englishman, and muttered something about this. He prescribed some special injection for my eyes. Then we were lined up, and were all dosed by a filthy Turk out of the same squirt, whatever our eye trouble was. This was a mistake, it appeared afterwards.

The next day, having hidden my trousers under my bed when I arrived (they always take away all one's kit on entering hospital) the guard was sent to get them. I put them on nevertheless, and then demanded to see the Director. It took all day to await my chance, but when the

posta was off the *qui vive* I ran along in my trousers and a
blue overall of the hospital towards his office.   It was a huge
building, and I got lost, but it was fatal to turn, so I went on
through numerous corridors with an increasing train of postas
at my heels, and finally fetched up in what appeared to be an
ante-chamber of the Director's wife.   The postas stopped
short and peered in at the door.   I apologized to the Turkish
lady, who was arguing with some Armenian maids.   She asked
why I was running away from the postas.   I assured her I
was doing nothing of the kind, but I was merely running to
the Director.   She was tickled by my having trousers, and
asked how I had managed it.   I explained that the Director
had given me a standing invitation to his office for any request
and that I had hidden my trousers to be able to do so.   She
rebuked me for breaking rules, and asked me what I could
possibly want.   I said I wanted to give some urgent information to the Chef d'Hôpital.   Finally, she conducted me to him.
He heard me coming, and I saw his face over the posta's
shoulder quite enraged and savage, and he said I was not to
enter.

It was spoken in Turkish.   I had, however, already
entered!   His face changed in a second, and he was the
crafty Director, professed huge surprise at my statement that
I had had no food and had not been allowed out of the room,
or to cash cheques, or to receive any attention, and that I
wanted to return to the garrison at Psamatia.   He promised
to remedy all things at once, and to send me " ée yemek "
(good food) at that very moment.   I extracted a promise to
depart next day.   How I loathed the place !   The Russians
alone made it unbearable, poor fellows.   They seemed on the
verge of suicide in that great empty room with hundreds of
beds in it.   Nothing else happened for two days except that
a Turkish doctor came and injected some serum into my eyes,
which he said was to happen three times a day.   The Director
himself came round next day, and tried to pretend he was
busy, when I went for him.   I made myself such a nuisance,
and torpedoed his dignity so successfully, that he finally un-
masked, and I knew him for the cruel, lying, and crafty type
of Turk, veneered with excellent manners, but a brute at heart.
It was the same fellow, as far as I can remember, who refused
a dying Russian officer's daily request for permission to have

one or two of his friends from Psamatia to see him in order
to make his will and provide for his wife and children. I had
been in Psamatia when our Russian friend (Roussine) had
daily asked for this from their end. Their letters were never
answered, but were destroyed by the old commandant, as
were the dying man's by the Director. He died. When he
had been dead some days the Director sent to Psamatia a
kind request to the officer to come and talk to his friend,
with private directions that they were to be told the man
had just died when they came.

Anyway, by the end of the third day after the "tor-
pedoing," my patience was at an end. I had learned, after
many weeks, how difficult it was to get out of a hospital once
one was in. After more scenes I left in the evening in an
arabana, bearing a letter in Turkish, saying I had been
excellently treated and had received the best attention
possible. On arrival at Psamatia my little sad room seemed
heaven again. I was alone, and the groaning of the Russians
was somewhere away.

The new commandant was haughty and somewhat Ger-
manic, but I found him a much better fellow, and straight.
He did what he promised. He heard my complaints about
the men, and rectified their pay and provisions, he got us
money, and sent me, on one occasion, a Polish book to read—
which tickled me. I found he meant well, and decided to culti-
vate his good graces, which I did in German. He had had
four years in Berlin, but sided against us in the war. Anyway,
he let me go to see Dr. König, a German eye specialist from
the *Goeben*, at a marine hospital around the harbour. *En route*,
the posta with me led me across the station, and in the crowd
I went to ascertain how to get a ticket, and found they would
have issued one to me right enough. Vesikas (passports), etc.,
were necessary, however, for the train, which went only so
far as San Stefano !

While awaiting Dr. König, I talked to a delightful old
French lady nurse, who was seventy years of age, and had
not been allowed to leave. I mixed freely with German
sailors from the *Goeben*, and heard of their escape from our
fleet. They thought they would win the war, but seemed less
confident than before for an early peace. They were all very
loyal, and stuck to it that their country was well provided for,

and " sehr billig." König I found a very capable and courteous officer, and quite efficient. He prescribed most carefully for my eyes, told me to avoid all glare, to follow his precautions, and I might prevent my eye trouble from becoming chronic. He explained my blurred vision and periodical darkness as nervous exhaustion, and related it to my spine, where it had been bumped by the shell explosion. He ordered rest and quiet, and sent me to his colleague, a nerve specialist. The net result was that I was not allowed to get the medicine as the shop recommended was not a Turk's, and I was sent to a Turkish nerve doctor, who mixed the whole thing up, and thought an operation on the eye was necessary, but, later on, said he had meant the other eye ! I felt like operating on both of his.

My visit to König, however, was momentous in one respect. On my way back I was stopped by an Englishman in mufti, and offered cigarettes. He seemed very kind, said he was a sailor man, and, before the posta intervened, gave me his address. We had to be careful, as the posta knew some English. In short, in five minutes we had agreed to escape. He was an interned civilian, taken at the outset of the war from his ship. I found out that church was the best meeting place. I hoped to further matters on my next day at the bath. I was now allowed out once a week. I found out which bath was best for my purposes by talking to the postas. The thing was to find one near the Galata Bridge. This was, however, out of bounds. I did the next best thing. Frequent visits to the commandant's room made me acquainted with the map of Stamboul. I found a bath, both hot and cheap, in the Turkish quarter but a mere five minutes' walk from the Galata Bridge. After two trips, and working the right posta with a heavy bribe of a two-lira dinner, I was allowed to a restaurant after the bath, but only on promising not to enter any shop. I stumbled most miraculously, however, into a Greek restaurant, which afterwards became quite a favourite centre of plots and plans. I eyed the place at once as very strategic. It was some steps down from the road, and not too conspicuous. One could see without being seen.

Two tables at the far end adjoining the wall had benches behind which one could slip letters, and I arranged for cushions to be placed there in which I could put letters in case the

posta searched, which he did more than once.   In the middle
of the door at the far end was a small pigeon-hole through
which the manager or his assistant shouted orders for food.
I gradually built up a disposition to order my own food.   A
few words were allowed.   Often I went up, and, completely
blocking the view, slipped in a letter.   I even went to the
extent of getting a message along the 'phone on the opposite
side of the street by two relays—the first from me to Theodore
in French, about food.   It was a great dodge to get some other
officer with one—*i.e.* to go in twos—and by some clear conversation with him in something the posta didn't understand,
give information to Theodore the manager.   In this way
we often ran a four-cornered conversation.   I paid heavily,
but money was forthcoming from my cheques, and the Dutch
Embassy's allowances came in regularly here.   Letters and
replies were received here from Dorst the sailor.   We formed
rendezvous for the church, if one could only get there.   The
Christmas season was approaching, and we assured Gelal Bey
we wanted to go to church.   We had asked very often for
months, but this had been refused.   However, the new
commandant allowed us this on certain severe conditions.

I shall never forget how restful and glorious it seemed to
get into the Crimean Memorial Church, an excellent chapel
built of stone off a side road in Pera.   An Englishman preached
most beautifully to us, and English people sat all around ;
but we were not allowed to speak or sit near them, and an
interpreter came to approve of the sermon.   Our money was
scrutinized to see if there was any writing on the notes.

I had a Burberry that I had dragged along with me on the
trek, and I often changed it for one very similar, having made
rents and marks similar on both.   One left at the door on
our entry would be substituted for the other, with notes
carefully sewn into the shoulders, underneath the lining.

On more than one occasion the crude efforts of our dear
countrymen and women to communicate with us brought us
within an ace of discovery and always intensified suspicions.
This often resulted in a redoubled guard or, greatest tragedy
of all, a blank week, when we were not allowed out at all
except along the wretched suburb of Yedi Kuhli.

But I proceed too rapidly.   All this took a long time.
Time for a prisoner with experiences such as mine behind one

is one terrible blank punctuated by moments that count. There is born a patience terrible with hope. To get out on Sunday we waited and planned all through the week, arranging appearances with postas, often waiting a whole day for a chance to speak a word freely to our brother officers, only possible when a certain posta was on duty at night. How seldom all the necessary elements of a setting to a single successful transaction are present, only a prisoner can know. But as I went homeward from that bath and restaurant and saw an avenue through that way to freedom, I felt hope once again stir within me.

In two or three weeks I had already got plans quite far advanced.

The scheme began to shape itself as follows :—

I would escape from barracks at Psamatia some Thursday night. This would give me a good start, as Friday is the Turkish Sunday, and inspections, etc., on that day are very slack ; in fact, the commandant did not always come out on that day. He also lived on the Asiatic side. The first step would have been impossible while I was in the garrison itself, as besides a permanent and personal guard on me there was one beneath my window, one at the foot of the staircase, and several on the door, besides one at each street corner. By complaining of the morning sun that poured into my room, and of the noise, I got a transfer to an old building opposite, the real reason being that my small room was watched and impossible.

The old building I had found out all about from a Russian who had been there before, and great was my delight in first getting over there. I had to pretend I was almost blind for days before I effected this. As a matter of fact my eyes were getting a little easier and only troubled me at times, so far as seeing went.

I had to be so very careful those first days. I was alone and all the postas watched every movement and seemed to suspect my very thoughts. So much so that I had never yet had an opportunity to go upstairs. After a few days I had got friendly with an old posta who generally came on duty very early. When he had got my cigarette well going I chased my kitten up the stairs. He helped me to catch it, and I had a good clear survey. A hammer to extract nails and screws from the window, and a rope to get on to the ground, were all that was necessary, provided we had a clear field. There were many difficulties, among which was the increasing of the guards, on account of a stampede of prisoners and the arrival of a whole regiment of Rumanians, that seemed to have surrendered intact. To make room for these the Russians were now moved from the Bastille at Psamatia and brought to my house upstairs. We were not allowed to talk to them, and guards to prevent this were stationed on the stairs. They could not be trusted, but Roussine certainly could. The others were curious to the point of being a nuisance, and while not on for escape themselves were not very sympathetic. Roussine was loyal, however, and most sporting. I spent long hours each day in watching every movement of the street and the habit of the neighbours. Near by, one old Turk, straight opposite our back windows, used to light his pipe about dusk and smoke well into the night, staring towards us. Another wretched fellow used the back road for his rendezvous with his sweetheart. After a few days I had collected a great amount of information and knew the routine of postas with their family details and homes ; they loved to talk of all this.

I became acquainted with the changes of police and the street traffic. My behaviour improved so much that I hoped the posta would soon be removed from our landing. I encouraged the habit of the postas meeting downstairs. This I did in various ways. One was by making huge cracks in the wall with an axe above where he stood. The cold was now acute. A little fire downstairs in an old kitchen, even after our frugal meal was finished, was a further inducement. A Turkish soldier loves to sit over a plate of hot cinders and dream of his fields and goats on the far-away uplands of Anatolia. They would not drink on duty, and seldom off.

A plan of the house was as follows :—

We were directly opposite the commandant's garrison, in about the middle of a street. The house on one side was, I believe, " to let " in its upper story. I formed wild notions of a secret tunnel through the wall from the inside of my cupboard, and a Monte Cristo chamber on the other side with a comfortable bed and excellent table, with an office for all kinds for secret-service meetings, with a free access to Stamboul through the back door by a change of kit. Alack and alas! the house proved very much inhabited, and often when I was spying on others I found they were spying on me. The basement of our house was only a cookhouse and a stairway that led up to the landing on the first floor, and up another flight to the Russian officers. On the second flight was a window-door, old and flimsy, that was nailed up. It led outside to a tiny landing that was surrounded by windows from other houses. Behind this landing was a tiny spare plot where a house had been burned down. Other windows high up in our lavatory looked down over roofs on to this section. I got through on several occasions and crawled on the tiles, which cracked like biscuits when one knelt not precisely at the sides. And this was very conspicuous, besides being right under the Russians' noses.

Doust and I had met once or twice at church. He had been in charge of a Turkish tug for months and knew the movements up to the harbour, ships' booms, the plans of mine-fields, and also replacements of guns at the Dardanelles. We intended to take these plans with us. He first of all promised an old launch to pick me up halfway to Galata, and go through the Bosphorus against the strong current. He was to bring Visikas (passes), and I was to go disguised with a fez. He said that the boom was open for hours each night, so that a small thing could get away. The whole plan had to be altered, however, on account of the Russian armistice and revolution. It was now the second week in December and the boom was closed all night.

Only traffic heavily searched was allowed through. This the Germans supervised, and they were thorough. I verified many of these facts from the German sailors themselves. In fact, quite often I wore my Burberry, and with my cap passed for a provincial German on several occasions with the German Tommies. Others thought I was a German American.

We altered our plan to that of going as fishermen, as these were still allowed out and in more freely. We should all be disguised as fishermen, get to a point inside the entrance, walk overland a few miles to the Black Sea, and then pick up the boat, which would be skippered by some reliable so-called fishermen through the actual entrance.

We only awaited a strong wind to enable us to get over

X

the distance in time, also some money, and the perfecting of the arrangement. I did exercises, tried to get fitter, and laid in a stock of necessaries and medicine for my eyes in case of exposure to the weather.

My difficulty was to see how to escape from my room just at the right moment. Neither part of the *bandobast* could wait for the other. Moreover, a chance had to be taken when offered, as everything depended on the right posta. To escape and hide in Stamboul seemed the best thing to do, but this meant that my chance of getting right away was lessened, as one would be sure to be missed after some hours, and at most after a day. This would be telegraphed all over the place and search would be redoubled. The ordinary risks were bad enough. Communication got very difficult owing to the capriciousness of the commandant, as he sometimes wouldn't allow me to go out, or only to a bath near by, and sometimes the posta was obdurate. On one occasion I crossed from one tramcar on to another and then back again on to the first, leaving my old posta revolving around helplessly. I had previously told him that if we lost each other, we should each go back at once to report. He was an old peasant from Anatolia, or I would not have dared this. I had promised him not to escape while with him. This I did first thing before he allowed me into the restaurant. A change of trams and swift walking brought me to Pera. I made plans and called at the rendezvous. Nothing happened. I left a letter and then drove back as hard as I could to Psamatia, passing the posta just before arriving there. He was weeping with fright and annoyance, but forgave me on seeing me again.

The new commandant gave me an orderly named Plaistow, from the Gloucestershire Yeomanry, and a very excellent fellow and good friend he was, although his cooking was not of the first grade. A night or so after this when he was rubbing my spine, from which I suffered acute neuralgia at intervals in the region of the bruise, the door opened and two British officers came in. Their physical condition and that of their kit marked them as just captured. One was a colonel named Newcombe, who had been captured north of Beersheba with a small striking desert force armed with machine-guns, during a phase of the battle of Gaza. On camels he had led the force, about sixty strong, without convoy, before the battle, by a circuitous route over the desert to the Turks' rear, and having captured cars and staff officers and generally enjoyed an excellent field day, he was himself taken after heavy casualties. A large Arab force, which by the Emir Feisul's influence should have co-operated, had let him down. I liked him at once. He seemed dead beat and very non-plussed, if not depressed, at being captured. He could not sleep, and I combated in my mind this new difficulty in my escape programme—of a colonel who could not sleep. A goodly number of the senior officers I had hitherto met in captivity were against escaping, some unsympathetic, some almost hostile, and one actually gave a written order to all officers junior to him not to escape. I was extracting secret delight from the fact that here at least was one colonel half asleep and little conscious of the fact that I was going that night, or certainly during the next few days, when, following a huge sigh, I heard the extraordinary words, " Mousley, what's the chance of bunking from this, do you know ? "

The colonel was eyeing me attentively. Gradually I acquainted him with how I had had designs to escape from the very first, but everything had been frustrated, that now once more I had a show on hand ready after much work and patience. We sat up in our respective beds, smoked many cigarettes, and planned. A bottle of bad whisky helped us. I found him a most interesting companion and very human. In fact, immediately after his capture he seems to have complained to Djemal Pasha about our men's treatment one moment, and the next to have proposed to Djemal's A.D.C., Ismed Bey, either to let him (Newcombe) escape or to let our Fleet into the Dardanelles, no matter which. We talked politics, and he put up all kinds of extraordinary and difficult schemes which we crystallized together. Actually I promised to let him join my escape plan with Doust, provided he agreed with the scheme and came under my orders so far as plans went. He agreed most readily.

This was necessary for many reasons, as I had trodden very delicate ground what with impersonating Germans, etc., and could not trust any one with the plans at that stage. He helped me most loyally and generously although not always effectively. To get out to Pera and Stamboul it was necessary to act, and act earnestly, before the commandant, and the colonel more than once abandoned the point and through lack of insistence lost the day. This meant hanging up things. My privileges of a bath and dentist had grown to be a regular thing, won single-handed after much struggle.

I had now to start afresh. To make matters worse some more officers, newly taken, now joined us. One was a fire-brand and tried shock tactics, such as kicking the postas. He did himself much harm and no one any good. Others were content to be told " Olmus " (Can't be done), but we old hands knew that by a judicious alternation of determined insistence and quiet submission one got ahead on the wave of the commandant's mood. My plans had to be altered on account of the extra guards put over us, and the heavy snowy weather. I managed after much difficulty to meet Doust and his friend, a youth named Castell, in a Turkish bath. Plans were ready. They cashed my cheque. The boat laden with oars, sails, provisions, and charts would come to a point half a mile from our camp the next night or two, depending on the weather. The signal was to be given by Castell passing at 2 p.m. precisely, smoking if we were to start and not smoking if it was off. He came and did not smoke.

After delay and trouble we got word from him that the wind had changed and it was impossible to get through the Bosphorus in time, before dawn, as the current was so tremen-dously strong, and the only way was somehow to contrive to reach a point by road about halfway along the Bosphorus, thus shortening the time. This meant more *bandobast*, more money, more contingencies, and more meetings with more interviews of the commandant.

By this time I was quite friendly with him and knew his politics. He was a German-hypnotized old Turk, too simple to be either clever or dishonest. He assumed the rôle of uncle to me. This I fostered and became a most unruly nephew constantly out of money (so as to get cheques cashed), full of pains (to get at a doctor—I mean Doust), persistent in wrong-doing, and contrite after commission.

My violin he quite loved (so he said), but while I played forte he little thought that the colonel was either pulling out nails from the escape window, or smashing the frame. I got a posta to help me haul up a bucket of water from the well at the foot of the stairs, and contrived to let it go with the end of rope and all. He certified this. We got a new rope. This we intended to use on the night.

About eight days before Christmas a change of plans had to be notified to Doust. Everything was "Yesak" (forbidden) on some new temporary order. I could not get out, so, much against my will, I trusted some one. Colonel Newcombe assured me that a Jewish Armenian interpreter who had just joined the garrison was absolutely trustworthy. He had carried several letters to the Embassy. I had written Castell (there was no time so I abandoned our code) a note giving a new sketch of our house, the section at the back, the place by which we would descend, and where Doust would meet us. Also I gave orders for a motor-car or arabana (Turkish carriage) to be half a mile off. We were to go hard for the Bosphorus point arranged. I put in urgent orders for roubles according to prearranged plan, also that the boat should have lifebelts (in case we had to swim for it at the entrance), charts, and certain food. Also bailers ! !

The letter was sealed and signed with the cryptic sign I used ⚭. This I gave to Newcombe, and, on his strong assurance, agreed to his giving it to the interpreter Fauad. He said he would take it. We waited for a reply.

Nothing happened for days. No reply or answering signal from Doust was forthcoming. We waited anxiously. About four days before Christmas, Fauad told me quietly after our evening meal (we were eating with the commandant and his staff, raw fish chiefly and soup beans) that he had posted the letter instead of delivering it. The censor had come to him secretly that night and for £1000 would keep quiet ! ! I tried to take this as coolly as possible, and announced as quietly that he would be hung at any rate for carrying the letter. This was to see if he was blackmailing. When we got back to my room we had a general council with the colonel and Gardiner, a captain of the Norfolk Regiment, whom I allowed to come with us. The colonel advised not taking him as he was not much used to the East, and he couldn't talk any language but his own. But I promised to let him come as he wanted to see his wife, and he was quite enthusiastic. It was a pleasure to me to see how keen he was and I admired him much for this. However, they both thought I should see the censor, and prevent him going to the commandant. I felt more and more strongly as I thought it over, that there was something unsatisfactory about the thing. The censor would not commit himself to Fauad and us. Moreover, would Fauad post it ? He was an Armenian and the Turks were against him. My friends insisted. I persisted.

For one thing I could not understand a Government censor, in a place so full of intrigues as Stamboul, playing with a noose to such an extent. But if Fauad was acting he did it well. A post-office official did visit him every day or so, but in spite of all, I could not get over the fact that Fauad had been quite cool when I had sprung it on him, that if the censor had seen it he, Fauad, would be hung. If the censor *had* seen it Fauad should have shivered. In the meantime I told Fauad we would pay a good sum, but not £1000, and pretending to be very frightened, showed him that we must be allowed to go to town often to get money. We would have paid a good deal even on the chance of the story being true, and intended doing so. However, I watched him carefully, and the more importunate he got, the more leave we obtained to town, where, needless to say, I strained every nerve to further and hasten our escape. We told Fauad we couldn't pay before a week, and hurried on our arrangements to get off before then. I grew more certain, day after day, that it was merely a scheme for getting money. He seemed to grow more anxious daily lest we should escape, but more, I believe, for fear he should lose the money than anything else. He tried to stop us from going to a certain bath where I had arranged a last rendezvous with Doust and Castell. At the last moment, through the innocence of some newly arrived subalterns, we nearly missed them. They wanted to go elsewhere as the bath was full—but I was undressed and through the door before they could get me back, and there I saw Doust and Castell. Fauad spied on me and followed me to the bath. I introduced him to Doust as an Armenian who would lend us the money in a few days, and thus I told a good deal of my story to Doust and Castell with Fauad not suspecting, and in fact being quite overjoyed about his money. A few moments alone when we got outside the bathroom, and our plans were ready. Fauad became rather suspicious, but I risked all.

When we got back I was greatly surprised to see a posta

PHOTO OF THE AUTHOR TAKEN SECRETLY WHILE A PRISONER IN STAMBOUL.

on the stairs and doors. The commandant knew nothing of this, but afterwards it appeared that Fauad had probably invented something vague about hearing us talking escaping, just to safeguard himself in case we went, and without divulging about the letter. This was a serious block. The stairs' posta had been taken off, and was now on again.

I had within three days to re-establish an entente with the commandant. We got ready. Our clothes we stuffed with cheese, oxo, cigarettes, and chiefly nuts and raisins. I wore my uniform under my mufti kit, as in certain quarters I wanted to pass as an interned civilian, in others as a German. I also had a fez.

By this time our plans for escape from the building were ready. The door could be opened noiselessly and on more than one occasion I got Colonel Newcombe to hold the rope while I went down to reconnoitre. I remember the exquisite feeling of being on the road outside the guard. I lay in hiding the opposite side of the wall and watched processions of people passing, the movement and change of sentries, and explored the street corners near by to see which were guarded. It was quite difficult to get back by the rope up the wall without knocking down old bricks or tiles. Doust failed me time and again on these occasions, partly through uncertainty whether to take a risk or not. As the day grew near we felt more and more our difficulty of communication. As I have said, I believe I was the first to have really a plan of escape in Kastamuni, and I can safely say that in no case of escape within my knowledge, was communication so very difficult. We had to have alternate plans.

Thus a tremendous storm burst at the entrance of the Bosphorus from the Black Sea and altered all the police arrangements. German reliefs changed the guard at the walls. I saw that the difficulty was to find an occasion when the auspices would be favourable both for getting out of my prison and getting away from Stamboul. On this account Doust promised to get me a secure place of hiding, in fact assured us both that in hulks lying in the harbour, or in quarters of Stamboul, it would be very easy and without risk to any one.

This latter consideration was my only deterrent from changing a life of wretched misery and oppression for comfort and rest, that the consequences for the unfortunate discovered sheltering us would be more than one could reasonably allow. Moreover I steadily avoided, so far as escape went, any assistance from women, let alone the kind and dear souls of the English fraternity who were in Stamboul. I considered it a selfish measure and one that no man has any right to accept from a woman unless she is professionally in the secret service. For a woman to risk the penalties of discovery in Stamboul might be a terrible ordeal. I had asked only to be shown an empty place, *e.g.* possible for a stowaway, and I would retrieve my own food.

In the meantime we had heard from Doust that he had suddenly decided to get married and would send, instead, a youth of about twenty, called Castell, more or less an English Levantine who could travel as a Turk or Greek, had a passport, and knew the country from Panderma to the coast. The plan had now been altered to the Dardanelles, failing which we were to make for Panderma and overland to Aivalik on the coast, thence to Mytelene.

The wind had been steadily east for days. No other craft was available except the sailer. But by leaving here, say Thursday night, and getting past the shipping zone by dawn and making the Dardanelles entrance late that (Friday) night, we should run the gauntlet through the narrow neck of Gallipoli past the unwary watchmen and lightship, and what with our capellas (Turkish officers' fezes) and a good German appearance of one of us, with a current of six knots plus the wind behind us, we thought it good enough. An hour or two later and we should be at Imbros, and pictured ourselves coming gaily along on a flood tide heading straight for our gunboats, probably attracting the fire of both our guns and the Turks'. Doust had verified that there were not very many surface mines, most, the nearest, being two feet deep. We drew about eighteen inches. Altogether it looked a most sporting chance and I can say that we enjoyed preparing our plans as much as schoolboys. The navigation was to be left to Colonel Newcombe, who made a quadrant, and to my excellent radium prismatic compass which I had retained from the retreat. Failing our reaching the Dardanelles in time, from stress of weather or other cause, we intended making for a point past Panderma, which we hoped to reach by next evening and from there march to the coast.

Just before Christmas the weather grew colder and more boisterous. I got leave to go to town and was allowed into the Maritza café. Here I found most urgent and useful news. Some fortnight before while walking with my posta, who was quite friendly towards me after his lira lunch, I told him I wanted to ask some German soldiers what mosques we could go to at Tchouka Bostan. Reluctantly he allowed me to speak to them. They took me for a civilian *interné*. I soon learned that German N.C.Os. often got along to the forbidden quarter, where were the usual nightly attractions for the troops, by pretending they were going to the *Korkovado*, a large Russian ship near the southern end of Galata Bridge, and used by the German General Staff Officers. Having got through the military police by saying they were off to the *Korkovado*, they swung past the ship around the bay. I intended to do the same, only to swing round out to sea. The restaurant man now verified this to be true.

The wind was so favourable and the position of our sailing boat, which had to be kept in an exposed bay in order to be ready, was so precarious that our friends sent us word that we must start Christmas Eve, notwithstanding the extreme cold. The idea of their arriving at the foot of the back wall was less to help us than to tell us whether the road was clear, *i.e.* on what streets the police sentries were, for as I have said, besides the garrison itself, a cordon of police surrounded most of the streets.

Doust and Castell came about six o'clock to the back street. As arranged, I had lowered a string down. Doust was to tie a note on the end if our plans were altered, and to smoke if we were to start.

Instead of this, however, they bungled badly, lost their direction in the dark, and jumped about in the most ridiculous fashion ; in fact, their proceedings were the most suspicious imaginable. They continued to grope in the wrong corner of the section and to take alarm at their own shadows. They had previously inspected the section and said they had located our rope. This they could not have done.

All this time I was on the ledge outside our house hiding, with Greeks and others peering towards me out of windows not eight feet away. One was smoking and washing up. I thanked Heaven it was dark. Once she called out asking if any one was outside. I could almost have reached her with a stick. The posta had cut off my retreat by going upstairs, but it appeared he did not know I was outside. I felt greatly amused at our sentry with fixed bayonet mounting guard on the stairs, his prisoner being a few feet away outside the house beyond the door, which I had shut after me. I heard my friends trying to get the posta downstairs. When his steps sounded as going downstairs I threw some small bits of clay towards Castell to show him where we were. He looked round helplessly. I dropped some just over our corner. It made a loud sound. Still he did not understand. Then I threw a large lump and hit him. He skipped like a jackal and took to his heels with a terrific clatter. Although it was annoying the whole show was so funny that I almost over-balanced with laughter.

I went after him down the rope and found postas and sentries wandering about us in all directions, but our friends had gone. Sentries being on all the streets and on the *qui vive*, I returned up the rope and sent my orderly to the bazaar. There he found Doust. They said they had only come to tell us that the boat had been smashed on the rocks near Psamatia and had also fouled the Galata Bridge. But we were to start next night and walk to Galata, risking the German police and so on.

This was Christmas Eve which we now proceeded to cele-brate, and determined to start next day. The other officers bearded the commandant's cat, a satanic beast that had stolen our food often. It combined all the cunning and resourceful-ness of a dozen cats. It broke several windows and went for several of us before we despatched it. As a matter of fact, I deprecated all this as it meant renewed guards.

But our escape was known only to me and two other officers, as more than one found the topic all engrossing, and the newly captured had no idea of the danger from the Turkish spy system of being overheard. I was feeling pretty done up with the tension of waiting and waiting for days on the point of going every moment. I did not go to church as I wanted rest, and we had had a boisterous night. They brought back a note from church saying we should be off that night. All this meant an appalling amount of anxiety, as we had to eat with the commandant opposite. However, at the last moment a posta appeared, and in any case the wind was unfavourable and no signal came. We opened our Christmas parcels from the English community at Pera, and the colonel and I smoked on still full of hope. The posta pacing outside my door kept me awake. Alarmed at this embarrassment to our escape I protested loudly with him and called the guard to stop him. It was maddening to any one in our state of nervous health (besides inconvenient for the escape).

First thing next morning I went to Gelal Bey, our commandant, and complained. He smiled and shook his head. It was necessary. We had been caught speaking in church. I assured him it was the Christmas season, a season of peace on earth, not of tramping postas, etc. He laughed and said he would take him off late in the night. I asked him if he thought I was going to escape. This completely disarmed him. He indignantly said " Of course not. My arrangements are complete. You cannot." And he took off the posta at once. We had dinner, intending to start as soon as we got back from the commandant's house. The whole crowd of officers and clerks was there with the commandant at the head of the table. Colonel Newcombe was so silent and thoughtful that I thought something would be spotted. I contributed some liveliness, however, and drew up elaborate schemes for to-morrow's marketing and getting boots mended, and the usual routine. On returning to our room the posta was off, as had been promised.

Now I had been marked as an escape officer, and had refused my parole several times, so I was not bound in any way. I therefore assumed my disguises. I bulged horribly with my double clothes. Parts of this diary I had around my waist, and some in a roll which I had sealed. I waited twenty minutes from my hiding place outside, disguised and ready. Should we start or was it another failure ? Then two highly-nervous figures passed at a quick walk, or run, beckoning us to come at once. At the last moment they abandoned all our careful plans, why, I never found out. I told them to wait a second and watch, as we heard sentries. They did not. We risked it. Half a word to the others and we were down the rope. I went first, then came the colonel dangling two legs

in the air in great style. We waited at the foot of the rope
while people passed. After a terrible delay Gardiner's little
stout figure appeared on the rope going round and round. I
reconnoitred and went ahead. Doust and Castell had simply
sprinted on ahead rather panicky. I set out to track them.
The others walking together tracked me. At last the two
appeared, and Doust on seeing me started at a run evidently
thinking me a German or sentry. It was awfully funny. I
called to him to walk quietly, but he could not. His was just
the way to attract notice. He led us miles round the seashore, and many people regarded us wonderingly. Finally,
in reducing our going to a normal walk, we lost Doust altogether. At last when we reached the most glaring quarter, to
our horror he came out in the main streets. Some one asked
for a light. I went on.

The night was rainy and sticky, and what with two suits,
a heavy trench burberry lined, and with about ten pounds of
food, I developed a most awful stitch in my side. The weight
of my coat I estimate at twenty pounds. The others felt the
walk less, but then I was a much older prisoner, and had been
solitarily confined for weeks and weeks, often without stretching my legs. More than one policeman looked at me. I wore
a fez, and at last Doust walked more slowly. With my
burberry on and field cap I passed as a German. While
carrying my burberry on my arm and wearing a mufti jacket
and fez, I passed for a local inhabitant. We adopted our own
pace and walked on opposite sides of the road. The colonel
most kindly changed coats with me, his being much lighter.
In the heart of the traffic by the tramway at Sedkigevy,
Doust stopped us to sign some document purporting to be
that he had helped us to escape, so he said! He gave us a box
of wedding cake at the same time, for he had been married
on Christmas Day. We put our names on the paper without
reading it as we were under every one's eye. Rather an unnecessary and totally unwise procedure I thought. We were
now nearing Galata Bridge. Passing Maritza café, now dark
and gloomy, I jocularly suggested a drink. It was, of course,
closed. Doust shook hands and left us. Castell had gone
ahead it seemed, and ought now to be paddling about disguised as a boatman near Galata. Early that evening he had
sent some one ahead with some bribes for the Turkish water

police, whose duties were to examine any one leaving the jetty by Galata Bridge. The German guard also was informed that some German officers were coming over to the *Korkovado*. I now walked on a hundred yards ahead alone, with a good Prussian swagger, wearing my burberry and cap. A Turk or two saluted me, and some Germans also. But one of the latter came boldly up to me and I thought I was discovered. The Germans would be the last to let us escape, although they often sympathised with us. I pretended, however, I was in a great rage. I roared out in German for a boat for the *Korkovado*, and spoke sharply to the police, asking them if they had nothing to do. The fellow then stopped, turned, and strode off on the regulation beat. A boat now came out from the ruck with several others behind it. I recognized Castell disguised as a ferryman, and got aboard.

A few moments afterwards, what seemed ages to me, the other two appeared, the police regarding us all. We pushed off. The water was choppy even here. We passed the *Korkovado* in the dark, the anchored boats, and what appeared to be a guardship. Here certain boats were challenged. Castell earlier in the evening by lying off for some time near these boats, had heard the password given by other boats on going past this point. He now used it once. As the water moved behind us, one felt that one was at last committed to the attempt for good or bad. Stamboul was behind us. We had now actually reached the Marmora Sea by steady rowing. It was about 8.30 p.m.

We had purposely not conversed until we were away from the jetty, and now took stock. Our dismay may be imagined when we found the money had not been brought, and for which we had given cheques. The boat we had bought. The life-belts had been forgotten. I had said we couldn't start without them. In fact, these and buckets for bailing I had repeatedly asked for, and was assured they were there. There was no spare mast, one faulty rowlock, a chart and telescope. We might have been going on a voyage of discovery to a new America!

I put the wedding cake down near our seat, and four dozen eggs Castell had brought were placed on another. Castell and Gardiner and I alternately sat on these. In fact the boat seemed full of eggs, and we joked about poultry farming.

Only two loaves had been brought.   Then I sat in some more eggs that were covered up by a coat.

We were now a mile or more out in a dark heaving sea, at this stage about a foot of water in the boat, which plunged violently especially as Castell's oars were generally in the trough of the sea just at the wrong time.   By the light of our lanterns it was a queer show altogether.   Gardiner moved about in a most unsteady fashion, with wedding cake sticking to his clothes, and we were all over egg.   I fell to eating them raw. Ever since the sporting days of my youth I have liked eggs. The others chaffed me about this, and we became quite jocular over the whole show.   The wind and sea now made progress difficult.   I opined that if we didn't get on, the commandant at dawn would see us from his window.   Castell had told us he knew everything about a boat.   In fact, he knew extraordinarily little.   He assured us that when we got out a bit more the wind from the Bosphorus would enable us to hoist a sail. We were a long while getting there, and more than once were very nearly upset.   The swell increased tremendously.   One second we saw the gloomy form of mosques and minarets, and lights, the next we were in the trough of the sea.

I had had the rudder, but now started to bail out with small tins.   It was useless to be angry with our well-meaning friends, but to put it simply, the whole *bandobast* was a horrible "let down."   I have before been in a storm without a bailer, which had been washed overboard, and almost lost my life through the same cause.   Gardiner nearly fell overboard more than once in shifting about.   I was trying to bail with one hand and keep the boat's head on to the sea, eating eggs in spare seconds.   The boat rose and fell and plunged severely.   Suddenly Castell's oars fell plop into the sea, and he vomited frightfully.   Here was our skipper sea-sick !   I am afraid I was bad-mannered enough to laugh outright.   Colonel Newcombe joined in.   Gardiner was silent, we learned why a few minutes later.   Colonel Newcombe pulled splendidly for some time, and then I, and then Gardiner.   The colonel and I bailed with all our might, bailing out eggs (the bad ones floated), wedding cake, cheese, and all kinds of garments. The boat was like a horse out of control.   And filling rapidly. Gardiner couldn't get both his oars into the water at the same time, or if he did they fouled his knees, and his legs beat the

LIEUT.-COL. S. F. NEWCOMBE, R.E., D.S.O., WHO ATTEMPTED TO ESCAPE WITH ME BY
BOAT OVER THE MARMORA SEA

bilge and air trying to recover his balance. Then Colonel Newcombe took the oars again, and we got along, although slowly. Subsequently our skipper decided on the sail. We ran it up, and the boat sprang before the wind in a most enthusiastic manner. The boat, I have forgotten to note, was about twelve feet long, and, of course, quite open. She cut through the water at a great pace, the black waves rushing past us like snakes. We were heading, however, between Haida Pasha and Principo instead of the open sea, and we thought of General Townshend asleep in his excellent bungalow, and some one suggested we paid him a visit.

I suggested at this juncture that the Dardanelles were not in this direction. We tried to get her around, but the wind was changing and varied greatly. It now came on to blow a gale. There was nothing for it but to tack. Our tacking, however, was much like a political speech of Mr. Asquith, chiefly zigzag, without much progress. The wind beat us up to the Bosphorus, and one tack very nearly landed us on a buoy. We were driven in the wrong direction, and I prophesied we would ultimately land in the Sultan's kitchen. Poor Gardiner now became very sea-sick, and said things to me for eating eggs. I said I enjoyed them, and that as a matter of fact I hadn't been able to afford eggs for ages.

Suddenly there was a loud report, as if some one had fired from close by. The boat nearly upset. We shipped a heavy wave that broke over us, and something wild and heavy smothered us. It was the sail. The mast had broken off short above the stays. We were very nearly wrecked, for the boat was heavily waterlogged and still leaking horribly. Hitherto our pace had kept her going. We all bailed for life, then Newcombe and I took the oars. There appeared to be no spare mast or cord. Then we bailed for life, while the colonel pulled magnificently.

When he was tired I took over, and found that, notwithstanding my back, I could pull fairly well.

To attempt to go on was ridiculous, even if possible. It was freshening to a heavy gale outside, and we had taken about two hours to get two or three miles. Castell proposed landing at Haida Pasha and walking to the coast, which, of course, was a most childish idea, meaning a huge and unnecessary march without arrangement. I proposed we all returned and got a place of hiding until a proper *bandobast* could be made. This had been faithfully promised us. It now appeared, however, that there was no arrangement made, and we were advised to go to Doust's house. This we all refused to do, as he was now a married man. We begged hard for some other hiding-place until a plan for escape could be made, but nothing seeming possible without implicating women, we decided to return.

Sadly we put the boat about, and made for the lights of Topkana. The water literally poured into the boat. After several narrow shaves we regained Galata Bridge, but instead of returning to the same jetty, I decided to cross under the bridge, and disembark the other side. This we did without mishap. Rendered bold by disaster, we were rash to the point of recklessness, and I set out to get a carriage, leaving the others by the quay. This I did by haranguing an Armenian driver in broken Turkish and German. He was to drive us back to the Arc Serai, a military quarter not far from Psamatia. The others clambered in with me.

We left Castell to do as he liked with the boat. Short of encumbering our English friends there was nowhere to go, although we had been assured there would be when we started, and we all realized only too well the double difficulty of making the opportunity of getting out of the house coincide with that of getting right away. We thanked Castell and said "good-bye." I first took the precaution to indicate the line of defence in case we all came up for trial about the letter.

We drove past police and sentries without mishap, and I thought how easy it would have been to have gone the same way.

The question now was how to get back to garrison. The colonel advocated driving to the commandant and saying we had been out for a " nuit joyeuse," a sort of supper and dance programme, in fact. Gardiner, on the other hand, advocated " benefit of clergy." We were to walk to the house of the Catholic padre, who had been very good to us, and get him to take us back like prodigals. Both of these courses I thought unnecessary, and determined to try to get back undiscovered.

We passed many police and sentries, who came out to look at us, but we kept talking French, and except for a *chokidar*, who followed us and kept hammering the street with a stick, and who eyed us most severely, we arrived at the back entrance without incident. I left my friends behind and reconnoitred, intending to get back if possible over the roofs. To my great astonishment, however, the rope was still there. Now, before starting, I had asked our friends left behind to pull the rope up between one-half and one hour after we had left. The reason was that I didn't want the rope discovered at dawn or by some night watchman, thus advertising the escape. And if, on the other hand, the strong cordon of police and guards round about the camp rendered escape impossible, we should be glad of the rope. It was, however, now long after midnight.

I asked the colonel to be especially cautious, as I felt certain there must be some reason for the rope being there.

He climbed up, leaving his coat with ours, which we tied with the end of the rope. In getting up, however, his foot went through a pane of glass. But he arrived at the top, peeped in, and said there was no posta, and the road was clear. Gardiner and I arrived up, in fact I helped him over the wall, as I found his nose, hands, and feet all together within a few inches of the top as he had tried to scale the wall like a steeplejack. He went inside and I remained to bring in the rope and coats. Laden with all these and twenty feet of rope I was just about to enter the door, when I saw a Turkish posta returning up the stairs. It afterwards appeared that he had been sent on duty shortly after we escaped, probably by a secret order of the commandant, and had only gone downstairs for a moment to see what caused the falling glass.

Dropping all my kit and the rope on the landing, and closing the door, I rushed downstairs as if coming from the Russians above, shouting that some one was ill. I managed, of course, to collide forcibly with the posta, knocking him and the lamp downstairs. While my friends arranged his injured feelings, I made for my room, tore off my clothes, and got into pyjamas.

It was now necessary for some one to go down the rope again to get some coats and disguises which had fallen down through some one's tying them to other coats in the loop instead of on to the rope. The colonel very sportingly insisted on going down the rope while I, in bare feet in the thinnest of pyjamas, made a violent demonstration downstairs, saying I insisted on going to the shops to get some brandy for an officer who was dangerously ill. As I expected, the posta downstairs, thinking I was escaping, called his friend

Y

from above, who came down, leaving the road clear. They both hung on to me and drew their bayonets. I managed to delegate one to ask the commandant for special leave, while the other was compelled to remain at the front door.

There is nothing like thoroughness on these occasions. This gave them a good fifteen minutes to get the coats, and hammer up the door, which had been hanging by a nail. We made some hot tea, one of the most glorious drinks of my life, and, quite exhausted, slept. The last words I heard when going to sleep were from Colonel Newcombe, who said, " For Heaven's sake let us never mention escape again." But an hour before the dawn he and I were both at work with a small hammer inside our charcoal cupboard, hammering a hole through the wall to next door, which we believed " to let."

We worked at this the whole of the following day, and except for the sentries being on duty permanently outside our door, no one visited us the whole day. This shows how well the plan for having a good start would have succeeded.[1]

[1] Col. Newcombe, Captain Gardiner and I received mention in the post-war despatch "for gallantry in escaping or attempting to escape while prisoners of war" (5.5.19).

CHAPTER XIV

DISCOVERY OF THE LETTER—BRUSA—COURT-MARTIAL—LIFE
IN A STAMBOUL PRISON—POLITICS AND INTRIGUE

ON the day following this, extra sentries were put on us, and all privileges stopped. Nothing was known, but it appeared that Fauad was suspicious, and had probably informed the captain of the guard. He was more importunate than ever for money. The crisis was precipitated by our discovery that he had appropriated large sums of money for cheques given to him by other officers. He said that the censor had become impatient, and that he had had to be paid with this money. I got Fauad to come to our room. I proposed to buy the letter off him, as it was stamped. He first swore that he had the letter, and on our producing the money, some only of which we wanted to give him, he started to blackmail us by refusing to say where the letter was until he got the whole sum. It ended up by me closing the door and saying I wanted the letter and proposed to take it. He was a tall but sloppily built fellow, and after a straight one on the point of his chin I back-twisted him over the iron bed. We searched him, but found nothing. It was at this point when he said the letter was known about, and when it seemed he would betray us in any case, that another officer caught him by the throat. But he managed one wild yell, which brought up the sentries. I was marched off with fixed bayonets for about the tenth time in my career as a prisoner of war, but had time to hand my pocket-book and papers to a friend before this happened.

The commandant kept me waiting a long time, and, of course, the letter was produced, but not a word was known of the escape. I believe they sent urgent telegrams to the mouth of the Bosphorus police, so that if we had actually got away to the Dardanelles, fortune would have assisted us with an extraordinary false scent. In the meantime, the commandant's wrath was terrific, in fact, as I explained to him, it was rather unnatural, seeing he had once said he would adopt me as his nephew. But, alas, he was beyond a joke.

I was remanded under a heavy guard, who inspected me about every five minutes, so that work at the hole had to cease, and two nights after, we were carpeted before a Court of Inquiry consisting of the commandant, another officer, and some one from headquarters. As we didn't know whether the letter actually existed now, there was no point in saying much. But the colonel, when asked why he wanted to go out, said " Pour une nuit joyeuse," comprising, presumably, a dinner at the Tokatlion and a fairy row on the Bosphorus. His countenance, however, and mine also, fell when the commandant produced the letter, all about our roubles and lifebelts, and the way to Russia. But when the commandant jeered at the colonel as being too old and past his prime for such undertakings, I laughed out aloud, for on our actual show, so far as physical serviceability went, the colonel was worth about six of us.

At the inquiry the others left the affairs to me. The net result was that by evasive answers and careful admission we were able, while sticking completely to the truth, to save the escape from being divulged. At the beginning of the inquiry we thought they had found out from Castell, who, we were informed, was under arrest. Our fears were allayed and our cautions justified when it turned out that nothing was known.

One was amused at hearing the old commandant's boast about his having made it too difficult for us to get out.

" Why didn't you start ? "

" We did not start for the Black Sea because you had got our letter of plans, and then it was difficult with our sentries," etc., etc. So I replied.

Masses of documents were compiled. The colonel was twitted about one so senior as he being led astray by me ! And I was locked up.

I had only got one message away, about trying to establish a hiding-place, and I feared I would be sent away now to camp. The others, after several false starts, left one night in a hurry with a heavy guard for Afion Kara Hissar, the camp away back near Konia. Col. Newcombe and I had patched up all sorts of schemes in the meantime. The difficulty now was how to communicate with him. One good scheme was by intercepting letters arriving from England for him after he had left, and adding words. In fact, more than once I took such a letter and extracting a bill, sent on news from England and from myself, which practice became general.

A week later I was, to my great delight, examined by a doctor for my spine—a concession due to the kindness of the commandant, whom I played to across the road one or two tunes he had informed me he liked.

One had to bank on there still being a soft place in his heart for me. But he resolutely refused to see me. I wrote him, saying he couldn't be more angry if I had got away ; yet, here I was, and might I not be allowed to stay in Psamatia— my parole, of course, being impossible. I got no answer, but to my delight he followed Dr. König's recommendations for me to go to the baths at Brusa, the Generals' camp, the reason he gave being that my former General (G. B. Smith) had no A.D.C., and I might join him. I was paid up to date (Gelal was an excellent fellow in this way) and in the early twilight, one snowy morning, with my sad little bundle of baggage in front on a donkey cart, I set out with a heavy guard, who watched me every second. My guard had evidently had terrific orders, but I managed to implicate them into a fray with some German soldiers, who didn't understand Turkish or that I was a prisoner. One of them gave me a *Tageblatt*, which I returned during the fight with a letter inside for the Dutch Embassy, containing news as to my departure. This I hoped would let every one concerned know at once where I was off to.

The steamer trip was wonderful after so many years away from a ship. I watched a German officer and a rather pretty German girl on board. They were quite polite, drank beer marked Münchener, and talked about friends on different fronts. It was roughish weather. We got to Panderma about 3 p.m., caught a tiny train that wound over pretty, undulating country for twenty miles, bringing us nearer and nearer to the snowy heights of Olympus. One and a half hours later I was put in a gharry (*quel luxe !*) and taken to the commandant, a youngish Mir Ali, who spoke a little

French and tried to appear kind. Our *entente cordiale* progressed considerably, he pointing out how he loved all his generals and other prisoners, and how they loved him, and how I must also get to deserve his affection, as he put it. He said we were all free, had a posta each—I already saw myself near Olympus, making a bee-line for the coast—and then he opened my confidential report from Gelal. The commandant's jaw fell, and he got black with rage at having taken me, as he said, for a *bon garçon*. I was, it seemed, a horrible "escape officer," and had come to stir up his flock to revolt, etc., etc. I should go to the bath only once a week, and not enjoy any privileges or walks, etc. Knowing the Turk by this time, and seeing much hope ahead, I said little. The generals were in what had been a hotel, and were divided into several messes. They had a garden in front of the house.

Captain Goldfrap, whom I remembered from Kut, came to take me up to General Delamain, who was kinder to me than I can say. He gave me dinner and some cognac. I was half frozen with the snow. I noticed that his first questions were about his officers and men. The generals had been cut off for long from all the rest of the Kut force, and I enlightened them considerably. General Evans, made a brigadier in the last days of Kut, was still as cynical as ever. On this first night of comparative comfort, I also talked to Major Hibbert, whom I had had a little to do with when on General Smith's Staff. They were all very, very kind to me. I didn't say a word about escaping just yet. General Delamain talked to me quite a long time after the others had gone. He was as cool and unruffled as ever, and weighed the political news I gave him very carefully. He was very much more *au courant* than most officers through having read German literature "on the passing show."

I rigged up a bed and slept. In the early hours of the dawn I felt more peace than I had had for years. Snow was still falling. I was very much impressed with every one's kindness to me, a subaltern, and, knowing how hard up they all were, decided to go on my own so far as possible. As I lay in bed shivering with cold, I found a figure rattling tea-things beside me. It was Namatullah, the faithful Mohammedan servant of General Smith, who had heard I was back. He was always the best of servants, and his delight at seeing me was a rare

HOTEL AT BRUSA
WHERE OUR GENERALS, WITH THEIR A.D.C., SPENT THEIR CAPITIVITY

treat. Later I got a servant to myself from the camp. The escape got abroad the next day, when orders came that I was not allowed to go out. But the generals one at a time took me for walks, or went bail for me.

Life here was more possible. They had books and papers not so very old. They had had over two years of uninterrupted study, and were very proficient in acquired languages. General Melliss I thought more aged than the rest. His captivity sat heavily upon him. He also was extremely kind to me, in fact, I might say that one of the most wonderful experiences of my many and varied phases of captivity was meeting these senior officers of our army in captivity. More than ever I saw deep into those traditions of the old British Army, where efficiency, quietness, and comradeship took first place. I felt that for these men captivity was even more serious than for me, for, although their careers were more or less perfected and mine broken off sharply at its beginning, still they had so much less time left.

I am writing this part in Brusa, some little time after, and want to give first place to this important record. I am tempted to remark with Stevenson on the glories of old age. Youth is uncharitable to youth, so coltish and impatient with short-comings, and so infinitely borable. My whole experience of captivity showed nothing to equal the brave resignation of these Christian men at Brusa, "their kindness and forbearance, their oversight of imperfections." And I had had the privilege of seeing their brigades in action, and knew them one and all by common report for men who would have had their own armies to command if they had been spared by fate for France. I only hope that if ever anything of all this is published they will not take amiss anything written herein.

Later.—Most of the notes of my life in Brusa have been lost. I must only record the gradual relaxation of my restrictions, and my earning, by good behaviour (!), the right to my own posta, who took me through the sights of old Brusa—for this was the former capital—to the Green Mosque, and some-times away to the near foothills. Brusa is a smiling valley. The high-road was forbidden, and it was only when we got a new posta that we could go there.

I discovered most excellent companions in Major Hibbert and Captain Goldfrap, who sometimes walked with me, and were most strenuous workers at languages. General Hamilton sometimes gave me tea and talked India and history, and General Smith talked chiefly fishing. He seemed much restored by his captivity, and walked at a tremendous pace. General Delamain I discovered was a chess player, and many were the excellent games we played together. He was very much stronger than I, but I improved, and managed to win about one in three later on, Queen's Pawn Opening being the only one that he ever succumbed to. We had frequent talks on politics and travel. He has many points of contact outside his profession, and is most exceptionally well read in foreign politics and international movements. On occasion at the football field I was sometimes privileged to discuss with him the larger game of chess that seemed to promise to pass from an apparent stalemate to decisive results. The collapse of Russia was now more than ever apparent. It was the fourth week of March, 1918.

I had got to know Brusa fairly well by now with a view to politics, and had sounded many of the prominent Turks there. It was seething with sedition and readiness for revolt.

Suddenly two pieces of news arrived simultaneously. Without notice I was ordered to Stamboul under a heavy guard, being told I was probably to be exchanged. . . .

And a heavy barrage of artillery had begun in France.

After dinner General Delamain took me into his room. We had some Brusa wine and a long talk. He pointed to the paper, and said he believed the beginning of the supreme test had arrived. Facts following on this showed how right his judgment was. He was most kind, and offered to lend me money, for which I thanked him sincerely, but said I had enough.

In fact, I told him I expected to be up either for a court-martial or else to be going home. We had a pleasant evening, and he wished me all luck.

General Melliss also gave me a tin bath and some good advice. I collected orders for articles wanted for when, if ever, I should return, and left at dawn.

The journey I made under a most undesirable character, called Mohammed Ali, a Turkish subaltern, thoroughly dishonest and treacherous, and a bully. We soon came to loggerheads, as I realized I would get no privileges from him except what I took. I was driven to the Brusa station in his gharry, for which he made me pay two liras. When we got to Modarnia I had to wait an age on the roadside in a biting wind. This, I remember, set my neuralgia going severely in my back. It was necessary to wait, he said, while he bargained for various hens and a lamb, which he proposed to turn over at a profit at Stamboul. Then, when I went for a meal to an exorbitant Greek, he wanted to stop my ordering from the waiter, even through him, and proposed to decide what I should eat, and this, when he proceeded on the usual presumption that I would pay for him. We did this on occasion, but the regular thing into which this custom had grown was often exploited against us. He ran up a huge bill of about two liras, which he was so certain of my paying that he started bullying beforehand. His face, when I didn't pay, was a study for Mr. Punch's artist.

The sea ran high and our boat left before we arrived. I hoped for many things if we could wait that night in Modernia, what with communications and plans useful in case I returned to Brusa. No one had ever stopped there. As bad luck had it, a terrible little produce boat turned up late in the evening, and, with many cattle and sheep and hens, we crouched down from the wind. It was the third week in March, and at this season the Marmora can be very rough.

White horses raced by, and cold spray dashed over us. Except in the sun it was almost freezing. We called at two or three little ports. The weather grew worse, and every one was seasick, including Mohammed Ali. It was a race as to who would be sick first. He eyed me helplessly. And, of course, no sooner had he been sick two minutes than I had a letter or two off. I felt sick, but was not actually so, and tried to hide it. Later, I was allowed into the captain's wheelhouse, and sat down. The sea was very rough, and got so bad that we had to lay to all night off an island, where we tossed and tossed. All the Turkish peasants, men and women, went through their toilet in the dark, and what with men smoking, women being seasick, and children—dozens of babies bawling their heads off—I had plenty of entertainment. I paid a lira for a place to stretch my legs and, later on, slept. Before morning I had appropriated a fat peasant for a pillow, in discovering which at dawn he was so honoured that he gave me some cigarettes. Here Mohammed Ali butted in and kicked him. However, I gave my place to him to finish my lira's worth, and at this Mohammed Ali became nearly mad with annoyance. During the previous day the cattle had stampeded from side to side, and as the boat heaved one went overboard, but was recovered. One was lost for good. More than once, when the tiny top deck was deserted except for my guard and myself, Ali edged away from the heaving side and eyed me most furtively. I saw what he was thinking of. I laughed, and caught hold of him, and he squealed and had his posta brought up. I informed them both that they must be careful, as the boat was rocking and the sea was rough and that one cow had gone overboard !

The next morning we awoke to a magnificent dawn, and all was still. Across a silver, warm, and sunny sea we cut a gleaming path towards Stamboul. Land was scarcely in sight, and I was alone with the sea. Things deep down within one stirred with a sympathy now long grown old. . . . The sea and destiny and the secrets ahead of us, known only to these both. . . . Here was I, returning to Stamboul either to the wonderful far-away world that lay before April 29th, 1916, or to prison. I knew not which.

At about 3 p.m. the minarets of Stamboul stood out of a glorious afternoon sky. I saw the scene of our adventure, and soon was ashore once more by Galata Bridge.

Here I found a whole *posse* of police to escort me, and began to realize I was not going back to London !

On shore I found the most indescribable bustling in the streets, and newspapers and bulletins were being bought everywhere. My guard, and, in fact, several people, shouted out to me as we went on, that England was "biti" (finished), that our French front had collapsed, and we had lost 40,000 in prisoners alone. This increased my guards' excitement so much that they walked at a fearful pace, and I told them that when their news was bad they went slowly, and when good they ran. This steadied them, and we clinked along over familiar streets, and I expected to be going to Psamatia again, but, instead, I was left with my guard outside the Ministry of War, in the large square known as Serasquerat, in the centre of which stood a very old tower, Yargun Kuhle. Here, after some delay, I was sent into a room, and some insolent Turkish officers gave contradictory orders. My kit was burst open and searched, and anything like a knife or matches, or razor, or even the commonest utensils such as a fork, were all taken from me, together with any written matter or books. Then I had another long wait in the central hall, while Staff officers came and went, all talking about the great news.

I was dead tired and hungry, having eaten only an egg and some bread since leaving Brusa, thirty-six hours before. My back gave such trouble I could hardly sit up straight. Ultimately I was taken to a building called the Marhbesana, a gaol where military and civil offenders languished and died. I had heard a lot about the place. Four British officers had been in it and one had died there. It was half full of Armenians, who were spared until they divulged where their money was, or of officers put on one side by Enver, and of scapegoats, a few of whom, no doubt, deserved being there— excluding myself. I went along hard stone passages to a fellow called Djemal Bey, acting commandant of the gaol, who wouldn't say anything about me, why I was there, or what I had to do. I grew very tired and impatient at another long wait of over an hour, standing up. Then I was put into a room with an old Arab and a dishonest-looking civilian Turk, and a renegade Egyptian. I was to be left here " a moment," so my escort said, as he went away, but the door was barred, and I realized that I was a prisoner in this wretched tiny dark room, with a window looking out on the passage and an appalling lavatory place opposite. A heavy guard on the door paced ceaselessly to and fro, and had strict orders about me. I was not to be allowed anything.

The Egyptian actually made me a cup of coffee. He was a cross-eyed sort of chicken-and-egg lad one sees in Port Said, but I preferred him to the rascally Turk, who was from Rumania, a clerk fellow, who called me Herr Leutnant, and, when he wanted anything, Herr Hauptmann. Shouting and roaring went on between these people. I got a sort of tiny wooden frame down and tried to sleep. One couldn't walk or move about while the others were there, for want of room. The Arab was evidently a man of some position from Aleppo. He proved a fanatic, and prayed every half-hour on his mat, working his lips the while.

He had all the fervour of the fanatic, and when he prayed his eyes assumed a Berserk look. I discovered him to be an old rascal, none the less. He gave me a little of his soup (gaol stuff), and then helped himself to some sugar and tea which I had brought in my pocket against emergencies. No one came near us with food all that day. I commenced to roar lustily through the bars. After some hours of this a man appeared the following day with some soup and bread at least twenty-four hours after I had arrived. My companions now laughed, and said I was to be court-martialled, and the old Arab, who seemed friendly with the guard, told me they had decided to try me for escaping, for sending letters home about Stamboul, and that they had got letters back from some " big men " in London to me which proved I had done so. At this I felt more resigned.

The Arab then commenced in all sorts of ways to sound me about helping him. He wanted a large sum of money to let loose a conspiracy, something about killing the Sultan, Enver, and a few more. It was very difficult to talk with him, as I didn't know Arabic and he didn't know Turkish, and he would only trust one old inaccessible man, who spoke French, to translate. The scheme set me thinking. That it was partly a feeler I had no doubt, but I began to glean direct intelligence of many matters of intrigue in Turkey.

All the elaborate caution of the East this old Arab showed when we talked together, pretending he was discussing food, and we had often to wait for hours until the others were asleep. This was March 27th, my birthday, and a terrible one it was. I felt very unwell. There was no food. I had no access to any one to ask for food, and my polite notes to the commandant were ignored. I managed to get a paper, and the news from France was bad. The German offensive was sweeping everything before it.

My guards and gaol companions amused themselves by showing literally how Germany was now walking over the French and us. I, however, awaited the counter-offensive, if we were not too broken, and, in any case, the moment when the German advance must be outdistanced owing to the elaborate communications required for pushing on the great masses of men and materials of modern war. It was a most miserable birthday, but in the evening we had a side show, which I encouraged. The Turk slammed a door on the Egyptian's heel, and then, in a second, the latter, who had been very forbearing, was at his throat with one hand and tried to brain him with an iron off the bed with the other. The Turk produced a knife. They fought, and knocked over the table. The old Arab came in to separate them, and got embroiled himself.

When the show was at its height and the guard came in, I stepped out and got a note on to a shelf in the washing-place. This was for a poor little subaltern of the R.A.F., who had been hauled into a room near mine, only he had some air and a good view of the Bosphorus. Thus correspondence started. I had had it ready, and when all the doors opened to see the fun I shouted a word to him. We exchanged notes in this way, although it took a long time for him to find the place. We exchanged money and other things.

The fight being over, our commandant came in. He thought I had had a hand in it, but the guard was loyal. I asked for a cell for myself. He was an inconsiderate beast, so I quoted the privileges of officers in captivity, and objected to being with an Arab and a Turk. The latter was eventually removed. Life went on. The plot of the Arab proved very subtle. He wanted an aeroplane to fly with gold into Turkey, and his party would meet it at a certain place, and then presto! up would go any building or bridge we liked. I found out the two sides to the Arab movement, the *coterie* round Enver, the Armenian gambit, the German supervision, and the extreme precariousness of Telaat's position as Grand Vizier. The movement was quite widespread throughout Turkey, but it all seemed so futile and nebulous. There was no head, and corruption was on every hand. Three or four days afterwards, I saw Gardiner's face around the passage beckoning violently to me. With him here it was now apparent what we were up for.

I got in touch with him by notes, and a day or so afterwards I was taken from my appalling room and put into his, a fine, large room, along a side alley and overlooking a courtyard with huge iron railings, but with a most magnificent view of Stamboul beneath us. It was a distinct change from the terrible place I had been in.

Beneath us was another storey where the worst criminals

were confined. Their lot must have been terrible. The tops only of their cell windows were above the ground.

Gardiner had been hauled away from camp at Afion Kara Hissar for " escaping." This was all he knew. He had come to prison about ten days after I had, and had had a much better time. He had made some arrangement for getting food outside by sending out a posta and giving heavy backsheesh.

Then, days later, we got the Kivas from the Dutch Embassy to visit us. He brought Yarmouth bloaters and tea and clothes. One day I bought a tin of cocoa, for which I paid £8 10s. After a few more days the commandant sent for me, and said an officer, who was interested in me, would like to talk.

I found a very polite Turk in naval uniform, who was evidently out for news. I remembered having seen him with Germans on occasions. What did I think of Stamboul, of its beauties, of its buildings, of its future after the war? He gave me news from the Western Front, and let me see the papers, as the tide of war just then was much against us. Had I seen Enver in Berlin? (They had evidently been reading some of my letters, including some intended deliberately for them.) Who was Earl Grey, was George Lloyd related to Lloyd George, and was Fitzmaurice—a secretary to the British Embassy before the war—in position in London? I merely told him that I had only just commenced to get food, after being neglected for some days, and if he would get me permission to have a bath I would be glad and happy to help him waste as little of his valuable time as possible.

This he did, and I was allowed to a bath—not my old one, worse luck!—close to the gaol. I also got a doctor to verify my former report to Dr. König that I needed baths, and there I hoped to begin planning again. On the promise of a consideration of these things, we talked hard. I told him I recognized he was out for news, of which I had none; but that, in other words, I was certain that unless Turkey made a separate peace she would have small say in any peace, as Germany would decide that for her. If she was for a separate peace, the time was now, before the counter-offensive began. I found out a good deal about the German hold on Turkey. With considerable cunning, the Commandant Djemal later confirmed my suspicions that the Turks, with all the capacity for intrigue for which they are famous, wanted to get in direct touch with England just to verify German accounts, and a strong party in the Turkish Cabinet was for this. Their motives were less those of *rapprochement*, than suspicion of their grasping ally.

The bath I had every week, writing many letters about it beforehand, or it was sure to be missed. We were allowed to walk in the courtyard, a hundred yards long, every day or two. Scanning the bars, I saw some British faces there, and some Indian soldiers who had escaped. The R.A.F. officers were brought to the prison just to be interrogated, and, after a few days, went to a camp.

Colonel Newcombe now arrived, and had the next room to us. We got in touch with him. He had just been allowed to go to Brusa with some other senior officers, and after three or four days there was brought here. He was most lugubrious about the French front, and said he feared Kemmel meant the collapse of Ypres, etc. We cheered him up, and sent him *yarhut*, the Turkish sour cream. He was most generous with the stores he had. We began communicating at our windows as we had postas on our doors. I now heard that Lieut. Sweet, who was to have escaped with me from Kastamuni, had died in Yozgad. He had been wounded in his escape.

Fearing we might be separated, we arranged that the defence of the case should be left to me, as it seemed still uncertain whether we were up for trial of the letter—*i.e.*, intent to escape—or whether they knew anything about the actual attempt.

Some days later I was sent for to the Taki-ki (Court of Inquiry), some quarter of a mile off. They wanted to know whether the fourth officer—referred to in *the* letter—was present. It seemed not. They then mixed up Galloway, who had given his parole, with another officer who had wanted to escape early in December, when the Black Sea affair was on, but not later, for the Dardanelles attempt. Galloway it was who had had a cheque stolen. My last memory of him from his former visit was that he complained of leaving Stamboul, which he liked. He had been sent for spectacles, but the Turks had sent him to bed in hospital, saying his eyes must be bad.

I answered nothing. Lieutenant Galloway turned up

weeks later, very indignant. He thought the prison much inferior to the almost absolute freedom at Gedhos, where those who had given their parole walked about practically free for miles.

We others didn't sympathize much with his grief, but got ready another plan for escaping while in town.

To our great amusement the parole wallas—those who have given their word of honour to the Turks not to escape—are infinitely touchy on this question, and prefer to call themselves Jurors, as distinguished from non-Jurors. We ragged them by pointing out that even a Bolshevik was only a nonconformist, and we re-named them the Abjurors, as distinguishing them from the Endurers. We heard that the Abjurors (parole wallas) on leaving Changri had been persuaded to " abjure " by promises of " palatial dwellings in Smyrna." These turned out to be huts at Gedos.

Then the trial started. The other two were had up separately. They said I wrote the letter, that it was entirely my plan, although they were coming, and how only I had managed to get the information it contained, and that the whole plans were left with me.

I went the next day, realizing I could postpone the trial if I wanted to. A colonel and four or five other officers were assembled around a table, and a very decent Turk, Ali Bey, who spoke excellent English—was a graduate of Edinburgh—talked to me. They were all most deferential, and I seemed rather a character to them. Many of my letters sent back from the Censor lay on the table. I explained that I could quickly tell them all they wanted to know, but wouldn't say a word until they realized I was a British officer, and before trial wanted some fair play. I wanted baths and massage for my spine. There were my medical certificates to prove this. I wanted food.

The therapeutic baths lay in Pera, far-famed Pera, which included the church, the Embassy, the baths. The latter gave me rest, and also chances of getting a *bandobast* for escaping, if necessary, alone. I actually got the court's leave to go here, after refusing to say a word. An hour or two afterwards I was striding along Pera with a military policeman at my heels. It was such an exceptional thing in these days to be allowed out from the gaol that my guard was impressed.

We found a bath the other end of Pera, a poor enough establishment, but one of the few places where one could get hot water. From here one managed to send out a note or two, although at first my guard wouldn't allow me to speak to any one alone. The bath people were awfully afraid, but I paid them well, and little privileges like a note to the Embassy meant cheques cashed and food available. The Germans were now nearly at La Fére, and the public grew more timid accordingly.

On my way back I was stopped at Galata Bridge by a tall figure in mufti. The voice sounded strangely familiar. It was Forkheimer, an intimate acquaintance of mine at Cambridge before the war. We had often canoed up and down the Cam, and had played some keen tennis together. I had missed keeping an appointment with him in Leipzig in 1914, and had been invited to visit him in Vienna. Had he been fighting? Yes! being a German-Austrian, *natürlich*, a captain of cavalry, he had had his portion of it all on the Russian-Austrian front. There was no time to say anything else but give me his phone number.

On returning to the prison I found our room had been changed, and of all people in the world I met there, Vicomte D'Arici, my Italian friend from Kastamuni. He had been brought to gaol for trial. He was a brave man, well read, an excellent linguist, and had done foreign secret service for Rome for years. He knew of people I had known in Germany. In fact, it was the most exquisite good fortune that brought us together in prison when the one aim of the commandant at Kastamuni had been to separate us. We talked German day and night. He was up for being in possession of plans of the Dardanelles forts, and of all kinds of intelligence which he had gathered at Adalia, where, being free for many months after the outbreak of hostilities, he had been in a position to do this. He had, I understood, got quite a lot through to the Italian Foreign Office.

Nothing but the barest reference to the adventures and intrigues that now followed is possible in this diary. He was still carrying excellent information of the internal state of Turkey, the army and navy, the inner politics, the German supervision. Through him I got acquainted with one De Nari, an Italian engineer of great influence and power and ability,

Z

a prominent man in the Committee of Union and Progress, and a close friend to Turkey. By dint of much work I continued to pay bogus visits to a doctor's apartments beneath de Nari's, and the posta believed this was my dentist. We discussed politics, and de Nari, who was most hospitable and kind, gave me information over coffee and smokes.

He was an intimate friend of Midhat Chukri Bey, the secretary of the Union and Progress, and of Telaat Pasha, the Grand Vizier. The latter was, it appears, quite interested in Newcombe and me, and had some idea of getting in touch with England direct. I had several offers made to me, and only too glad would I have been to take any offer direct through to our Foreign Office, especially as Telaat wouldn't trust any ordinary envoy from Turkey. As the Germans had all the codes, to begin *pourparlers* by means of a prisoner would be the most secretive. I became quickly *au courant* with politics there. I was told that when peace was in sight I was to be sent home with an offer. I did not, however, like the great influence that De Nari had in the councils of things, and it seemed that the whole cabinet was a mass of infidelity and intrigue. A few decided and definite men could have persuaded Turkey out of the war, and, personally, I think it a great pity we didn't bomb fortified Stamboul years before.

D'Arici's wife had been stranded in Panderma, where all her goods were searched. I managed to get through to her some letters from d'Arici, and to effect her transfer to Stamboul. Moreover, d'Arici, sport that he was, had still with him some valuable plans of mines, and much secret information about politics with reference to Bulgaria. These he wanted to get rid of to his wife, and not to destroy. Having satisfied myself with his outline of defence in case things went wrong, I hunted and found his wife, after many adventures, in the heart of Pera. The guard followed, believing her the proprietress of a therapeutic bath. We had arranged a rendezvous in the waiting-room. I had to bring the packet back, as no chance offered for giving it, and it was, of course, certain death for her and for him, if not for me, to have been in possession of such interesting documents. I felt my weight of responsibility, but resolved to try again. The second time she was dressed quite differently. I found her flat, and racing up the stairs ahead of the posta, burst in and gave her the packet. She pushed this down her blouse, and the next second the posta very angrily forced the door open. While he was suspiciously looking around I bolted off again, and, of course, he had to follow me. My excuse that I was hungry was fairly feeble. Anyway he was appeased with a good meal, and I intended not to have him again if I could help. D'Arici was delighted, and I, on the other hand, now relied on getting away politically without escaping. The next day I got a private message from Ismid Bey, a tall, smart, and very modernized Turk doing A.D.C. to Djemal Pasha. He was very occupied with keeping up the importance of his chief, whose influence on the Triumvirate wavered at times. He had just returned from a voyage on the Black Sea, and in his cute Turkish way was most interesting as well as eager for news. He was half French. On entering he barked at my posta, who, startled and terrified beyond words at my claiming acquaintance with so august a person, literally cowed down, and waited outside.

We were in the Florence Restaurant, and had more or less privacy. There I learned for the first time of the outer expression of Bolshevism. Everywhere around the Black Sea where he had been, murders had just taken place on a wholesale scale. He told me a story of his difficulty in getting an interview with people in the southern ports. They were invariably killed just before, the reason, he was told, being that any one who wanted to interview a man wearing a collar must be anti-Bolshevik. Ismid showed me excellent and recent photos of the French front, and assured me that from personal inspection, he thought the German *bandobast* so gigantic and their defences so colossal that we could never get through. It was, however, all to an end. He wanted me to interpret to him the British official attitude to Turkey, and gave me to understand that for himself he wanted peace ; in fact, he had just come from a peace meeting, but Enver was against all this. We had as yet no big victory in the West that might justify a Turkish *bouleversement*. He spoke of financial difficulties, and how much depended on a new arrangement of parties immediately. Djemal had quarrelled with the German commander in Palestine, and wanted Turkey to seize the whole of the Adrianople *vilayet*. In fact, against German orders he had insisted on a full Turkish Army Corps being stationed there, and he disliked the German military preponderance in the capital.

As for the Russian Fleet, Ismid indignantly denied that they were German, and said the Turks had seized them on threat of engagement, as the Germans had hoisted the German flag on the fleet after putting German crews aboard. He despised the German as being too stolid to understand Turkish mentality. This bore out what he had told Newcombe, that the Germans imposed tactics of too high a tactical standard on the Turkish forces after Gaza. I got a good deal more information, which I hoped Newcombe and I might turn to account.

D'Arici was amused at all this. We played bridge and plotted for more news. In the meantime I had visited Forkheimer's home, and persuaded the posta to remain downstairs. My life now was as different as possible from what it had been during all the preceding years.

I cashed £50 in cheques a month, and got out twice or three times a week. Turks began to know me in the street. Forkheimer and I, seated on his balcony overlooking the Bosphorus, sometimes snatched a few short minutes from captivity. We both wondered what our mutual acquaintance, Goodhart, an American we knew at Cambridge, was now doing. His people gave me most excellent tea. I was much interested in the pertinacity of these good people in believing Germany was absolutely right in the war, and we quite wrong. One avoided as much politics as possible, but they were rather keen.

About this time Colonel Newcombe and I formulated a scheme by which the British Government and our brother officers might be saved a considerable amount of money. The exchange at this time with the Dutch Embassy was 130, and in the bazaar privately as much as 200 could be got. These cheques could be exchanged again at a huge profit in Switzerland, and a great deal went into the pockets of foreign changers. Our plan was to get a loan of 10,000 liras a month, or 50,000 in a lump sum from the Ottoman Bank on the security of British officers and approved of by the senior British officer, at the rate of 250.

The *Chef de Renseignement* of the Ottoman Bank was agreeable. In fact, the bank would have made largely on the

DJEMAL PACHA, ONE OF THE TRIUMVIRATE WHOSE A.D.C., ISMID BEY,
MET ME SECRETLY IN STAMBOUL

transaction, and, while helping us by ready money, and saving the Home Government over 100 per cent. on the exchange, have kept it out of Germany's hands, and would not have got any meantime advantage, as repayment of the loan would have been delayed until after the war. Every one was most enthusiastic. Senior officers at Brusa were willing to support the scheme, but the Turks wanted General Townshend's signature. We drafted a letter from our prison asking for his support and approval, and, if possible, to enlist the sympathies of the Dutch Embassy where English cheques were paid only at market rate, British officers getting about one-third to a quarter value (exchange was 500 at the armistice). The general frequently dined in Stamboul, and had a launch at his disposal, so I was informed by a Turkish naval officer, who had been with him for some time, and although no doubt considerably watched, would have many more opportunities than any one else.

After considerable trouble I managed to get a letter through to the general, with a covering one to be given to him at a dinner in Pera. The reply was long in forthcoming, and was most disappointing.

General Townshend wrote through his A.D.C., pointing out that the Turks weren't philanthropists, and if the scheme had been thought practicable it would have been tried before. Still, one must suppose the general knows best, as he dines out frequently and sees quite an amount of Stamboul personages.

I understand from de Nari, however, that General Townshend is more stalked than stalking. In a small photo of the general, with his A.D.C., Mrs. Forkheimer, and a young Austrian lady, taken on the rocks at Principo, we saw the first of our general for years. He looked extraordinarily fit and well. Some weeks later I passed him in Galata with an officer, and he looked exceptionally fit then. We envied him his opportunities, even if he were closely watched. Of one thing I was certain, that he either did not or could not know of the appalling sufferings and mortality of his division.

About this time I received a kind letter from Lord Islington in reply to the letter I had sent in the water-bottle. It contained, to my joy, the signal I had asked him to put if the letter was ever received and dealt with, and contained also some personal inquiries about my health. This letter landed

me in for another inquiry, which I survived all right.   In fact,
I pointed out that it was known in London I had been neglected,
and so I was allowed to visit Dr. König again and extend my
visit to the baths.   The German doctor was now quite angry
with the Turks.   I got my bi-weekly bath at Pera, and built
up a regular visit to certain places.   De Nari and I were now
well acquainted.   He was a very able and strenuous worker,
and although keen on Turkish affairs, and fond of Turks even
to the point of being hand in glove with the Union and Progress
party, he was a keen and loyal Italian from all I saw of him.

Politics progressed rapidly.   The second German offensive
was well under way.   So successful was it that, according to
de Nari, my chance of going home on a special embassy grew
less.   The Turk in victory does not do himself bare justice.
He revives instincts from his uplands in Central Asia.   The
Germans would be in Paris in two weeks, and Turkey would
have back Egypt ! etc., etc.

This man, de Nari, was a type to admire.   An adventurer,
brave, fearless, able, far-seeing, yet with much of the gambler
in his nature, he belonged to the strain of Italy's brightest
history.   I remember one day having left the posta downstairs,
and I came up by another door.   De Nari's tall figure entered
the room where a piano and 'cello lay amongst his papers and
plots.   He pulled his small black beard, and said with an
anxious sigh, " Eh, bien ! Un jour plus ! "

I noticed a revolver in his hip pocket.   This man had just
been to a meeting with the chief spirits of the Union and
Progress Committee, and had had to talk around the big
heavy Telaat.

Apart from our political moves I tried to the very best of
my powers to persuade him to get d'Arici out of prison.   But
d'Arici's machiavellian spirit had so many ramifications that
I think he was commonly feared by all parties.   I knew him,
however, as a brave and reliable man once one understood his
code.   He was still within measurable distance of death, yet
he dared to give me written information to carry outside.
This would have completed the noose, and I was fully conscious
of it when I carried the packet around.   In fact, the day I
took it I had resolved that at any cost I wouldn't allow the
posta to get it.

Great days.   De Nari brought me messages from this Turk

GENERAL TOWNSHEND ON HIS ISLAND (PRINCIPO) WITH VISITORS

and that. I told nothing, but waited. I felt that with a very little the Turks could be persuaded to give in, and said I was ready to take their suggestions and to promise to return to captivity if nothing happened. But against all that the set Government party wanted, or that the Union and Progress wanted, was the solid rebellious faction without a head, some against the Germans, some against the cost of living, some for the old regime, some for Bouharneddin, and some for the new party. Turkey in faith and tradition is too disciplined to be Bolshevik. Otherwise her rebellious factions would have united and hurled out the war cabinet in twenty-four hours. It was on one of these factions I had stumbled through the old Arab in the prison. Their scheme had now grown to blowing up Bilijik Viaduct, thus stopping the German offensive against Baghdad, a wholesale slaughter in Stamboul (d'Arici and I resolved how in this case we would floor postas and escape in their kit), and the opening of the Dardanelles. The police were seething with disaffection. The garrison at the Dardanelles had quarrelled with the Germans there, and a hundred or so of the latter had become casualties. This was confirmed from several sources. We began to hope for a sortie of the Dardanelles Turkish Garrison. But the success of the German offensive nullified this. Then came more quarrelling about the Black Sea Russian Fleet. The Turks insisted on taking it from the Germans. The latter had long since altered their cry from Berlin to Baghdad into Baku-Bokhara, and here got at loggerheads with the Turkish advertised programme. Turkish finance was in a deplorable state. Everything pointed to peace. But the German management that had kept Turkey in so long was efficient beyond words. A little opening, a little altering of the disposition of troops, and Turkey was out. Such was the state of Stamboul in May, 1918. I went to tea on more than one occasion at my friend Forkheimer's home. We talked Cambridge and the phenomenon of war as if we had been back among the cloistral stillnesses beside the Cam. He told me frankly what state Austria was in.

In the middle of all this political welter I was suddenly summoned to the court-martial. Arrived there one morning with my guard, I was shown into a passage, and the first person's head I saw among those peering around the corner was Castell's. He was heavily guarded. The place swarmed with sentries and spies. By making several requests in English and French I soon found no one there understood these languages. A little kitten had been playing in the room. I enticed it to come and talked to it and played with it with a piece of string. The Turks all became most interested, and thus talking to the little kitten I informed Castell exactly as to the stage of the case, and what was not known. I told him that it was my opinion nothing was known of the actual attempt, and that he must give guarded answers and evade every question that might divulge this. Our procedure was to avoid implicating the restaurant, who had had little or nothing directly to do with us. This I had purposely arranged beforehand. Also I wanted our stories to agree in evasion, as it was useless for me to evade one question, if he did not.

He had, it appeared, been transported to Angora, and had been kept under the closest confinement there, until one day, when he was informed he was to go to the war prison at Stamboul for court-martial for assisting British officers to escape. He was thus dreadfully in the dark, and had an idea the whole scheme was out. The other officer had kept inside the margin of my statement, and I intended Castell to do the same.

While keeping strictly to the truth in any statement, I intended to block and confuse their prosecution as much as possible. I now ordered Castell to abandon a scheme for hiding his identity which he had made months before. He was from Smyrna, and very little proof of his identity seemed forthcoming. He had intended taking the name of a British officer who had died on the trek. This was to save his neck, if imperilled, as he had some doubts whether, in spite of his British nationality, the Turks would not hang him without further ado as a Turkish subject. Much of Turkish justice depended on the state of the German offensive, which now seemed to have partly fizzled out. The Turks appeared to know it was the last bolt.

I was taken into a room with even more officials present than before. The court arose and bowed, and I saluted them. They gave me cigarettes, and inquired of my bath. I thanked them, and pointed out that this happened to be a bath day. An old judge smiled amusedly, as if I had already been ordered to be shot and tendered a petition for reprieve on account of its being my bath day.

They took particulars, and, showing me the letter, asked many questions at once. I informed the court, through Ali Bey, that I would do my best not to waste these gentlemen's time if they first allowed me to ask a question or two. After some discussion they agreed. Pointing to the letter, I asked if this, and this alone, was the only matter in issue, and if all questions and answers were to be concerned with it, or did they want to go into Gelal Bey's inquiry, and many other letters I had written ? They looked puzzled, and would not commit themselves. However, after an hour of futile questioning about something or other in the letter, I gave them all kinds of contradictory statements and meetings with other persons, and about a dozen plans of escape, as if I were keen on making a clean breast of all my delinquencies. This they took down letter by letter, and, of course, actually found out on cross-examining me that these things related to other letters and other individuals, and led us into most interesting sidelights about our earlier letters to Bach Pacha, and Heaven knows what, but did not advance the case in hand. At last, mopping their brows—it was a hot day, and we had been at it over two hours—they said very severely that the trial was only concerned with the attempt to escape, and with the particular letter. This eased my conscience, as it cut out the actual attempt, and confined matters to the Black Sea affair. Except when they grew tired (I sympathized with them), they were quite pleasant, and my eyes pouring with water, an old colonel examined them, and went into an account of how his eyes had been similar once in the Caucasus. This I made lead to a digression on the war in the Caucasus and German propaganda there. (Germans were in hospital at Haida Pacha, with bad eyes, had they come from there ?)   We got on to the French Front, and the whole court crowded around to hear my opinion of the situation there. . . . I quoted the generals from Brusa, that they predicted an early dislocation of the German push. We got on to politics, and, later in the afternoon, after a most enjoyable day, marred only by the proximity of certain questions to embarrassing ones, I had managed to explain that the letter had been sent to Castell, c/o. the Embassy, as I didn't know his address. I had first seen him in church holding the plate. I didn't say where I had last seen him, which had been in the boat. Also I managed to save Doust, who had been a starter in the original scheme, although his name wasn't mentioned, by not answering, saying it was not decided as to who would go, but we had left a place for a spare passenger. As a matter of fact, one officer had changed his mind at the last moment. The Turks got to this point before at Psamatia, but instead of sending for officers concerned, they sent for Lieutenant Galloway, an officer who had given his parole, and was sunning himself pleasantly at the parole camp at Gedos. But as it was merely his travelling a few miles against a chance of Doust's neck, we three in the know were inwardly conscience easy.

The Turks congratulated me on my statement and one called me a *shaitan* (devil) to his colleague. I was to return to Brusa shortly, provided I answered the most important question. What matter? said I. Having answered so many, what was one extra for so great a boon? In fact, if they offered to return me to England I wouldn't mind repeating the whole performance. They clapped me on the shoulder, and then, amid a deathly silence, asked me to explain how it was the rope was actually seen down the wall. (They had evidently mixed up the occasion.) I said if they would produce the person who saw it I would endeavour to extract the reason from him, the wisdom of putting down a rope to escape when the plan had not only not been delivered, but, on the contrary, discovered.

This answer delighted the old judge, who said I was *birinji* (first-class), and wouldn't have me hectored further. I have forgotten to record that early in the trial they had admitted that Fauad, the interpreter, had played a most villainous game, that the letter had never been to the censor, that he had stamped it, taken it to a post-office to have a post-mark put on it, and then, tearing it open, had reappeared with it days later, saying it had cost him so many hundreds of pounds, etc. I now congratulated myself on having been so circumspective about the case, and that my opinions and theory had been so extraordinarily correct.

A door opened, and then, after some shuffling, question two was put to some one : "Do you know who this is?" A screen was suddenly moved, and there I saw Castell, looking white and scared. They had got very little out of me as to our meetings, etc., and I had said that he was the man who took the plate round in church, and had been unknown to me before, and that I had been informed that he was anxious to escape.

He looked helpless at being asked who I was, but the screen was hardly removed, when *I* said aloud for Castell to hear, " Why, that's the man at the church ; I didn't know him before then." The court jumped up, and guards came over to seize me ; I hadn't been meant to speak, as they had intended asking Castell who I was, etc. But the opportunity was too good to be missed. Castell was much relieved at this satisfactory announcement, showing how little the court-martial had progressed with the escape proceedings. The old judge roared with delight, and altogether we were quite entertained.

The proceedings had not stated what offence had been committed, although it seemed to embrace :—

(1) My intention to escape with news, general spying, and " undermining the fidelity of Turkish guards " (?).

(2) Castell's guilt in helping me to escape. He was technically a civil prisoner himself.

(3) Fauad's guilt as a Turkish posta. He was wearing uniform.

It began by my informing them these were not offences for which an officer, who had refused his parole, could be punished. It ended by my giving a general tirade on international law as regards prisoners of war, and showing that there were certain acts from which a prisoner of war could be restrained from committing, but for which he could not legally be punished. For instance, I might be much more useful to my country as a prisoner propagandist, and that with a sufficient audience of postas I might start a revolution. They were amused at this, and asked me what, from my point of view, would be a remedy for this ? I suggested exchanging me !

I had been asked by Gelal Bey to pay for the replacement of two of Fauad's teeth that I had knocked out. I agreed willingly, and now suggested that I would like him to carry this souvenir of his treachery. The court, however, said they would not require this, provided I did not regard him as a Turkish soldier, although he was in uniform.

They shook hands with me. I had much cause to be thankful that the inquiry had been so unsuccessful in finding out more.

I now returned to prison pending trial of the others. Castell was moved near me. This meant he was acquitted. A day or two afterwards the state of our rooms was so unsanitary that we feared an outbreak of fever. Castell left for hospital with typhus, and another man died. The smell from the drains and lavatories was overpowering. We were between this and the stench from the prisoners in the cellars beneath our window.

Colonel Newcombe now went sick. His skin broke out into a fiery rash, which increased, and he felt unwell. I tried daily for three or four days to get some one to see him, but the commandant took no notice. At last one doctor came and said it was merely bug-bites. By dint of perseverance we got another Turkish doctor who ordered him to hospital, it being actually smallpox. The colonel went off very depressed at our dividing, as we had all sorts of plans on foot for an escape from Brusa. He hoped, however, to get to the hospital where his lady friends might be permitted to visit him.

D'Arici and I now got down to work. I collected a complete compendium of news about the state of Turkey, statistics of the army, shipping, transport, exchange, loans, and especially inside politics. Dissensions between party and party were increasing daily, and now that the offensive, wonderful as it had been, was held up, the Turks on all sides were for peace. Yet the official hold continued.

By intelligence of this nature, carefully corroborated and up to date, I hoped to be able to render some service to our authorities when, as I fully believed, we should come to enter Stamboul. As yet no Turk can believe this will happen.

The others were sent to Afion. I continued on for a week or two. D'Arici and I had made great progress with our Intelligence. I loved to listen to his adventures and travels and his light-hearted view of life, including as it had for him great danger, varying discomfort, and uncertain rewards. Yet whether on a duel or trying to raise the wind, the artist was not far beneath, and he often treated us to selections from grand opera. His voice was an excellent baritone of great purity and power.

With the other officers removed, I was now more free, and got into touch with two well-known English Levantines, Hadkinson, father and son, who were in the next room to ours. The former was a fine type of manhood, white-haired, and approaching seventy-five. They had been confined for over eighteen months as suspects in spying at Smyrna for our fleet. Young Hadkinson, the son, was much *au fait*, and helped me gather many facts about the course of Turkish politics during the war, and the many factions working secretly for the overthrow of Enver. We hatched all kinds of plots, and finally adopted a scheme fitting in with the old Arab's, by which a certain Turk was to be sent to Brusa to act as our messenger to and from Stamboul (it was only six hours' journey). Thus we could perfect our scheme. There are parts of these schemes and plots which it may be early to publish, but one startling proposition was for a certain powerful faction to open the Dardanelles to our fleet by a revolution among the Fort garrisons. It was amusing to think of me, a prisoner, carrying answers from and to Turkish generals at the head of many thousands of Turks in all the services, for a conspiracy to open the Dardanelles. Nor was this so unfeasible as it appeared. The army of the Dardanelles was anti-Enver. It was the Union and Progress Party alone that prevented every move. The movement wanted money, and was going to commence with a general massacre of the Turkish Cabinet. At this stage I left for Brusa again, the capital where many prominent Turks even then were in hiding!

CHAPTER XV

ARRIVED I found my room next General Delamain
had been pounced upon, and I took up my quarters
with the other officers at a building known as the
American School, in a garden high up above the town. Here
some of the senior officers from other camps had arrived.
They included Colonel Lethbridge, Colonel Lodge, Colonel
Broke-Smith, who for a time had commanded the 10th Field
Artillery Brigade in Kut. He was just the same cheery good
fellow as when I had first seen him under fire, wearing a tam-
o'-shanter in his bivouac at Azizie, seated alongside his slowly
dwindling " peg." He grew more interesting as he got into
the night, and the more interesting he grew the nearer his
nose sank towards his glass resting always on the table.
About 4 a.m., towards the end of his anecdotes, his nose
generally peeped over the rim.

I was severely watched, and not allowed much freedom.
We had less restrictions in some ways, and some officers were
actually allowed to fish. Most of us took to making rods and
lines and flies. General Smith, easily the best fisherman
there, made most beautiful flies, some of which he gave me.

Major Hibbert and I shared a primitive rod I had brought
back from Stamboul. I was allowed to go fishing once by
mistake. Postas *shikared* me so severely that I had little fishing,
but my brother officers were most sporting and kind in not
minding a little inconvenience. They, too, however, went not
to fish so much as to get a walk three miles outside the limits
tramped over for so long.

We went to see the football twice a week, and on these

occasions General Delamain and I sometimes exchanged political notes on Europe. The third offensive had begun, but changed immediately into a counter-offensive. I shared a room with a Major Julius, a staff officer of considerable reputation in India. It is significant that from some meagre news of cavalry and artillery movement on the French front, he calmly and deliberately prophesied that the great day had come, and an offensive would follow. It did. In a few days we had got Peronne, and went on and on.

Colonel Newcombe arrived two weeks after me, and now came to my house. We worked letters to Stamboul, and I kept privately in touch with de Nari. This was expensive, as we paid a person's passage weekly, there and back, with a reward. The colonel now proceeded to lose his heart to the young lady who had nursed him in hospital.

Communication to Stamboul from Brusa remained difficult, owing to the risk. Forkheimer had kindly written a note to the Consul at Brusa, and through this channel I managed, once or twice, to get communication through to de Nari about money and news, although I did not send any intelligence matter through this channel, as being unfair to the other side ; and in fact I promised to that effect. The Consul's daughters were most sporting and kind. We met them, on occasion, in the bazaar, and Greenwood, who had now turned up at Brusa, and who had made much progress as a disciple, frequently did sleight of hand tricks over a basket of apples in some one's stall with one of them, thus getting a note through about Embassy money or something. I managed to get letters through to Forkheimer to recover for me a medical certificate which Dr. König had formerly written me, but which had gone astray, except one piece perfectly undecipherable.

A Committee of Prisoners' Exchange now arrived, and we all fortified ourselves with statements of our cases. I knew they would prevent my going for political reasons, unless and until de Nari's schemes were ready.

More and more I saw only too clearly how all other schemes and policies came back to the U. & P.'s programme. That notorious party, bad as it was, remained the one strong faction with anything like a programme or that knew what it wanted. It retained the reins of government merely because everything outside it was vacillating, indefinite, inarticulate ; because the

policy of parties that revolved around it was either tyrannized
by intrigue or hampered by personal jealousies. And so these
parties made no progress towards translating their general
ideals into realities, but vaporized over their respective
watchwords. For instance, the Itihad or Union faction was
for bridging the artificial distinction of Young and Old Turk.
They wanted a Turkey for all Turks. Another faction, rather
a lesser circle enclosed by the last, was the Peace and Salvation
Society which was for immediate cessation of hostilities,
abandoning the scimitar for the wheels of industry and general
social development. These dreamed of the Prince Subaheddine and wanted his recall. The Prince had had to leave Turkey at the peril of his life, and after doing useful work for
us in Greece went to Switzerland. He seems an idealist of
good intentions, and with a love of his country, but, unless
under the shelter of our guns, to lack both the vigour, nerve
and determination necessary to cope with such as Enver a soldier
of fortune, Telaat a promoted telegraph clerk, Djemal a throw-
back to the primitive Tartar, all enjoying a snatched executive
authority at the point of a revolver. There had been with me
in the prison in Stamboul a Turkish major brought up for
appropriating goods. From him I learned something of the
appalling nature of the corruption in Turkey. Take Giahid
Bey, for example, who was appointed to stop profiteering. He
merely steered profits into his own pocket and that of Enver
& Co. I heard from a first-hand source that on the second
sack of Erzerum, property worth three million liras was
divided between the triumvirate and remains invested in
various countries against an international finance débacle
later on.

Take Jemal, the Governor of Stamboul (Commandant de la
Place), formerly Enver's A.D.C., a man in whose hands rested
the lives of practically all the political prisoners of Turkey.
Not one spark of justice remains to such. Not only had he
to fulfil the mandates of the triumvirate, but, outside that, he
utilized every opportunity for his own advancement. That
is possible in Stamboul probably more than anywhere in
Europe, not even excepting Russia. To seek advancement at
the expense of the public weal and justice, it is only necessary
to enter the arena of intrigue boldly, and, armed with the
possession of as many facts as possible of other intrigues, by

a general compromise of blackmail, to retain this advancement. Added to which there is the difficulty of foreign policy, left as a most tangled legacy of personal intrigue by Abdul Hamid. The problem of Russia, Turkey's external fear both for Constantinople and her eastern flank, of the Balkans with their vulture propensities awaiting the fall of Turkey, and the necessity of Turkey having at least one friend in Europe, are a sufficient handful without the increased embarrassment she gets from internal questions like that of the Armenians and the Arabs. And over all these problems, without and within, mined like high explosives around every important structure of the State, there is usually flung the shadow of some daring ambassador presiding by intrigue and threat of application of the match. Wangenheim was such a one.

One heard it said on every hand that our ambassadorial representation before the war was so weak that it flung Turkey into the arms of Germany. There must be some truth in this from the universality of its utterance, and yet imagine to what state a country, as seething with intrigue and corruption as is Turkey, must be reduced by being bombarded with the courtship of the leading Powers ?

The third German offensive now became our offensive, and once more the tide of battle ended in our favour. Once more on the French front we redug our trenches among the earlier dead. We seemed still far from getting back to England. The exchange that should have happened two years before has been held up partly by the instigation of Germany, and partly by the weakness of our own delegates on the Prisoner of War Committee in Switzerland, two or three years before. Eighteen months after Turkish prisoners in Egypt had got their treatment agreed upon, we were left *in statu quo*, and when we saw for the first time the regulations to which both England and Turkey were bound, there were outbursts of indignation on every hand. If our representatives on the Prisoner of War Committee had included some efficient soldier, who had known, by practical dealings, the methods and delays and subterfuges of the Turks, we would have had some safeguards, and it would not have been possible to keep British officers in underground typhus cells for nine months, awaiting trial for an offence of escaping, the penalty of which was only two weeks, and the inspection of camps would

2 A

not have been a farce. For instance, a list was allowed to be presented by the Turks saying all camps had no complaints, when we had not even been visited up to date (July, 1918).

At times I have imagined that the lot of imprisonment, such as ours, must have a purifying influence and help one to see beneath the surface of the passing show into the deeper, eternal currents that flow along translucently below.

Sometimes, if rarely, I had managed to entice my posta above Brusa town and from a hill beheld the rising beauty of Olympus. Going to my bath on one occasion in the hot month of August, I was too tired and seedy to get there in time, and so, sitting down by the roadside where the more fortunate were allowed to walk daily, I wrote these lines—

SONNET

CAPTIVITY

One day I sought a tree beside the road
   Sad, dusty road, well known of captive feet—
   My mind obedient but my heart with heat
Rebelled pulsating 'gainst the captor's goad.
So my tired eyes closed on the ' foreign field '
   That reached around me to the starlight's verge,
   One brief respite from weary years to urge
Me to forget—and see some good concealed.
   But skyward then scarred deep with ages long
   I saw Olympus and his shoulders strong
Rise o'er the patterned destinies of all the years
   Marked with God's finger by the will of Heaven—
   Tracks men shall tread, with only Time for leaven—
That we might see with eyes keen after tears.

Brusa, July 16th, 1918.

But these moments were few, and the pressure of existence and shikar for food and money, and general bandobast of plots and plans and pots and pans engrossed much attention. The Austrian Consul's house I visited for a few seconds through the posta confusing it with the council offices. I usually arranged not to go to the house, but after I had built up a system Colonel Newcombe over used it. His young lady friend, who had nursed him in Stamboul, came on a visit to

Brusa, and rendezvoused him once too often here. They confused him with me and I got punishment for both. This left Colonel Newcombe free still to carry on our plans, although he was very averse to letting me pay his penalty. Any other proceeding was, of course, futile for both of us.

We had several plans, all of which failed. Then we decided to get back to Stamboul once again. So changed was the political outlook for Turkey that escape from there was now much easier, and to live in hiding was possible. He arranged to get there by the help of this young lady.

The exchange selections of officers were made and remade, and finally all kinds of people were put down including one colonel who was hard of hearing, which he described as gun deafness. He managed to be deaf while his examination was on, but forgot not to hear when they said he was to go. We all did this more or less. However, I realized the board was all a hoax and insisted on going back to Stamboul for treatment to my spine, as there was no specialist in Brusa. By dint of great persistence I managed this. An interpreter, Zia Effendi, from the American College, Smyrna, I found deeply versed in politics, and although he was not reliable, was undoubtedly in touch with some movements and was useful to a degree.

It was now August, 1918. The faster the Germans went back, the more the German alliance was criticized and the Government openly attacked. A financial panic occurred in Stamboul. Jealousies raged over the Doubrouja, half of which Germany gave to Bulgaria leaving the rest in abeyance. And Turkey wanted the Maritza even if Bulgaria had the half of the Doubrouja. Germany used this fact as a bribe. Then trouble commenced over Batum. Germany, in seizing Odessa, indicated her independence of Turkey on her way to the East. Popular feeling, that had only wanted a leading motive, now became articulate over this. Feeling ran high. Telaat went to Berlin, collecting souvenirs and welcomes from Bulgaria and Austria *en route*. There, as had been expected, Turkish claims were admitted after a theatrical tussle put up by Germany, on the condition that Turkey remained in the war.

In the meantime Bulgaria began to plot to be the first rat from the sinking ship. The first rat has the best chance.

Meanwhile Newcombe's plan to escape to Stamboul was

difficult owing to the extra posta in the garden. This was due to the Consular affair. He disguised himself as an Arab, and, except that he walked as if in Regent Street, did not make a bad one. The plans he left largely to me. On my suggestion he kept to his bed for some days beforehand on pretence of being ill. Then, on the night, I rushed down to one posta and sent him off with a letter to the commandant. The other was suspicious, but after some scene I managed to cajole this fellow, Abdul Khadir by name, whom we all detested, and made my peace with him. Sincere acting was necessary as we heard the cracks of a tile, and I knew Newcombe would be caught if Abdul went another yard. I shook him by both hands and prevented him from going, telling him that now I had forgiven him. This was true. The man was a sneak in many ways and I took delight in thinking how I was enabling Newcombe to get away even as we spoke, and that it was this posta of all who should be on guard. Then Greenwood and I decoyed with several drinks of mastik, the curious people, including a colonel, who wanted to see Newcombe. I lay in Colonel Newcombe's bed at night. The next day I told the old Turkish officer in charge of the place that Newcombe did not want to see any one, which was probably true. (He was by this time well on his way to Stamboul.) I then got into his bed knowing the Turk, being suspicious, would come. Greenwood made me look like Newcombe's figure. Meals, half-eaten, lay by the bedside. I had eaten them so as not to let even the orderlies know. I heard the door open and the Turk peep in. A few groans sent him out again.

The next night we had much to do with keeping abreast of the general curiosity. But it was essential to give him a good start. Then, the following morning, I took in to Colonel Lethbridge, our C.O., a letter of explanation that Colonel Newcombe had left with me for the purpose.

Of all people it was I who was delegated to tell the Turk. In as many words I merely said the Colonel had fled. The old Turk screamed with rage and terror, seized his sword, put on his fez and jacket, and, forgetting his trousers, rushed outside screaming to his postas and looking under every bush.

This continued at intervals all day. We all were locked up, but this only lasted a day or two. A few days later I got permission to go to Haida Pasha Hospital in Constantinople, and heard privately that Newcombe had arrived in Stamboul, and was in hiding through the assistance of his lady friend. Meeting General Delamain on the football ground, I said that I believed this was my *Heimkehr*, or in other words, that in any case hostilities were near an end. He thought so too. I listened to him on the military situation in France and Bulgaria and we discussed the emergence of new political formations in Europe, the new distribution of the balance of power necessitated by the hiatus of Russia, of the Balkans, possibly of Austria.

We talked of the tendency of small movements to merge into large, of the awakening of similar thought in all men, of chaos revolving around chaos that could not become cosmos before the centre of political gravity were ascertained, and equilibrium adjusted once more. Looking back on captivity one felt that the change in one had become spiritual even more than physical. The pattern of destiny stood out very plainly for us all.

We said " Good-bye," and that night my brother officers gave me an awfully good send off, and Colonel Broke-Smith produced an extra bottle of mastik. I had a long talk with our senior officer, Colonel Lethbridge of the Oxfords, whose quiet, restful attitude was still undisturbed. I left before the dawn in an arabana, some of my friends coming to the wagon. I felt certain this was the last occasion of my departing from Brusa.

Except for one old Jew and a very pretty daughter on board the boat, the voyage was without incident. She sat by me, and after waiting an hour I managed to put a letter into her pocket when the posta turned away. She was to deliver it to Colonel Newcombe. Much depended on this.

We arrived at Galata Bridge, and this time, different from the last, excited crowds were reading news of the victorious arms of the Entente. *Le Journal d'Orient* spoke out plainly and bitterly against Germany, and was for a separate peace at once. Everything had changed.

I was hustled to Haida Pasha Hospital and went through the same performance as of old, having my clothes taken from me with all my kit and food I had brought with me, and spending the first night in a bathroom. The noise saw maddening and I could not sleep.

The whole hospital talked of one, Jones, an officer of the Volunteer Battery whose guns I had brought back from the front line in Kut, at night, on a momentous occasion. I had heard before that he had pretended he was mad so enthusiastically, that he had gone mad in fact. He was now here hating Englishmen hard, and in fact it was dangerous for him to meet them. Most of the Turks said he was mad. I woke after a troubled sleep to the startling announcement by a Turk, from an adjoining bed, that during my sleep Jones had been standing over me silently for a long time. The repetition of this got on my nerves. He wouldn't sleep in the same room with an Englishman, so I moved to a large ward, where I was quite alone.

In the middle of the night I saw a ghoulish figure, wearing a large, black mantle and with stark, staring eyes, stalking me from bed to bed. With all the uncanny anticipation of one's every movement that usually happens only in a nightmare he divined my every move, for I also tried to get to the door. Then I started to talk German. At this an attendant came for him. I breathed freely as he left. I thought what a pity it was after all my experiences to meet my end from a mad fellow-prisoner. After this he fled on seeing me, although I kept up the German identity. Then I got a note written to me from him, a veritable mad document assuring me he hated the English and that he feared I was going to kill him. This arrived just after I had met him in daylight. He wore a black overall, a yard of which he had picked into threads, which his busy fingers did incessantly. His hair was long, he wore a beard, and his white, sunken cheeks gave him a ghastly appearance.

I had wished him a polite "Good evening" in Turkish, and then the note had arrived. I replied to it in German, and he replied again that he didn't know German, and if I didn't promise not to kill him he would kill himself. We met alone, and, in an extraordinary way, with some postas looking on, I discovered Jones to be quite sane.

It is a wonderful story. I refer only casually to it here. From this moment we acted consistently when together, he pretending he hated all of us except me, and at periods even me, if postas were difficult. He had had a most lonely time for months. The strain had been awful. He had heard of my adventures and regretted, he said, that we had not been together in a camp to try some escape. He told me of his long story, commencing with spiritualistic séances at Yozgad, which the commandant attended, and how he had almost persuaded the commandant to take him to the Black Sea in search of treasure, the whereabouts the spook had revealed to Jones. The fate of the Turk before the treasure was found seemed to have promised to be a watery grave or bondage. That fizzled out, and then he and another subaltern named Hill, also pretending he was mad, acted with such persistence that they were finally sent for medical treatment to Stamboul. On the way they were spied on and Jones, besides pulling out all his teeth, had, with Hill, pretended to hang himself, kicking off from a table as they heard the guard entering. This, he explained, was necessary to convince the Turk. They had arrived in Stamboul a few months before. On the preceding Monday Hill had left on exchange and Jones, who had had to act he didn't want to go to England as he was a Turk, had either overdone it or else one or two Turkish doctors believed him more or less sane. There can be little doubt that more than one medical officer and possibly the commandant of the hospital, saw through Jones' pretence, excellent as it was.

Some Turk suggested to me, with a most confiding smile, that Jones, in pretending for so long he was mad, was actually going mad, and by the armistice would be so mad then that he would have to be exchanged!! The *Chef d'Hôpital*, a very decent fellow, discussed Jones at great length with me. Jones, he said, would not return because he feared a court-martial, as one mule had had a grudge against him for getting his guns in a mess at Kut, and that as I had rescued him I was the only Englishman Jones would tolerate. The commandant was quite baffled about the mule, which, on inquiry, turned out to be Colonel Maule. On the plea that I was also down for exchange, in fact had passed both examinations for this in the hospital, and that I believed I could get Jones along with me if I said I would defend him and get him off at the court martial, the commandant asked permission from head-quarters for us to go. Jones continued to make himself so troublesome through the whole hospital, knocking people into wells and doing and undoing jobs, that they allowed us together on the plea that we were to concoct a defence. Jones had already purposely written about twenty volumes of rubbish on this. He was a daring actor but not quite finished, and more than once I thought just overdid it before the commandant. Once alone over our law books, with a huge kettle of tea and some food from parcels that now were arriving, we talked of our plans and of his great loneliness for months. I knew more than he did of local politics, but he was very useful and altogether a first-rate companion.

Mademoiselle X, Colonel Newcombe's friend, now visited me in hospital with another lady who had been kind on occasion. She showed me her engagement ring, and told me how the Colonel had turned up with a basket of fish after getting across the Marmora in a fishing boat, and had gone into hiding there. He seems to have had a sporting time of it and displayed considerable daring. I had posted him pretty well up to date with news for de Nari, and I now heard he had more or less supplanted me as to going home, owing to my disinclination to support any party programme of Turks or any one else.

The next day I got out to Pera for my baths. To accomplish this takes hours of patient waiting for a chance to remind the commandant, and heavy bribery inside the hospital. I found that the city was seething with intrigue, that I was watched, that Enver and Telaat were preparing to flee, that Rahmi Bey, a clever but notorious Albanian at Smyrna, was trying to commence *pourparlers*. General Townshend who had, so the papers said, become Turcophile, and had frequently acknowledged his good treatment by the Turks, was now rumoured to be enthusiastic to go out with the terms of peace. His agent, the lady who had visited me in hospital, had now got more or less in touch with de Nari, *i.e.* my line of communications. I was sorry so many things did not seem understood by well-meaning senior officers in captivity. After some hours with my friend de Nari, the posta being outside, and reading between the lines, it appeared that certain parties were stalking Enver and Telaat, who now resigned. That these parties were stalked by General Townshend, and he, in turn, was stalked by de Nari representing the U. and P. and Italy. Some one was required to stalk him.

The U. and P. were most immensely unpopular. Marshal Izzet Pasha, a soldier of standing, became Grand Vizier after

Tewfiq Pasha, the friend of England and ambassador in London before the war, had refused. But while the U. and P. was supposed to be definitely ousted from the war cabinet that has brought and kept Turkey in the war, I found that their elaborate spy system had definitely obscured the political identity of certain politicians until then. These, wearing no outward badge but secretly U. and P., now had a preponderance in the cabinet, although not a heavy one. The *Journal d'Orient* (run by Carossa, the millionaire) and the *Ak Sham* spoke out strongly for peace.

We were now on the Somme and the Bulgarians were being hammered back. The dying cries of the *Osmanisher Lloyd*, a blatant Prussian paper that had crowed over Stamboul all the war, were very humorous.

I went into town day after day. Regulations were relaxed, and although I had a posta, I was more free. The universal ruin that threatened seemed to invite every one to make a little backsheesh first. Day after day I saw Forkheimer, who was as kind and sporting as ever. He seemed to have no idea of the extent of the calamity that must threaten his country and Germany if, as it seemed, this was the end. He was disgusted at the state of Turkish policy and put me *au courant* with much news that helped me and could not damage them. They had seen a lot.

It is now October 20th. Exchange is panicking, politics in a frightful tangle. The exchange of prisoners is hung up. Marshal d'Esperey, with British and French forces, is still thrashing the Bulgarians, who are reported likely to make peace at any moment. Other political parties here want to forestall them. Zia Bey, the interpreter from Brusa, has helped me to get in touch with the Prince Subaheddine's party, whose chief virtue is that it is opposing political profiteers.

October 21st.—I have seen Newcombe with his *fiancée*, and de Nari in the Petit Champs in Pera. The colonel came out of hiding and walks about free. I have seen a note in the *Journal d'Orient* describing him as a Turcophile (at which he would be most annoyed) and saying that he had escaped to Stamboul from Brusa, and would follow General Townshend on a political mission. I now saw de Nari every day and realized one thing very surely, viz. that he stood to represent the interests of the U. and P. and particularly Italy. I saw most of his private communications from Shefkut Pasha and Midhat Chukri Bey (the able secretary of the U. and P.). He was more than ever concerned lest the *pourparlers* should get out of his hand. He engaged the ear of the U. and P. in the cabinet, yet as an Entente subject resident in Turkey during the war, his path was more or less difficult. It seemed to me he was sending Colonel Newcombe with his, de Nari's, wishes, put as representing the Turkish Cabinet. He was largely interested in Adalia, the Italian settlement, and wanted at all costs to get that for Italy. We crossed swords in a friendly way over methods, and he realized I wouldn't carry his representation, which seemed to me unofficial and unauthorized. Nevertheless, Colonel Newcombe has an excellent understanding of the position here, and he does know what few British officers know, what is in the mind of the Turks.

Turkey is outflanked. The Chatalja lines that held up the Bulgarian forces are useless against the concentration of modern artillery fire, and most Turks realize this. I knew from d'Arici who was there on the occasion of that battle, how easily the Bulgarians could have entered behind a heavy moving barrage.

October 23rd.—Townshend left a few days ago for Smyrna. De Nari assured me the public wanted to know what chance his terms had, and questioned me about the possibility of my taking other terms through after Newcombe had left on his errand. I pointed out for his sense of humour that in this way the whole remnant of the prisoners might ultimately get out of Turkey. He was a delightful man, and, with all his arduous schemings, had a large margin for laughter. I informed him that I had no desire to take through his suggestions without adding my own notes. I had now got in touch with the Prince Subaheddine's Party. They were sending a delegate to the fleet to try and get permission to send him to Switzerland for the Prince. I assured them that all their influential following would avail them nothing, but that on one condition I would get his embassy put before the fleet, and possibly take their delegate to London. Also that I was the only one who could do it. The delegate was to meet me in Smyrna in case I left first for there, which I expected to do any day with Jones.

My condition was that complete intelligence on all matters

financial, economical, political, naval and military be collected on the heads I gave them. The English governess of the Prince's daughter, Fatteh, unfortunately, I did not meet through posta difficulties. De Nari knew I was in touch, and hurried Colonel Newcombe off. I tried to put the latter *au courant*, but he was too much elated at his embassy to think of what it contained, and, after all, as he said, de Nari's party was a very real one, and a factor to be reckoned with.

October 26th.—I have omitted to note an excellent air-raid over Stamboul, the second of two attacks in the same week. About 2 p.m. from the hospital I heard the sound of explosions in Stamboul. People were running on all sides to get a good view of the attack, and the Turkish officers of the hospital, many of whom had not seen a shot fired during the war, rushed down below to their basement floors. They came on, a flight of seven very fast machines, and were met by a steady barrage, which began at San Stephano, and continued across Stamboul.

Their bombing could be located by the white bursts. To my delight they seemed quite close to the Ministry of War. As they swept towards Pera, they bombed Galata Bridge, and the German Embassy. The sky was thick with artillery bursts, but the machines were very fast. As they circled around, keeping a beautiful line, and came towards Haida Pasha, heavy German guns opened on them vigorously. This hospital, the largest in Turkey, has a big white crescent painted on the roof, but as German artillery was close by, a mitrailleuse alongside in the Crimean Veterans' garden, and the Haida Pasha Station yard about two hundred yards off our boundary, we saw quite an amount of bombing. The hospital was spared, but a bomb got the barracks close by. The Turks in the hospital pointed with pride to a Turkish aeroplane which got up to attack our planes. It was a glorious opportunity for a spectacular event such as the Turks love.

Above the silver sea there appeared seven shivering planes, flying in formation like sand-grouse across a blue sky dotted by the white puffs of artillery fire. As the Turk arose the fire ceased. Two of our fellows detached themselves to beat him off. He came down wounded a few moments later.

A good deal of propaganda has been dropped, showing

the precise position of the Entente and Allied Armies. From
all reports the bombing was not good. They got very few
soldiers. One colonel was killed. But as Stamboul is
heavily armed and protected, according to the development
in practice of modern war it seems justifiable.

The moral effect was the most wonderful imaginable. The
Chef d'Hôpital asked our advice. For the first time in its
history the sacred city of Stamboul, sheltering with all its
intrigue behind the locked gates of the Bosphorus and Dardanelles, is no longer inviolate, but assailable from the skies.
It is ten thousand pities we did not resort to this a year before.
When one realizes how slender was the official hold that kept
Turkey in the war over many crises, how indifferent provincial
Turkey was about entering, and how averse to continuing
for the sake of Germany, one can realize how air propaganda
and attacks would have brought before them the meaning of
this war.

I pointed out that they had to thank the Germans for the
bombing, firstly, in that she had commenced to break the
rules of war, and secondly, that she was their ally. To bomb
Germany it was necessary to risk hitting the Turks. The
Germans—not the Turks—had used this warfare from the
first. This I circulated to the Press, and it reached a good
many channels, besides some prominent members of Parliament. The passions of the Turks came uppermost. The
next morning I was in Pera. Many Germans had been
assaulted, and more than one Turkish woman had flourished
her knife at German officers.

I saw instances of sharp expression of feeling myself. The
planes came again, dropping propaganda this time, and not
bombing. The propaganda notified that German armies
are surrendering wholesale, and we have more than reached
the original point whence the great German offensive started,
and are still thrusting them back ; that Bulgarian armies are
broken, and communication between Germany and Turkey
cut ; and that, unless all Germans have orders to move out
of Stamboul at once, bombing will continue. I had ascertained the extreme importance and likelihood of advantage
in this propaganda, and had asked a captured R.A.F. officer
with me in prison months before to get it through at once.
He had a code, and the first letters of new prisoners were now

expedited. He sent it. This time public rage and dissatisfaction was more intensified than ever, and the Press was outspoken.

General Townshend's offers of mediator, as advertised by certain political parties, no one takes seriously who is acquainted with the political manœuvring of Turkish parties for position. They are prepared to use his " good graces," as they put it, just so far and no more as he can recommend leniency for them, or rather, give to the fortunate parties, successful in manœuvring for the privilege of commencing *pourparlers,* the chance of having first word.

Moreover, the Turks refer in the Press to their excellent treatment of the General as giving them a sort of right to expect his " good graces." One is tempted to ask, like the soldier in *L'Aiglon,* what about the rank and file ?

It is the Entente thrust towards Nish, the rumour that we have flying columns near Lala Burgas, and that, failing a surrender, a landing will be made at Dedogatch, that is making up the Turkish mind. It is the collapse of Germany on the western front, the decision in the main theatre of war, that has crumpled up Turkey. In other words, there can be no mediation here any more than there was when Kut fell.

October 31st.—I have been too busy to write my notes. Jones and I have worked very hard for hours a day with an inexhaustible patience to try to prove his insanity. It is now admitted that he is insane and believes he is to go home to be court-martialled for some offence, and I am to take him away on the pretext of defending him. It would take many hundreds of pages to write down the history of these four weeks. I have the offer of living freely with de Nari, but I do not care to accept a semi-freedom. Nor do I want to stay here until the fleet enters, as it must. I want to get down to Smyrna. By then, if the delegate from the Prince's party arrives, I can take him to the fleet, or otherwise go alone. I became acquainted the other day with de Nari's terms and suggestions carried by Newcombe, who is to have direct communication with Turkey, but only through de Nari by a code. I have a letter from de Nari to Newcombe, saying I am also to use the code and to have access to his channel of communication, if necessary. After Colonel Newcombe had gone, de Nari's scheme did not appear to him so rosy, and he realized how the situation was getting out of his hand.

The Germans have been pouring into Stamboul from Anatolia and Syria.   I have heard of their stand alone against Allenby's forces when the Turks were demoralized and the Arabs attacked them as anti-Islam.

Conflicts are frequent between the Germans and Turks in Stamboul.   The German troops are ransacking the houses, and removing everything, from locks, windows and telephones, to motor-cars and vehicles.   They move about in bodies.   A number of German privates besieged by some Turks near here, put up an excellent defence, fought their way to a ship, captured her, and steamed out to the Black Sea.

We were to have left to-day, but final receipts and passports were overlooked until the last moment, and Jones' was a difficult case.   I wouldn't go without him.   He thanked me again and again, and assured me, "Mousley, but for you I should be left here possibly weeks after the fleet enters."

Everything is excitement and disorder.   Centuries of captivity are falling from me every second.   I am outwardly calm, and too busy to psychologize much on the great end of this awful eternity.   This may be because I am busy.   But in odd moments I realize that vision in Mosul, seemingly so many millions of years ago, was true, and that given enough patience, the stream of Time must carry us away past even the most terrible moment.

CHAPTER XVI

SMYRNA, November 4th.—Thank God ! After colossal trouble and planning to bring Jones along, we were allowed to go on the evening of November 3rd, having been delayed just enough to miss the boat of several days earlier—I believe purposely.

Exquisite joy and suspense of that last night ! I had seen Gelal Bey recently in Stamboul, and he spoke kindly to me. It brought my terrible Psamatia days back, and I fled. Jones and I arrived at the quay by Galata Bridge in the afternoon with a guard. I got leave to take farewell of de Nari. Before the boat left I was overjoyed to see aboard d'Arici, who had been freed a few days before, and had sought me everywhere. With all his delightful light-heartedness he expressed his profound gratitude for the services I had done him. He gave me advice, very useful, about Rahmi Bey, the prominent ex-Governor of Smyrna, to whom I had a letter from de Nari, and who was leaving by the same boat. A sharp and polished Oriental, he appeared to me, but well equipped with cunning and Eastern dalliance. Ali Bey, who had been sympathetic at my court-martial, was there also to say farewell, and bid me back to Stamboul as soon as possible. We all drank German beer obtained in the saloon at a lira a bottle.

I met Hadkinson the son, of prison memories, having heard much news about his plans from d'Arici. He was also travelling to Smyrna. I procured for Jones and myself a tiny double-berth cabin, where he was permitted to cease playing he was mad, poor fellow ! and we had a glorious meal of tinned meats, and cake and tea.

We saw the last of Stamboul from the deck after our affectionate farewells were over, when we had got under way. As the blanket of Night wrapped Stamboul from our view, we saw disappear first the outlines of the great mosques, and then the minarets. It was still too close to watch. . . . We adjourned to our cabin with a pipe each and a brandy, luxury of luxuries ! Jones and I sat side by side on the bunk, listening to the splash of waves outside the porthole. We went on deck. Far away in our wake a few lights flickered upon the waves. It was Stamboul : the City of the Eternities, the Beautiful, the Terrible.

Jones was a philosopher. We were silent, or swore beneath our breath.

I left him to see Rahmi, who had sent me a message. We had a long conversation in French. For some reason he did not want to talk English. He believed Turkey would do best if given great chances. He admitted they were finished. All depended on England. He would assist me in getting away if he could.

Hadkinson and I then made some plans. He was a man of forty, had lived in Smyrna all his life, would also help me to get away, and, in fact, contribute himself to the information I had. He had also got in touch with Satvet Lutfi, the friend and confidential adviser of the Prince Subaheddine, the patron of the Peace and Salvation Society, who was to leave Stamboul in two days' time, and had not already left, as I had heard.

We planned deep into the night, then Jones and I slept.

We awoke lying alongside the jetty among the rocky hills of Panderma. I took Jones on to a train for which we waited an hour or two. He still acted all he could that he was mad, and would, until he got on board, so he said. We got into a crowded carriage, and after a journey lasting all day, reached Smyrna the next morning without mishap from bandits, who had been stopping many trains and holding prominent citizens to ransom. The country was uncultivated, and had been left to run wild. The people remaining were Turks and Greeks. At Smyrna the Dutch Consulate assisted and gave us money. One batch of prisoners had left that morning, and another would leave in two or three days.

Jones and I found apartments along the bay where General Melliss had been. The generals had come straight from Brusa here, and some already had departed. I had got the local operator to repair the wireless station that had been closed down for years. We got into touch with one Commander Heathcote-Smith, formerly Consul at Smyrna, now at Mytilene, and through him we got into communication with the fleet at Mudros. For permission to use this wireless I found de Nari's letter very useful. Mr. Whitall offered me a launch, which, however, would have meant getting to Mytilene, and no further.

The moments of waiting for the reply to our wireless were exquisite. At last, in direct touch with the outside world! Newcombe had been hung up for days here, and had left a few hours only before we arrived. Our wireless answer said that a gunboat was to arrive, and I would then be enabled to get in touch with naval circles direct. That day, Hadkinson invited us out to his father's suburban villa perched high on a hill overlooking a wonderful harbour. One or two officers were here I had known in Kut. They had found their way to Smyrna unassisted in the general chaos.

That afternoon the Monitor 29 entered Smyrna. The once familiar grey of England's Navy—for us a very strange sight indeed—filled us with feelings indescribable. Her two 6-inch guns were elevated. She was spick and span. As the blue uniforms appeared we beheld our first sight as free men. We went on board for a moment. I learned that the captain had very strict instructions that no one was to leave Smyrna without orders. He was there to stand by. He would go to the vacant British Consulate.

I returned at a more leisurely moment, hours later, and in the wardroom had my first respectable whisky. The officers were inordinately kind to all of us, told us news for the twentieth time, and gave us of their best. One of them, a Mr. Underwood, I found knew some friends of mine. He came to dine with Jones and me in the town.

That night a telegram reached us from Constantinople that Satvet Lutfi Bey—the personal friend and secretary of the Prince Subaheddine before the war, during most of which he had been in various prisons, and now hoped to rejoin the Prince and to bring him back as the light of Turkey—would

2 B

arrive at dawn. Satvet had collected first-rate matters of intelligence from the actual sources, and owing to the duplicity of the police, had got first-hand information of all descriptions.

Before the dawn Hadkinson and I went together to see Lutfi. Our postas we had now shaken off for good. We refused to recognize them. Satvet was a well-bred, well-dressed Turk. His quietness and pale face impressed me. He was a serious and earnest man. We took him along to the Military Governor, who turned out to be Nureddin Pasha, the general who had unsuccessfully tried to take Kut early in the siege. He was delighted to meet me, and delayed a whole queue of Turks and Greeks who were waiting to see him while he described to me what happened on December 25th, 1915. I got his permission to leave the harbour with Satvet. Armed with this I saw Commander Dixon of the Monitor 29 at the Consulate. Dixon was a typical naval officer, physically and mentally robust. He literally pulled me to pieces and my intentions, or as much as he could get out of me, and finally allowed me to send some wireless messages to Mudros, and, if satisfactory replies were forthcoming, to send us there himself. He came to tea with us that night, and told us the reply had come, and that it was fixed that we should leave at dawn in a captured Turkish gunboat manned by officers and crew off the M. 29.

Commander Dixon was a most entertaining and entertainable person. He was delighted to get away from Mudros, which he described as " Fleet, fleet, fleet, with bare hills all around." I was very elated as this was my last night in Turkey. We crowded around the piano and sang glees and songs. I drove back with Dixon to the Consulate to get some directions. As we went along, the town stood at attention, so great was the prestige of the fleet even through this diminutive representative, the monitor.

The scene when the M. 29 entered was one of the greatest enthusiasm imaginable. Crowds jammed the quays and waited there hours. All around the ship the sea was black with boats loaded with people anxious for a glimpse. The Greeks, however, seized the opportunity of getting their own back on the Turk, and made attacks largely unprovoked. They hoisted huge Greek flags over many public buildings, including the

THE FIRST WARSHIP IN TURKISH WATERS. H.M.S. MONITOR 29, WHICH DESPATCHED PRINCE'S DELEGATE WITH AUTHOR TO THE FLEET

hotel where Commander Dixon was staying. This led to blows, and it looked like a general riot.

Dixon, however, with commendable promptness, had a manifesto printed in about six languages, and posted up by daybreak, warning any one against making any demonstrations whatever.

That night Jones assumed partial sanity among some British officers. This was necessary, as some recent prisoners seemed in a hurry to supplant those of long standing. I had tried to take him with me, but this was not permitted. But it was agreed at the Consulate he was to go with the first batch. On this condition I felt my convoy of him was at an end, especially as I was travelling on duty. We had a cheerful last evening, and on our way to the town met some of the officers we had known in Kut, separated from us by years of captivity. Major Harvey, our adjutant, was among them.

Prisoners now began to flock into the town every hour. I was under orders of secrecy, and managed to slip away quietly with Satvet Lutfi. A party of prominent Turkish supporters with him, Hadkinson and I, all lunched together.

Further delay was necessary, as the heavily-mined harbour had been only partially swept, and a few mines had got loose.

We waited on the gunboat till about 4 p.m. Commander Dixon came and wished us good luck, and that I might be found useful to the Staff at Mudros. A brisk and simple good-bye, and we got on board. The officer accompanying us saluted his commander, the engines started, a rope fell, we were under way. I gazed with the intoxication of a mysterious ecstasy at the widening strip of green water between us and the quay, where, in white uniforms, Commander Dixon and his officers and one or two officials of Smyrna waved us good-bye.

.   .   ..

The Lieut.-Commander clapped me on the back and asked me to have a drink as a free man on board a British ship. I drank deep and prayerfully!

Later, we went on deck. It was a wintry evening, but the sky was very clear and the harbour magnificent. We followed the golden path westward towards the setting sun. Here and there we saw some sunken ships that had been mined, and others that had been used to block the channels. A small detail was the discovery by our skipper that this old Turkish gunboat had been wrongly described. We drew eight feet instead of six, and mines lay at nine !

Who cared ? One would have been free ! And that drink ! Satvet Lutfi, immersed in gloom, sat in a heap in the tiny cabin eyeing the coast. I spoke to him. He replied to me very sadly. Pointing to the sunset, he said the sun was setting on Turkey, and he believed one hope only remained. That was his Prince. From politics we passed to his experiences. He located, far away to the south-west, an old stone prison quite alone on the rocks. There he had been a prisoner for years before the war and years during the war.

He told me how he had been intended to die there. They had no water, only a central pool in a dungeon collected from the rain, thick with slime and teeming with insects and worms. There he had got his pale cheeks and left his constitution. And yet, after all his sufferings, he never had hesitated to pronounce what he believed was for the good of Turkey, regardless of cost. I know enough of his history to know he spoke the bare truth. However, his eloquence about ideals for Turkey grew less as, on emerging from the entrance, we entered an increasing swell. A few moments before he had declaimed passionately about the sea, its freedom and beauty. He now became silent, and, like many a better man, evidently felt seasick.

The naval lieutenant and I talked long. The night swallowed us up. I slept on the floor of the cabin. It grew more rough and the wind increased to a steady roar.

At about midnight we reached a point where an armed " Drifter " was waiting to take us further on ; but the sea was so rough that we had to stand by until the dawn before we could tranship our small cargo or come alongside.

As it grew light I discovered us to be alongside a North Sea whaler, with a great, rising bow, fast engines, besides mast and sails, and armed with 3-inch guns, anti-aircraft guns, and loaded up with deep-sea charges. The skipper was a very rough but efficient and kind man from North Scotland, who swore lustily at all things. He related interesting experiences about submarines he had got rid of with his last depth charge. The sea grew worse. It was impossible to tranship the cargo, so we proceeded to Mytilene, where we arrived about 8 a.m., and immediately went on board another monitor.

Her commander and officers had heard of our coming, and had everything ready—a bath and breakfast. Sweet nectar of the gods this to me! Privilege to meet freely again cheerful and free men, to move about the polished decks, handle a knife and fork once more. I had breakfast on deck. The wardroom amused me. These lonely officers had cut out from home papers various pictures of the *Stage* and the *Field*. These they had shaved down to the actual figures and pasted on the walls in all kinds of glorious dresses and attitudes. It seemed as if they were all alive and just arrested midway in some pose or movement. My naval friends saw me regarding them in silence.

" Well, what do you think of them ? "

" I wasn't thinking, but wishing they were all alive."

Heathcote-Smith, wearing a commander's uniform of the R.N.V.R., came to see me. We had a long talk. He was *au courant* with local affairs, but much in the dark as regards Stamboul. I answered a good many inquiries of his, and told him a good deal that surprised him. He took a few notes, and thought I should push on at once to the Admiral, which I was under orders to do. Hadkinson stayed here, as he had some important local business to settle, and the delegate and I left in the armed drifter about nine-thirty.

Mudros, Nov. 15*th*.—We left the island bay with the monitor scintillating in the wintry sun, and got at once into a heavy swell. I was still among the realities of a dream. As we headed for the open sea, now full of strange, new knowledge of the great things that had been away from us so long, one fact impressed itself in my mind. It was that there was no precise outside information of facts political and otherwise in Turkey, and particularly in Constantinople.

In other words, in my first contact with the outside world I had not known for so long, I began to realize that this world was totally out of touch with the inside (Turkey) from which I had just emerged. I was making for the fleet with a Turkish delegate of good standing, straight and loyal, who had suffered severe imprisonment for his opinions and fidelity to England. This fleet, for the first time for ages, was now unlocking the Middle East, and when it entered the Dardanelles would enter a sea of problems and difficulties—some existing since Islam, some invented and concocted for the occasion. I hoped Satvet and I would be able to be of use. Lutfi became more discursive as we went on, and gave me his files to read and his papers to see. He offered to do all I wanted.

It was terrible weather, and we were both seedy. About dark, however, we reached the entrance of the great harbour of Mudros, heavily boomed and mined. We sped by a light-ship, the drifter having only one dim glim at her masthead. One heard submarines were still on the look-out.

It was too dark to see anything except here and there red or green lights at intervals. We went dead slow. The lights grew thicker. Suddenly, on rounding a bend we saw before us thousands of lights, many of them twinkling with the Morse code, messages from ship to ship. They were the lights of the Entente fleet. We were swept by a searchlight, and got into touch with H.M.S. *Europa*, the depôt ship that had called up our wireless at sea, and ordered us to report there. We were taken on board, where we met Captain Pearce, R.N., Commandant of the Base. After some inquiries he communicated with the flagship.

The admiral (Sir Arthur Calthorpe) wanted to see us. We went, accordingly, to H.M.S. *Superb,* a spick and span battleship of the *Temeraire* class, carrying 12-inch guns. We were taken down to the wardroom to wait a few moments, as Admiral Calthorpe had just got into wireless communication with London on some urgent matters. Here officers swarmed around us. Some asked for news of their friends, a few of whom had been captured in flights from Mudros to Stamboul, or who had been taken down the coast years before. They gave us news of home, and all seemed very keen on getting into Stamboul and rounding up the Turk, as they put it. The while we drank whiskies and soda. They liked Satvet Lutfi, who was quiet and collected in the face of what he called " *Quelle destinée !* "

The admiral sent his flag-lieutenant, saying he was suddenly urgently engaged. I was to go to Admiral Seymour and Captain Burmester, R.N., Chief of Staff. I presented Satvet and his embassy, as I had promised. He spoke indifferent French, which was indifferently understood. I assisted in indifferent French and Turkish. The admiral supplemented his French with English, and Satvet his Turkish with French. He produced letters from many Turks, including the Grand Vizier and from the ex-Ambassador Tewfik Pasha. He wanted permission to go to Switzerland to bring the Prince Subaheddine back, or failing that, to be allowed to meet him in London on the approval of our Foreign Office, or, failing that, permission to make communication to our Foreign Office for transmission to the Prince. Permission for this was necessary from our Foreign Office. Having heard his credentials, the admiral agreed to wire.

Among letters for the Prince Subaheddine is the following from Marshal Izzet Pasha, the last Grand Vizier of Turkey before the fleet entered. It fell to the lot of this patriot and renowned soldier, after the flight of Telaat and Enver, to survey the ruins of the Ottoman Empire.

Translation.—Letter from the Grand Vizier, Ahmed Izzet Pasha, to Prince Sabah-ed-Din Bey.

Respectfully submitted :

Under physical and moral suffering, I write to your Highness from the bed to which I am confined by sickness. I have obeyed the desire of his Imperial Majesty by accepting the offer of the Grand Vizierate, in the hope that I may be able to render some service, however small, to my country, in the appalling straits into which it has fallen, and to relieve the painful trials now come upon us. At this time, the assurance of future existence depends upon whether every man will labour for the common cause in a spirit of patriotism and self-sacrifice, with one mind and purpose, and divesting himself of all personal feeling. Most earnestly I beg for the favour and support of your Highness, who has so great a share in the welfare of the country. As for a long while past you have been in political relations with the statesmen of the Great Powers of Europe, 1 trust that you may be able to render valuable services in that direction. A communication on this subject will be sent to the Minister at Berne.

The moment that the state of the country is somewhat more normal, steps will be taken to carry out perfectly independent elections, and it is hoped that, under God's favour, we may be successful in forming a Government—no matter who may be its head—on right lines and of a natural character.

Again assuring your Highness of my entire devotion and loyal friendship, I have, etc.

(*Signed*)   AHMED IZZET.

4th November. 1918.

On being asked why it was so necessary that the Prince should return, the Turk became most illuminative. The admiral and his Chief of Staff were most interested, and heard some startling information. Satvet told them of the hopeless chaos politically, and how the Prince would unite enough parties to form a strong, reconstructive Government. He explained such a Government would be most useful to the Allies, that unless Stamboul politics were rescued from the adventurers who had manœuvred themselves even into the new Cabinet, the Allies would find that nothing short of a great army would keep Stamboul. Captain Burmester, R.N., a most penetrating questioner, cross-examined Satvet, and made some notes. The admiral promised to wire London.

Useful as was the information that was forthcoming, I do not think half the available use was made of Satvet's possibilities. Matters of intelligence concerning plots, flooding of mines, issue of false notes, and German spies were really much less important than the gambits of political tricksters. Afterwards, I had a talk with Captain Burmester, and gave him some details of the intelligence I had collected, and of some which had been added by Satvet. It included the circulation of false issues of notes, the plot to deposit fresh mines in the Dardanelles and Bosphorus from vessels, the intended flooding of the Aregli coal mine and others near the Black Sea, the removal of property by the Germans still in Stamboul, above all, the secret machinations of the U. and P. for a pan-Islam propaganda in Egypt, Palestine, India, Mesopotamia, Persia, and their machinations with Bolshevism. The latter, incredible as it may seem, was quite true, and could be located in various committees and agencies of U. and P.

Russia, it is true, has always been, and is still, the eternal *bête noir* and dread of the Ottomans ; but certain of their political tricksters hope, by a spread of the Bolshevik contagion, to undo the victory of the Allies. The world is tired. If Russia and Central Europe and the Ottomans require not only to be beaten in the field, but to be conquered and subdued, is there the wherewithal to do it in the Entente? Whether the success of Russia would mean the annexation of Turkey the Turks would, they say, ignore, for Turkey is very deep in the mud ; just as Enver, Midhat and Co. ignored the fact that the success of Germany meant the ultimate erasion of Turkey.

The gambit of Italy in requiring the Adalia coast without much justification, the gambit of forcing the issue about Smyrna and the Levant by Greece, the so-called competition between England, France, and America for the economic control of the Dardanelles, make the situation ripe with possibilities of intrigue. To solve the Turkish problem, in my opinion, it would be necessary to give first place to it, to treat it as a single issue. It is a situation that cannot admit of compromise. America is rumoured as being out to capture the trade resources of the Black Sea empires, in so far as it leaves her Monroe doctrine intact, which seems to mean privileges without duties. The French are not so popular as they were, although French traditional popularity is reviving in Constantinople just now. And most Turks are convinced that an international policy of Stamboul would be impracticable. It would go to the nation with most trade, the biggest fleet of warships and mercantile marine, *i.e.* England or America. If *not* internationalized, the financial basis, which is mostly French, would give France the lead. But while this process of "becoming" goes on, Turkey will be left to her own devices with direful results to the world.

The admiral and his Chief of Staff were most kind to me, and, busy as they were, found time to inquire about our captivity. General Townshend had been through just before. I was asked to see the Director of Naval Intelligence, Colonel Temple, on shore, whither I went with Satvet, after enjoying some conversation and drinks provided for us by the " Flag," whom the admiral ordered to take us to the wardroom for some refreshment, of which mine was chiefly whisky, and Satvet's port. He kept looking around at the excellent furnishings, and saying "*quelle destinée !*"

Every one was busy, and the fleet was evidently sailing very soon. We went ashore to some naval officers' quarters, where a most excellent mess, full of all good fellows and good things, entertained us. I had very little kit, and was short of blankets.

My tiny room was very cold, but we borrowed what we wanted. Officers crowded around us in the mess, and asked us questions. It was, however, very late, but I didn't go to bed until I had arranged a room for Satvet. My room I shared with a war correspondent from London, who was much on the *qui vive* for news. I told him very little, and ordered Satvet not to speak to him except in my presence. This correspondent was very grateful for such news as we had to give, and by permission I drafted for him the first cable concerning Stamboul, for the Associated Press, which duly passed the censor. He gave me much news of home, and wanted my experiences, which I didn't care to say much about just then. I remember that my first night on shore, outside Turkey, was so cold that I couldn't sleep very well in my tiny bunk. The next day I inspected the harbour and surrounding hills, where circular marks lett on the black hillsides showed the site of the great camp of New Zealanders and Australians for the Gallipoli operations.

The giant fleet, including over forty first-class fighting ships alone, lay silent and still below me. One distinguished the peculiar turrets of the American ships, the line of the Italian, and two big clumsy Greek cruisers. One's feelings of thankfulness of release were overwhelming. The vast assembly of ships stood for victory ; but they were also invested to a great degree with a fascinating political significance that only one versed in Stamboul intrigue during the war could appreciate. Here was I with a long pilgrimage of loneliness, forced inaction, suffering, and sickness behind me, at last free. Yet, instead of rushing away home by the first boat, I found myself content to wait here at the door of the Dardanelles, fascinated with the phenomenon of the Iron Key about to open the gate of Constantine. Released from the perpetual convoy of postas, and paralysis, mental and physical, that is conseq ırnt on captivity, one might imagine I would be eager to look only forward. And yet, even before being re-introduced to the old world, I found myself taking an all-absorbing interest in the problem that I had just left behind.

That morning I made another long report to Colonel Temple, who was supervising Naval Intelligence, and I gave him the piecemeal information he sought, to the best of my ability. Enver and Telaat had left for Germany. A double of the former had cleverly put quite a number off the scent. Many Turkish officials who were to meet the fleet and accuse the U. and P. as the source of the downfall of Turkey, were themselves sleeping partners of the U. and P. oppositon to the Entente that had continued the murder of Armenians, sheltering of spies, even refusal to say who and where were the chief delinquents. This was all proceeding apace, *sub rosa*. From what I had seen in Stamboul just before leaving, I thought the Turks there preparing for the arrival of the fleet much like a very naughty lower fourth form at school, hatching all kinds of devilries for the arrival of their new master.

Satvet and I had lunch in H.M.S. *Europa* with Captain Pearce, who was exceedingly kind to us, and very sympathetic with Satvet's impatience in awaiting the reply cable from the Foreign Office. It was a very cheerful meal, and even Satvet bucked up, and eventually said he would hand over to me his embassy and all his papers if it would help the fleet to find out who was who.

Colonel Temple sent for me that night and afterwards had another interview with Satvet for Intelligence. He then kindly wrote me a letter saying I was proceeding home on urgent political matters, and immediate passage was requested. He asked with a smile if I would care to return to Stamboul with the fleet. I found that prospect, however, rather too exacting, and, besides, I seemed to promise more usefulness by going home at once. He informed me confidentially that the fleet would sail that night for Constantinople, and was very anxious to know what was the feeling there about the Greeks. At Smyrna the Greeks had certainly sought to make trouble, what with their gigantic Greek flags and public demonstration.

That night the gigantic fleet prepared to move. In the early dawn of the 12th one heard answering signals. Their lights moved out to sea. When we awoke not a sign was to be seen of them. Only H.M.S. *Europa* and a few dozen gunboats, with a cruiser or two, and some old ships remained. The next day there was still no reply. I went out to dine with the officers of the Air Force, which was very strongly represented there. They were very eager to hear an account of their recent bombing raids on Stamboul. All the machines had flown from here. Afterwards I saw some of the wonderful developments in the plane of modern war. That evening some ships arrived from Dedogatch, and I heard much of the preparations for landing here in case the Turks further delayed surrender. And heavily as the place is fortified there is no doubt but that we could easily land and, with a march or two, cut off the Gallipoli peninsula, so depleted are the Turkish forces.

On the 13th Satvet went sick and was removed to a hospital boat. He sent in a short letter in French to the Grand Vizier, explaining how he had been held up. The next day he was better and got discharged. He was chafing about the delay of his embassy to the Prince. I now got a room for us both. There had been a tremendous amount of influenza in the fleet and I was not certain I hadn't got it myself.

I got permission for him to wire the Commander-in-Chief of the fleet in Stamboul for immediate leave, either to come to London or to return to Stamboul. In the meantime we made ourselves useful to Captain Pearce, now S.N.O.A., who requested us to visit a large camp of Turkish prisoners. Their work was to paint and clean the fleet with a host of other minor fatigues. They wanted to return to Turkey, as English prisoners, they said, were returning home. They wouldn't work, so we harangued them, and Satvet told them plainly what a state their country was in, how short of food the capital was, and what was more, how they had been betrayed. They were sullen but ultimately agreed to work for a time. They certainly looked fighting fit and fat, and well-clothed. I couldn't help comparing their lot with that of our own poor fellows. Satvet then communicated with Tewfik Pasha, who now replaced Izzet Pasha as Grand Vizier, informing him that he had handed over to me the letters from Izzet Pasha for our Foreign Office, and for the Prince, and letters from a score or so of leading men in Stamboul to the Prince with other matters for the perusal of our Foreign Office and wrote that he would return to Stamboul. A telegram from the Foreign Office confirmed this.

CHAPTER XVIII

*M*UDROS, *Nov. 20th*, 1918.—Two days ago we lunched again with the Commandant of the Base on board the *Europa*. The commander of the *Sikh*, one of the fastest T.B.D.'s in the fleet, was there also. He left Portsmouth the evening of the armistice and declared how England had gone quite mad on armistice night. It was wonderful to meet some one so fresh from home. He had now been to the fleet and returned. The entry had been magnificent. In battle line ahead it had passed through the Dardanelles, sweepers in front, without mishap through the mine-fields, although two or three sweepers had been blown up previously in sweeping and the survivors of the crew of one had just before reached Mudros. The fleet passed on to Stamboul in a solemn procession of battleships, cruisers, and light craft in line ahead reaching 16½ miles. First came the British, then the French, the Italian, and Greek. The Greeks had most tactlessly hoisted huge flags but were promptly dealt with. Then a detachment went to the Bosphorus while the main fleet went to their prepared anchorage at Ismid some miles off. They are now preparing to enter the Black Sea.

I equipped Satvet with a few local luxuries and he went on board a steam yacht. At the last moment, however, owing to mines breaking away, he could not sail, and lay in harbour when Heathcote-Smith came from Mytilene *en route* for Stamboul to assist the Commander-in-Chief. By this time it was beginning to be realized in Stamboul what were the difficulties, and Heathcote-Smith was glad to find out all he could about partisans there, and how few people were sincere. The first Press reports were certainly misleading. Fitzmaurice,

whose name was more than a terror to the Turks, ought
to have been sent back at once. He had been First
Secretary to the Embassy preceding hostilities, and knew a
good deal of Turkish under-currents. On our entry, there
was too much disposition to listen to Turks on the spot instead of sorting them out. Turkish exchange, so far from
falling, is rising, and although we have landed a heavy force
at the Dardanelles, the Turks seem all out for a " try-on."
Heathcote-Smith left that night, but Satvet's small yacht was
still weather-bound. I have definitely taken over his mission
and said " Good-bye " to him.

RETURN—On the 23rd I boarded H.M.S. *Rowan*, an armed
charge-layer captained by the ex-chief officer of the *Mauretania*.
We were weather-bound for two days further. Then the
weather suddenly cleared, although the seas were still heavy.
We arrived at Malta, where I had to report to General Temple,
Director Intelligence Mediterranean Naval Squadron. He
gave me a through pass to press on urgently to Rome and
Paris, then on to the Admiralty and Foreign Office with a
letter saying I was carrying urgent despatches and required
urgent passage. I took some despatches for him also. I
dined that night with an officer of the Intelligence Department
named Latouche, who afterwards played the piano to me
in his rooms above the moonlight waters of Valetta, dotted
with lights of warships. Then we saw part of La Traviata,
made a final report to General Temple, and I slept in the
Orontes with my despatches from Mudros and Malta, besides
all Satvet's affair. A number of kind invitations reached
me but I regretted I had no time to stay. One was from an
old friend of Newcombe's who wanted news. I wrote to the
colonel, who had evidently abandoned his mission at Mudros
and gone to Egypt. I was extremely lucky in getting my
passage at once, as the gunboat to have taken us had to go
elsewhere. We left at dawn. It was a stormy passage. We
arrived at Taranto across the barrage on the 30th, where
an exceedingly kind letter and telegram from Lord Islington
awaited me, congratulating me on being free and hoping to
see me in a few days. At Taranto I found heavy blockage
of officials, troops, and ex-prisoners of war, arriving from all
quarters, all held up here in camps. Some had been here weeks,

I went on board H.M.S. *Queen*, where Admiral Hannay, having considered my papers, told me that he with his Staff was leaving that night for Rome direct and Paris. He offered to make room for me. We left that night about eight o'clock. A great crowd of naval and military people, both British and Italian, came to say good-bye to the admiral. I was fortunate to secure half the compartment of the King's Naval Messenger, who proved a most useful companion. His frequent journeys had acquainted him with all the stopping places and cafés. That night Admiral Hannay and several of his officers came into our coupé. We made a most excellent meal from various baskets and bottles, and they asked me an account of my travels in Turkey. I found it impossible to talk of any but the humorous side of it all, the serious history of these long, shadowy years being like night-mists over tideless marshes, silent, lifeless and secret. The admiral laughed gaily at the idea of generals getting C.B. (confined to barracks), and said I had had a most unique experience. We had quite a night of it. At dawn we were running through that delightful country of Southern Italy, of pleasant semi-wooded plains, dotted every now and then with abrupt little hills on the top of each of which stands a village crowned by an ancient castle, walled and steepled. The sight of these hilltop villages, familiar to every traveller in Italy, catching the rays of the morning sun I thought most wonderful. We ran past them for hours, dazzling like bright coins on a green carpet.

About 10 a.m. we arrived at Rome. The hotel accommodation was overcrowded. I had a bath and meal at the Continental Hotel near the station, for which I paid the best part of a sovereign. Then I visited the Excelsior Hotel with my papers, and later went to the British Embassy with some papers for Commander de Grey of the English Mission there. He had just left for England, but I enjoyed a most pleasant hour or so there in conversation with some English ladies from the mission. Rome was delightful. I drove and drove and drove to feel myself free once again. I had tea at an extraordinary little cake-shop, where pretty women like butterflies came and went. I smoked from my cab in the gardens. In the early moonlight I drove past the Coliseum, but quickly. It stood for history. I didn't want history just then. In a freakish moment I visited the Forum again.

That was history to be sure. But more so it was philosophy. It invited one to peer into the Future. This spot that once ruled the world. This world now at sixes and sevens, that owned no dominion. . . .

So far as Rome went, I quickly noticed a Bolshevist element in the Press, in the street, at the station. The nation was strung up and some were getting out of hand. In one quarter a fire appeared to be proceeding and some people obstructing the firemen, although I didn't verify what was the real cause of the violent rioting in so prominent a street.

I was now beginning to shake off the coma that had undoubtedly settled upon me. Of one thing I am sure. Rip van Winkle, after his twenty years of sleep, felt much less strange than I after my two and a half years.

The station porters were all on strike, so Major Molson and I wheeled our barrows ourselves. He also was an old Emmanuel man and going home to stand for Parliament. We travelled together on the same train as the admiral's suite. At Genoa and Turin we got in touch with soldiers returning from other fronts. The latter place was feet deep in snow, and icicles hung from the verandahs. At Modan we had to change, and in the restaurant I found myself sitting opposite a face I knew well, and was very troubled at not knowing who it was. I had forgotten much. It was a Major Murray, from one of the batteries at Hyderabad, who had been with me before leaving India. I learned from him that a good many of my friends were casualties, the survivors all over the world, and that few had counted me as alive. He had been badly knocked about by a shell himself.

We arrived at Paris in early morning and again wheeled our kit. I learned here that General Cox, to whom also I was to report, had been accidentally drowned just before. He was one of the most brilliant Intelligence Officers of the Entente, and every one was deploring his loss. He had been a close friend of Colonel Newcombe, and apart from my intelligence duties, I had looked forward to giving him an account of the colonel, who had asked me to do so the first moment possible. This was only the prelude to many rude shocks I was to get. One might say that for me the casualties had happened in one night, for I heard news now for the first time of casualties that had happened in early 1915, and casualties had been going on ever since. The first thing I saw in *Le Temps* was that Rostand, the great French writer, had died. Like Cyrano, he had left, so he said, to carry word of victory to the great French dead.

I finished my duties at Paris and left that evening. For a meal at the Café Amercain I paid a gold sovereign. The place was full of Americans, and all other places were also crowded. France was tired. Since I had left there in November, 1914, she had aged and the last of her pretty frocks had been put away.

As I was travelling on a naval pass they read me for Captain, R.N., instead of R.F.A., the former ranking as a brigadier in the army. This meant a seat in a packed train. Molson and I left for Boulogne that night and arrived at dawn. Other politicians were *en route*. The magic word was to be " Coalition." We had a long discussion as to the merits of coalition, I holding that in time of war it was good, as in home politics there was only the question of union. But when peace comes the international or foreign policy becomes constructive, and criticism in the ascertainment of the centre of political gravity is necessary. To me it seems true that many of the ideals of the war already have to be exchanged for the hard fact of compromise. Compromise is always bad and weak and muddlesome beyond a certain point. But the problems of the world I have recently left can admit of no compromise ! The Turkish problem must be solved or left !

Boulogne also has changed a great deal. Hotels have become hospitals and it seems very English.

We left by boat in the fogs at early dawn, a number of senior officers returning on short leave being on board. I was astonished at the youth of many of them. It told me of the drainage of the war.

About ten o'clock I saw again the thin line of white cliffs—England. A few quick moments and I stood on the quay at Folkestone. An hour later in a refreshment car ! It was a carriage for the most part of silent men from all fronts. Out of the window, hedges, fields, crows, trees, England flew by. I had a desire to get out and walk every yard. I had an impulse. No, it is too private to record.

I was free. England, England, England.

2 C

EPILOGUE

OXFORD and Cambridge Club, March, 1921.—The publication of the foregoing, which awaited the recovery of some of the manuscript from Turkey, has been still further delayed owing to my having been cut off from communications in Persia last year.

Several months after the Armistice I married, and with my wife returned to Baghdad, where I took up the post of Chief Legislative Draftsman to the Judicial Department. To have returned to the past scene of the events of my captivity is an odd experience, and my friends have asked me for a recent impression. This, however, might lead to controversial matters, and for such there is here neither place nor room.

However! On our return in November last year we stopped at Kut for two days. I add a last note from my diary.

P.O.'s Quarters, Kut, November 8th, 1920.—We left Baghdad by train about 7 a.m. on November 6th, day travelling being necessary on account of the recent revolt. The whole line is heavily blockhoused. It lies along the route of our historic retreat after Ctesiphon back to Kut. Somewhere beneath the desert dust is the double trail of bones ; bones of the men who fell in the retreat, and bones of the men who fell or crawled six months later in the captive columns.

We are staying with the Political Officer, a tremendously kind and interesting fellow. My wife was most curious to behold first hand the precincts of our doings in the siege, some of which I had described to her from my captivity. The foreshore has quite changed. My artillery observation posts of sandbags, that once, tattered and battered with shell fire, defied the Turkish marksmanship to the end, has given place to a fine street, and this house stands where the garrison gunners kept a similar vigil, and where our flag, shot into ribbons, was hauled down on the fateful day. I had no difficulty, however, in locating many familiar scenes. We visited General Townshend's house, where, as the Jewish occupant explained, " the General issued his communiqués ! " It suffered from our own guns after the Turks entered, and the minaret also was damaged by some accidental shot.

My wife knew several of our garrison when her father's regiment, the 24th S.W.B.'s, was in India years ago. I entertained her with stories of the amusing side of Kut. She was highly delighted at the little Arab boy's question as to whether she also had been in the siege !

We climbed the roof. The pattern of the shell burst that killed poor Colonel Courtenay and Garnett and Begg is still there. Then we visited the horse lines and took a car over the crumbling trenches to the Brick Kilns, where General Smith and I had our first dug-out. It seemed strange, indeed, to go along " on top " in a car where for so long to show even a *topee* was to offer a dead mark to the Turks over the river.

The Brick Kilns most of all retain and impart to one again the spirit of Kut. The dug-out is still dug out, and bits of blown-up guns all round about. The position of Colonel Broke-Smith's Battery (63rd R.F.A.) I located near by. One seemed to hear his genial voice as he stumped along these very trenches to see if his guns were on their night lines. He was a magnificent gunner, and neither the siege nor captivity sapped far into his joyous indifference. I remember delivering a message to him under a sharp fire in the action of Um-al-Tabul, glorious to Townshend's memory. Shells were bursting all around as he sat up his limber pole. I should think it impossible for any voice to sound more gleeful and exhilarating, and at the same time with more whip in it than his. He had got the precise range of that glorious target of crowded Turks, surprised at 1000 yards. Under each burst of his shrapnel I saw the running figures suddenly changed to flat black patches. In fact, we could distinguish bursts by gaps suddenly appearing in the black horde. He came to lunch at my club on our meeting in the War Office after the Armistice, and admitted that when the Turks were particularly troublesome in his captivity, he used to recall with much satisfaction that glorious target.

As we walked to position after position, incidents long forgotten came up to the surface of my mind. Here was where we made the ramp for the debouch, there where poor Bombardier X was sniped. This was where the floods burst in over the bank and flooded us out.   That where we made our last line.   We came across a patch on the *maidan*, thick with shell cases and pieces of segment.   This to my delight I located as the position of my old battery, the 76th R.F.A. The six gun emplacements are clearly discernible, and my dug-out, in which I had spent so many weird hours, gaped eloquently before me.   Grass grew on the walls.

The picturesque position of 86th R.F.A. in the palms is overgrown, but the smashed trees and shell-pierced wall and dug-outs gave me my bearings.   The fort has been erased.

Last of all I succeeded in finding in the town the billet of the Sixth Divisional Ammunition Column, which later on I had shared with Tudway and Mellor.   The upper story that had been partly demolished by the shell which occasioned the bruise to my back has now been cut away.   The front door was barred and the billet vacant.   By entering through an adjoining house, and scaling the wall on top over which the Turks had swarmed, I got down and forced the door for my wife and Major Jeffery to enter.   The cupboard which I had filled with bricks was still there, as also the room in which the shells had entered four and a half years before.   Only four and a half years, and yet how far had I walked and seen since then !   The back wall over which we used to peep at the Tigris is smashed down by bombardment, and the whole place bespattered with bullet marks.

The last glimpse I had had here was of my poor Don Juan's black tail on the verandah post, and of triumphant Turks kicking our orderly.   To stand here once again, but as a free man accompanied by my wife and a Political Officer in that fire-changed scene, in that spot of long-enforced soliloquy, was surely more wonderful than coincidence.   Cocky would have called it Destiny, and Tudway, " Outside chance."

While we were talking, an Arab from next door burst in, greatly excited.   " Sahib chunet hina fil mahassere ? "   (" Was Sahib here in the siege ? ")   I answered him : " Naam.   Kasr mali fil mahassere."   (" Yes—my palace of the siege.")   He laughed.   Kasr means palace.   We remembered each other perfectly.   He continued to salaam at my feet as something too wonderful.   He said he remembered selling us some date juice (at an enormous figure, by the way).

He was surprised I had learned to speak to him in Arabic,

and we had a long talk on old days. He recounted their troubles and persecutions after the Turks entered. A small Arab boy here at the P.O.'s house remembers me up in my observation post. An excellent little fellow, he has followed me about everywhere, or waited at my door—"Arid ashuf Sahib. Ma'arid backsheesh." "I want to see Sahib. I do not want backsheesh."

10 *p.m.*—An hour ago I was about to go to bed, but the moon was floating on the Tigris. Two moons ; one in the sky, one in the water, just as of old. It was irresistible, so I went forth with a pipe.

Once again Kut is asleep. Over the river Woolpress throws its familiar shadow, only a little more dilapidated and shattered. Beyond that, beyond the palms and the town, all around, skirting the desert, encircling—the trenches are falling. History fades. The desert encroaches once more.

Since last here I have lived centuries of time, at no moment very far from, and in some precious moments very close to, the silent Heart of the East. Silent yet not inaudible its murmurs can reach a patient and humble listener. And into two or three years of captivity "from within" may be crowded the revelation of the experience of many years. In these precious moments the whisperings remain largely inarticulate, and then in our difficulty we mistakenly identify the desert with its effect on us. Robert Hichens clothes it with mystery, and Chu Chin Chow with the transmutability of bright colours.

Here in this very spot, the first British army of history to do so, its dauntless heroism and sacrifice unavailing, succumbed to the finiteness of mortals. From this spot the survivors were trailed in dying columns across the ancient routes of the East, an object-lesson of the assailability of our prestige. It will take more than a successful campaign to erase that memory. The moral is we should not attempt what we are not prepared to carry through.

To-night, then, in this moment of a complete cycle in my history, I would like to think the advancement we have made in this country is consolidated and permanent. Is it ? Apart from the fact that the arrangements for this country exist under the Treaty of Versailles, a treaty largely inoperative on account of divergence in the Entente, do we yet realize that a good deal of the recent rebellion is a national movement in a country extraordinarily hard to contain with a depleted army ? Is it yet fully realized that for the first time in the history of an Empire we have in this country—mandate though it be—a nursling territory with every flank, except a mile or two of sea, politically open ?

On one side awakened Russia, adjoining Persia of grandee or gentleman bandit government ; on the north, the hornet's nest of the Highlands of Kurdistan ; on the west, the illimitable eternity of the Arab's desert.

Adequate garrisoning is out of the question for financial reasons, and we are just realizing here, as in Ireland, that to conquer a country is one thing and to police it another. General Townshend's advance represented the high-water mark of his conquest—until he was cut off ! But now " they are all about us." To impose any programme on these people —as is the case also with the Turks—which they do not absolutely endorse, must involve policing. How earnestly did people at the Armistice, who knew Turkey and Turkish intrigues, urge this fact on our advisers at home ! And now, two years afterwards, I see that the Treaty of Sèvres is to be modified in favour of the Turks. How very clearly this was foreseen as inevitable by some of us ! The desert and Mohammedan question must be examined *ab initio*. It should not be contingent on or sequential to other matters of European politics—because it is of a different world.

The fact is that, in the desert, nature is at a minimum. There is no mountain ravine, no forest to determine the path of man. Here are the Great Silence, the Great Solitude, Illimitable Space, and a Sea of Time. Here introspection is at a premium, the mind is unfettered and chainless. Perhaps it is free. And in this world of Stillness and Emptiness man moves as a considerable object. From the desert came all the prophets. Cities and customs arise and disappear into the sand. Dynasty succeeds dynasty, as conquest succeeds conquest. In the end you have the sand and the horizon as at first.

Can it be wondered at, therefore, that in such soil a transplanted mushroom of civilization cannot be expected to flourish ? In 1914 Mesopotamia was much as two thousand years ago. An advanced civilization with elaborate impedimenta is deposited on to it. This civilization, then, must either have an army adequate to protect it or it must conform to whatever standard of efficiency, to whatever degree of perfection, the local inhabitant will tolerate.

This cardinal fact has been obscured by a mass of controversy and interesting side issues, *e.g.* to what extent the possibilities of this country can ever be realized unless we enter on a gigantic irrigation scheme and plug up the hills at the source of these rivers. But the farther afield and the more elaborate our development, the more this cardinal fact holds good.

Goethe tells us to take the duty nearest to us. But this is precisely what the hard-working officials of the Civil Administration have done. We went from commitment to commitment, and this duty led to that, this problem to the one adjoining. Which may make for good progress in war, but for a programme of peace it overlooks the cardinal principle. Nor do I think that the Arab can be expected to appreciate the fact that pending the arrival of a definite Treaty with Turkey, the spirit of government and development must be expected to be arbitrary—for we declared otherwise in our proclamation to them. Greater clairvoyance and experience in the direction of policy might have borne steadily in view this cardinal fact instead of relentlessly pursuing the god Efficiency. The god Efficiency was invented by Prussia, and with all its completeness and perfection the war found it to be only a machine. It overlooked human factors ; it missed cardinal facts.

Yet, coming back to Kut once more ! None of our beleaguered garrison on this Babylonian plain could have believed it humanly possible to effect such a metamorphosis in this land in so short a space of time. Wharves, shipping, and railway systems, electric light and fans, Courts of Justice, Revenue, Agricultural and Finance Departments, Government Press, British and Arab daily papers—it has been built up by great and unsparing effort, and so far as earnestness and will to succeed went, the officers of the Civil Administration have worked tremendously hard. My own chief, Sir Edgar Bonham-Carter, I have known work continuously all through the heat from early morning until late into the night.

.   .   .   .

It was from this bank in December, 1915, that, previous to his arrival recently as a High Commissioner, I last saw

Sir Percy Cox, then Chief Political Officer, as he left by the last boat for downstream. I talked with him this week before leaving Baghdad, and found him much older. He must have had a long spell of work without leave. The Persian Treaty which he made for us at Teheran is, I hear, moribund, and this must have been a great disappointment to him.

Nevertheless, he has undertaken the enormous responsibility and difficulties here most courageously. The Arab welcome to him on his arrival the other day was little short of homage to a king. It has changed the situation a good deal.

To-morrow we go from here by paddle-boat to Basra, en route for home on leave.

Bacon tells us that writing maketh an exact man. Perhaps to know when one has said enough is to be exact.

Let us then away from Kut at once and for ever.

.   .   .   .

London, March, 1921 (*continued*).—Kuttavi!—I have cut. Or rather, Kuttaverunt, the doctors have, as they think I should not return to the climate of Mesopotamia.

I am back in this dear sweet land, beautiful even in all her sorrows. Back, round the pivot of palm trees to where I was before the war, behind me the eloquent vacuum through which the world has rolled. It is almost a complete vacuum, as *Punch* might say, a host of flitting, fading shadows.

But at times I see a long, wide river winding over endless plains, with here and there a solitary palm. And I hear the long cry proceeding from the dark figure crouching in the bows as he takes the soundings, " Bahout pa-a-ni ! "—the long, lone cry that ever and anon by day and night floats intermittently to the ears of the traveller in that ancient land.

It, too, has borrowed from the desert something that is deterministic and ineffaceable.

Back to this window. And so, " Another cycle is complete ! "

THE END

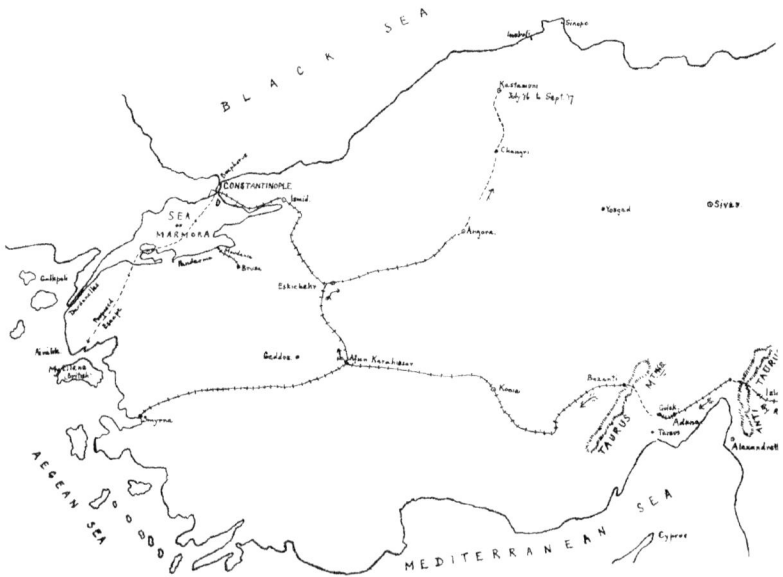

MAP OF TREK
(including plan of escape)

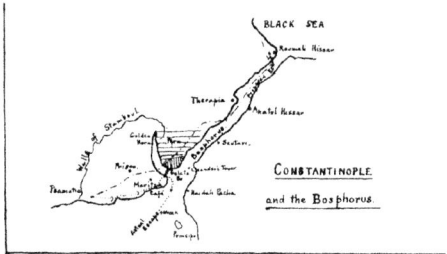

BLACK SEA

CONSTANTINOPLE
and the Bosphorus.

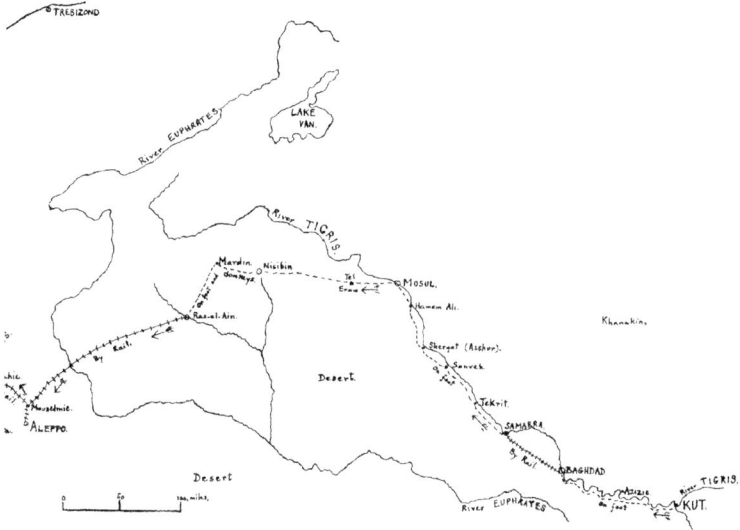

TREBIZOND

River EUPHRATES

LAKE VAN.

River TIGRIS

Mardin Nisibin

MOSUL.

Ras-el-Ain.

Desert.

Khanakin.

Shergat (Aschur).

Tekrit.

SAMARRA

Desert

BAGHDAD

River EUPHRATES

River TIGRIS.

KUT.

ALEPPO.

Desert

Printed in Great Britain
by Amazon

52524608R00261